Canada and the United States

CANADA *and the*

UNITED STATES

Some Aspects of *Their Historical Relations*

Hugh Ll. Keenleyside, M.A., PH.D., LL.D.

REVISED AND ENLARGED EDITION PREPARED BY

Hugh Ll. Keenleyside

AND

Gerald S. Brown, PH.D.

INTRODUCTION BY

W. P. M. KENNEDY, M.A., LITT.D.

PROFESSOR OF LAW AND POLITICAL INSTITUTIONS
IN THE UNIVERSITY OF TORONTO

New York: Alfred·A·Knopf: *1952*

L. C. catalog card number: 51-13225

THIS IS A BORZOI BOOK,
PUBLISHED BY ALFRED A. KNOPF, INC.

FIRST EDITION, PUBLISHED 1929
SECOND EDITION, REVISED, ENLARGED,
RESET, AND PRINTED FROM NEW PLATES, 1952

TO

Margaret Louise Keenleyside
Ellis William Keenleyside

MOST DELIGHTFUL OF PARENTS

Introduction

That knowledge and intelligent study of international affairs constitute important elements in the peaceful progress of the world is a political and social commonplace. A fact, however, of this nature is none the less valuable for being a commonplace; and it is extremely important that it should be emphasized with sincerity and honesty during a period such as this, with a cataclysm in the immediate background, with fears and with failings of hearts making wise decisions more than ever difficult and tending to obscure future international understandings. Too frequently in the past the commonplace has in truth degenerated into intellectual vulgarity, in that superficiality has passed for learning, acquaintanceship for intimacy, and platform and after-dinner affability for that critical insight which ought to guide men of different nations if they would follow the paths of ordered peace and mutual progress. In relation to the United States and Canada all this has been far too prominent. A common language, a common sharing in the economic development of a continent, a common tradition in public and private law and in democratic government and suchlike have been overemphasized at the expense of that deeper and more profound knowledge which in reality constitutes international understanding. Indeed, it is not too much to say that the very width of those things which the United States and Canada have in common has been influential in befogging the past, in charging the present with friction, and in loading the future with apprehension. In addition, it is quite evident that the relations between the two nations have been studied and discussed as though they were solely and exclusively Anglo-American. In other words, scholars, statesmen, and public writers and speakers have tended to lay stress on the European or imperial aspect in them at the expense of the ever developing point of view of British North America. The Canadian community, with its peculiar social, economic, and political values, while not being neglected, has suffered through being viewed too much from London. There was necessary then a study in which a great commonplace should be dignified, and in which the emphasis would be rightly placed. I venture to think, without indeed committing myself either to Dr. Keenleyside's facts or to his interpretations, that this book in its conception and form will fill a long-felt want.

Dr. Keenleyside moves along sound lines. First of all, he realizes that the present and future relations between the two nations lie deep in the past. He is, I need hardly say, too fine a scholar to believe in historical determinism; but he does recognize that a national "personality" cannot be divorced from its origins and evolution if understanding of it is to emerge, any more than would be the case in that of a natural person. Thus, then, he sets his whole work in a frame of history to which he has brought sound original research and not a little insight, which ought to do valiant service in ridding the whole subject of cant. Secondly, he is not afraid of critical interpretation. I may not, many of his readers may not, agree with him in detail. Be that as it may, Canadian-American relations cannot be explained, much less understood, when governed by a polite and conventional smugness which only covers the inevitable rivalries with a thin veneer of international hypocrisy. Thirdly, he is not afraid to treat the present, to see it in such reality as the spirit within him allows, and to interpret it with such objectivity as human frailty will permit.

No one, then, can read Dr. Keenleyside's study without being convinced of the soundness of his methods and of his general success in accomplishment. I believe that he has set down nought in malice. Little good—indeed, great harm—is done when such phrases as "the unguarded line," "blood is thicker than water," "kindred peoples," and so on, do duty for that patient search for truth, that sincerity of knowledge, and that spirit of criticism which wise men ordinarily give to their own affairs. Such search, such sincerity, and such spirit are emphatically necessary amid those vaster activities which we call international; and they are of the very essence of wisdom where our common heritages are so liable to obscure our vast differences. Dr. Keenleyside has done valuable work for civilized progress; for this cannot be without truth, frankness, and insight. It is on these that the real security of Canadian-American relations must be based, and this book will perform an international service of immense importance.

In its æonian processes nature has endowed the United States and Canada with vast economic resources, thus making possible the development side by side of two cultural groups separated politically by the processes of human history. On the other hand, we have daily before our eyes the evidence that forces of interdependence are at work which in the pedestrian affairs of life may tend to cloud realities. It is the function of the scholar and the thinker to see all the forces—to see municipal law and international law, cultural idiosyncrasies and cultural likenesses, the foundations and superstructures of separate political integrity and the foundations and superstructures of moral unity in the things that are more excellent. In a word his quest is philosophical: to relate the many to the one. That quest must be pursued with all the honesty of purpose available if reality of aim is to be realized. I believe that Dr. Keenleyside's book will do much to lift the relationships of the United States and Canada to a plane

Introduction

of sane dignity, removing them from empty verbiage, uninformed deductions, and doctrinaire theories. In so far as it accomplishes such an end it will have contributed to that future of mutual understanding and peaceful self-respect, each country secure in its independence, which are essential if the facts of interdependence are to bring forth the fruits of a world-wide civilization parallel with the domestic civilization of each state. "A nation is the workshop of the world."

W. P. M. KENNEDY

Baldwin House
University of Toronto
February 2, 1929

Preface

When *Canada and the United States* was produced in 1929, it was the first published attempt at a comprehensive review of the history of the contacts between these two North American neighbors. Its reception indicated the existence of a rather surprising interest in the subject.

During the last twenty years the subject of Canadian-American relations has been a constant theme in historical writing on this continent. Individual volumes of high merit have been published. Above all, as a result of the generosity of the Carnegie Endowment for International Peace, the imaginative editorial ability of that distinguished American of Canadian birth Dr. James T. Shotwell, and the high standards of scholarship of a large group of Canadian and American scholars, there was published a long succession of admirable volumes dealing with many aspects of the same basic theme. This series, under the general title "The Relations of Canada and the United States," has resulted in a great expansion of our knowledge of the intercourse between the two countries, has corrected many earlier misconceptions, and has provided a storehouse of detailed information that will be of inestimable value to scholars for many decades to come. It is probable that today there is a more complete knowledge of the relations of Canada and the United States than of any other two countries in the world.

All of this activity in the field covered by *Canada and the United States* appears to have stimulated rather than satiated both the scholarly and the general interest in the subject. From time to time since the exhaustion of the first edition, there have been suggestions that a new and enlarged volume would be of interest and value. It is as a result of these proposals and of my own continuing interest in the subject that the present revision has been written.

In preparing the second edition I have had the invaluable co-operation of Dr. Gerald S. Brown, of the University of Michigan, who has been responsible for the incorporation of much of the new material and many of the new evaluations that have resulted from the tremendous research of the last two decades. It is our hope that this book will give clear evidence of the value of the work that has been done by other hands in the years between the two editions.

The second edition has also been brought up to date by the inclusion of material covering the 1930's and 1940's. In many ways this is the most exciting as well as the most important period in the whole history of the two nations. While some of the events of these decades must await their final evaluation in the years ahead, there is much that is of significance for the present and the immediate future.

One question of content gave the authors considerable concern. Chapter x deals with the effects of the First World War on Canadian-American relations. At first they considered the advisability of dropping this chapter entirely because, from the perspective of 1952, many of the facts that loomed large in 1929 carry a reduced inportance. In the end, however, it was decided to keep the chapter in a revised form partly because of the significance of the events it describes and partly to emphasize the change that has since marked the relations of the two countries. The contrast between the effects of the First and Second World Wars is of very real interest, particularly because of the way in which it illustrates the increased maturity of the Canadian people.

In addition to the great contribution of my collaborator and the patience of my publishers, I am indebted to many persons for assistance and encouragement in the preparation of this edition during a period of great personal preoccupation with other matters. My first acknowledgment should be to those many scholars who, in the Carnegie series or in individual publications, have provided new knowledge and a stimulus to renewed thought and interest. I should renew also my acknowledgment of indebtedness to all who helped so wisely and well in the preparation of the original edition and who are mentioned in the Acknowledgments in that volume, reprinted herein.

Particular encouragement and assistance in the development of the present text has been received from the indefatigable George W. Brown, whose work at the University of Toronto and as editor of the *Canadian Historical Review* has made all Canadian scholars his debtors. Mr. Stewart Bates, Deputy Minister of Fisheries, and Mr. S. V. Ozere, of the same Department, were most helpful in connection with the expansion of the chapter on fisheries. With the approval of Colonel Laval Fortier, the Deputy Minister, Miss A. E. Horne and her colleagues of the Canadian Department of Citizenship and Immigration were of the greatest assistance in the revision and extension of the chapters on Immigration and Emigration. Mrs. P. Ross Kidd, Miss Gwenda Stephens, and Miss Jacqueline Carr of the staff of the United Nations helped immeasurably at many points in the preparation of the text. Above all, as in the preparation of the first edition, I am indebted to my wife for constant and discriminating encouragement and support.

In this edition much of the obtrusive paraphernalia of scholarship has been discarded, without, it is hoped, reducing the critical standards that my collaborator and I have sought to maintain. It is hoped that this will make for easier and less interrupted reading. Most of the footnotes have been omitted, and a small selective bibliography has been appended.

H. L. K.

Preface

Geographically the United States and Canada form a single unit; politically and to some extent socially they are divided and unique. The international boundary, cutting laterally through the continent, has in physiographic terms no logical or rational explanation; it is a thoroughly human product. Invisible and illogical as that boundary is, however, it has in certain ways acted as a barrier more effective than a mountain range; marked divisions more radical than an ocean need produce.

The proximity of the United States forms a constant and a serious problem to Canadians. Comparatively weak in numbers, limited in present wealth, of secondary importance in world affairs, Canada cannot escape the inevitable comparison with her colossal, wealthy, and potent neighbor. Americans, on the other hand, are seldom reminded of the existence of their northern kinsmen in spite of the fact that the Dominion ranks first among the customers of the United States, that it sells more to the Republic than does any other state, that it is the locus of more than one fourth of all American foreign investments, and that the total trade between the two countries far exceeds that of any other trading communities.

Canadians can neither forget nor ignore the United States; the influence of the Republic may be seen in every aspect of their lives. In literature and in education, in science and in art, in social standards and in religious concepts, in legislation and, above all, in economics, the enormous pressure of American custom impinges upon those who reside north of the forty-ninth parallel.

In studying the history of American-Canadian relations, therefore, it is not surprising to find that the Canadian people have generally known a great deal more about American conditions and have been far more interested in American actions than Americans have known or cared to know about the situation in the Dominion. The United States is the only foreign country in

xiv

which Canadians are vitally interested, as it is the only country in a position seriously to influence the course of Canadian history. To Americans, on the other hand, Canada is only one of many foreign states in which they are about equally interested. In Canada public opinion is extremely sensitive to American conditions. This situation is not a recent development; it was even more true in the early history of the Republic and of British North America. The present book, therefore, will present much more about Canadian opinions and Canadian conditions than about the conditions and opinions of the United States.

In preparing this study of some aspects of the history of North American relations, I am well aware that I am treading on highly debatable ground. Every incident here discussed has been the center of a more or less serious conflict—a conflict that has enlisted historians as well as politicians or soldiers. Differences of opinion still exist, even among those who cannot be accused of tempering their historical technique to gratify their nationalistic impulses. Under such circumstances the most that any writer can do is to examine the material available, write what he conceives to be the truth—and concede the same liberty to his critics.

Another difficulty that has had to be faced is that resulting from the innumerable ramifications of the subject. Each chapter could easily have been expanded into a book, each sentence to a chapter. Greater difficulties of selection and elimination could hardly be imagined: the very plenitude of the materials has been a source of difficulty and of trial.

No attempt has been made here to live up to the implications of the remark of Hardy's Spirit Sinister, whose "argument was that War makes rattling good history; but Peace is poor reading." War and threats of war must be recorded in relating the history of Canada and the United States, but of much greater importance are the accomplishments and intercourse of peace.

In bringing together this material in what I hope will prove to be a convenient form, I have endeavored to make a small contribution to rational thinking on the subject of international rela-

Preface

tions. It is only on a sound knowledge of the past that a genuine plan for future decency in the relations of the two states can be based. If this book serves in any degree to aid in the attainment of that knowledge, my hopes will be realized.

Ottawa, Ontario
January 1929

xvi

Acknowledgments

The number of persons who have, in one way or another, assisted in the preparation of this book is so large that it is quite impossible adequately to acknowledge their aid, deeply and sincerely as it is appreciated.

I should be truly ungrateful, however, if I failed to take this opportunity to express my thanks to Dr. George H. Blakeslee, of Clark University, and Professor Harry Elmer Barnes, of Smith College. It was on the suggestion of Dr. Blakeslee that the work was originally undertaken, and his kindly encouragement and invaluable critical assistance have been a constant support and an unfailing corrective. The encyclopedic range of knowledge and the stimulating friendship of Dr. Barnes have been of the utmost assistance from the beginning to the end of the whole undertaking. No trouble has been too great, no detail too small for his never failing kindness.

Special mention must also be made of the aid rendered in the final stages of preparation by Dr. George W. Brown, of the University of Toronto, assistant editor of the *Canadian Historical Review*. At a considerable personal sacrifice Dr. Brown went over the whole manuscript and gave me the benefit of his exceptional knowledge of Canadian history and his unusual powers of critical discrimination. I must also acknowledge the assistance of Professor Frederick H. Soward, of the University of British Columbia, who examined the first three chapters in detail, and whose friendship and criticism were equally appreciated.

Certain sections of the manuscript were read and annotated by the following gentlemen, whose special knowledge was united to my great benefit—with unusual kindness: Professor W. Stewart Wallace read the chapter on the Loyalists; Professor W. N. Sage read the sections on the Oregon Boundary and the Annexation Movement in British Columbia; Mr. William A. Found, Director of Fisheries for the Dominion of Canada, read the chapter on the Fisheries Dispute; Professor George M. Jones read the sections on the Rebellions of 1837–8 and the Annexation Movement of 1849; Professor D. A. McArthur and Professor Kenneth W. Taylor read the chapter on Commercial Intercourse; Professor Edwin P. Tanner read the whole manuscript but devoted particular attention to Chapters i and iii; and Professor George M. Smith read Chapter x. Mr. Charles A. Magrath, Chairman of the Canadian section of the International Joint Commission, and Mr. Laurence J. Burpee, secretary of that organization, read the pages dealing with the organization and work of the commission. These gentlemen are not, of course, to be held responsible for any misstatement of fact or failure in interpretation; these are the exclusive responsibility of the author.

Professor Carl Wittke, of Ohio State University, whose *History of Canada* had recently been published, was good enough to read the original manuscript—an almost impossible task—and his suggestions were of the highest value. The same is true of Professor A. E. Martin, of Pennsylvania State College. I am also deeply indebted to Dr. Mack Eastman, of the International Labour Office, Geneva, under whose inspiration I first caught a glimpse of the fascination of historical study; to Dr. O. D. Skelton, Under-Secretary of State for External Affairs, Ottawa; to Professor Walter C. Barnes, of the University of Oregon; to Dr. Verner W. Crane, of Brown University; to Professor Ross W. Collins, of Syracuse University; to Dr. Julius Klein, of

xviii

the Department of Commerce, Washington; to Mr. R. H. Coats, Dominion Statistician, Ottawa; and to many others who have given of their time and their knowledge to assist one who had no just claim upon either.

Mr. Hugh S. Eayrs, president of the Macmillan Company of Canada, has assisted most generously in the surmounting of obstacles having to do both with the text itself and with its preparation for the printer.

Mention should also be made of the kindness of the members of the staff of the Widener Library at Harvard University; of the Congressional Library, Washington, D.C.; of the American Antiquarian Society Library, Worcester; of the Dominion Archives, Ottawa; and of the Provincial Libraries at Toronto, Winnipeg, Regina, and Victoria.

I must also express my deep gratitude for the highly efficient, painstaking, and generous assistance of Miss Alison Ewart of the University of Toronto. It would be very difficult indeed to find a more competent research assistant.

Above all I must acknowledge the invaluable contributions of my wife, Katherine Hall Keenleyside. At every stage in the preparation of the manuscript her critical advice has been of the greatest value, while without her practical assistance and constant encouragement the task might never have been completed.

Finally, I would acknowledge my indebtedness to Miss Isabel Abercrombie for willing and careful assistance with the typing.

H. L. K.

Ottawa
January 1929

Contents

xxi

Contents

April 13th

April 27th Mid-Term

May 4th

xxii

Contents

May 11th

—week

Map, Tables, and Charts

Map of the United States and Canada   2

TABLES

CHARTS

Canada and the United States

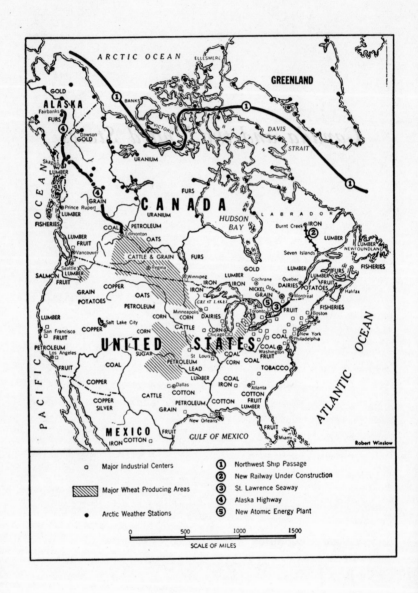

ARCTIC OCEAN   ELLESMERE

GREENLAND

GOLD
ALASKA
Fairbanks
FURS   ④   Dawson
Skagway   GOLD
LUMBER
URANIUM
FISHERIES
Prince Rupert
LUMBER   ④   GRAIN
SALMON   Seattle
LUMBER
FRUIT

BANKS   ①

VICTORIA

①

DAVIS

STRAIT

URANIUM

FURS

CANADA

HUDSON
BAY

LABRADOR

Burnt Creek IRON
②
Seven Islands

LUMBER
NEWFOUNDLAND
LUMBER
FISHERIES

COAL   PETROLEUM
Edmonton
OATS
CATTLE & GRAIN   FURS
Regina
Winnipeg   LUMBER
COPPER   IRON   IRON
OATS   PETROLEUM   IRON
POTATOES   GRAIN
CORN   CORN   DAIRIES
Minneapolis
Salt Lake City   CORN   CATTLE
COPPER   CORN
SUGAR   PETROLEUM
LEAD   St Louis
COAL
CORN   COAL

GOLD
Cochrane
NICKEL Ottawa   Quebec
⑤   GRAIN   Montreal
Toronto ③
⑤   FRUIT
FISHERIES

DAIRIES POTATOES
LUMBER FRUIT
FURS
Halifax
Boston

New York
Philadelphia
Washington
COAL   FRUIT

TOBACCO

UNITED   STATES

LUMBER
San Francisco
FRUIT
PETROLEUM
Los Angeles

FRUIT

COAL

COPPER

COPPER
SILVER

CATTLE

MEXICO   FRUIT
IRON COTTON

Dallas

COTTON
PETROLEUM
GRAIN

CORN   COAL
IRON   Atlanta
COTTON
COTTON   FRUIT
LUMBER

New Orleans

FRUIT
Miami

GULF OF MEXICO

PACIFIC   OCEAN

ATLANTIC   OCEAN

Robert Winslow

▫	Major Industrial Centers	① Northwest Ship Passage
▨	Major Wheat Producing Areas	② New Railway Under Construction
		③ St. Lawrence Seaway
●	Arctic Weather Stations	④ Alaska Highway
		⑤ New Atomic Energy Plant

0   500   1000   1500

SCALE OF MILES

I

Canada and the American Revolution

I. The Background of the Revolution

The American Revolution divided the English-speaking peoples into two distinct competing nations. On the continent of North America this division has taken little cognizance of geographical factors, and a territory essentially homogeneous has been bisected by arbitrary political and economic barriers. One result of this condition has been a continuous succession of geographic, economic, and political problems—problems that have on occasion led the countries to the verge of war, and that once did result in armed conflict. The genesis of these international difficulties is to be found in the civil war that disrupted the British Empire in 1783.

To appreciate the national viewpoint of Canada, or of the United States, and to understand the principles upon which these nations were founded, a knowledge of the causes and issues of the American Revolution is essential.

On 18 September 1759 the fortress of Quebec surrendered to Great Britain. Less than four years later France finally renounced all claim to Canada, and the Treaty of Paris, signed on 10 February 1763, marked the termination of one of the most momentous epochs in the political and military history of the world. The Seven Years' War resulted, in its immediate effect, in

3

the relegation of France to the position of a second-rate colonial power, and presaged the world dominance of the so-called Anglo-Saxons—a dominance that is only now being challenged by the rise of militant communism. In its immediate effect on the continent of North America, the war resulted in the expulsion of the French government from Quebec, and the establishment in its stead of British rule.

Terminating the struggle between two world empires, the Treaty of Paris raised the curtain on civil war. Before 1763 the imminence of French aggressive power had made vitally necessary the protection that the British army and fleet alone could afford the American colonies; but with the foreign foe defeated and peace attained, the ministers of the King found opportunity to institute those internal reforms which the satisfaction of the imperial ideal and the financial embarrassments incurred through the recent war alike demanded.

Imperial reorganization was rendered imperative by the burdens contracted during the lengthy struggle—burdens of administration and of finance, involving a vast territory and varied nationalities. The public debt of Great Britain had risen, by 1763, to the sum of £130,000,000, and this debt was due in large part to the war in the American colonies.

In an attempt to ensure at least the partial payment of this debt by those in whose behalf it had been chiefly incurred, the government of George III decided upon the strict enforcement of the Regulatory Laws. Many of these laws had been on the statute book since the days of Cromwell and Charles II, but had never been seriously enforced. They were, as was natural, based upon the mercantilist theory—an economic doctrine that was accepted without argument by the statesmen and economists of the day. Restrictive laws were, therefore, supplemented in number and made effective in practice.

Intercolonial feuds—for even during the French war the colonies had never united in any lasting community of purpose—and, what was even more important, the addition of Canada and the

Mississippi Valley to the British holdings in North America, made administrative reform essential. The demands of this reorganization required the presence in America of British civil and military officials. Thus not only did the new regulations react unfavorably upon the business interests of the colonies, but a bureaucratic social caste was strengthened. The philosophy of this class inevitably conflicted with the doctrines of individualism and equality which were inherent in a society characterized by frontier conditions.

The background of the American opposition to the new laws is to be discovered in the considerable period during which the colonies had been almost completely free from external regulation. Between 1660 and 1763 the American colonies had enjoyed an economic freedom unknown in any other colonial system of the period. Legally, the Regulatory Laws of 1660 were operative during this period, but in fact they were consistently ignored. Thus, the colonists had become accustomed to a status of self-government, and representative institutions had developed to a stage far beyond that attained in England itself. They had controlled their executive through the "bargain and sale" procedure, and had enjoyed an economic and legislative freedom which was an exact reversal of the practice in French and Spanish colonies. It was therefore logically impossible to expect that the colonists would peacefully agree to accept the restrictions which enforcement of the existing laws would entail. Habit and interest were both opposed. As Van Tyne has said, "Great Britain had given the colonies free rein for too long a period to make it safe or practicable to attempt the enforcement of any important and extensive restrictive regulations, however legally or morally just they may have been."

Thus every action of the British government was obnoxious to the long unrestricted colonists and, judged by the standards of today, these actions were unduly repressive and altogether unjustified. Given the economic theory of the time, however, they were the just and unavoidable result of the new problems forced

5

upon imperial Britain after 1763. It was not a matter for censure or praise; it was the logical result of the existing conditions. Or again, as Van Tyne well expressed it:

"after a century of great laxity towards the colonies,—a century in which the colonists were favored by political privileges shared by no other people of that age; after environment had established new social conditions, and remoteness and isolation had created a local and individual hatred of restraint; after the absence of traditions had made possible the institution of representation by population, and self-government had taken on a new meaning in the world; after a great gulf had been fixed between the social, political and economic institutions of the two parts of the British Empire—only then did the British government enter upon a policy intended to make the empire a unity."

Psychologically the colonists had long been independent; it required only an overt act on the part of Great Britain to arouse a demand for legal freedom. But the reorganization of 1763 to 1775 represented more than simply a renewed effort to enforce the mercantile system as set down in the Navigation Acts from 1661 onward.

After the great victory of 1763 the rulers of imperial Britain looked with some awe at the Empire that they had acquired, as Seeley later said, "in a fit of absence of mind." They felt, not unnaturally, that something should be done to rationalize the administration of their great new estate. So British imperial policy became a search for a system that could comprehend and control an Empire of a diversity and extent that surpassed anything known to the precedents of history. The methods of territorial imperialism seemed to offer the solution. These methods were in direct conflict with the insistence of the American colonial leaders that the Empire was a federal structure. Thus the Revolution when it came was a revolt against centralization as well as against economic injustice.

6

From this background, hastened and provoked by the personal ambitions and antipathies of the leaders, arose the American Revolution. Colonist turned against Englishman, and the Empire so recently acquired was rent apart by civil strife. In the American Revolution, Americans and Canadians as such for the first time came face to face in conflict.

2. *Canada after the British Conquest*

When Quebec surrendered to the British in 1759, Canada had a French population of approximately 70,000. The vast majority of this total were the habitants—simple peasant farmers, kindly in spirit, industrious, and devout. They were, primarily, tillers of the soil and, in a small way, trappers; yet when occasion demanded, they had been ready to exchange the hoe for a musket and, under the leadership of their semi-feudal overlords, to go forth to battle against the hated foreigner. "A strong healthy race," wrote Governor Murray, "plain in their dress, virtuous in their morals; temperate in their living." Nominally occupying a political and social status comparable with that of the medieval peasant of Europe, the French-Canadian habitant enjoyed in fact a more worthy position. It is true that he was unlearned and credulous; but it is also true that he was very largely free from feudal dues and services. He had a simple, firm, and direct belief in a personal Devil, a literal hell, and the innate wickedness of man, but in this he was not unique. His economic situation was, in the main, satisfactory, and if he was at times dragged away to unwelcome military service or oppressed by a petty tyrant among his superiors, his general lot was infinitely superior to that of his European cousin. His land was protected by legal agreements, his services to seigneur and priest were clearly understood and might not be lightly altered either to his detriment or to his

7

benefit. He was neither educated nor free, but he was busy and, on the whole, content.[1]

The nobility of New France was a miscellaneous class. From the military and executive officials of Quebec to the simple seigneur of the Yamaska River was a far longer descent than that from the latter to the lowly habitant. Many of the seigneurs worked as hard and lived almost as humbly as did their legal inferiors. It was an honor to be a seigneur, but hardly a privilege. To be an official of the Crown was, however, another matter. This class, accustomed to the Old World prerogatives of their order, did not lose the feudal spirit in their new surroundings. Rulers in peace and leaders in war, they did not suffer defeat gladly, and many of them returned to France in 1763.

Occupying a position more powerful than either habitants or noblesse were the clergy of the Roman Catholic Church. The secular and regular clergy combined to control not only the conscience, but, to a lesser degree, even the person and possessions of their ignorant communicants. All education and much of the local government were directly in the hands of the clergy. Living, in many instances, brave, self-sacrificing, and adventurous lives, they were acquainted also with the sources of power, the paths of wealth. The influence of the clergy was so great that few, even of the most exalted administrators or nobles, cared to offend the priest in holy orders. The absence of the printing press was no inconsiderable factor in the maintenance of their control. With the coming of the British, their power was weakened, but was not annulled.

For the greater part of the history of New France trade had been a governmental or a private monopoly, and in consequence no strong commercial middle class had developed. The few important merchants domiciled in the colony were closely allied with the political and military leaders. For many years before the coming of the British, graft, jobbery, and corruption were

---

[1] It should be noted that religious unity was maintained and economic and social progress retarded by the laws prohibiting entry of Huguenots and other heretics as settlers in New France.

not uncommon in Canadian life. The habitant was oppressed by every method of political and commercial chicanery, with the result that moral degenerates, such as Bigot, and fools, such as Vaudreuil, were enabled to live in luxury and lascivious extravagance. Against these conditions the honorable and able Montcalm had fought in vain, and on the Governor and the Intendant rests, and should rest, a large part of the immediate blame for the success of British arms in the capture of New France.

On the other hand, it must be recognized that in New France, as elsewhere in North America, the frontier did exert a democratizing influence on life and institutions. The *coureurs de bois* represented escape from the control of established authority, and the figure of the captain of the militia embodied the seed of local autonomy. As compared with the thirteen colonies, however, New France even in 1763 could still be described as a controlled society.

This, then, was the colonial organism against which the British fought, and in its political and economic aspects it was overthrown by the invaders. A military government was at once established under General James Murray, the most unusual of all rulers—a tolerant militarist. Under his reasonable and kindly control the habitants enjoyed a freedom from military burdens and a security against unjust taxation to which they had long been strangers. Strict financial probity was demanded of the British officials; feudal dues were abolished; freedom of worship, including the abolition of compulsory tithes, was assured; and many French Canadians were employed in the legal and political administration.

Following the establishment of the British rule, traders, both from the homeland and from the American colonies, began to appear in Canada. Almost immediately, in an effort to exploit the one and thwart the other, this new element entered into conflict with both the French people and the British military officials. In their striving for wealth they were violently impatient of all obstacles. General Murray characterized the traders of Montreal as "the most immoral collection of men I ever

9

knew." Later on, Governor Guy Carleton, who was of a similar opinion, added to the bitterness of the new arrivals by depriving the justices of the peace of their civil jurisdiction—a power that he believed them to be using to the detriment of the habitants. Making full allowance for the differences that were bound to arise between the military and the commercial interests in the colony, for the exasperation that colored the reports of Murray and Carleton, and for the insufficiency of proof available regarding the integrity of some individual merchants, it still may be admitted that the Governor was probably exaggerating very little when he wrote that these traders "all have their fortunes to make, and are little solicitous about the means." It is not an unusual attitude. They were—and it is not peculiar to their day or occupation—more concerned with results than with methods.

With the advent of the English minority at the conquest, the theme of the rivalry of the Hudson and the St. Lawrence as the two routes capable of tapping the great mid-continental area of North America enters upon a new phase. The English minority aspired to the same ambitions that the government-controlled French fur empire had treasured. Englishmen coming from the seaboard now became the supreme advocates of the Dominion of the North. To use the St. Lawrence, with Montreal as the business capital, to tap the fur trade of a whole continent became their design. So the Proclamation of 7 October 1763, cutting off the West, was anathema to them; the Quebec Act, adding the West to their domain, was triumph. New England versus New France had been the theme down to 1763. Now, after the conquest, English merchants succeeded French administrators as the leaders of the great North American rivalry. It is an ironical reflection that the proclamation granted an assembly and cut off the West; the Quebec Act added the West and vetoed an assembly. Consequently, neither imperial solution was wholly acceptable to the English minority in the new colony.

In August 1764 the military regime was ended and a civil administration substituted. By the terms of the proclamation marking this change, the supreme executive powers were placed in the hands of the Governor-in-Chief, appointed by the Crown and supported by a council with whose "advice and consent" he was expected to act. The proclamation established English civil as well as military law; required an oath of loyalty and a declaration against transubstantiation of all who would seek office or exercise the franchise; and professed to hope for the establishment of a representative form of government "as soon as the state and circumstances of the said colonies will admit." The execution of this last suggestion was obviously impracticable so long as the civil disabilities remained to disqualify Roman Catholics. In 1764 a representative system of government in Canada would have meant that a few hundred English Protestants would have elected representatives to legislate for more than seventy thousand Catholic Canadians. Impossible as such a condition would have been, the British traders of Montreal and Quebec continually demanded the fulfillment of this "promise" and kept the colony in a state of turmoil for many years.

In spite of the best efforts of Governor Murray, and later of Sir Guy Carleton, to administer justice to all classes in the community, conditions grew steadily worse during the decade following 1764. The clergy was displeased by the abolition of compulsory tithing; the power of the nobles was shattered by English civil law; the British citizens clamored for representative government; and the habitants, disturbed by the general unrest, felt a logical dislike for the foreign conquerors and disapproved such radical innovations as trial by jury. So unsatisfactory was the whole situation that Carleton finally returned to London and, by persistent and powerful lobbying, succeeded in securing the passage of a new legal instrument for the government of Canada. The principles of the famous Quebec Act of 1774 were very largely the product of his mind, and its passage was primarily due to his efforts.[2]

[2] It should not be overlooked, however, that the situation in the thirteen colonies also influenced the British government in drafting the terms of the act. This influence was most clearly shown in the clauses extending the boundaries of Canada to include the Ohio and Mississippi valleys. As Professor D. A. McArthur has said, the British government had "one eye on Boston, the other on Quebec."

Quebec. The privileges and restrictions of the law were alike denounced, and in time many of the peasantry began to understand the implications of "that damned word, Liberty." On the whole, however, the habitants appear to have been indifferent rather than opposed, although the revival of the compulsory tithe, so pleasing to the priesthood, was a matter of dissatisfaction to the peasants. Of some of the latter it can probably be justly said that this act "which was supposed to comprise all they either wished or wanted, had become the first object of their discontent and dislike." But this was true only of a minority, though the number steadily increased as a result of the ceaseless propaganda carried on by the British traders—a propaganda that did much to make the soil receptive to arguments of the emissaries of the Continental Congress, and later of the American soldiery.

It is worth noting that all the chief features of the Quebec Act were clearly formulated before 1773. It was not, therefore, in the eyes of the British government at least, one of the coercive acts promulgated as a result of the Boston Tea Party of December of that year.

In spite of the criticisms of the Quebec Act, it did improve the immediate conditions in Canada. Whether or not the policy of conciliation toward French-Canadian culture here adopted has been advantageous to Canada, viewing the national history as a whole, is a question yet unanswered. It is clear, however, that any other course would have created immensely greater difficulties in the eighteenth century.

3. *Canada and the Committees of Correspondence*

This, then, was the situation in Canada when, on 5 September 1774 the first Continental Congress met in Philadelphia.

14

Inasmuch as Canadian conditions had formed the subject of many and vigorous complaints on the part of American radical leaders from 1763 down to the date of the Congress, it was logical that the position of Canada should be seriously discussed at that famous gathering. Nor was the subject forgotten by the press and platform of the day. Throughout the thirteen colonies there was a real desire for the inclusion of Canada in any scheme of opposition to Great Britain. American leaders and people alike were convinced that Canada should be included if federation and rebellion were resolved upon. The Congress took immediate action to meet this popular desire. On 26 October an address was ordered to be printed for distribution in Canada. This document spoke largely of the "transcendent nature of freedom," which was to overcome all differences of language and religion. It went on to invite assistance in united opposition to the arbitrary actions of Great Britain. In closing, it even went so far as to suggest that punishment would follow in the event of a refusal to co-operate. It is estimated that over two thousand copies of this document were circulated in Canada by the following March. Its effect was strengthened by American emissaries who went among the Canadians, playing on their fears with tales of the Inquisition that the British were about to establish; of oppressive taxes to be imposed; and of foreign wars in which the manhood of New France would be sacrificed.

During October 1774 the British residents of Canada gave a practical demonstration of their sympathy for the revolutionary leaders. Aroused by reports of royal oppression in Boston, many of the merchants of Montreal and Quebec combined to collect and ship a contribution of grain and money to the New England port.

Early in February 1775 the leaders of the American patriots decided to issue a more formal invitation to Canada to join in the struggle against Great Britain. Congress referred the matter to the Boston Committee of Correspondence. This committee met on 20 February and Samuel Adams was instructed to draw up a letter to the merchants of Montreal. The letter as finally

drawn contained a statement of the economic and political grievances of New England; a denunciation of the Quebec Act as a
despotic imposition against which all loyal Canadians should
revolt; an invitation to send delegates to the second session of
the Congress, which was to meet in Philadelphia on 10 May; and
a request "for the return of this message with your own sentiments."

The reply from Montreal was sympathetic but hopeless. Canada was depicted as being in worse condition than New England,
and the administration as too strongly entrenched for attack.
Interpreted in the light of modern knowledge, this meant that
Walker and the other merchants of Montreal, though sympathetic with the cause of revolt, knew that such a solution was
impossible in Canada at that time, and that the only result would
be the loss of a very lucrative fur trade.

A third letter, following the same lines as its predecessors,
was written by John Jay on 29 May 1775 and forwarded to the
"oppressed inhabitants of Canada."

When it had become apparent that no real assistance could be
expected from Canada, and when the appeal to arms had finally
been made, the patriot leaders began to look with apprehension
toward the northern boundary of the colonies. As something of
the ability and energy of Sir Guy Carleton was known by reputation, the fear of an invasion from the north was a constantly
growing anxiety. In reality, Carleton was in no position to wage
an offensive war, as his forces had been reduced to the danger
point in favor of General Gage, who was campaigning in New
England. Moreover, the habitants in many districts were dem-
onstrating a decided disinclination to obey orders. The failure
of the British leaders to recognize the situation in Canada is
clearly evidenced by the instructions sent to Carleton in 1775,
inviting him to enroll six thousand French Canadians for immediate service. Sixty willing recruits would have surprised him
at the time. But the American Congress, failing to recognize the
impotence of the Canadian Governor, came to agree with Arnold
in his declaration that an invasion of Canada was made necessary

by a "due regard to our defence." Congress hoped by one strong action to defeat an enemy, conquer a country, remove the fear of a flank attack, gain recruits, and liberate a people.

4. *The American Invasion of Canada*

An invasion having been determined upon, General Schuyler was appointed commander at Ticonderoga. This post, which had been captured by the energy and initiative of Ethan Allen and Benedict Arnold, now became the rendezvous of the American forces. The plan of campaign provided for simultaneous attacks upon Montreal and Quebec. It was hoped that Quebec could be taken while Carleton was defending Montreal, a development that would inevitably result in his subsequent surrender and a complete conquest of Canada. The fatal weakness in this plan lay in discounting British sea-control, which made a real blockade of Quebec impossible.

The first care of General Schuyler was to send emissaries into Canada to observe the temper of the inhabitants and to report on the military situation. The information obtained by General Schuyler, together with the letters of Carleton, Cramahé, and other British officials give a vivid, if overdrawn, picture of Canadian feeling. John Brown, Schuyler's personal representative, reported that everywhere he was received with the greatest kindness, and that the inhabitants appeared unitedly favorable to the American cause. Schuyler wrote to Washington that "accounts from all quarters agree that the Canadians are friendly to us," and a little later he reported to the New York Congress that "they are friendly to us and join us in great numbers." On 21 September 1775 Cramahé wrote to Carleton that many Canadians were actually serving with the Americans. "No means have been left untried," he said, "to bring the Canadian peasantry to a sense of their duty, and engage them to take up arms in defense of the Province, but all to no purpose." On the same day Carleton himself reported that "the Americans have been more successful with them and have assembled them in great numbers."

Reassured by the reports of their agents, the American forces moved forward into Canada. Over a thousand men under Arnold started from Cambridge to attack Quebec, while the main force under Schuyler followed the old French route along Lake Champlain and the Richelieu and St. Lawrence rivers in the direction of Montreal. The British made their first defense at Fort St. John's, some twenty-five miles southeast of Montreal, and a protracted siege ensued. Here General Schuyler, lacking the physical energy demanded by winter campaigning, and suffering from a disease that gave him little respite, was forced to give up his command and was succeeded by the brilliant and impetuous Montgomery. On 1 November St. John's fell, and with it the Americans captured about two thirds of all the regular troops in Canada.

The way was now open to Montreal, and Montgomery entered the city on 13 November, capturing stores and ammunition that had been collected for the use of Carleton's troops. Carleton himself had left the city during the night, taking all the boats that were in condition to sail. The ships, however, were becalmed a few miles below the city, and Montgomery sent troops and guns to stop them at the point near Sorel where the river narrowed. But Carleton outwitted his enemies, escaping during the night in a small boat that drifted past the American patrols, and rowing with muffled oars, silently, in the shadows of the bank.

The American successes at St. John's and Montreal still further influenced the wavering Canadians. In spite of the influence and vigorous loyalty of the Roman Catholic priesthood, who even went so far as to refuse absolution to all traitors, the American battalions daily increased as the Canadian militia melted away. In his report from Montreal on 24 November, Montgomery wrote that he "could have as many Canadians as I know how to maintain"; then wisely added: "at least I think so, while affairs wear so promising a prospect." Montgomery's difficulty was financial: he could "maintain" very few. Had he been strongly supported with "hard" money, so that he could have taken full advantage of the favorable conditions, the whole history of the continent might have been vitally affected. Carleton, as he wrote to Lord Dartmouth, could do little to offset the drawing power of American success, since he lacked both financial and military strength.

On 19 November Carleton arrived in Quebec, after an adventurous journey from Montreal. His appearance was hailed with "unspeakable joy" by "the friends of the government," but it met with "the utter dismay of the abettors of sedition and rebellion." A third greeting also awaited him—a greeting from the muskets of an investing army of some five hundred and fifty Americans under the resolute leadership of Benedict Arnold.

Much has been written upon the strategic importance of the city of Quebec. As well as being the only post in Canada that "had the least claim to be called a fortified place," it was the key to the defenses of the colony, and until it was captured, Canada was unconquered. The taking of Quebec was, then, the fundamental object of American strategy. To this end Washington had dispatched Arnold, with eleven hundred picked men from Massachusetts, overland to the St. Lawrence. At Quebec he was to join forces with Montgomery, descending from Montreal, and together they were to possess themselves of the key to continental power.

In spite of the lurid exaggerations so commonly employed in describing Arnold's march, the event does deserve a high place in the annals of military achievement. Leaving Cambridge with more than one thousand sturdy men, he struggled for three hundred miles through the autumnal wilderness, by swift streams and long portages, through the pathless forest and over wind-swept hills, soaked by day and freezing by night, harassed by accident and desertion, ever menaced by hostile Indians, and with a diminishing supply of food. Finally exhausted, their clothing torn and their shoes in shreds, weak with hunger and disease, and leaving one third of their number dead on the way, he and his men accomplished their journey and sighted their objective.

After a short stay among the friendly habitants in order to recuperate strength and repair equipment, the Americans advanced to the river and on 8 November prepared to cross. But for three days they were delayed by inclement weather—a delay that was to spell the doom of their hopes, for during that brief respite Colonel MacLean, the picturesque and energetic military defender of Quebec, was organizing his defenses and collecting necessary supplies. When Arnold finally succeeded in crossing the river, he was confronted by an opponent who, in spite of the positive disloyalty of many of his troops, and the covert hostility of some of the citizens of the city, was prepared to offer a resolute defense. Facing these conditions, and lacking a naval force to make a blockade fully effective, Arnold could only await the coming of Montgomery.

On the same day that word was first received in Quebec of the coming of Arnold, Cramahé, the commandant, had received a letter from General Howe in Boston. This lazy and incompetent commander declared that no aid could possibly be sent to Canada until spring. In his reply Cramahé declared: "There is too much reason to apprehend the affair will soon be over." It was at this depressing moment that Colonel MacLean appeared in Quebec with a force of two hundred Highlanders. These recruits had been obtained as the result of a daring and adventurous trip not only in Canada but in several revolting colonies as well. The impetuous Scot, taking control from the weaker hands of Cramahé, began to organize a systematic defense. "Those vagabonds," he had earlier told the burghers, "come with no other view than that of plunder and pillage." Such statements as this, combined with the ragged appearance of the American troops, very shortly had an appreciable effect on the attitude of the more wealthy citizens. The admission to the city of six hundred half-starved and desperate men was not lightly to be connived at, even by those who were politically sympathetic to the republican cause.

On 14 November Arnold wrote to Cramahé demanding the evacuation of Quebec, stating that "on the surrender of the city the property of every individual shall be secured to him; but if I am obliged to carry the town by storm, you may expect every severity practised on such occasions." Under the influence of Colonel MacLean, Cramahé answered this demand from the mouth of a cannon. The American leaders thereupon undertook to blockade the city.

Despite the unhesitating rejection of the American offer, all was not well in Quebec. Of the six thousand inhabitants, many openly favored the American cause; the militia was halfhearted or openly insubordinate; the defenses were old and in many places insecure; and the troops, though well armed, were few in number. Chaos reigned and no one knew what each succeeding day might bring forth. In the midst of this confusion, and to the great joy of the Loyalists, Governor Carleton arrived from Montreal. Three days later he issued a proclamation stating that "in order to rid the town of all useless, disloyal, and treacherous persons," those who refused to serve in arms "must quit the town in four days."

The city having been thus purged, Carleton and MacLean set their forces to work on the defenses, hoping to get them into condition to withstand an attack. In order to gain time, a rumor was circulated to the effect that the British were preparing for a sortie against Arnold's lines. The Americans, with ammunition reduced to five rounds for each man and still suffering from the effects of their long march, determined to retreat up the river to Pointe aux Trembles, there to recuperate their strength and await the arrival of Montgomery. This withdrawal made Carleton's task more simple, and he worked steadily to collect supplies and to strengthen the ramparts of the city. By the enlistment of every able-bodied citizen he succeeded in marshaling a body of over eighteen hundred men. Five hundred and thirty-one of these, however, were French-Canadian militia of very doubtful loyalty.

Meanwhile General Montgomery had been having troubles

of his own at Montreal. Having followed the usual American custom of enlisting recruits for certain definite periods, the General was faced, shortly after the capture of that city, by the prospect of losing the greater part of his forces. Fatigued by a strenuous campaign, unpaid and poorly equipped, their immediate object accomplished, and the term of their enlistment expiring, the American soldiery viewed with rapidly vanishing enthusiasm the prospects of a winter campaign against Quebec. Nor did the true sons of Massachusetts and New Hampshire respond with alacrity and pleasure to the commands of a general from New York. Refusal of duty was a daily problem among officers as among the men, and "sick parades" were well attended by those whose only desire was to escape further campaigning. It was not until a Congressional committee had arrived in Montreal and had promised increased pay, bonuses, and new equipment, that Montgomery was in a position to advance with three hundred men to reinforce Benedict Arnold—an advance that was made the more desirable by reason of the growing friction between the citizens of Montreal and the occupying forces. Montgomery and Arnold joined forces on 2 December, and three days later they encamped before Quebec. The city was now completely blockaded, and Montgomery, in command of approximately one thousand Americans and about five hundred Canadian volunteers, prepared for the final clash.

5. *The Assault on Quebec*

Another tragic drama was now to be staged under the grim walls of old Quebec. It was rapidly enacted. On the day following his arrival Montgomery wrote to Carleton demanding an immediate capitulation. "You have," he said, "a great extent of works from their nature incapable of defense, manned by a motley crew of sailors, the greatest part our friends, or of citizens

22

who wish to see us within their walls, and a few of the worst troops who ever styled themselves soldiers." The Governor refused even to receive communications from a former British officer, once his friend, now a traitor. Attempts to arouse the citizens to make a demonstration favorable to the Americans met with no success. Carleton's control was complete. As the siege continued, the situation of the republican troops, improperly housed, suffering severely from the cold, poorly supplied with food, and inadequately protected by artillery, became more and more desperate. The New York troops, moreover, had given warning that they would not remain after the end of the year, when their period of enlistment expired. Montgomery attempted to encourage his soldiers with promises of plunder after the conquest of the city. This, however, afforded little immediate comfort. On 20 December the supreme disaster occurred: smallpox was reported in the American camp.

Action, immediate and final, was now imperative. A hurried consultation among the American leaders resulted in plans for a surprise attack. Scaling ladders were prepared, ammunition was collected, and the men were organized for the great adventure. After many delays and much indecision the attack was finally launched under the protecting cover of a turbulent snowstorm on the last night of the year.

Arnold, with the major portion of the troops, attired for the most part in British uniforms captured at St. John's, attacked where the defenses of the Lower Town dropped to the St. Charles; Montgomery led a smaller party against the southwest corner of the Lower Town, below Cape Diamond. They were to join within the city and carry the citadel from below.

Through the darkness, under a stormracked sky, the two detachments struggled toward their objectives. Between four thirty and five o'clock a rocket shot up from Cape Diamond: the attack had been launched. Quebec became an inferno of noise. Between the storm-gusts could be heard the clangor of bells from church and convent, the rattle of musketry, the cries of wounded men; while deep and resonant came the sound of firing cannon. Montgomery and his little force dashed for the barricade that stretched across their way—a barricade whose position they knew, but which they could not see. But success lay not that way. The burly skipper whose duty it was to guard this path had trained his largest gun upon the clear approach. Warned that the Americans were approaching, he fired into the murk and darkness of the storm. His effort was crowned with amazing success: the gallant Montgomery and many of his men were killed by the first discharge; the remainder had no choice but to retreat. The following day the body of the American leader was recovered from its shroud of ice and snow, to receive honorable burial at the hands of his foes.

Arnold's plight was but little better. Wounded himself at the first barricade, he handed over the command to Captain Daniel Morgan, who, taking the place of his fallen leader, drove the British to their second rampart. Here the defenders stood their ground until, a circling movement having been accomplished, the Americans found themselves attacked from the rear. Their ammunition exhausted, and now with no hope of success, four hundred and thirty-one of Arnold's men surrendered. The attack was over, Quebec and Canada were saved, and the British loss was thirty killed and wounded.

6. The Changing Attitude of the Canadians

The American defeat at Quebec was indeed the crucial event in the struggle for possession of Canada. Larger bodies of troops were placed in the field in 1776, but never again did the danger to Quebec appear imminent. Never again did the habitants, disillusioned by this defeat, risk their lives and property, in comparable numbers, on behalf of a losing cause. British authority was here established, to remain unquestioned for more than three decades.

Despite his wound and the clouded aspect of American fortunes, General Arnold and the remnants of his force attempted to maintain the siege. Washington urged him on and sent what troops he could spare, though not the five thousand requested by Arnold. Carleton, realizing that the elements were fighting for the British, made no attempt to break the blockade.

Arnold's position was indeed precarious. Suffering from scurvy and smallpox, with food supplies rapidly dwindling, the mutinous spirit of his troops became dangerous, and this condition was gravely aggravated by his inability to pay their allowances.

An even more fundamental misfortune was the rapidly changing attitude of the Canadian populace. The military mind is never conducive to good relations between soldier and civilian. When to this professional attribute is added a distinct consciousness of racial superiority, such as the Americans felt toward the unenlightened French Canadians, pleasant intercourse cannot long be maintained. After the American defeat at Quebec the Canadians had little need to refrain from the expression of their sentiments, and the weary, undisciplined, ragged Continentals were no longer objects of respect. American offenses, which had previously been glossed over or condoned, were now bitterly resented. As the resentment of the Canadians grew, so increased the causes for complaint. "The licentiousness of our troops," wrote Schuyler, "is not easily to be described, nor have all my efforts been able to put a stop to these scandalous excesses." Another American general subsequently stated that "few of the inhabitants have escaped abuse, either in their persons or their property . . . court martials are vain when officers connive at the depredations of the men." Not only personal abuse, but the regulations rendered essential by the military occupation weighed heavily on the Canadians, and when Arnold was forced, on 4 March 1776, to declare all who refused Continental money to be "enemies," their indignation was violently expressed.

A final cause of animosity was the attitude of the American soldiery toward the Roman Catholic Church. Flamboyant in his zealous Protestantism, the recruit from New England or New

York found no little difficulty in obeying the order to treat all religious persons and buildings with punctilious respect. Thus resentment spread, and the American leaders found it ever more difficult to maintain friendly relations with the "oppressed" people whom they had come to free. A Congressional committee including the arch-diplomat Franklin and a Jesuit priest, John Carroll, was sent to Montreal to smooth out the existing difficulties. The mission brought with them the first printing press to enter Canada. It was set up in Montreal, where it was used to publish material favorable to the American cause. Not even the abilities of Franklin and his colleagues, however, were sufficient to alter the Canadian attitude.

7. The Final Defeat

Faced by constantly increasing difficulties, Arnold remained at his post throughout the winter. Reinforcements arrived in the spring, but such was the condition of the American forces that no offensive measures could be immediately initiated. On 1 May General John Thomas reached Arnold's camp with eight regiments; but five days later Quebec was relieved by the arrival of British ships. The first ship to reach the city was commanded by Sir Charles Douglas, and it was but the forerunner of a fleet with ten thousand men. Carleton, however, availing himself of the assistance of two hundred men from Sir Charles's ship, waited for no further aid but, placing himself at the head of his forces, issued forth to give battle.

In the American camp all was confusion: a condition aggravated by the pretensions and inexperience of General Thomas. With the approach of the British troops under the leader whose ability the Americans had come to know only too well, all thought of defense was abandoned, and each soldier for himself sought safety in flight. In this situation Sir Guy Carleton displayed another facet of his many-sided character. Showing a humanity that gave a luster to his name which military achievement alone could never confer, he recalled his troops from the pursuit and sent word to all the farmers between Quebec and Montreal ordering them to treat the Americans with every kindness. Search parties were organized to bring in the sick and exhausted, and not only did he care for his enemies in their weakness, but, having cured their diseases and healed their wounds, he set them at liberty to return to their homes. Such acts of mercy fittingly crowned the first military defense of Canada.

At the same time that he himself was defeating the Americans in the east, Governor Carleton arranged for an attack on American power in the west. This blow was struck by Captain Foster against the invaders' post at The Cedars, forty-five miles southwest of Montreal, and was entirely successful.

The scattered American troops found a rendezvous at Three Rivers, and there their leaders planned to make a stand against the advancing British. Here General Thomas died of smallpox and was succeeded in command first by General Thompson and then by General Sullivan. Hardly had the latter organized his command and made tentative but hopeful plans for the future, when the British attacked. On 14 June the Americans began a second retreat—a movement that did not make a lasting stop until Crown Point was reached. By 25 July the only American soldiers left in Canada were prisoners in the citadel, and patients in the hospitals of Quebec.

More slowly Carleton followed his retreating foe, and the American forces were able to embark safely on Lake Champlain. Carleton's failure to press his pursuit sharply reflected the statesman in him more than the soldier. The Declaration of Independence was still in the future, and many Americans hesitated to take the final step. Carleton might well have considered that a severe military reverse would harden opinion and push Americans into the irrevocable act of independence. The British advance ended at the northern end of Lake Champlain, and on that inland sea a curious conflict took place. Arnold at one end of the lake and officers of the Royal Navy at the other undertook to carve ships of war from the forests bordering the shore. By October the fleets were ready and on the 11th of that month a naval battle commenced, in which the Americans, outnumbered and more lightly armed, were completely defeated after a prolonged and vigorous engagement. In the larger view, however, Arnold's tactics were successful. His brilliant defense had so delayed the progress of the British forces that winter was now at hand and a further advance was impossible. Having reconnoitered the surrounding districts, General Carleton led his troops back to Canada. Mahan regards Arnold's action on Lake Champlain as one of the decisive battles of the war.

8. *The Denouement*

Thus ended the first American invasion of British Canada. In seeking the causes of defeat, due importance must be given to the natural difficulties of the undertaking; to the unstable quality of the American troops; to the military ability of General Carleton; and to the attitude of the clergy, who felt safer with Great Britain under the Quebec Act, than with the thirteen colonies. More significant than any of these causes, however, was the fundamental error of the American leaders. Had Schuyler and Montgomery prepared and executed comprehensive plans for the utilization of the potential strength of the friendly Canadians; had this force been enlisted and trained for even a short period; and had Congress given Montgomery the financial support necessary to carry out these plans; the conquest of Canada might well have been assured. As it was, however, as soon as disaster overtook the invading forces, the few Canadian auxiliaries deserted and the general populace, with no apparent stake in American success, either lost interest or became actively hostile. In June 1776 General Washington wrote that many of the American misfortunes "can be attributed to a want of discipline and a proper regard to the conduct of our soldiery." Had he written with full cognizance of all the factors involved, he would have had to place the primary condemnation on those generals and politicians who neither succeeded in nor strongly attempted capitalizing the friendly attitude of the Canadian population.

The victories of 1776 ended the direct connection of Canada with the American Revolutionary War. Subsequent interest in the struggle was only incidental. An attempt was made in 1777 to organize a winter campaign against Canada. General Gates, president of the American Board of War, appointed Lafayette to command this expedition, but gave no further support. The movement never progressed beyond its American base. There now seems good reason to believe that the whole plan was simply an attempt on the part of General Gates to lower the brilliant Frenchman in the esteem of George Washington. The opposition of the latter to such a scheme was widely known. In the following year an abortive attempt was made to enlist a brigade of Canadians under French officers. According to the general plan of which this was a part, France was to equip an expedition against Halifax and Quebec, while American troops were to advance on Detroit, Niagara, Oswego, and Montreal. This plan was endorsed by Congress, but was subsequently vetoed by the strong common sense of General Washington.

A few of the habitants who had enlisted under Arnold and Montgomery remained with the American forces until the end of the war; but at no time did the vital interests or ultimate safety of Canada become seriously involved. Apart from the military difficulties to be faced by an invading army in Canada, the American leaders would have been faced by another problem had they attempted such a movement. This difficulty was tersely described by Franklin as the "want of a sufficient quantity of hard money." "The Canadians," he wrote, "are afraid of paper and never would take the Congress money. To enter a country that you mean to make a friend of with an army that must have occasion every day for fresh provisions, horses, carriage labor of every kind, having no acceptable money to pay those that serve you, and to be obliged therefore from the necessity of the case to take that service by force, is the sure way to disgust, offend, and by degrees make enemies of the whole people, after which all your operations will be more difficult, all your motions discovered and every endeavor used to have you driven back out of the country."

The formal entrance of France into the Anglo-American struggle ended all real prospect of a second American invasion of Canada. The French wanted no part of a successful attempt by the revolutionaries to take Canada. They preferred to guarantee Canada to the British Empire, because they felt that with Canada the prospective United States would be too independent. France wanted a United States dependent upon herself.

Among some sections of the Canadian population disaffection continued to smolder throughout the war, and in consequence Governor Haldimand was frequently to be found reporting in a pessimistic vein. But on the whole conditions steadily improved. The clergy gradually regained their ascendancy through the use of pulpit and school; and the imperative demands of personal duties, together with the reasonably just rule of British officials, gradually bred forgetfulness. The dream of republican liberty was slowly forgotten in the press of concrete facts.

American interest in Canada did not, however, end with military defeat. Force having proved ineffective, the subtler methods of diplomacy were brought into action. For this purpose few more competent agents could have been found than John Jay, John Adams, and Benjamin Franklin, the American commissioners at Paris in 1783. Congress had instructed these diplomats to persuade the British representatives to incorporate the cession of Canada to the United States in the treaty of peace. This was "a difficult errand in diplomacy . . . demanding wariness and adroitness if not even craft and dissimulation."

It appeared at first as though the American diplomats would be successful, as Oswald, the head of one group of British commissioners, was a weakling, unversed in such negotiations, and lacking in detailed knowledge of North American conditions—in spite of extensive possessions in the New World. When Mr. Strachey—a new commissioner—arrived in Paris, however, conditions changed, and at the same time the British government emphatically reiterated its earlier orders against any such surrender. The United States had demanded the cession of Canada as part of the reparation for losses during the war; to prevent future wars; and as compensation for indemnifying the Tories or Loyalists. In reply, Great Britain refused to pay any reparations; stated that there were other ways of preventing war; and declared that the Loyalists must be provided for in any case if a treaty was to be made.

The strategic position of Canada, as well as the value of the fisheries, the fur trade, and the lumber resources of the colony, made it a particularly valuable possession, and all Franklin's logic and sauve manipulation proved unavailing. The statesmen of Great Britain recognized some truth in Washington's statement that the loss of Canada "would be a deadly blow to her trade and empire." The refusal of France to support the American demands was an interesting commentary on the relations of the erstwhile allies. Congress, realizing that American independence was not yet assured, had wisely refrained from making the cession of Canada a *sine qua non*. The American representatives turned to more promising discussions.

Apart from recognizing the complete independence of the American colonies, the Treaty of Paris embodied a number of other clauses that were to be of great importance to the history of Canadian-American relations. Among these were the provisions designed to protect the Loyalists and to prevent the collection of pre-Revolutionary debts. The treaty also defined the boundary between British and American territory, and defined it in such terms that its precise location inevitably became a cause of bitter and extended discord. Similarly the clauses relating to the North Atlantic fisheries introduced a subject that became a recurrent theme of international controversy.

2

The Influence of the United Empire Loyalists

1. The Loyalists

The American Revolution won independence for the thirteen colonies; and, in a very real sense, it created British Canada.

The migration to Canada of thousands of colonials who had opposed the Revolution gave to the northern colony a solid basis of British stock which was of fundamental importance in guaranteeing the existence and persistence of Anglo-Saxon civilization in what had been, before this time, simply a conquered French province.

The importance of the United Empire Loyalists—the Tories of the Revolutionary days—has sometimes been exaggerated in Canada, but it has been sadly neglected to the histories of the United States.

Second only to the American Revolution itself in its effect upon the history of the continent was the formation and persistence of the Canadian nation; and in both the establishment and the preservation of this political and cultural entity the Loyalists played a conspicuous role. The more nationalistic historians of the United States have been content to anathematize the Tory as a traitor, while Canadian textbooks paid him passing tribute as a martyr and a hero. But neither Americans nor Canadians have sufficiently recognized in the Loyalists a force that has played a vital part in molding and directing the history of a continent. Yet had it not been for the Loyalist pioneers, imbued as they were with a bitter hatred for things American, it is altogether probable that Canada would have fallen before the republican assaults in 1812, and that it would be today a political division of the United States. The indignities they had endured had burned into the souls of the Loyalists a hatred of Americans which, bequeathed to succeeding generations, has not been negligible in its influence upon modern Canadian history. In the early and critical days it was a determining force.

Few movements in history have been more distorted in the popular mind than the American Revolution. It is not to be supposed—as has been done so often—that the response of the American colonists to the arbitrary actions of a harried and stupid imperial government was spontaneous, spectacular, and unanimous. Society in the colonies was divided gradually, and by the interaction of many influences, into two groups; but within each group was to be found a wide diversity of sentiment. It was only after years of conflict, economic, political, and military, that a majority of the people came to favor independence. The greater number were at first opposed to separation, and many retained such sentiments even after 4 July 1776. At least one hundred thousand residents of the various states maintained their opposition so clearly that they were forced by the zeal of the Patriots to leave the colonies. These individuals, who through their support of the imperial cause lost their homes and possessions, later became known, by decree of their sovereign as the United Empire Loyalists. The causes leading to their extraordinary display of fealty were as varied as the individuals themselves and the facts with which they were confronted.

In every society are to be found two classes: those who fear change more than they dislike the faults of the existing order, and those whose emotional or rational hostility toward contemporary conditions leads them to a desire for radical alteration. In

33

the early days of revolutionary agitation the conservatives of American society were altogether opposed to any plan of separation from the Empire. Many of them were willing to take part in non-importation agreements and other forms of economic and political argument, but they thoroughly condemned physical force and the agitation for independence. They argued, with some truth, that the British colonial system tended to stabilize business conditions, to strengthen the moral code, to introduce social refinements, and to add to the amenities of life. Thus the conservative tendency was altogether in the direction of loyalism, many going so far as to oppose all criticism of imperial measures. Gradually, however, as British regulations widened their scope and increased in severity, many of these conservatives, feeling the pinch themselves, becoming accustomed to conflict, and fearing classification as Loyalists, tended to condone and finally to join in active support of the Patriot policies. Large numbers of this class, nevertheless, maintained their opposition to the Revolution, and oppression served only to inflame their hostility to the "rebels." In the end the extremists among them found difficulty in distinguishing between a legitimate desire for reform and treason.

In addition to these "natural conservatives," there were many other classes whose loyalty to the Empire was a product of the immediate social and economic conditions: officeholders under the Crown; clergymen of the established church; the more prominent and successful of the professional classes; and those, in general, whose economic prosperity and social prestige depended upon the continuation of the existing order. There were many colonists, moreover, who objected to rebellion on religious grounds: who believed with Dr. Myles Cooper that "the principles of submission and obedience to lawful authority are as inseparable from a sound, genuine member of the Church . . . as any religious principles." Religious authority was not a negligible force in eighteenth-century America. Finally, the sentimental attachment that characterizes many English-Canadians or Australians today in their attitude toward the mother country was no small factor in adding members to the Loyalist party in 1776.

The Loyalists, in large part, were "the prosperous and contented men, the men without a grievance. Conservatism was the only policy that one could expect from them; men do not rebel to rid themselves of prosperity. The Loyalist obeyed his nature as truly as the patriot, but, as events proved, chose the ill-fated side." Yet this is not altogether true. The Loyalist party contained men and women from all classes in society, from governor to cobbler, and from priest to tavern-keeper. It contained, again, men of varied nationality—Dutch, Irish, Indian, German, and Scotch—who had joined for even more varied reasons. It is true that habit, fear of change, local jealousies, sentiment, and hope of profit all contributed their quota, yet social, political, and economic vested interests really explain the strength of the Loyalist cause. The Loyalists were not men of peculiar virtue, nor of excessive vice; they were ordinary human beings seeking to protect their own interests.

Generally speaking, the wealthier Loyalists and their servants went by sea to Nova Scotia and New Brunswick. Farmers from New England and New York followed the established frontier tradition and moved west to Upper Canada.

Had the Crown triumphed in its struggle with the thirteen colonies, the almost universal condemnation that has been visited upon the Tories would have fallen instead upon the patriots; the victors have enjoyed the spoils of approbation. *Ut mos est hominum!*

2. The Treatment of the Loyalists

It was not until after the signing of the Declaration of Independence that the cleavage between Patriot and Loyalist became pronounced. Prior to that time there was much shifting from one side to the other, and the majority of the people were definitely and finally committed to neither party. As the struggle between the colonies and the Crown became intensified, however, the Revolutionary leaders labored under the imperative necessity of assuring to themselves the co-operation and support of the people. Adherence to the Crown could not be tolerated in the newly formed state, and expediency demanded a policy both harsh and effective. By legislative enactment, social pressure, and mob compulsion the ideal of uniformity was sought.

One of the first important actions of the Revolutionary Congress and the local state committees was the passage of a series of Test Laws designed to reveal the political complexion of those whose loyalty was in doubt. The justice or injustice of these laws is still a matter of dispute, and, as is usual in such matters, logical arguments can be advanced on either side. To the Patriot, King George III was no longer the supreme authority in the free states, and those who still paid him homage were traitors to the newly formed and independent Republic. The Loyalist, on the other hand, denied that the Crown had lost its power, and denounced as rebels those who signed the Declaration of Independence. To the Patriot leaders, Test Laws appeared necessary for the preservation of the new freedom; to the Tory, they were unauthorized measures of oppression, enforced by extra-legal organizations. Granting its premise, each argument was sound; but, just or unjust, such laws were inevitable.

Supplementing the Test Laws were hundreds of regulatory enactments designed to eliminate loyalism or, at worst, to weaken the Tory cause.

Varying slightly from colony to colony, the Regulatory and Test Laws contained, in essence, the same provisions. Loyalists were barred from all civil rights; they could neither collect debts nor claim legal protection from slander, assault, or blackmail. They could not hold land, make a will, or present a gift. The professions were closed to them, and military service in the Whig ranks was frequently demanded. Freedom of speech, press, and travel were rigidly curtailed, and, on the charge of treason, Loyalists were hanged, exiled, or imprisoned. On the same charge property was confiscated. Heavy fines and forced donations were levied, and in many districts those suspected of Tory sympathies were herded together in concentration camps, some of which compared unfavorably with the worst of British prison ships. The extent to which these laws were enforced depended on local political and military conditions. Their incidence varied directly as the strength of the Patriot cause.

Administered with justice and with judicial care, many of these laws could not fairly be criticized, in view of the conditions of the time; but enforced as they were by local Committees of Public Safety composed, for the most part, of the most violent members of their respective communities, they were intolerably oppressive. Thousands of Loyalists were driven from their homes to seek asylum in such Tory strongholds as New York and Philadelphia. Arnold Toynbee has written that never before had any group suffered so much for purely political reasons.

The intensity of the feeling against the Loyalists can with difficulty be exaggerated. They were accused, often quite justly, of acting as spies for the British army, of supplying it with food and munitions, of counterfeiting American currency, and of enlisting bands to attack Patriot strongholds. General Washington declared them to be "abominable pests of society" and advised against their execution only from fear of retaliation on Patriot prisoners. He urged all Tories to commit suicide. John Adams "strenuously recommended" hanging all those who were inimical to the progress of the Revolution. Even the philosophic Franklin became vigorous in denunciation, though he himself had long opposed the idea of independence. To the rabble of town and city the plight of wealthy Loyalists was an invitation to pillage and destruction. In such cases espionage, informing, slander, and robbery were praised as virtues and as evidence of patriotic zeal.

Persecution of the Loyalists was not confined to the legal enactment of the various Revolutionary bodies. The factors most important in giving rise to the bitter hatred with which the Loyalists came to regard the United States were the indignities that many of them suffered at the hands of Whig mobs. On suspicion of loyalty to the Crown, the homes of reputable citizens were broken open, hoodlums from the worst elements of the community ransacked the rooms, closets, desks, even women's clothing; and frequently such raids culminated in the destruction of the house by fire. Property was destroyed, women were insulted, and men were subjected to every conceivable brutality. Against these excesses such leaders as John Jay, General Greene, and Alexander Hamilton protested in vain, for such acts received the enthusiastic applause and approbation of the noisy majority.

But the evil was not all on one side. When opportunity offered, the Loyalists, in their turn, were responsible for brutal and mischievous actions. The failure of the British leaders to utilize the potential strength of their Loyalist supporters led to the organization of independent and irresponsible bands such as that headed by the fanatic Fanning. The Loyalists, moreover, were confident of ultimate victory and they despised and derided their opponents. They could not conceive that the power of the British Empire would ever be defeated by "rascally mobs" drawn from the lower classes of colonial society. This social snobbery added to the fury of the Whigs. The Loyalists have long been accused of cruelty and excess because of their employment of Indian allies, and this criticism is not without foundation. In this, however, they were not unique. As Channing has pointed out, the Patriots also employed the redskins, and throughout the war every effort was made by each side to enlist the Indian tribes. It was sheer hypocrisy for either Whig or Tory to inveigh against such employment, for the colonies had long been using Indians in their wars against the French.

The methods used by both parties in this civil war were far from justifiable, but, owing to the greater possibilities presented to them, the Patriots excelled the Loyalists in the amount and degree of suffering they caused. As the war continued and the Revolutionary party grew in strength, the attacks on the Loyalists increased in severity.

3. The Emigration of the Loyalists

The American Revolution was ended by the signing of the Treaty of Paris on 3 September 1783. The pressure of British public opinion had forced the King's delegates at Paris to insist upon the inclusion in the treaty of some clause protecting the Loyalists. Thus Article V was evolved. In it the American negotiators agreed that Congress would "recommend" to the various states that all persecution of the Loyalists should cease; that the property of those who had not actually taken up arms should be restored; and that all Loyalists should be allowed to return to their homes for the period of one year in order to settle their affairs.

It soon became evident, however, that the state, county, and civic bodies in America would pay little attention to the Congressional recommendation. With the exception of South Carolina, no state made any real effort to carry out the recommendations of the commissioners. When, relying on the treaty, many of the Tories attempted to return to their homes, they were met with indignant, organized, and virulent opposition. The Whigs made little attempt to discriminate; the name Tory sufficed to arouse the popular frenzy. The indignities suffered by the Loyalists after the signing of the treaty of peace were even more brutal and degrading than their miseries during the war itself. Referring to these excesses of the Whig mobs, John Adams wrote: "profaneness, intemperance, thefts, robberies, murders and treason; cursing, swearing, gluttony, drunkenness, lewdness, trespassing, mains are necessarily involved in them. Besides they render the populace, the rabble, the scum of the earth, insolent and disorderly, impudent and abusive. They give rise to lying, hypocrisy, chicanery and even perjuring among the people." Death was the port of more than one returning Loyalist.[1]

[1] "Lynch law" was a term first used at the time of the Loyalist persecutions.

Many of the hardships suffered by the Loyalists during the war may be condoned as unavoidable under the difficult circumstances of that time; but few extenuating facts can be adduced to excuse the postwar activities of the Revolutionary mobs. A large number of the Loyalists had left America during the Revolution. The formal end of the contest failed to bring peace to those who remained. The harsh treatment continued, and thousands more—many from the best educated and most respectable classes in the community—were forced to join the swollen stream of emigration and to seek new homes in Great Britain, the West Indies, or Canada.

To appreciate adequately the effects of the Loyalist emigration on Canada, it is essential to understand the conditions of the country at the time during which it took place. Before the coming of the Loyalists, Nova Scotia and Prince Edward Island together had a population of approximately 13,000. By 1790, Loyalist immigrants had raised this to 35,000. To the 700 settlers in New Brunswick were added 10,000 exiles. The western settlements, later known as Upper Canada, with practically no permanent white settlers before this time, became the new home of 6,000 Loyalists—a number that was increased to about 12,000 before 1800.

The movement of the Loyalists into the Canadian provinces began in the early days of the Revolution, but it was during the years 1782, 1783, and 1784 that it reached the greatest proportions. The British government, which very properly held itself responsible for the welfare of those who had suffered for their loyalty, during these years found it a difficult task to provide food and shelter for these claiments upon its bounty. Under the efficient supervision of Governors Haldimand and Carleton, however, the settlements in the northern wilderness progressed more rapidly than could reasonably have been expected. To tide over the first years of low production—and it should be remembered that many of the Loyalists knew little or nothing of the arts of farming—the government made grants of land, food, seed, tools, and stock. The Loyalists, moreover, were not backward in demanding indemnities for the hardships they had suffered and the losses they had sustained in the revolted colonies. These claims were supported by many Englishmen in Parliament and elsewhere, with the result that a royal commission was appointed to inquire into the losses and to arrange a proportionate indemnity. Thus encouraged, many of the Loyalists sullied their hitherto excellent records by the most shameless "padding" of their claims. The commission did its work thoroughly, and generous payments were finally made to those who could prove actual and serious loss. As a balm to his wounded dignity, the Loyalist was privileged to suffix to his name the letters "U.E.," alluding to his great principle, the unity of Empire."

In spite of these material and psychological aids, however, the newly arrived settlers had to undergo many hardships. Privations such as they had never known were now their daily lot, and the long snowbound winter nights they were forced to spend in rough log huts or army tents gave ample opportunity for bitter thought in reference to the authors of their misfortunes. The fierce anger with which they had resented the indignities of war gave place to a deep and acrid hatred, which pervaded every aspect of their lives and constituted one of the strongest influences in molding the outlook of their children.

Another early element in the population of Upper Canada, and an element immbued with ideals and prejudices very similar to those of the Loyalists, was composed of military officers and men introduced and organized into communities by the energy of that ardent imperialist Sir John Simcoe, first Lieutentant-Governor of Upper Canada.

The settlers in Canada proper were at first under the direct control of the government at Quebec, but by the Constitutional Act of 1791 their political autonomy was attained, under the title of Upper Canada. This act was required because after the passage of the Declaratory Act of 1778 the British government could not impose taxes except through an assembly. Such an assembly was provided, but it was hedged about with every conceivable restriction. In fact, it sought to create in North America the very image of the British Constitution of that day. It was, in consequence, quite unsuited to the conditions of the frontier.

Nova Scotia and New Brunswick had their own political, legal, and religious institutions from the start, and the conservative tendencies of the upper-class Loyalist immigrants were soon reflected in a bureaucratic government and an established church.

4. The Loyalists in Canada, 1784—1812

The influence of the Loyalists on Canadian-American relations was most obviously exerted during the years between 1784 and 1815, and it reached its climax during the first critical weeks of the War of 1812. From the time of their migration to the outbreak of the war, the Canadian Loyalists were occupied in the clearing and cultivation of their new lands, in the opening of routes of travel and communication, and in the formation, development, and finally the crystallization of a social and political organism. The innate conservatism of the settlers to some extent triumphed over frontier conditions, and the society that developed in Nova Scotia, in New Brunswick, and in Upper Canada was more orderly, more stratified, and far less progressive than similar communities in the United States. There is an interesting parallel to be discerned, however, between the views of the conservative Canadian community and those of the Federalist element in the United States. The social system developed in Upper Canada, with its inequalities and injustice, was to some extent, at least, the natural result of the Loyalist tradition; and it was not until after the rebellions of 1837–8 that this system was radically modified.

The Loyalists maintained, as a cardinal factor in their creed, their hostility toward the United States. To this hostility gradually became linked a firm belief in the moral and political depravity of those who had left the Empire. The popular acclaim with which the majority of Americans greeted the French Revolution; the religious agnosticism that characterized many republican leaders; the turbulent assertiveness of the lower orders and the radical spirit in its social, political, and religious manifestations in the United States were the criteria upon which the Canadian based his immutable belief in the decadence of American society. Thus contempt was added to hatred.

Many Americans, in their turn, were supercilious and scornful in their attitude toward the royalist, reactionary, and religiously orthodox Canadians. On the other hand it is interesting to observe that many of the Federalist leaders in the United States shared the Canadian prejudice against the more radical elements in American life.

During the early years of the nineteenth century a new element was gradually appearing in the fertile acres of Upper Canada. The generous land policy of the government, combined with the excellence of the soil, and the rapidly improving means of communication, proved irresistible attractions to many of the more enterprising American farmers. Many of them crossed the boundary and took up farms in the newly organized districts and townships. Some of these newcomers were known as "late Loyalists." They were men who had been willing to try life in the new Republic but had finally decided to migrate. For the majority of these farmers this migration was made simpler by the firm belief, which was ingrained in their minds, that before many years Canada would become an integral part of the United States. As was to be expected, the new settlers tended to favor the American form of government and were little influenced by any sentiment of loyalty toward Great Britain. For some time, however, the exigencies of frontier life precluded any opportunity of their taking part in political matters, but as soon as the necessity of continuous physical labor was overcome, they entered more and more into the discussion of public affairs. As their numbers increased, they became more assertive, and by 1812 leaders such as Mallory (who, it might be noticed, had been a Loyalist), Marcle, and Willcocks claimed to represent at least one third of the population of Upper Canada. In the crisis of 1812 many of these settlers sided with the Americans and were nearly successful in handing over the province of Upper Canada to General Hull.

It is worth noting that throughout nearly the whole period of controversy and strain in relations between Canada and the United States, there was almost uninterrupted freedom of transit for permanent or temporary migrants across the international boundary. It is only since 1924 that there have been any serious obstacles raised against this movement.

When war threatened during the years from 1805 to 1812, the presence of these settlers in Upper Canada and the tenor of their reports to the American government led Congress to the assurance of an easy conquest, should the invasion of Canada be resolved upon.

The influence of the Loyalists at the critical moment in 1812, and throughout the remainder of the war, was a prominent factor in the successful Canadian defense. The Executive Council that so ably assisted General Brock, the commander in Upper Canada, was composed almost entirely of Loyalists; what effective measures had been passed by the Assembly were largely the work of members of similar antecedents, and, above all, the enthusiastic support of the Loyalist settlers alone made possible the consummation of the plans of the executive. Had they been halfhearted or fearful when the first shock came, Upper Canada could hardly have been saved. The defeat of General Hull and his invading force was the crucial test of the whole war for Canada. This early victory reassured the Canadians and steeled them to withstand every attack of the powerful but disunited enemy. The vigor and success of their defense did much to ensure the continued existence of Canada.

It is probably just to declare that, had there been no Loyalist migration to Canada at the close of the American Revolution, the republican armies would in all likelihood have been successful in the War of 1812—in spite of French-Canadian loyalty. Great Britain, involved in a death struggle with Napoleon, could afford during 1812 and 1813 neither men nor material to defend a colony of doubtful value. Upon the Canadians themselves fell the burden of defense, and the vitality of their resistance was supplied, in large part, by the United Empire Loyalists. As the War of 1812 marked the final independence of the United States, so it marked the permanent foundation of a British state in North America. For the problems arising from this second fact Americans, according to Goldwin Smith, "have to thank their ancestors who refused amnesty to the vanquished in a Civil War." The harvest sown in 1783 was reaped in the defeats of 1812.

5. *The Loyalist Tradition*

With the close of the Napoleonic Wars a great tide of British immigrants swept into Canada and the Maritime Provinces. The virile element thus added to the population, while it was less emphatic in its attachment to the Empire than were the Loyalists, did much in fostering the latter's predominant influence toward imperial solidarity in the colonies. Moreover, as the original Loyalists passed from the scene, there went with them their direct and dynamic personal hostility against the United States, and there rose in its stead a traditional and sentimental antipathy, which exercised an undoubted influence, but which was less malignant than the hatred of the veteran of 1776. From this time on, the exact extent of the Loyalist influence is a matter for speculation rather than for concrete demonstration. More and more it became merged in the common loyalty felt alike by the British immigrant and the naturalized American. The Loyalist tradition, however, did not die. At every period of Canadian crisis—in the rebellions of 1837 and 1838; in the dispute of 1842 between Maine and New Brunswick; during the annexation discussions of 1849; at the time of the Fenian raids;

in disrupting the Canada First movement of 1871; and in the political battle of 1911; in trade movements, in diplomacy, and in politics—it has been a potent factor. Schoolbooks, orators, and patriotic societies have done much to perpetuate the Loyalist tradition.

As is usual in such cases, the virtues of the founders of the tradition have been acclaimed and their weaknesses or failures overlooked. The Loyalists were very far from being perfect, and it serves no good end to overlook their faults. They were in most instances undemocratic, antisocial in business affairs, hidebound and intolerant in their religious convictions, unprogressive industrially, given to the excessive use of hard spirits, and in almost every way opposed to what is known as the "modern spirit." They were the inevitable product of their heritage and their environment and were neither more vicious nor more virtuous than their neighbors. It is amusing in this connection to compare the publications of the United Empire Loyalist Association with those of the Daughters of the American Revolution.

No candid student of international relations can review the history of American-Canadian contacts without realizing that there has always been in Canada a considerable body of public opinion hostile to the United States. Economic causes have been predominantly responsible for this fact, but more than casual importance must be attributed to the influence of the Loyalists.

3
The War of 1812

1. The Causes of the War

The second and the most important military conflict between Americans and Canadians occurred in the years 1812 to 1815. The War of 1812 at first divided, but subsequently united, public opinion in the United States. It completed the work begun in the Revolution by stimulating American nationalism, and it finally destroyed any possibility of reunion with the British Empire. Moreover, by its encouragement of native industry it went far toward breaking the economic ties between England and America—a fact that is evidenced by the development of the protective tariff in 1816.

The War of 1812 aroused little interest and was not taken very seriously in Great Britain, but in Canada it aroused in the provinces of British North America the beginnings of a consciousness of nationhood.

A by-product of the Napoleonic struggle for the domination of Europe and the world, the War of 1812 increased the existing irritation between the United States and Great Britain and settled none of the real grievances existing in North America. To Great Britain, fighting, as she believed, for the liberties of Europe, the American declaration of war savored of treachery. The United States, injured commercially by the Franco-British blockade of Europe, its "national honor" involved in the question of impressment, and urged on, above all else, by the desire of the West for conquest and trade, disregarded the wider implications of the European conflict; disregarded also the grave injuries suffered at the hands of France; and declared war to maintain in battle the American interpretation of the freedom of the seas. Selecting Great Britain as their foe—both because her offenses were more serious and because England was their "traditional" enemy, France their earliest friend—the leaders of the American people advocated the conquest of Canada as a compensation for national losses, a vindication of national worth. Careless of the danger that their action might involve for the liberties of Europe, they seized the moment of Britain's extremity to assert American dignity, and to drive, if possible, the last remnants of British monarchical rule from the continent partially won in 1783. It is true that many leading Americans vigorously opposed the declaration of war and endorsed Pickering's well-known toast: "The world's last hope—Britain's fast-anchored isle." But these men were not in power and their counsel was overruled. The desires of the Canadian people were not considered; the provinces were looked upon merely as possessions of Great Britain and not as peaceful neighboring states. To Canadians themselves, of course, the causes of the war were as foreign as the war itself was undesired. But loyalty to the Empire and the Crown, satisfaction with the rule of British justice, and the Loyalist repugnance to any form of union with the United States led the Canadians to engage in a counter-struggle, which resulted in the birth of Canada as a nation, and the continued hold of Great Britain on the continent of North America.

The causes of the War of 1812 were four: British interference with the European trade of the United States; the impressment of American sailors by the forces of the Royal Navy; the determination of the American frontiersmen to defend their borders against the Indian allies of Great Britain; and an imperialistic lust for the conquest of Canada. But these causes were not so simple as they appear and as their usual treatment would suggest.

Between 1798 and 1812 Napoleon Bonaparte was making a remarkably successful attempt to conquer the whole of Europe. One by one his adversaries were brought into subjection or alliance, until among the major powers of Europe the vacillating Alexander of Russia, chaotic Spain, and the island kingdom of Great Britain alone remained in active opposition. As the intensity of the struggle increased, every possible means of pressure was employed by the antagonists. Maritime blockade, as one of the more obvious weapons of economic warfare, was resorted to early in the conflict. The Berlin and Milan decrees of Napoleon ordered the confiscation of any vessel trading with Great Britain, while the British Orders in Council forbade commercial intercourse, except by special permit, with any continental port under the control of the French Emperor. These regulations applied not only to belligerent but also to neutral vessels. Between the upper and the nether millstones thus provided, neutral commerce was threatened with disaster. Because Great Britain, by reason of her naval superiority, was able to enforce her decrees to their logical extreme, upon her was showered the more violent abuse. These restrictions bore most heavily upon the trade of the United States, and under the leadership of Jefferson and Madison the American government protested with frequency and vigor. This proving ineffectual, an embargo was placed on all trade with the two major belligerents. When Napoleon later formally withdrew his decrees, the embargo was continued against Great Britain alone. The British government, faced by conditions comparable only with those of 1914–18 or 1940–5, persisted in its course, ever widening the scope and tightening the enforcement of its restrictive measures. Finally, however, as a result of the repeated and emphatic protests of the United States, and wishing to avoid war with that country, the British Orders in Council were repealed on 23 June 1812. President Madison, however, had reclared war before news of this action

49

reached America. When the news did finally cross the Atlantic, Admiral Warren, in command of the British fleet in American waters, at once offered to make peace; but as he could give no guarantee that impressment would be abandoned, the President decided that the war should continue.

Judged by the interpretations of maritime law which were enforced by the Allied and associated powers in the First and Second World Wars, the restrictions applied by Great Britain in 1812 were lenient to the point of negligence. But judged by the chaotic juridical dicta of the early nineteenth century, a period during which an American Secretary of State could frankly argue that "free ships make free goods," it was difficult to defend the British actions.

These trade restrictions, however, were not so important in arousing the national temper of the United States as was the British policy of impressment. The Royal Navy, grown pompous and overconfident since the victory at Trafalgar, declined thereafter to a low ebb of discipline and training. The ships had suffered from neglect, the officers suffered from pride, and the crews suffered from lack of sanitation, decent food, and discipline. These conditions produced an inevitable deterioration in the quality of the personnel. So miserable was life aboard a British man-of-war that hundreds of sailors deserted when opportunity offered. This usually occurred, for obvious reasons, in American ports, and there the deserters found naturalization papers easily obtainable; on the docks at Baltimore, for example, at a cost of one dollar each. Many of the deserters shipped again immediately, this time as members of an American crew. The British authorities were naturally aroused by these desertions and, refusing to recognize the validity of any form of naturalization, made strenuous efforts to stop the abuse. Naval vessels stopped American ships on the high seas, and on the slightest evidence the royal officers seized men whom they believed to be deserters and carried them off to the British men-of-war. Not only was this procedure illegal under the maritime code of the time, but many and grave acts of injustice inevitably occurred.

The United States protested frequently and forcibly, but without satisfactory results. In reply, Great Britain demanded that the United States adopt some effectual method of returning British deserters and abandon her support of the principles of naturalization and certification. A deadlock ensued.

These two factors: interference with American trade and impressment, have usually been given as the real causes of the War of 1812, and this opinion still persists in many quarters. The authoritative *Cambridge History of British Foreign Policy* declares that the war was "almost entirely" due to those two causes. Recent investigations, however, have radically altered this interpretation. Two other causes must also be recognized.

The Indian problem was a legacy of the War of Independence. By means of presents, the payment of comparatively high prices for furs, and, on the whole, reasonably fair treatment, the British authorities had managed to win and to hold the friendship of the Indians. In every dispute with American settlers in the territory beyond the Alleghenies, moreover, the British had supported the native claims. The Americans declared that British agents not only had supplied the Indians with weapons, but had urged them to attack and pillage the frontier settlements of the United States. The first accusation was certainly true, and it is probable that some of the more irresponsible British traders did encourage the Indians to raid American outposts. Certainly the Western Americans had good cause to complain of the British relations with the Indians and, indeed, of the whole of British policy in the West. The American commissioners at Ghent, however, failed to produce any evidence in support of the accusation, and there is no proof of any official encouragement of the Indians by the British authorities. The desire to settle the Indian problem, to seize the Indians' lands, and to force the British to relinquish their forts in the upper Mississippi Valley in accordance with the terms of the Treaty of 1783 was undoubtedly a strong factor in convincing the Western states of the necessity of war in 1812. It is significant that the American delegates at Ghent at the close of the war refused to agree to the delineation of any boundary line separating the territory of the United States from the lands claimed by the Indian nations.

The three causes mentioned above were of first importance in justifying the American declaration of war. Most contemporary authorities believe that the interference with American overseas trade was the major cause of the conflict. There are still some historians, however, who will argue that the determination of the Western American frontiersmen to expand the borders of their states and to free themselves forever from the stifling competition of the British fur traders was the fundamental explanation of the War of 1812. As Pratt has demonstrated, it was not the representatives of the harassed commercial interests of the East, it was frontiersmen from the South and West who forced through Congress the declaration of war. "Nothing could better demonstrate the frontier character of the war spirit than to observe its progressive decline as we pass from the rim of the crescent (i.e., the frontier states) to its center at the national capital."

Possibly the two arguments can be reconciled if it is recognized that the Southern frontiersmen were greatly and directly interested not only in expansion for expansion's sake, but also in maintaining an open sea route to European markets for their great staple crops.

The desire to obtain Canada and to drive Great Britain forever from the continent was the natural result of the philosophy of the American Revolution and the passions engendered by it. But it was more than that. It was a symbol of the imperialistic desire for expansion inherent in a young, confident, and successful nation. Even apart from the economic factors involved, it was natural, therefore, that the most ardent advocates of war should be found among the Westerners, frontiersmen, men whose own lives were a proof of the dynamic expansive power of American society. They were the real democrats, the typical product of the new frontier. In the eyes of such Americans, aggressive action against Great Britain was peculiarly justified and thoroughly acceptable. The British Crown was the hereditary enemy, the malign representative of aristocracy and reaction; and blows struck against Great Britain were blows for liberty and democracy. Monarchy and republicanism could not thrive as neighbors, and until the last vestige of British control in America was removed, the Union would be insecure. Furthermore, the acquisition of the Canadian provinces would compensate the United States for injuries suffered at the hands of Great Britain, and it would open a new and convenient waterway for Western commerce, the St. Lawrence River.

A final incentive toward the conquest was the reputed desire of the Canadians to be freed from British oppression and to be allowed to enter the American Union. That Canada was united in desiring this consummation was vouched for by Henry Clay and his followers—those impetuous advocates of expansion known as the War Hawks.

These, then, were the causes of the War of 1812—causes in the creation of which the Canadian people had little part. In the result of the war, however, the Canadian provinces, as elements of the British Empire, and as the objectives of American attack, were vitally interested and deeply involved.

2. The Canadian Attitude toward the War of 1812

To understand the attitude of the Canadian people in 1812 it is important to recall the ethnic composition of the colonial population.

As has been shown above, the inhabitants of the Maritime Provinces were, at this time, still largely of Loyalist descent. Some few thousand pre-Revolutionary immigrants from the American colonies together with a much smaller number of French Canadians—returned Acadians, or descendants of those who had escaped the expulsion—were the only other important elements in the population. New Brunswick in particular was still almost exclusively the home of Loyalists. The French-Canadian habitants, both in Nova Scotia and in Lower Canada, remained loyal to the British cause. The Roman Catholic priesthood, whose privileges and power rested very largely upon the continuance of British rule, and who were utterly antipathetic toward the skeptical, free-thinking attitude apparently so common in the early United States, were primarily responsible for the fostering of this anti-American sentiment. The memory of American excesses during the invasion of 1776 was also a contributing factor.

The Maritime Provinces played little part in the War of 1812. The authorities in Maine and New Brunswick by concurrent proclamation, issued during the summer of 1812, prevented any military activities on that section of the international border. This truce within a war lasted until 1814, when, after the defeat of Napoleon, it was abrogated by the British, and offensive measures were undertaken with the assistance of veteran troops newly arrived from Europe. Nova Scotia not only escaped suffering in the war, but actually prospered exceedingly. Halifax, the British naval station on the North American coast, was busily employed in repairing and equipping His Majesty's ships, while privateering under letters of marque gave profitable employment to many a "Bluenose" crew. Supplies from the Canadian army, purchased in New England and New York, found entrance into Canada through the ports and border towns of the Maritime Provinces. Inasmuch as a very considerable proportion of the rations and equipment for the Canadian forces was obtained from the United States, this trade was highly lucrative for those engaged in it. Indeed, many of the traders of Nova Scotia and New England alike prospered during the war to an unexampled extent, while peace was temporarily disastrous.

These commercial relations between the Maritime Provinces and New England did not, however, lessen in any appreciable degree the hostility evidenced by the far-eastern Canadians toward American institutions and ideals. The people of Nova Scotia, Prince Edward Island, and New Brunswick were not less forward than their compatriots in Upper Canada in the denunciation of the political and territorial ambitions of Henry Clay and John C. Calhoun. The Assemblies of Nova Scotia and New Brunswick voted large sums of money and prepared their militia for active service in defense of their country. The Assembly of the latter province declared that it was "ready and determined to repel every aggression which the infatuated policy of the American government may induce it to commence on the soil of New Brunswick." During the critical period of the war the 104th Regiment, recruited in large part from the Loyalist districts of the Maritime Provinces, made a heroic winter march through the wilderness from Halifax to Montreal, in order to aid their hard-pressed comrades in Canada.

No accurate statistics relating to the population of Upper and Lower Canada in 1812 are obtainable. The census is a comparatively modern innovation on this continent. As a compromise among the many estimates, the following figures may be accepted as substantially correct:

Lower Canada (Quebec)	325,000	of whom the vast majority were of French descent
Upper Canada (Ontario)	100,000	made up approximately as follows:

Loyalists and their descendants	20,000
American settlers	40,000
Other immigrants, largely British	20,000

The United Empire Loyalists, if not the most numerous, were, individually, still the most influential element in the population of Upper Canada, and Upper Canada was destined to be the main theater of the war.

The Canadian attitude toward the War of 1812 may be said to have been determined by five outstanding factors: (1) the ingrained dislike for the United States originating with and fostered by the Loyalists; (2) the natural loyalty of a weak and dependent colony to the motherland to which it is bound by ties of affection, tradition, and self-interest; (3) the favor with which the British rule was accepted by the Roman Catholic hierarchy, which in turn controlled the opinions of the vast majority of the inhabitants of Lower Canada; (4) Canadian resentment of the partiality they felt was displayed in the savage attacks of the press and politicians of the United States against Great Britain, while France, though apparently guilty of similar offenses against the Republic, was mildly reprimanded or even publicly applauded; (5) the conviction, which grew as the war progressed and as propaganda produced its usual wartime effects, that the Canadian volunteers were fighting to uphold the honor of their country and the safety of their homes and to preserve their ideals and their religion. This struggle, it was believed, was against an invader devoid of responsibility, subject to mob rule, blackened by the atheism of republican France—a nation led astray by the philosophy of Jefferson, Voltaire, and Paine.

The influence of the Loyalists was the most decisive factor in molding public opinion in the early and critical days of the war.

The imperial loyalty of Canadians was strengthened by the imminence of a stronger and more populous neighbor. The fact that this neighbor was not always unselfish and friendly strengthened the imperial bonds. Love of Great Britain was linked with and dependent on a sense of security in the protection afforded by British power, while the later development of an independent spirit in Canada was synchronous with the growth of self-confidence. Before the outbreak of war in 1812, perfect reliance was placed on the ability and willingness of the motherland to protect her domains in North America. "To expect that Great Britain would submit to see the allegiance of her subjects stolen from her," wrote a Canadian editor, "is to accuse her of imbecility, blindness and decrepitude." The Canadian people were convinced that "the government as well as the people of the United States who are perfectly aware of the growing prosperity of Canada are devising means to thwart it." Against such an eventuality Canada looked to the motherland for protection and assistance. A citizen of Montreal, writing to the famous Montreal *Gazette*, declared that Great Britain had given to Canada "liberty and all the blessings arising from the protection and paternal affection of the best and happiest government the world has ever seen." If war should now be necessary, "Let government but give the word and Canadians will convince their enemies that they are loyal and brave people ready to defend their holy religion, their laws, their liberty, and their country, against any invader." Such was the spirit of Canada.

The methods by which the British administration had gained the good will of the Roman Catholic Church—the guaranteeing of tithes, the freedom of worship and instruction, and complete self-government—are too well known to need recapitulation. After the American Revolution, British policy generally in relation to the remaining colonies was designed to maintain them in a position of dependence, giving only such measures of independence as became progressively unavoidable.

The final influence in forming the Canadian attitude toward the War of 1812 was that arising from the differences between society in the two nations. The difference was not nearly so marked as Canadians popularly believed. The Virginia dynasty and the New England Adamses who ruled the United States until the advent of Andrew Jackson were just about as conservative in their attitudes, if not always in their expressed views, as were the members of the Family Compact itself.

The Canadians, however, firmly believed that great differences in custom and philosophy did exist. This conviction certainly influenced their attitude toward the war. And it is arguable that there was *some* justification for the Canadian position.

In the Loyalist immigration Canada received a foundation of conservatism which was of value during the early years of the formative period. It made possible the establishment of an orderly society, the foundation of those institutions by which civilization is commonly judged—although the Loyalists' interest in education, for example, was not so extensive as is frequently supposed—and it made certain the adherence of the new nation to the established, traditional authority, that of the British Crown. Thus a bulwark of imperial authority was erected on the continent of North America. Respect for law, obedience to the government, attachment to the church, and loyalty to the Empire were characteristic of early Canada. This statement, of course, has to be read in the light of the general standards of an early nineteenth-century frontier community. It is a relative, not an absolute standard that is used.

Conditions in the United States were somewhat different. Here the forces of law and order had indeed won a victory in the establishment of the Constitution, but the hostility toward authority that had been engendered and expressed by the Revolution was still everywhere evident. The forty years following the War of Independence were characterized by an excessive hostility to legal and, to a certain extent, moral restrictions. The Federalist leaders—Washington, Hamilton, Adams, and Jay—had favored a strong centralized government and had vigorously opposed anything approximating mob rule, but they could not control the particularist activities of the citizens as a whole. The spirit of the time was individualistic, aggressive, and confident, and, as almost invariably, the period of war was followed by a general relaxation of the ethical code of the nation—a psychological reaction after a period of moral and physical stress. That this relaxation did not affect the Loyalists to an equal degree was due to the conditions of their new environment. Hard and continuous labor is not conducive, among groups with the social and religious traditions of the Loyalists, to lax morality.

To some extent the differences between society in Canada and in the United States were more apparent, or perhaps verbal, than real. It would probably be accurate to say that the Canadians talked more conservatively and the Americans talked more radically than they acted. Each certainly believed that major differences existed. Canadians looked on the announced political, social, and religious liberalism of the United States as symptoms of degeneracy and decay. The Reverend John Strachan, the able but violent bishop of the Anglican Church in Upper Canada, declared that the seceded colonies, "instead of possessing the happiest government in the world, possess one of the worst, for who is so ignorant as not to know that the unhappy country is subject to a Virginia oligarchy? We may despise this degenerate government, equally destitute of national honor and virtue, and leave them in silent contempt to brood over their selfish and iniquitous proceedings." Nourished on such sentiments from a pulpit consecrated to the service of the Prince of Peace, and from the pen of one whose duty it was to proclaim the brotherhood of man as well as the fatherhood of God, it need cause little surprise to find that the Canadians were convinced that in 1812 they were fighting against a nation whose society was governed by evil and whose moral standards were debauched.

3. The Attitude of the United States

Pity, not unmixed with contempt, was the general attitude of Americans toward the Canadian colonists. Having themselves battled against and overthrown the power of the British Crown within their respective states, the Americans could not understand the attachment of Canadians to the "effete" monarchy of Great Britain, and laid the cause to a lack of energy, initiative, and valor. Thus it was that in planning the conquest of Canada the American leaders sincerely believed that they were conferring a favor on the less vigorous inhabitants of North America. It was to be a crusade to spread the culture of the democratic Republic. That the Canadians might not wish such liberty and culture, or that the American armies would be faced with any great difficulty in accomplishing their task, was beyond the comprehension of the democrats of Kentucky or New Jersey. There were, of course, other attractions in this plan of conquest: the Indian trouble would be settled as the Americans desired, the addition of a rich and extensive territory would add to American prestige, and, above all, Americans once again would be fighting against the hereditary foe; and all the auguries and portents promised victory.

The people and government of the United States were alike completely misled in regard to the sentiment of the Canadians. Americans could not comprehend how any people could prefer the monarchical system of Great Britain, with its restrictive colonial regulation, to the free, independent, and democratic political economy of the United States. The American settlers in Upper Canada added to the delusion. Segregated to a great extent in townships of their own, these emigrants soon came to believe that their own desire for union with the Republic was shared by all Canadians. They so reported to the United States government, leading Jefferson to speak of Canada "which wants to enter the Union." Eustis, American Secretary of War, after an examination of all the information obtainable, declared: "We can take Canada without soldiers! we have only to send officers into the Provinces, and the people, already disaffected toward their own government, will rally to our standard." John Henry, sent into the United States by Governor-General Prevost on a mission of observation, reported that Americans unanimously considered "the disposition of Canadians as friendly to them," while John Mellish, an American who visited Canada in 1811, declared that "were five thousand men to be sent into the Province with the Proclamation of Independence the great mass of the people would join the American government." Colonel Cruikshank, a Canadian historian who has done invaluable work on this period, has written that "travellers from the United States, who visited Upper Canada during the first decade of the nineteenth century, generally agreed in reporting that they had observed among the inhabitants a determined partiality to the United States, and an avowed hostility to the British government." Many Americans, moreover, believed that even Great Britain itself would not be averse to an American-Canadian union. "That the Canadas should be attached to the United

States was the unanimous opinion of all intelligent statesmen in Great Britain in the years 1809–1811," declared the *National Intelligencer*. These opinions, both American and Canadian, are further proof of the old adage that men believe what they want to believe.

Not only did Americans believe that Canada would welcome intervention by the United States, but they were confident that should any defense of Canada be attempted, the American forces could easily overcome the opposition. A comparison of the relative strength of the combatants goes far to explain the inevitability of such a conclusion.

In 1812 the British colonies in North America possessed a practically undefended boundary line one thousand miles in length; and a population of less than 500,000, of whom only some 80,000 were domiciled in Upper Canada, the inevitable point of attack. To defend this territory there were in Canada 4,450 regular soldiers, and a possible militia strength of about 65,000 men. Of these Upper Canada could provide, at most, 11,000. Canada did, in truth, appear to be in no condition for self-defense.

In the United States, on the other hand, was a white population of over 6,000,000. In April 1808 the American standing army had been increased to about 6,000 men, and on 6 June 1812 there were under arms a total of 6,744 men. But the potential strength of the country was shown by the war measures and the militia returns. An order of 11 January 1812 provided for the enlistment of 25,000 additional men, and other acts authorized the President to raise this total to 50,000 and to demand of the states 100,000 militia. The total militia enrollment (on paper) at this time reached the enormous number of 694,735. Fortunate it was for Canada that, through the opposition of New England and the almost complete lack of competent leaders, this huge strength could not be exerted on the northern frontier.

Thomas Jefferson characterized the proposed conquest as "a mere matter of marching"; Calhoun declared that "in four weeks from the time that a declaration of war is heard on our frontiers the whole of Upper Canada and a part of Lower Canada will be in our possession." But it was left to Andrew Jackson to picture the conquest in its most alluring colors:

"We are going [he declared] to vindicate our right to the fur trade, and to open a market for the productions of our soil . . . to seek some indemnity for past injuries by the conquest of all the British dominions upon the continent of North America. Should the conquest of Canada be resolved, how pleasing the prospect that would open to the young volunteer, while performing a military promenade into a distant country. A succession of new and interesting objects would perpetually fill and delight his imagination, the effect of which would be heightened by the warlike appearances, the martial music, and the grand evolutions of an army of fifty thousand men. But why should these inducements be held out to the young men of America? They need them not, animated as they are to rival the exploits of Rome, they will never prefer an inglorious sloth, a supine inactivity to the honorable toil of carrying the Republican standard to the Heights of Abraham."

It is obvious that the American interpretation of the Canadian viewpoint was incorrect, and it was so proved by the outcome of the invasion.

All of the United States, however, did not view the projected war with such enthusiasm. It is an extraordinary fact that the very persons on whose behalf the war was nominally being fought (the harassed shopkeepers of New England and New York) were the leaders in opposition to the war policy. Evidently the influence of the Western "expansionists" was greater than has sometimes been suggested. The merchants of New England and New York, whose commerce had been so seriously disrupted by Jefferson's embargo and the Non-Intercourse Act enacted by the Madison administration, were almost unanimous in their opposition. The British Orders in Council and policy of impressment were annoying, but they feared that war, with

62

Great Britain in command of the seas and the British market closed, was likely to prove disastrous. "Nothing but their fears," wrote General Dearborn in regard to the citizens of Massachusetts, "prevent them from going to all lengths" in opposition to the government. Two weeks after the declaration of war the general reported again: "There has been nothing yet done in New England that indicates an actual state of war, but every means that can be devised by the Tories is in operation to depress the spirits of the country." The Governors of Massachusetts and Connecticut refused to supply the militia necessary to guard the coast, and the former issued a proclamation (26 June) for a public fast in consequence of the federal declaration of war—a wrong committed "against the nation from which we are descended and which for many generations has been the bulwark of the religion we profess." The Governor of Vermont threatened to use force if the federal government attempted to compel that state to aid in the prosecution of the war. Under the vigorous leadership of Josiah Quincy the Federalists openly and violently accused Madison and Monroe of having sold the honor of the United States to France. New England Congressmen who had voted for the war were publicly insulted; the Massachusetts House of Representatives issued an address proclaiming the war a wanton sacrifice and advising the people to organize locally to "express your sentiments without fear, and let the sound of your disapprobation . . . be loud and deep . . . let there be no volunteers except for defensive war." An attempt made to call a state convention to arrange for the withdrawal of Massachusetts from the Union was narrowly defeated. The action of President Madison in denouncing the armistice arranged by Governor Prevost and General Dearborn (in consequence of the repeal of the British Orders in Council) provided the Federalists with further ammunition. New England Puritanism, still extant in some degree, was as vigorously opposed to a war that strengthened the hands of "atheistic France" as was Canada itself.

New England was, perhaps, even more opposed to the Republican (Jeffersonian Democratic) Party than it was to the war, but this does not alter the fact that the opposition was a vital factor in restricting the energies of the United States, and the movement continued to grow after 1812, to culminate in the Hartford Convention of 1814. But the Federalists, defeated and discredited in the country at large, could produce no effect on the national policy, could not prevent the Southern and Western states from waging an offensive war.

4. *Waging the War*

War was declared by the United States on 18 June 1812. When the news reached America that the British government had revoked its Orders in Council, President Madison refused to agree to an armistice, but he did authorize Jonathan Russell, American chargé in London, to offer definite terms of peace. Lord Castlereagh, however, expecting Admiral Warren and President Madison to settle the whole problem in America itself, refused to negotiate with Russell. This deadlock wasted so much time that the continuation of the war became inevitable. Moreover, the problem of impressment still required solution.

The exposed situation of Upper Canada led inevitably to its selection as the theater of war. With its long and undefended border, its weak military strength, the large percentage of Americans in its population, and its difficult communications, Upper Canada appeared to be incapable of any resolute defense. Almost every prospect appeared to favor a speedy and practically uncontested victory for the American forces. Internal dissensions in the United States, and the enthusiasm with which the Loyalists of Upper Canada supported General Isaac Brock, who was probably the most capable leader to participate in the war, alone indicated the possibility of a successful defense of Canada.

The enthusiasm and determination of the Loyalists, however,

did not alter the fact that by 1812 they were a numerical minority. The declaration of war precipitated a real crisis in Upper Canada. General Brock, apart from his 1,450 regulars, was forced to rely upon a scanty militia force, which in many districts refused to obey his orders, and a legislature so evenly divided between Loyalists and American sympathizers as to be practically useless. His troops, moreover, were lacking in the essential materials of war; their artillery was weak, supplies were meager, uniforms and shoes were not available for all. Thus Canada was defended in its most vulnerable spot by less than two thousand soldiers and a populace at least one third of which was in sympathy with the invaders. The only favorable omens, as noted above, were the hostility of New England to the war, the character and ability of General Brock, and the enthusiastic co-operation of the Loyalists and their sons. The American leaders in their optimistic references to the conquest of Canada had forgotten the exiles of 1783. The Loyalists had suffered too acutely to forget with such dispatch.

War had been declared on 18 June 1812. On 12 July General Hull, a venerable relic of the Revolutionary struggle, advanced with some two thousand men from Detroit into Upper Canada. The settlers on the western end of the Ontario peninsula offered little resistance, and within two days his cavalry had penetrated one hundred miles into British territory. One of the first acts of General Hull after the invasion started was to issue a grandiloquent proclamation to the Canadian people, offering them freedom, justice, and the other prerogatives of a republican people if they would refrain from interfering with his operations against the minions of British tyranny. General Brock replied with a counter-proclamation and ordered out the militia. This order was obeyed only in the Loyalist districts, and the apparent success of General Hull tended to make the people as a whole disheartened and fearful. The pro-American element rejoiced, and on 26 July General Brock reported that "numbers had already joined the invading army."

In this predicament the British commander saw the necessity

of rallying public opinion behind his efforts, and on 27 July he summoned an extraordinary session of the Assembly.

The legislative body that assembled at York in answer to the summons of General Brock was divided almost equally between Loyalists and representatives who either did not wish or feared to oppose the American advance. Five months previously Brock had appeared before this same body and had urged immediate action to place the country in a position of defense. Specifically he had demanded the recruiting of a larger militia force, suspension of habeas corpus, the promulgation of a law against aliens, and more effective machinery for the apprehension and punishment of military offenders. The legislation that resulted had been entirely unsatisfactory. "The many doubtful characters in the militia," wrote General Brock, "made me anxious to introduce the oath of adjuration into the Bill. It was lost by the casting vote of the Chairman. The great influence which the numerous settlers from the United States possess over the decisions of the Lower House is truly alarming, and ought, immediately, by every practical means, to be diminished." The session had ended in discord and chaos.

When the Assembly reconvened, on 27 July, the same difficulties arose. Again it refused to repeal the act of habeas corpus, and "appeared by its proceedings rather to court the favor of the enemy than fearlessly to perform its duty." The spirit of the pro-American leaders was beginning to permeate the mass of the people. "My position is most critical," wrote General Brock, "not from anything the enemy can do but from the disposition of the people. A full belief possesses them that the province must inevitably succumb."

The critical moment had now arrived. Canada was invaded; the American settlers were offering no resistance to the enemy— many of them were actually assisting the invaders; large bodies of militia had refused to serve; and opposition in the Assembly blocked all energetic measures of defense. The Loyalists, however, were still united in their hostility toward the Americans; they needed only a leader.

The leader demanded by the danger of the situation was found in General Brock. Almost by force the necessary money bills were rushed through the Assembly, which was then summarily dismissed. Calling together the Executive Council, Brock outlined the situation and, with its hearty concurrence, declared martial law. Orders in Council were promulgated to provide for the control of aliens and the deportation of those who refused to take the oath of abjuration and allegiance. Imbued with their traditional antipathy toward Americans, and inspired by the challenge of Brock's leadership, the loyal elements of the Upper Canadian population rallied against the invaders. Troops and supplies were collected, with a new enthusiasm regulars and militia united, and between the 4th and 27th of August the timid and incompetent Hull was forced to retire over the border; Detroit was invested and captured; Upper Canada was consolidated and made secure.

The expulsion of General Hull and the capture of Detroit constitute one of the most extraordinary feats in the military history of Canada. Brock's force was barely half the size of the American army, but it was disciplined, enthusiastic, and brilliantly led. General Hull was subsequently court-martialed and sentenced to death. On account of services in the Revolution, however, he was pardoned by President Madison.

The success of General Brock in this action against Detroit was greatly facilitated by the capture of Fort Michilimackinac by a small detail of soldiers under Captain Roberts—a bold operation that confirmed the Western Indians in their allegiance to Great Britain. The dilatory tactics of another incompetent republican—General Dearborn—who had been expected to aid Hull by vigorous action on the Niagara frontier, also contributed to the American defeat. The only American success in the early weeks of the war was a minor victory at Fort Erie.

The second attack upon Canada was launched at Queenstown Heights by Generals Smyth and Van Rensselaer. Having collected 5,000 men on the American side of the Niagara River, they crossed over and succeeded in occupying the heights above the Canadian village. Owing, however, to a difference of opinion between the commanders, the refusal of the New York troops to leave the territory of their own state, and the energetic and able opposition of Generals Brock and Sheaffe, the Americans were expelled from the heights they had captured, and were driven into the river or forced to surrender. The Canadians captured 900 prisoners, but the death of General Brock was heavy payment for their victory.[1]

In the early months of the war Russia proposed to mediate between the combatants, but, as in the case of the armistice desired by Admiral Warren, no assurance was forthcoming from the British government that the policy of impressment would be abandoned, and President Madison in consequence refused to discuss peace. It is only just to add that the war enthusiasm, which had by this time affected the majority of the American people, including the leaders of the government, made them impatient of any peace proposals. Less than three years later they accepted terms that they had refused to consider in 1812.

After the defeat at Queenstown Heights, Van Rensselaer retired and General Smyth took complete command of the American troops on the Niagara frontier. He immediately assured himself of a prominent place in the records of military incompetence. Although he had 4,000 troops in his command, he was badly defeated—by a force of 400 Canadians—in a second attempt to cross the river into British territory. This travesty on the art of warfare occurred at Black Rock, and General Smyth was shortly afterwards relieved of his duties. It was now too late in the year for profitable campaigning, and except for a few small and unimportant engagements both armies retired to winter quarters.

In contrast with these defeats by inferior forces on land, the record of the small and largely disregarded American navy was replete with brilliant victories. The inventive genius of the Republic had produced a type of frigate that was heavier in con-

---

[1] One of the chivalrous actions of the war was the salute fired by order of General Van Rensselaer on the day of Brock's funeral.

struction, better adapted for speed, designed to carry more men and to mount more guns, than vessels of the same nominal class in the French and British fleets. The superior power of the American frigates, while it excuses to some extent the defeat of individual British ships, does not in any sense exonerate the British navy as a whole. The navy was caught unprepared; the incompetence of its higher command cost the lives of many valiant seamen and severely damaged the national reputation. Trafalgar had killed Nelson and put the Lords of the Admiralty to sleep. The American ships, moreover, were manned by volunteers, the majority of whom had been trained in the mercantile service of the Eastern states. Too many of the British crews, on the other hand, were the offscourings of city slums—the type most likely to constitute the "catch" of the press-gangs. Three great American frigates—the *Constitution,* the *President,* and the *United States* —during the first few months of the war won decisive victories over the hitherto undefeated vessels of the British navy. Their success in these single combats aroused intense enthusiasm in the United States, while defeat came as a stupefying shock to the British. The Duke of Wellington wrote: "I have been very uneasy about the American naval success. I think we should have peace with America before the season for opening the campaign in Canada if we could take one or two of these damned frigates." These spectacular victories, however, had very little real effect on the course of the war as a whole, and after January 1813 the British navy not only controlled the seas by reason of its superior numbers, but also retrieved some of its lost prestige by victories in single combats. In 1813 and 1814 the American coast was securely blockaded by a vast fleet of vessels under the White Ensign.

The naval policy of the United States in 1813 was aimed primarily at gaining control of Lake Erie and Lake Ontario. In this way it was hoped to facilitate the military occupation of Upper Canada. Captain Chauncey was sent to Lake Ontario and under circumstances of great difficulty he constructed, armed, and manned a small fleet. Across the lake at Kingston, Commodore

Yeo was engaged on a similar task. The result was a stalemate; neither officer wished to risk the chance of a decisive defeat, and no serious engagement took place. A different result was obtained on Lake Erie. Here Commander Perry succeeded in building a fleet that was definitely superior to that of his British opponent, Captain Barclay. In the Battle of Lake Erie the Americans were completely victorious. As a result of this battle the United States gained full control of the lake, and consequently was able to force the British troops to retire eastward, abandoning Detroit and Amherstburg.

On land the United States was somewhat more successful in 1813 than it had been in 1812, although the final balance was not materially altered. General Harrison, now in command of the American forces in the Northwest, advanced his troops toward Upper Canada in three divisions. General Winchester, in command of 1,000 men, took the most westerly route. Near the village of Frenchtown, at the extremity of Lake Erie, he was met and defeated by General Procter, who had a force of 500 regulars and a similar number of Indians. Some 560 of Winchester's men were captured, and the British were accused of allowing their Indian allies to kill many of the American wounded. After his victory at Frenchtown, General Procter twice crossed Lake Erie to attack the pompous but timid Harrison (at Forts Meigs and Sandusky), but actually succeeded in capturing only a few American militiamen. After Perry's victory on Lake Erie, Procter was forced to retire. General Harrison followed and defeated him at Moravian Town, where the famous Tecumseh, a national hero in the history of Canada, was killed. This battle destroyed the reputation of General Procter but failed to provide one for Harrison. The latter had, however, in conjunction with Perry, regained control of the Michigan Territory for the United States. He now transferred his troops to the Niagara frontier.

In this region the first important action of the year was the capture and partial destruction of York (now Toronto), the capital of Upper Canada, by the combined forces of General Dearborn and Commodore Chauncey. The Library and Parliament buildings were burned, the public records were destroyed, plate was carried off from the churches, and many private dwellings were pillaged by the American soldiery. It is probable, in the light of recent researches, that the American commanders did not order or even encourage this destruction, but they cannot be held blameless for the actions of their troops. On the other hand, the American General McClure declared after the war that York had been officially destroyed in reprisal for the burning of Washington by the British. The amusing feature of this testimony is found in the fact that York was destroyed in 1813, Washington in 1814.

After the reduction of York, General Dearborn proceeded to Fort George, which he captured with little difficulty. But while these events were taking place, Governor-General Prevost sought to create a diversion by crossing the lake in Yeo's squadron to raid the American naval base at Sackett's Harbor. No startling success was achieved, though one ship that was building was destroyed on the stocks.

When General Dearborn captured Fort George, he drove out the British commander, General Vincent, who was in charge of a force of 1,600 regulars and volunteers. Generals Winder and Chandler with 3,000 men were sent in pursuit. Vincent retired as far as Stony Creek, where he took up a defensive position. Acting on the advice of Lieutenant-Colonel Harvey, a conceited but energetic subordinate, General Vincent sanctioned a night attack on the American forces. Under the command of Harvey himself, this attack was carried out on the night of 5–6 June with complete success. Once again American leadership had failed, while the Canadian volunteers, as always when fighting defensive actions in Canada, were valorous and effective. The Canadian forces now divided, thus paving the way for one of the most spectacular events of the war. The main body encamped at Beaver Dam, while Lieutenant FitzGibbon with fifty men took up an advanced position some miles away.

Having been warned that he was about to be attacked by a force of over 600 men, FitzGibbon placed his fifty followers in

71

ambush and, with the aid of a small band of Indians, succeeded in deluding the American leader as to the number of his opponents. As a result the whole column surrendered.

In August 1813 General Wilkinson, a pompous and incompetent militarist, arrived at Sackett's Harbor to take command of the American armies in the West. All of the available troops were collected here in preparation for a descent on Montreal by way of the St. Lawrence River. This was the classic design for North American campaigns: northward to Montreal in the Seven Years' War; southward from Montreal in the War for American Independence. Wilkinson's advance was to be made in conjunction with the forces of General Hampton—the latter entering Canada from his headquarters at Plattsburg, on Lake Champlain. At last success seemed ready to crown the American efforts. An imposing force had been collected, and an intelligent plan of action had been developed. But once again the stupidity of American generals, combined with the enthusiastic and persistent defense of Canadian volunteers, saved Canada from the threatened disaster and blasted the hope of American success.

On 26 October a force of about 1,000 Canadians, under the command of a French-Canadian officer, Colonel De Salaberry, ambushed and defeated Hampton's army at Chateauguay. A few weeks later General Wilkinson, having allowed his army to become divided, was badly defeated on the banks of the St. Lawrence, at Chrystler's Farm. Had Wilkinson been blessed with the virtue of courage, he might still have pushed on. His forces were scattered but not destroyed. Hearing, however, that General Hampton had retreated, he followed suit. The close of the year's operations was marked by the withdrawal of the American forces from Canadian territory along the Niagara River, after a harsh display of useless severity at Newark and the burning of Sandwich by General McClure. Fort Niagara, on the American side of the river, was captured by the Canadians, and a number of small villages were destroyed as retaliation for Sandwich, York, and Newark. Fort Niagara was retained under Canadian control until the end of the war.

In the campaigns of the next year (1814) the American troops, for the first time in this war, were led by reasonably competent commanders. In the summer of that year, fortunately for Canada, British reinforcements, released from European duty by the banishment of Napoleon to Elba, began to arrive in North America. But Yeo and Chauncey still disputed, without deciding, the supremacy of Lake Ontario. American invasions of Canada were again repulsed, while Great Britain maintained and made even more secure her control of the sea.

The first important movement of the year was initiated by one of the newly appointed American leaders, General Brown. With 4,500 soldiers under his command, he crossed the Niagara and on 5 July defeated General Riall, who with 1,500 men was awaiting him at Chippewa. Owing to the failure of Commodore Chauncey to bring his naval forces into proper co-operation, General Brown was unable to profit by this victory and retired westward to the Niagara. At Lundy's Lane, within sound of the cataract itself, was fought the most bitter engagement of the whole war. The battle began late in the afternoon, and neither army had any great preponderance of either guns or men. At first the Americans were victorious; they drove the British from their positions and captured guns and ammunition. Under the leadership of General Drummond, reinforced and reinspired, the Canadians returned to the attack at nine in the evening and continued the hostilities until midnight. Both sides were thoroughly worn out, but it was the Americans who retired; the Canadians were left in possession of the field. The next morning the American camp was found deserted. General Brown had withdrawn to Fort Erie. This post was soon abandoned, and at the end of the year Amherstburg and Malden alone of Canadian towns remained under American control.

In August 1814 Sir George Prevost found himself at the head of more than 11,000 seasoned troops, veterans of the Peninsular campaign. Having decided on an aggressive movement against the United States by way of Lake Champlain, he moved slowly across the border and invested and captured Plattsburg with little opposition. There he hesitated, waiting for Captain Downie, who was in command of the British naval forces on the lake, to defeat the American squadron and thus assure the safety of the British lines of communication. Unfortunately for his plans, Downie was killed and the British ships were defeated by an American flotilla under the command of Thomas Macdonough. Thereupon Prevost departed at once for Canada. Although this retreat was partially condoned by Wellington himself, it seems obvious that had an able, determined, and resourceful commander occupied Prevost's position, the 1,500 Americans who opposed him and the temporary loss of control on Lake Champlain would not have stopped the finest army ever collected (up to that time) on American soil.

The final naval action of the war on Lake Ontario occurred in October 1814. In that month Yeo, having constructed a great vessel of 102 guns (the *St. Lawrence*), blockaded Chauncey in Sackett's Harbor. This blockade was maintained during the few remaining months of the war.

Throughout 1814 the British navy controlled almost completely the eastern coast of the United States. Raids were made at many places along the seaboard, and these culminated in the Battle of Bladensburg and the capture of Washington. For some unknown reason no provision had been made for the defense of the capital. The hastily gathered militia fled at the first volley, and as a result Sir George Cockburn and Admiral Cochrane had little difficulty in taking the city. The Capitol, the Library, and the President's mansion were burned, though no private property was destroyed, nor were personal injuries suffered by any of the citizens. Admiral Cochrane wrote to Secretary of State Monroe that this action was taken as a measure of retaliation for the atrocities committed by American troops in the destruction of Canadian towns and the mistreatment of inhabitants. This explanation has been generally accepted by British historians; but while the destruction of government property is permissible under the laws of war, there are few reasonable men who applaud this or similar actions of the War of 1812. It is particularly difficult to find any real excuse for the destruction of the Congressional Library. This, in common with the American actions at Sandwich and the other excesses of the war, must simply be charged to the antisocial insanity, the destruction psychosis, that is an invariable accompaniment of war. An abortive attack on Baltimore ended the warfare on the eastern coast.[2]

On 17 December 1813 the American Congress had passed a new Embargo Act designed to prevent the trade that had grown up between New England and the enemy ports and fleet. As a result this illegal trade began to decline in volume, and Sir John Sherbrooke, Governor of New Brunswick, was ordered to invade Maine. It was hoped that in this way a new trade channel would be opened. The Americans offered little opposition, as the conquest gave promise of peace and increased commerce. The territory thus captured—the whole eastern section of Maine—was retained until the end of the war.

The Battle of New Orleans was the final land action of the war. It took place after the signing of the treaty of peace, but before the news of this event reached America, and it resulted in the decisive defeat of General Pakenham and his European veterans. It also resulted, ultimately, in providing a new candidate for the American Presidency: General Andrew Jackson.

By the middle of 1814 both nations were heartily sick of the war, and in August peace negotiations were opened at Ghent. A treaty was agreed upon and ratifications were exchanged on 18 February 1815. In the negotiation of the Treaty of Ghent, British diplomacy is seen at its lowest ebb. Castlereagh, Liverpool, and the others influential in deciding British foreign policy were concentrating their attention on the Congress of Vienna and had little time to spare for what they considered to be the minor drama of Ghent. By all rules of logic and the precedent of diplomacy, Great Britain should have been able to enforce her claim at least in regard to the cession of northern Maine. The British navy was in command of the sea and was enforcing a

[2] An incident in this attack was the event that inspired the author of *The Star-Spangled Banner.*

fairly complete blockade along the whole eastern coast of the United States; the British army held a large part of Maine and several posts on the American side of the Niagara frontier, and controlled the Oregon territory. Amherstburg and Malden alone of Canadian towns were in American hands. The cession to Canada of the northern half of Maine would have linked up the Maritime Provinces with Canada in a direct way, and had the cession been insisted upon, it might well have been achieved. The demand was made, but quickly withdrawn. Gambier, Goulburn, and Adams were men of little ability, less experience, and no determination. They were further weakened in their handling of the negotiations by the knowledge that the Duke of Wellington had expressed the opinion that it would require a concentration of all British power to bring the war to a more successful conclusion. This the British government was not prepared to face; after nearly twenty years of almost continuous warfare Britain wanted peace. For Wellington the crux of the matter was naval superiority on the Lakes. He doubted that this could be established, and his conclusion was: "In regard to your present negotiations I confess that I think you have no right to demand any concession of territory from America."

The United States, on the contrary, was represented by an exceptionally able group of men: Gallatin, Clay, Russell, Bayard, and John Quincy Adams composed what was probably the strongest diplomatic delegation in American history. Gallatin and Adams alone were more than a match for the British delegates. They did not succeed in persuading Great Britain to abandon Canada to the United States, nor did they gain a specific undertaking that Britain would end the system of impressment, but they did succeed in gaining peace without paying by concessions. Canada was not directly represented at Ghent.

The treaty was signed on 14 December 1814. It decreed a complete return to the *status quo ante bellum*. Impressment was not mentioned, nor was the subject of blockade. The boundaries and fisheries problems were postponed, to be settled, or so the

76

government hoped, in the negotiations that led to the Convention of 1818.

It is important here to emphasize that the Treaty of Ghent carried forward, in Canadian-American relations, the principle of Jay's Treaty. Commissions were set up to determine controverted points with respect to boundaries and fisheries. Also, both the United States and Great Britain were to make peace with the Indians, and thus this issue finally ceased to vex Canadian-American relations. The force of the humanitarian impulse was seen in a common declaration against the international slave trade.

5. *The Results of the War*

The War of 1812 had little or no effect on the history or constitution of Great Britain; it was a minor problem quickly forgotten in the rush of stirring events on the continent of Europe. But on the United States and Canada and on the relations of the two it had a vital and enduring influence.

During the early months of the war there appeared to be some real danger of its destroying the American Union. New England openly talked of secession. As the struggle continued, however, more and more of the Federalists united with the Democrats in support of the national policy. Those who continued in opposition were finally defeated in the hour of victory—as most Americans considered it—when the Hartford Convention, designed as the first step toward secession, ended as a fiasco on the arrival of the news of peace. The Convention might almost be described as the wake of the Federalist Party. On the signing of the Treaty of Ghent, differences of opinion were submerged in common rejoicing over the "victory." The Democratic candidate, Monroe, was returned in the election of 1816 by an electoral vote of 183 to 34, and this triumph inaugurated the national "Era of Good Feeling." From this time on, the American people "felt and acted more as a nation . . . they were more Americans." The new nationalism produced by the war was characterized by a greatly increased emphasis on the centralization of authority in the national capital. The American system sponsored by Clay and Calhoun now came into effective being. It was also characterized by the introduction of permanent military and naval establishments, and by the inauguration of that great political and economic institution the high protective tariff. It also marked the beginning of federal aid for internal development and improvement projects. Thus the military, economic, and sentimental life of the nation joined with the political interests in centralization at Washington. It is, then, true in more than one way that "the country entered the war distracted, indifferent and particularistic; it emerged from it united, enthusiastic and national."

Important as was the effect of the war upon the United States, it was even more vital in its influence on the history of the British colonies in North America. The defense of Canada was so unexpectedly successful, and was carried out in the face of such enormous odds, that the War of 1812 has become a national tradition. Before the war Canada had consisted of five geographically separate and politically independent colonies—all weak, all undeveloped, all apparently destined to ultimate absorption in the United States. At the close of the successful war of defense the colonies were still disunited, but they possessed a common tradition of more than ordinary virility, and a remembrance of victory against overwhelming odds, which gave confidence to the present and assurance to the coming generation. With the record of 1812 before him, no future Canadian had cause for despair. The struggle had been, in Canadian eyes, a desperate defense of home and political integrity; a fight for liberty against submersion in the American Union; a defensive war against a foreign invader. In the struggle French and British Canadians were drawn together as would not have happened in fifty years of peace—"it did more than any other event, or series of events, could have done to reconcile the two rival races within Canada to each other." Although the Canadian nation was not formally inaugurated until half a century later, the political divisions then united found their common basis on the fields of Chateauguay and Lundy's Lane. To the War of 1812 the British Empire owed a debt of gratitude too often unrecognized. It is still something of a national epic in Canada.

In one respect, however, the effect of the war on Canada was seriously detrimental: it retarded the growth of responsible government by at least a generation. Democracy, as an American invention, was in serious disrepute, and the leaders in the movement for constitutional reform were inevitably denounced as annexationists in disguise. Indeed, this tendency among a certain class of Canadians to condemn all political changes as American inventions still exists—in spite of the fact that today Great Britain, from a political and economic point of view, is considerably more radical than is the United States.

The effects of the war, so far as the relations of Canada and the United States were concerned, were most unhappy. The schism between the two branches of the Anglo-Saxon race was broadened and intensified. Mutual charges of atrocity were exchanged, confirming Americans in their hatred of Great Britain; while in Canada "two generations did not suffice to efface the evil memories of 1812." Thomas Jefferson declared that the British had indulged "in acts of barbarism which do not belong to a civilized age"; Canadians were "convinced of the future necessity of keeping their neighbors at a respectable distance, whether in peace or war." The influence of the Loyalists became more pronounced, and at the same time there was increased acceptance of their creed and its essential foundation: opposition to the United States. The bitterness engendered by the Revolution was renewed and intensified by the War of 1812.

4

Moments of Crisis

1. *Introduction*

The century of continuous peace that has been maintained between the United States and Canada has so often been eulogized by the professional orator that there is danger that its real significance will be unduly discounted. It was a true achievement in the conduct of international affairs, and the record is even more remarkable in view of the possibilities of conflict presented by the historical, geographical, and economic contacts of the two nations. Had there been no incentive to war, peace could hardly have been called a virtue.

On more than one occasion since 1815 the maintenance of peace has been by no means easy or automatic. Chronic dislike, fanned into glowing hostility by some unfortunate series of circumstances or some unusually knavish politician, has seemed potent with the threat of war. In 1838, in 1842, in 1846, the tranquil intercourse of the two peoples was rudely destroyed, and only by the determined efforts of true patriots in Great Britain, Canada, and the United States were armed conflicts averted. American exponents of the theory of Manifest Destiny (the rationalization that justifies the casting of covetous eyes upon all territories from the North Pole to Panama) have ever seen in the annexation of Canada a logical and mutually bene-

80

ficial step toward the consummation of their desires. A considerable segment of American opinion was represented by the orator who foresaw the eventual power of the United States extending not only from the Atlantic to the Pacific but also "from Tierra del Fuego to the Aurora borealis!" During these times of crisis in the history of British North America—in the rebellions of 1837-8, in the extreme depression of 1849, in the critical days of British Columbia from 1868 to 1871, in the election campaign of 1911—these advocates of expansion have tended to aid that party in Canada which seemed most likely to favor union with the United States. More than once such aid took the form of money and of arms. The net effect of this aid and comfort to a party in Canada supposed to favor annexation has usually been to strengthen Canadian nationalism or to bring increased emphasis to the imperial connection. The development and solution of problems thus aroused form no small part of the history of the relations of the two countries. It is desirable to have some knowledge of the more important of these critical periods.

2. The United States and the Canadian Rebellions

Long before the War of 1812 the more radical among the settlers of Upper Canada were protesting against both the form and the spirit of their government. The great power vested in the person of the Governor and the strength of the appointed Executive Council far outweighed the limited rights accorded to the elected Assembly. Many of those who were dissatisfied had been accustomed to the more democratic conditions that had pertained in some of the American colonies, and they now objected strongly to a governmental system that was neither responsible nor even fully representative.

For some years after their great migration the leaders of the Loyalists found no one in Upper Canada to dispute their rule, but the gradual influx of other settlers foreshadowed the coming attack upon their control. As the less wealthy among the Loyalists and the later settlers from the United States and Great Britain slowly overcame the hardships of their pioneer life, they found more time to devote to political affairs, and their challenge to the bureaucracy became audible.

The War of 1812 at first appeared to have welded Canadian society into a homogeneous unit, but with the relaxation of external pressure after the signing of the Treaty of Ghent, the cohesive bonds were sundered, and criticism again became vigorous and insistent. But the leading Loyalists, conscious of their patriotic service in the defense of Canada during the war, were more than ever imbued with a spirit that caused them to look upon Upper Canada as their "special heritage," and its government as their prescriptive right. Related in some instances by ties of blood, but bound together far more effectively by their social, political, and economic interests, the "Family Compact" held in one central authority the attributes of social prestige, economic advantage, and political control. Into this circumscribed body were admitted some of the more able, forceful, or genteel of the immigrants from the British Isles, while the Royal Governor became, perforce, a part of the system. This resulted not only from his natural sympathy for the social ideals of the Family Compact group, but also because, his term of office being short, he quite naturally looked to the permanent bureaucracy for guidance. The whole spirit of the Constitutional Act of 1791 was conservative, and it was designed, as far as the remainder of the British Empire was concerned, to prevent a recurrence of the troubles of the 1770's. The evils of the bureaucratic system that was thus developed were followed by the inevitable protests of those whose ambitions were fettered by their exclusion from the charmed circle. The criticism became more and more widespread, and many of the Loyalists themselves took part in the attacks upon the ruling clique. As the criticism increased, the grasp of the bureaucracy upon law, finance, state, and church became more tense. Revolution was inherent in the situation that developed.

As is frequently the case, the most perfect example of reactionary control was found in the church. By the Constitutional Act of 1791 large land endowments had been set aside for the benefit of the "Protestant clergy." This term was interpreted by the colonial officials to refer only to the members of the Church of England, although it was later modified to include the Church of Scotland. Not only were nonconformist bodies refused assistance from this endowment, but they were forced to labor under other restrictions as well. As late as 1828, Methodist ministers were not allowed to conduct the marriage ceremony, although the nonconformists far surpassed the Anglicans in number. Especially under the leadership of the famous Bishop Strachan, the established church interfered in political and social matters and displayed a bigotry almost as tyrannical, if not so complete, as that of the church in early New England.

Canadian opposition to the despotic political and social controls under which they suffered was stimulated by contrasting conditions in the United States. There the influence of the frontier was culminating in manhood suffrage, the election of judges, restrictions on the power of the commercial banks, and the other factors that characterized Jacksonian democracy. At the same time that the Westerners were taking possession of the White House in Washington, a Royal Governor, supported by an appointed and despotic Council, ruled Upper Canada from the capital in "Muddy York." Against this system of entrenched privilege members of the elected Assembly railed in vain.

For over twenty years this governmental system prevailed, in spite of protests and active opposition. From every district came the voice of remonstrance, but for a quarter of a century, in spite of bureaucratic interference and absolutism, the citizens of Upper Canada endured without violence, though the black clouds of protest bore witness to a coming storm. Opposition was crushed

83

by legal or illegal means, by persuasion, bribery, and force. Here, as ever, extreme conservatism was forcing revolution.

Yet it must not be supposed that the Canadian populace was unanimous in opposition to the Family Compact, or that there was always even a majority against the existing rule. By the use of one magic word, assisted, it is true, by a high technical perfection in the arts of political manipulation, many a hostile district had been won to enthusiastic support of the existing regime. The magic word was "Loyalty." The record of the bureaucracy was consistent in this matter: it had not varied in its support of the imperial bond and had opposed with unrelenting vigor any scheme of independence, any thought of annexation. Its hostility to the United States was ingrained and bitter, and this was the one issue upon which Canadian opinion, of whatever social or economic strata, approached unanimity. (The only serious exceptions were found in certain frontier groups in western Ontario where sympathy with American ideals was not uncommon.) With consummate skill the leaders of the Tory group cast doubt upon the loyalty of everyone who offered criticism—a protest against the Clergy Reserves was invariably followed by an attack upon the protestant as a propagator of American doctrine, as an advocate of annexation. Thus the prejudice of the people was utilized by the government, and for many years with great success. The task of the administration was made more simple when in 1835 William Lyon Mackenzie, the picturesque and fiery Scotchman who had led the forces of opposition, driven to desperation by his fifth illegal expulsion from the Assembly, enthusiastic for the doctrines of Hume and other English liberals whom he had met during an unsuccessful pilgrimage to London, and still moved by the biting logic of Tom Paine and his colleagues of the Revolution, threw off all restraint and became an open advocate of independence.

Throughout this period the attitude of Canada toward the United States was one of hostility, and this sentiment not only permeated the press, pulpit, and legislature, but was fundamental in the people themselves. They felt, and with some show of reason, that the United States was not only willing but eager to take advantage of any favorable opportunity to annex the British provinces. Many Americans could not feel comfortable until "British despotism" was finally removed from this continent. To any close relationship, either political or economic, the Canadian people were distinctly opposed, and the record of hostility that characterized the Canadian attitude toward the American contentions in fishery, boundary, and trade discussions from 1815 to 1846 was, in no small measure, a result of this ingrained national sentiment. Revolutionary America's treatment of the Loyalists was still bearing fruit. Not only did Canadians fear armed aggression from the United States, but they were keenly alive to the danger of permitting the establishment of a large American community in the Upper Province, the possibility of "peaceful penetration," and the introduction of the "loose demoralizing principles" of the Republic.

American opinion of Canada throughout the same period was very far from complimentary, and American newspapers and journals have been no more noted for reticence in the statement of popular prejudices than has the press of Canada. The sympathy of the Union, so far as Americans knew what was happening in Canada, was naturally bestowed upon the radical and anti-imperial elements in the Canadian population. Any movement that seemed to promise opposition to British or Loyalist authority received hearty encouragement from "across the line." Willcocks, a Canadian traitor of the War of 1812, had escaped to the United States, whence he devoted himself to the task of influencing Canadian opinion in favor of annexation. This he tried to accomplish by a sheet known as the *Upper Canada Guardian*, which he published in the United States and circulated in Canada. The whole venture was financed by American funds. In Plattsburg, New York, was published *L'Ami du Peuple*, a paper intended for the consumption of the French-Canadian habitant, and designed to stir him to rebellion by its recital of

85

the diabolical plots in preparation by the British government. Generalization is always difficult and seldom exact, but it is probably safe to say that the majority of the American people in 1835 not only favored the annexation of Canada but felt that any indirect aid that could be given to Canadian revolutionists would be not only justifiable but highly praiseworthy. Thus during the conflicts of 1837–8 there was very little popular objection to the violation of Canadian territory by armed American bands. On the other hand, the greatest enthusiasm was aroused by the presence of Mackenzie, Nelson, Papineau, and other Canadian rebels in American cities. The American as a rule rather despised the Canadian as a man without spirit who allowed himself to be ruled by a tyrannous and "effete" monarchy. The revolutionists were Canadians in whom "the slumbering genius of freedom" had at last awakened. Moreover, independence with Canada in its then existing condition meant inevitable annexation. Sentiment and interest united to mold American opinion.

So matters stood when writs were issued for the election of members to the Upper Canada Assembly in 1835. Mackenzie had been irritated into declaring for independence, and this fact had alienated the vast majority of the voters, in spite of the appeal held forth by his demand for internal reform. Even ardent liberals such as Dr. Ryerson and Alexander Perry evidenced the popular belief that in this election the people were "called upon to decide the question of separation by their votes." The inevitable result was achieved. By an overwhelming majority the Family Compact was confirmed in its position. Mackenzie himself was defeated.

The convocation of the Assembly was followed by some months of futile debate, in which the cause of reform was hopelessly beaten. Gradually, however, public opinion, in its reaction from the patriotic heat of the election, regained its old attitude of hostility toward the existing order. But Mackenzie was now ready for more drastic measures, and he was energetically preparing for the employment of force to accomplish his desires.

86

When, as a result of an armed insurrection under Papineau and Dr. Wolfred Nelson in Lower Canada,[1] the regular troops had all been moved to Montreal, he seized the opportunity presented to him. Against the advice of many of his friends and advisers, on 4 December 1837 Mackenzie organized a provisional executive, raised the standard of revolt, and called upon the citizens to support a democratic government. Meanwhile the revolt in Lower Canada very quickly petered out.

From the first the enterprise was doomed to dismal defeat. The government sent out a call for loyal volunteers, and these poured into Toronto in almost unmanageable numbers. A few insignificant skirmishes, one real fight at Montgomery's Tavern, and the rebels were completely routed.

Mackenzie himself escaped to the United States, and at Buffalo his movement received cordial and material support. Here four public meetings were held with the object of gaining volunteers and supplies for the Canadian rebels. One of these meetings was the largest gathering held, up to that time, in the city of Buffalo. The utmost enthusiasm prevailed, and the representatives of the federal government, if they did not sympathize, at least made no attempt to preserve the strict neutrality of the United States. Mackenzie made an eloquent appeal for supplies, for arms, and for volunteers. Many of the audience enlisted immediately; ammunition and field pieces were taken from the United States arsenal without any show of opposition. The number of recruits increased during the following week until a full thousand men were under arms, and "General" Rensselaer Van Rensselaer, of Albany, took over the command.

On the other side, however, notice must be given to a meeting of the American-born residents of Montreal at which a resolution was passed declaring that neither their support nor their sym-

---

[1] This rebellion was put down during the month of November. There were powerful forces in the old province of Quebec who saw dangers to the survival of French-Canadian culture in the Papineau rebellion: those who feared the anticlericalism of Papineau's younger followers, and those who feared that annexation to the United States would be the end of a distinctive French-Canadian nationalism.

pathy would be given to the rebels. But at a score of places across the American border—at Troy, Burlington, Middlebury, Rochester, Ogdensburg, Montpelier—this resolution was denounced and votes of money and supplies were passed in favor of the Canadian "patriots."

Mackenzie and his supporters were now determined to carry on the struggle from an American base, "secure in the protection of American unfriendliness to Canada." To give an appearance of legality, however, Navy Island, a Canadian possession in the Niagara River situated a short distance above the falls, was fortified as a base. Thence was issued a Canadian Declaration of Independence. This document offered land and money to all who would join the new government. On the American side, volunteers gathered in considerable numbers; material of every sort was provided by individuals, by societies, and by town and city officials. The encampment at Navy Island was of little importance—the real work was performed at Buffalo and Black Rock on the American shore. "The whole border" was in arms or was supporting those who had enlisted.

Throughout the Northeastern states "Hunter's Lodges" were organized, membership being contigent upon subscription to an oath "never to rest until all tyrants of Great Britain cease to have any Dominion or footing whatever in North America." There can, of course, be no question whatever as to the total illegality of the raids that ensued—raids organized by Americans, on American territory, and directed against a neighboring country with which the United States was not at war. The American government, moreover, was distinctly negligent in failing to take effective action to the end of checking these enterprises. It is true that orders prohibiting actions contrary to international law were issued, but they were not adequately enforced. No vigorous action was taken until after the destruction of the *Caroline*.

It is of interest to note, however, that the United States government and even state agencies were very much more circumspect in their recognition of the obligations of neutrality along the Canadian border than they were in their concurrent dealings

88

with Mexico. The seizure of Texas had no counterpart in the North, where a still potent imperial power could be seen behind the weak and exposed frontier community.

3. *The* Caroline *Incident*

The *Caroline* incident added to the already violent prejudice cultivated against Great Britain by the authors and politicians of the United States. At the same time it equally inflamed the Canadian hostility to the Republic.

The Navy Island base was supplied with all necessary materials by small boats loaded on the American side of the river. One of these vessels, a steamer known as the *Caroline,* was used by the insurgents to transport men and ammunition from Fort Schlosser in the United States to the island headquarters. Faced with the necessity of destroying this rendezvous, on 30 December 1837 a party of Canadian soldiers under Captain Drew crossed the river in small boats, cut the *Caroline* from her moorings at the wharf of Fort Schlosser, and towed her to the middle of the stream—whence, a burning wreck, she drifted toward the falls. In the skirmish on the American side at least one citizen of the United States was killed.

This action produced a violent repercussion in the United States. For a short time it appeared as though the border counties would themselves promote a war against Upper Canada. At last the President was forced to action; the militia of New York were placed on duty, General Winfield Scott was sent to the border, and orders were issued providing for the strict enforcement of the laws of neutrality. The American government then demanded redress from Great Britain for the violation of American territory. Great Britain in replying justified the action on the ground that it was a necessary precaution undertaken in defense of the realm, and legal under the rules of international law.

For three years the controversy this reply aroused was carried on by the two governments, while the excitement on each side of the border gradually subsided. In 1840, however, the whole problem was again dramatically brought to the public attention by the arrest of a certain Alexander McLeod, who, apparently in a fit of drunken bravado, had boasted in a New York saloon that he had killed an American in the attack on the *Caroline.* The British government requested that McLeod be immediately released on the ground that whatever he had done had been done under the orders of his superior officer, and that the British Crown itself assumed all entailed responsibility. The "national honor" was involved. The Department of State replied that the American government was unable to interfere in a state trial, and once more war seemed to be the only solution of the impasse.

A United States district attorney was supplied to McLeod as counsel in an attempt to assure his acquittal, although Governor Seward and other ardent patriots vehemently protested. Fortunately it was proved at the trial that if McLeod had ever made the alleged boast, he was a conceited liar, for at the time of the raid he had not even been near Fort Schlosser. He was finally released.

The discussion then returned to the original question of the legality of the invasion of American soil. Calhoun led the public attack upon the Canadian case, stating that it could in no sense be claimed to have resulted from necessity, and that it was, therefore, illegal. The matter was finally considered by Daniel Webster and Lord Ashburton in 1842. Webster insisted that to justify the action Great Britain must show "a necessity of self-defense, instant, overwhelming, and leaving no choice of means, and no moment for deliberation." Further, the British agents must not have been guilty of any "unreasonable and excessive" action. Lord Ashburton agreed with this statement of the legal principle, and declared that all these conditions were evident in the case in hand. Viewed objectively, this statement must be considered too sweeping, for the Canadian forces might easily have delayed and accomplished their purpose at a more seasonable time. Navy

Island might have been taken from the Canadian shore without troubling to scuttle the *Caroline*. The difficulty was finally settled when Ashburton "expressed regret that explanation and apology for the occurrence was not immediately made," and there the matter was left.

This was one of the infrequent cases in the history of international relations in which a sovereign power publicly confessed its sins. The British government did it again in the case of the *Alabama* claims a generation later.

For some time after the destruction of the *Caroline*, untoward incidents continued to occur along the Canadian border. President Van Buren's proclamation urging the observance of strict neutrality was of little avail, though at first an honest effort had been made to carry it into effect. Raids into Canadian territory were finally stopped by a realization of their futility and by the severe treatment accorded prisoners by the Canadian authorities. These raiders had, in reality, the status of brigands, so severe punishment was legally just. A number of them were executed and over one hundred and fifty were deported to Van Diemen's Land. Whether or not the British officials might have displayed more leniency is still a topic of historical debate. A recognition of the efficiency of Canadian methods is found in the following resolution passed by a public meeting in the city of Buffalo: Resolved "that Great Britain, in hanging, shooting or transporting American citizens who were assisting the Canadian revolutionists has infringed upon the rights of free men."

Thus was ended one of the most critical periods in the history of American-Canadian relations. That it did not result in war is decidedly creditable to those political leaders who braved the anger of the mob in order to preserve international peace. Internal conditions in the United States, especially after the burning of the *Caroline*, might very easily have plunged the English-speaking world into war. Here was a people proud, exultant, youthful; still glorying in the winning of their freedom from the world's greatest empire; filled with a passion for republican institutions; and still looking with disfavor upon the authors of their ancient wrongs. On the northern side of the boundary dwelt a people of equally intense pride, a people who had created a new nation in a wilderness because of ill-treatment suffered at the hands of their southern neighbors, and because of loyalty to their king. The Canadian nation was divided in race, and gripped in the travail precedent to the birth of free and responsible institutions. On neither side of the border was prudence held in high esteem. It was a time of hot words and energetic action; it was not a time of reason and philosophic calm. It is fortunate, and even surprising, that war did not ensue.

4. The Annexation Movement of 1849

The importance in Canadian history of the revolutionary movements of 1837 and 1838 is to be found not in the events themselves, but rather in the psychological result produced by the revolts. So effectively did these eruptions in the body politic draw the attention of the statesmen of Great Britain to the problem of Canadian government that Lord Durham, soon to become an outstanding figure in British imperial history, was delegated to proceed to the American colonies, to inquire into and report on conditions there existing.

It was no simple problem with which Lord Durham had to deal, and though in its ultimate effect the result of his counsel was beneficial to the colony, the political and especially the economic disturbances of the decade following his appointment as Governor-General led Canada in 1849 to the serious consideration of annexation to the United States.

One of the first acts of Lord Durham upon taking office as Governor-General was to issue a general pardon to all those who had taken part in the late revolts, with the exception of some few leaders, including Papineau, Nelson, and Mackenzie. At the same time he was conducting an extensive inquiry into the causes of political and social unrest in both Upper and Lower Canada. Late in 1839, failing to receive the support from the home authorities which his haughty spirit demanded and which he might reasonably have expected, Durham resigned. But his report, soon to become one of the celebrated documents of Canadian constitutional history, was already in the final stages of preparation. On his return to Great Britain his recommendations were presented to the ministry at Westminster.

Ultimately the most significant aspect of Lord Durham's report was his recommendation in favor of responsible government, but the most immediately important item was his proposal to unite the provinces of Upper Canada and Lower Canada in a legislative union. This recommendation was made effectual in the Act of Union of 1840. Even before the act became effective Lord John Russell, in a dispatch dated the 16 October 1839, declared that appointments to the Executive Council were no longer to be considered life appointments. Executive councilors were to be replaced "as often as any sufficient motives of public policy may suggest the expediency of that measure." Thus a system of semi-responsible government was provided, and by liberal interpretation and insistence the practices of real responsibility were gradually introduced, strengthened, and accorded the authority of precedent. In 1847 the appointment as Governor-General of Lord Elgin, who was a son-in-law of Durham, and thoroughly in sympathy with the full logic of responsible government, indicated beyond all possibility of mistake that the British government was now prepared to permit the establishment in Canada of a thoroughly responsible system of government. In the general elections in January 1848 the Governor-General assumed a strictly impartial attitude and largely as a result of this fact, the Tory Party was decisively defeated. The Reformers were returned to power, and a ministry was formed from among their leaders.

Now for the first time the power of the Family Compact, and of the "Chateau Clique" in Lower Canada, was shattered; a Reform administration was in office and an impartial Governor-

General occupied the official residence. This was a bitter experience for those who had long enjoyed the perquisites of office and authority; who had come to view themselves as the sole Canadian repositories of loyalty; and who now perceived that the government of their country had fallen into the hands of those whom they considered the low-born and the malcontent. Some explanation of this dramatic overturn was necessary, and the Tories found the explanation they desired in the almost solid delegation sent to swell the Reform majority *from French-Canadian constituencies.* Immediately the cry of "French domination" was raised throughout the land, and the decades of Anglo-French dissension—dissension that is still far too common in Ontario and Quebec—can be traced in no small measure to the bitterness here engendered.

The new ministry introduced as one of its first measures a bill to indemnify the citizens of Lower Canada for losses sustained in the outbreaks of 1837 and 1838. Similar legislation had already been enacted in Upper Canada, but the new bill was violently opposed by the Tories on the ground that, owing to the widespread nature of the revolts in Lower Canada, the proposed indemnity would in fact be subsidizing revolution.

The attack on the Rebellion Losses Bill was characterized by a bitterness and a violence never since equalled in a political struggle in Canada. Amid the fierce protests against "French rule," and accusations of personal corruption, began to be heard the prophecy of armed revolt, the muttered wish for annexation. The threats used a decade before by Papineau and Mackenzie were now heard in the mouths of Tories—many of the ultra-Loyalists of 1837 were flirting with revolt in 1849. If the Reformers had been extravagant in their denunciation of the government in 1837, the Tories were no more rational now—and they had infinitely less excuse for violence. "Civil war is an evil," wrote one Tory editor, "but it is not the worst of evils, and we say without hesitation that it would be better for the British people in Canada to have a twelvemonth of fighting . . . and lose five thousand lives, than submit for ten years longer to misgovernment induced by French domination." Another paper was reported by Lord Elgin to have said: "When we can stand tyranny no longer, we shall see whether good bayonets in Saxon hands will not be more than a match for a race and a majority." As Lord Durham had half foreseen, the Tories' hostility to the French was so great that many of them in order "to remain English" were willing "to cease being British." For reasons that will shortly become more apparent, Montreal was the center of the disloyal movement. In March 1849 the Toronto *Patriot* declared that there was an "undercurrent leaning of the Anglo-Saxons there [in Montreal] towards an annexation with their brethren of the United States." But the agitation was not entirely confined to Lower Canada. In Kingston a petition in favor of annexation was circulated, while the Toronto *Mirror* and the Hamilton *Spectator* advocated "an alliance with a kindred race." But Montreal was the center of the disturbance, and both the *Colonist* and the *Spectator* declared that a continuance of the existing situation would inevitably lead to separation from Great Britain and union with the United States.

The dispossessed Tories focused their attacks most pertinaciously and most violently against the government's Rebellion Losses Bill; their leader, Sir Allan McNab, declared on one occasion that he would rather join the United States than agree to its passage. A part of this opposition was undoubtedly caused by a genuine fear of French control, but it is not unfair to consider this a comparatively minor factor in the situation. The real explanation of the attitude of the Tories is probably to be found in their chagrin at the loss of office after so many years of uninterrupted power, in an intense desire to discredit the government, and in the hope of intimidating Lord Elgin into vetoing the bill.

In spite of all opposition, the government persisted, the bill was passed, and Lord Elgin gave his consent. Thereupon ensued the most disgraceful scenes in all Canadian political history. Lord Elgin's carriage was stoned, the Governor-General himself was insulted and reviled, and as a final act of revenge the Tory mob stormed and fired the Parliament buildings. Since that day no provincial or federal legislature has been convened in Montreal.

As might be expected, such actions as these merely served further to inflame the popular passions. The editor of the Quebec *Gazette* declared that the Tories had "destroyed their own reputation for consistent loyalty, ruined the character and credit of the country abroad, and retarded its prosperity. . . ." George Brown, the father of Canadian liberalism and editor of the Toronto *Globe*, had some justification for writing that "the Tories have not been a year out of office, yet they are at the rebellion point. . . . Withdraw the supplies and the Tory soon lets you know it is not the man or his principles which he loved, but the solid pudding which he could administer."

It would, of course, be manifestly unjust to hold the whole Tory Party responsible for the statements of its leaders or the actions of its mobs. The vital fact in the Canadian political situation in 1849 was the existence of a violently inflamed hostility between the two major parties—a condition so acute that many members of the party that had always been foremost in voicing its loyalty were now ready to discuss annexation to the United States, to toy with the idea of revolt.

The Canadian disorders of 1849, however, were not solely the result of political and constitutional difficulties. These difficulties were inevitable, but economic causes made them important. By the year 1846 the political and economic philosophy of the "Manchester school" had triumphed in Great Britain. In that year the Corn Laws were repealed, and during 1847 and 1848 tariff duties were removed from practically all commodities of commerce and industry. The reaction of this British policy on Canadian economic life was almost immediately disastrous. Prior to 1846 Canadian farm and forest products had enjoyed preferential treatment in British markets, a fact that gave assurance to the farmer or lumberman and facilitated the procuring of credit. Now this preference was wiped away and the products of Canada were forced into competition with the output of the United States and other countries. Lord Elgin, in writing to the

Colonial Secretary, described the conditions in Canada as follows:

"I do not think that you are blind to the hardships which Canada is now enduring; but, I must own, I doubt much whether you fully appreciate their magnitude, or are aware of how directly they are chargeable on Imperial legislation. Stanley's Bill of 1843 attracted all the produce of the West to the St. Lawrence, and fixed all the disposable capital of the province in grinding mills, warehouses and forwarding establishments. Peel's Bill of 1846 drives the whole produce down the New York channels of communication, destroying the revenue which Canada expected to derive from canal dues, and ruining at once mill-owners, forwarders and merchants. The consequence is that private property is unsaleable in Canada, and not a shilling can be raised on the credit of the province. . . .

"What makes it more serious is that all the prosperity of which Canada is thus robbed is transplanted to the other side of the line, as if to make Canadians feel more bitterly how much kinder England is to the children who desert her, than to those who remain faithful. . . . I believe that the conviction that they would be better off if they were 'annexed' is almost universal among the commercial classes at present, and the peaceful condition of the province under all the circumstances of the time is, I must confess, often a matter of great astonishment to myself."

Elgin put his finger here on one of the most fundamental developments of these years. The merchants of Montreal and other mercantile interests had since 1763 treasured the design of funneling out by the great St. Lawrence waterway the staple products of mid-continental North America. This design had been based on fur, on timber, and on wheat. The great rival of the commercial empire of the St. Lawrence had been the Erie Canal and the outlet to the ocean at New York. Down to the adoption by Great Britain of a free-trade policy in the forties, the merchant group had continued to hope and to work for a victory

97

of the St. Lawrence system over the Erie system. An essential element in any prospective victory was the continuance by Great Britain of imperial preferences, which tended to attract American wheat through Montreal. When Great Britain abandoned the last elements of mercantilism between 1846 and 1849, the merchant Tory group felt they and their grand design had been betrayed. Their anger turned toward the imperial connection.

The difficulty was enhanced, moreover, by the fact that colonial shipping was still hampered by the Navigation Acts—acts already famous as major causes of the American Revolution. Canadian protests against the new British policy were unavailing, and to many observers separation from the mother country and union with the United States, whose tariff wall was one of the chief obstacles to Canadian prosperity, seemed inevitable. Banks refused to extend credit to the farmer, for he was no longer certain of a market for his grain and fruit. The lumbering and dairying industries were faced with a similar problem, while exporting firms and allied corporations were forced into liquidation. To quote Lord Elgin again:

> "Property in most of the Canadian towns and more especially in the capital, has fallen fifty per cent in value within the last three years. Three quarters of the commercial men are bankrupt, owing to Free-Trade; a large proportion of the exportable produce of Canada is obliged to seek a market in the States. It pays a duty of twenty per cent on the frontier. How long can such a state of things be expected to endure?"

The British government, realizing the difficulties that were besetting its premier colony, was seeking means that would alleviate this distress and at the same time enable the government to remain true to its own politico-economic philosophy. The repeal of the Navigation Laws seemed to fulfill both requirements, and in consequence this was done. The St. Lawrence River was now thrown open to the traders of the world and *ultimately* this action conferred important benefits on Canada. It was some months, however, before foreign powers took advantage of their new opportunity, and the immediate effect was almost negligible.

The late forties and fifties witnessed fundamental changes in the whole North American economy. The age of wood, wind, and water was ending, and the age of steel, steam, and speed was beginning. The Industrial Revolution had burst the bounds of Europe and was building new problems in the Western Hemisphere. Thus political tensions and their economic causes struck suddenly and dramatically at the weak fabric of the Canadian state.

The most direct and obvious means of ameliorating Canadian conditions was that suggested by the British Ambassador at Washington, who, at the instigation of Canadian advisers, proposed the negotiation of a reciprocal trade agreement with the United States. The effect of such an enactment would be to open the American market to Canadian raw material, and the United States would supplant Britain as Canada's chief customer. To this proposal the American administration agreed and a bill to implement the agreement was introduced and passed by the House of Representatives in 1848. Owing to a general lack of interest and the pressure of other business, however, the session closed before the Senate had taken any action with regard to it. An equally abortive effort marked the following session.

While the Senators procrastinated at Washington, conditions on the St. Lawrence grew steadily worse, and sentiment in favor of annexation became more and more common as the economic situation became more stringent.

Nor was the condition of the loyal Canadian made easier by the news now emnating from Great Britain, for the London *Times*, the *Edinburgh Review*, and other equally prominent journals were giving voice to the colonial philosophy of Cobden and Bright. Loyalty to the Empire was no longer considered—even in the heart of the Empire—to be, of necessity, a virtue. Political leaders and public opinion seemed at one in resigning colonial destiny to the colonies themselves. Lord John Russell, Prime Minister of Great Britain, declared with the applause of

99

a full House that "he looked forward to the day when the ties which he was endeavoring to render so easy and mutually advantageous would be severed"; he and the people of England generally assumed that "the colonial relation was incompatible with maturity and full development." Other English politicians favored separation on the ground of expense. Indeed, the reaction against Tory imperialism seemed complete, and it was not surprising to find a Canadian annexationist editor summarizing it thus: "The whole current of opinion among England's most influential statesmen is evidently tending toward that point when they will bid adieu to the colonies, with wishes for their prosperity and hopes for continued friendship." As became evident later, British opinion was not united in willingness to bid the colonies adieu, but there was enough of this spirit extant and expressed to give real cause for worry to the Canadian opponents of separation.

In spite of these conditions, however, Canada was by no means ready for immediate annexation to the United States. Lord Elgin in describing conditions declared:

"There has been a vast deal of talk about annexation as is unfortunately the case when there is anything to agitate the public mind. If half the talk on this subject were sincere I should consider an attempt to keep up the connection with Great Britain as Utopian in the extreme. . . . A great deal of this talk is, however, bravado, and a great deal more the mere product of thoughtlessness. Undoubtedly it is in some quarters the utterance of very serious conviction; and if England will not make the sacrifices which are absolutely necessary to put the Colonists here in as good a position commercially as the citizens of the United States . . . the end may be nearer than we wot of."

It was at this juncture in Canadian affairs, early in the year 1849, that the British American League was organized at Brockville, whence its headquarters were shortly moved to Montreal. The League was organized by the Honorable George Moffatt, and its objectives were stated to be: the promotion of the commercial and industrial life of the colony; the organization of the moderate elements of the British population into one party; and a united opposition to French-Canadian domination. The advertisement issued by the League further proclaimed that "to maintain the British connection inviolate, has been, and still is, the ardent wish of every member of the League." The latter statement, however, was soon proved to be far from accurate.

The League was, in fact, a conglomerate body, composed of all the elements in Canadian society hostile to the existing regime, and it included Annexationists, Tories, Independents (those desiring Canadian independence but not annexation), Federal Unionists (proponents of a union including the Maritime Provinces and Newfoundland), and Provincial Partitionists (those in favor of annulling the Act of Union of 1840). One of the vice-presidents was an American citizen who openly favored annexation.

An organization composed of such discordant elements could not long resist the centrifugal forces embodied in itself. A convention was called, and when it became evident that the majority of delegates supported the British connection, many members left to join another body, known as the Annexation Association. At this convention, held in Kingston, the tenets of the League were expressed in the formula: "Protection, Retrenchment, and Union." This, for the time being, ended the attacks upon the loyalty of the League.

The agitation for annexation was centered in Montreal, and it was here on 10 October that an *Annexation Manifesto* was prepared and published. This document contrasted conditions in the United States and in Canada; placed the responsibility for the prevailing depression in the latter country on the British government; considered and discarded all proposals for relief which included membership in the Empire; and concluded that a true solution could be found only in "a friendly and peaceful separation from the British connection, and a union upon equitable terms with the great North American Confederacy of sovereign

States." The benefits to be derived from such a union were then enlarged upon, and the manifesto ended with an appeal to all true citizens to unite under the banner of the Annexation Association in working out the "common destiny" of the North American continent. In ten days over one thousand names were appended to this document, and many of them were those of leaders in the social and commercial life of Lower Canada. Combined with these were the signatures of Americans, extremists of the anti-imperialist Rouge party in Lower Canada, and others who had suffered politically, economically, or both, by the recent events.

The publication of the *Annexation Manifesto* served to bring the problem directly to public attention, and it did much to crystallize opinion both for and against the movement. The combination of forces favoring annexation was indeed a strange one. The business interests of Montreal—predominantly British by birth and extreme conservatives in politics—were, on this one question, linked with the ultra-radical elements of the French-Canadian populace, although on every other conceivable issue the two groups were diametrically opposed. Many members of the Tory Party, fearful of French domination, enraged by their own expulsion from office, and bitterly incensed over the enactment of the Rebellion Losses Bill, were united in the advocacy of annexation with those who had been their most fervent opponents on all other issues. Only an economic revival could reduce the fever of disloyalty.

The Montreal press at once became involved. The *Witness,* religious in tone and Tory in spirit, endeavored to give the sanction of theology to the proposed union: "It is precisely because we think the indications of Divine Providence are pointing directly, constanly and urgently in the direction of annexation that we have felt constrained to discuss it." So wrote the editor on 5 October 1849. The *Herald, Courier,* and *Gazette* favored annexation, while the *Transcript* and *Pilot* remained loyal to the British connection. The French-Canadian papers were similarly divided.

Although many of the more radical French-Canadian democrats were in favor of annexation, the majority of the French
populace was hostile to the movement. Following the leadership
of their church officials, these citizens of Lower Canada were
definitely opposed to a policy that would have led to their submersion in the huge population of the United States. They felt,
and probably with justice, that no American Congress would ever
grant to any section of its populace the peculiar rights that
Britain had granted to the inhabitants of Quebec. As one of their
own historians has expressed it:

> *"Les Canadiens-Français n'avaient aucune sympathie pour
> les Américains avec lesquels leurs ancêtres avaient été
> souvent aux prises sur le champ de bataille. Monarchiste
> et conservateur par leurs institutions, leurs mœurs et leur
> éducation, ils détestaient les principes républicains. Ils sa-
> vaient que, sous le drapeau britannique, ils trouveraient une
> sécurité parfaite pour leurs institutions et leurs privilèges,
> tandis qu'avec l'annexion, leur existence national courrait de
> grands dangers."*

Apart from Montreal, the movement in Lower Canada was
centered in the eastern townships. The movement, on the whole,
as subsequent developments clearly demonstrated, was not the
expression of a united public sentiment, but rather the action of
an ardent minority coerced from their old beliefs and convictions
by the pangs of a bitter experience, and temporarily beguiled by
the specious arguments of those few individuals to whom annexation really appeared to be the logical, inevitable, and attractive
destiny of British North America.

The publication of the manifesto did more than arouse public
opinion; it introduced the very practical problem of ways and
means. And this in turn demanded a discussion of the *terms* upon
which union should be based. The Montreal *Gazette* had at first
favored union, but it soon came to the point of declaring: "We
must have an opportunity to understand what we are called upon
to participate in before we can with prudence or honour throw

ourselves unreservedly into the annexation fad." This discussion of terms did something toward cooling the excitement of the more volatile annexationists, and it served to arouse many of the old anti-American prejudices of those whose Loyalist traditions had been momentarily forgotten in a temporary hostility toward Great Britain. Nevertheless, the movement did not collapse. The manifesto was followed by the formation of a political party; papers were published, pamphlets printed and distributed, and a platform campaign was carried on throughout the country.

As the campaign went on, the two sides drew farther and farther apart. The members of the government issued a vigorous denunciation of the Annexationists, and all officials of the state who had been in any way connected with the movement were summarily dismissed—an action that was vigorously supported and defended by Elgin in Canada and Grey in England. This step, however, was severely criticized by the parliamentary opposition and even some of the Reform Party felt that it was somewhat too drastic. But for the most part the press and people applauded the action of the administration; the Annexationists were apparently losing ground. Early in October prominent members of the British American League joined with the Loyalists of Montreal in issuing a counter-manifesto which received one thousand signatures without the formality of a canvass.

The Canadian Orangemen, though the vast majority of them were intensely opposed to the existing government, declared themselves in favor of unswerving allegiance to the British Crown. Many of those who had signed the original manifesto refused to continue their support. An enormous harvest and a slight stimulation to trade began to create an interest in business and to lessen the interest in political affairs. Conditions were such that the Montreal correspondent of the London *Times* felt justified in writing to his paper that he was becoming

"more confident every day that the late movement is a bubble which will have burst before next summer. . . . Nine-tenths at least of the Annexationists are so reluctantly.

They believe that this incorporation with the United States will act in a magical manner on the value of property and labour in Canada, and on commerce; that it will, in short, restore their own dilapidated fortunes. Show them a revival of prosperity without it, and annexation will be laid on the shelf until the next rainy day."

Doubtful as was the reception of the *Annexation Manifesto* in Montreal, it was received with even less enthusiasm in Upper Canada. The Toronto papers were almost unanimous in opposition to the proposal, the *Church* even going so far as to reassert the Revolutionary Loyalists' doctrine of indefeasible allegiance. Lord Elgin, nevertheless, was of the opinion that the large majority of those persons in Upper Canada who were protesting against the manifesto "firmly believe that their annexation to the United States would add one-fourth to the value of the produce of their farms." The attacks on the annexation movement were not, in general, based on economic grounds. The *Globe* and the *Patriot* reiterated time after time in good Loyalist style the old charges against the morals, religion, and civilization of the United States, paying particular attention to the question of slavery.

At this juncture a most interesting event occurred. William Lyon Mackenzie, the exiled revolutionary leader of 1837, in a letter from New York to the Toronto *Examiner*, stated that his

"sojourn in the United States had wrought a disillusionment. American democracy as it presented itself in the form of political corruption, crass materialism and human slavery, filled his soul with righteous indignation. He was convinced that the vaunted liberty of the United States was merely a sham; that neither the grandiloquent principles of the Declaration of Independence, nor the unctuous guarantees of the American constitution assured to the private citizen the same measure of civil and political freedom as was enjoyed by the humblest Canadian subject under the British Constitution."

This from the man who a decade before had favored annexation and had led a rebellion against the representatives of the Crown! Throughout the Upper Canadian peninsula this sentiment prevailed, the proponents of annexation being few and scattered. The British American League, both in convention and by vote of the local chapters, expressed itself as definitely opposed to union with the United States.

One of the strongest arguments of the annexation party, and one that was used with considerable effect, was that many British leaders had expressed themselves as favorable to Canadian separation, and that England, in effect, would be glad to see Canada go. This argument was finally overthrown in January 1850, when Earl Grey, the British Colonial Secretary, stated that the Queen was prepared "to assert all the authority which belongs to her for the purpose of maintaining the connection of Canada" with the mother country. This declaration went far toward ending the discussion; the practical difficulties were now too great to be overcome.

The session of the Assembly which opened on 18 January 1850 was to see the final defeat of the annexation movement. Only seven annexationists had been elected to the House in a total membership of eighty-three. Motions in favor of both independence and annexation were presented and overwhelmingly defeated. But the fundamental reason for the ending of interest in annexation, which took place during the spring and summer of 1850, was the revival of trade consequent upon the discovery of the Canadian market by foreign purchasing agents, and the activity of American buyers in taking up the immense Canadian crop of 1849. As soon as navigation opened, the St. Lawrence became crowded with shipping, and the grain deliveries presaged a great revival in every branch of commerce. Credit was again obtainable, property value increased, and a wave of confidence swept over the whole country.

The annexation movement of 1849 was merely one of the growing-pains of Canadian evolution. It was based on no fundamental hostility to the British connection, or on any compelling and persistent desire for union with the United States. The progress from colonial to dominion status in Canada, and from protection to free trade in Great Britain, produced a natural, but temporary, dislocation of the economic and political vested interests in the colony. The movement failed because it was—in a fundamental sense—insincere. As Sir John A. Macdonald said at a later time, the leaders of the movement, chagrined at their loss of political power and suffering from serious economic difficulties, temporarily "lost their heads." The fact is that the vast majority of Canadians were too much satisfied with their recently gained autonomy to be willing to sacrifice it by annexation to the United States. As Elgin wrote, "the existence to an unwonted degree of political contentment among the masses has prevented the cry for annexation from spreading . . . through the Province."

Supplementary explanations of the defeat of annexation may be found in the following facts: (1) The party favoring union with the United States was composed of totally irreconcilable elements, with no common ground except hostility to the government of the day. (2) The firm attitude adopted by the Baldwin-Lafontaine government, the tireless efforts of Lord Elgin, and the tardy but powerful support of the British Colonial Office strongly checked the movement. (3) The inherited and deeply rooted dislike for American institutions and people so firmly implanted in the minds of Canadians—a dislike made more potent by the influence of the Roman Catholic Church, and crystallized by recent developments in connection with slavery in the United States—was a deterrent. (4) Finally, and most decisive, was the revival of trade in the spring and summer of 1850. The winning of reciprocity in 1854 gave to Canada most of the advantages of annexation without its defects.

In the Maritime Provinces an agitation somewhat similar to that in Canada was carried on during 1849 and 1850. The principal grievance here was the removal of the tariff preference hitherto extended to New Brunswick lumber by Great Britain. The whole economic fabric of the colony may be said to have been based on this trade. Here, also, the old conservative bureaucracy had been defeated upon the introduction of responsible government, and its discontent synchronized with that of the commercial classes. The revival of trade and the successful working of responsible government ended "the silly fever of annexation which had prevailed for a time" among a disappointed clique, "for the Colonists had no liking for American slavery."

What, during this time of stress in Canada, was the attitude of the United States?

The Republic at this time was going through a period of militaristic expansion comparable in American history only with the course of events immediately following 1898. Texas, New Mexico, and California had lately been annexed to the Union, as had also a considerable portion of the long-debated Oregon Territory. It was not alone the oratorical patriots of the period who could visualize a continent over which the Stars and Stripes should wave alone, supreme. With the coming struggle over slavery and states' rights casting its ominous shadow before, political leaders were not averse to directing the public gaze toward foreign affairs. New York and New England merchants were glancing with covetous eyes upon the Canadian trade, and they were ever ready to welcome the northern provinces within the American customs wall. General Winfield Scott, whose previous connections with Canadian affairs had been marked by a high degree of intelligence and understanding, now published an open letter advocating the annexation of the provinces— by agreement with Great Britain, if possible. For a time this proposal threatened to become a plank in the Whig platform, for, as a politician of the time declared, "it would be a great honour and glory at this time to deliver Canada from the British yoke, for a great part of the Canadian people, and all of Lower Canada, have been despoiled of their political liberties." Certainly it may be said that a firm and unequivocal belief in the "manifest destiny" of the United States possessed the majority of the American people. "Both Cuba and the British Colonies," said a Washington paper, "at the proper time and in the proper manner will ultimately be annexed to the American Union." Secretary Seward, recognizing the tendency of the times, wrote that "the popular passion for territorial aggrandizement is irresistible." The old antipathy toward England, aroused by the many recent controversies, had not been allowed to die down, and an American correspondent of the London *Times* is found writing that "to fight the Britishers, all the States are one."

Native-born Americans, however, were not alone in their interest in Canada. French-Canadian immigration to the United States had already become an important movement, and at a meeting held in New York a society was formed by members of this group, with the object of bringing about a political union of the two countries. An address was prepared urging all Frenchmen in Canada and in the United States to band together to achieve this object. The address was circulated throughout the continent, and branch societies were formed in many of the Northern states.

It was, very naturally, in the Northern states of the Union that the Canadian question became most prominent. American papers quoted the *Annexation Manifesto* and all the information they could acquire tending to prove the dissatisfaction of Canadians with British rule and their desire for union with the United States. The Democratic State Convention, held in Montpelier, Vermont, adopted the following resolution:

"That, in the true spirit of Democracy, deeply sympathizing with the downtrodden, oppressed, and over-restricted of every clime and country, we hail with joy the rising spirit of liberty in the provinces of Canada as expressed recently in the published opinions of its citizens on the subject of annexation; that we appreciate the efforts and emulate the movements of the friends of Republicanism in Canada, and that we cordially extend to them the hand of friendship, fellowship, and brotherly love; that we will use all peaceable means in our power to further their object in becoming members of this our glorious union of free, independent and sovereign states."

Not to be outdone, the Whigs of Vermont adopted a similar motion. The Burlington *Sentinel* was even prepared to use force in the accomplishment of this glorious act of liberty, "after a fair trial" of "other means." The Legislative Assembly of New York resolved "that the annexation of Canada, and other provinces of Great Britain in North America . . . is an object of incalculable importance to the people of the United States."

President Taylor was scrupulously correct in his attitude toward the whole problem. He even made strenuous efforts to pass the Reciprocity Bill, which was designed to aid Canada by fostering the return of prosperity. This bill was defeated, however, because of poor management in Congress and because the Southern Representatives feared that it would lead to annexation, which they did not desire (Canada being "free soil"), and because a few of the Northern Congressmen believed that annexation, which they did desire, could best be obtained by making Canada realize the hardships of separate existence. The slave states approved the annexation of Cuba, which was slave territory, but opposed the taking of Canada; in the North the converse was largely true.

The United States was at this time engaged in an effort to solve the problem of the status of slavery in the territories recently acquired from Mexico. This was the period of the great debate in Congress on the slavery issue which led up to the Compromise of 1850. Nature barred slavery in Oregon as it did in British North America. To add so greatly to the expanse of territory devoted to freedom would have called forth strong Southern opposition and have added fuel to sectional tensions.

Such was the annexation movement of 1849. True, it was not an event of primary importance, for from the first its prospects of success were far from convincing. Nevertheless, it deserves more attention than is generally paid to it in conventional his-

tories, for it signalized the entrance of Canada on free and equal
terms into the ranks of commercial nations. No longer were the
provinces a commercial adjunct of the mother country. Moreover, the movement gave a glimpse into the thoughts that were
in the background of Canadian minds for many years; and at
the same time it gave American imperialists the opportunity to
express themselves yet again on the "manifest destiny" of the
United States. It was not until almost the beginning of the
twentieth century that loyal Canadians ceased to fear the possibility of absorption by the United States; and even today public-
opinion polls seem to indicate that many Americans believe that
the Constitution will ultimately apply to the whole of North
America.

5. *The American Civil War and the Fenian Raids*

A. *The Civil War and the British Empire.* In 1860 British-
American relations appeared to be more firmly established on a
basis of mutual toleration than they had been at any time since
the American Revolution. True, there was no great cordiality
either expressed or instinct between the two peoples. Many Brit-
ons still looked upon the American as an uncouth and boisterous
ruffian, engaged in a political experiment that was doomed to
failure and dissolution. On the other hand, the American saw
the British aristocracy as the product of many centuries of disastrous inbreeding—"effete," "decadent," and "rapacious." In
spite of these mutually uncomplimentary estimates, however, the
American Department of State and the British Foreign Office
had at last succeeded in settling the outstanding difficulties that
had embarrassed the two nations since 1776, and for a time there

appeared to be no necessity of propagating an anti-American or anti-British sentiment in either country. The various boundary problems had been settled; Britain had virtually abandoned the right of search; the fisheries dispute was temporarily dormant; and in general the future gave promise of a more peaceful intercourse than had marked the past.

Relations between the United States and Canada were particularly satisfactory as a result of the mutual benefits being derived from the reciprocity agreement of 1854. Trade was flourishing, Canadian raw materials were finding ready sale in American markets, and Canada was becoming an increasingly important customer for manufactured goods from the United States.

Yet in the five years from 1861 to 1866 these conditions were utterly changed. By the latter year the reciprocity treaty was abrogated; the American people were seriously considering the advisability of war against Great Britain; notice of repeal of the Rush-Bagot agreement had been sent to London, and the tension on the Canadian border exceeded that of 1837–8.

The causes for this abrupt and all-inclusive change are almost too well known to need recapitulation. During the American Civil War, Great Britain came to be so generally hated by both the North and the South that there was a very real possibility that the two sections of the Union might join in an offensive war against the common and "hereditary" foe. The Northern enmity was based on Great Britain's recognition of Confederate belligerency; on official laxity in allowing the escape of the *Alabama* and other cruisers; on the Confederate raids from Canada; on the consistent policy of blockade-running fostered by the British navy; on the generally expressed sympathy for the South common in British "society"; and, above all, on the action taken by Great Britain in the case of the S.S. *Trent*. The basis of Southern hostility was found in the refusal of Great Britain to join France in recognizing the Confederacy, and her refusal to intervene on behalf of the South even for the sake of cotton, the lack of which had paralyzed industry in northern Britain.² It was largely on the hope of British and French aid that the South had built her confidence of success, and when the formal neutrality of the British government made a Confederate victory impossible, the Southern hostility became correspondingly bitter.

The result of this feeling in the United States was, at the close of the Civil War, viewed with some concern in Canada. If a rapprochement had been consummated between the recent foes for the purpose of attacking Great Britain, Canada and the Maritime Provinces would have been the first points of attack. And many reports from south of the border served to convince Canadians that the people of the United States, as well as many of the more violent public officials, would not be averse to such a conflict. As a Northern marching song expressed it in a popular version of *Yankee Doodle:*

> *Secession first he would put down*
> *Wholly and forever,*
> *And afterwards from Britain's crown*
> *He Canada would sever.*

Even Secretary Seward, at the conclusion of hostilities, was persuaded that a foreign war would be the quickest method of uniting the North and South.

As a result of this attitude on the part of the American people, the reciprocity treaty was abrogated in 1866, and a bill was actually introduced in Congress to allow the entrance of Canada and the other provinces into the Union—a proceeding that was expected to result from the cancellation of the trade agreement. The real effect of this move was far different, for it was one of the prime factors in causing the formation of the Dominion ³ of

² It is an interesting fact that Great Britain, for comparatively trivial offenses against the Union in this war, is still condemned in the United States; while France, whose offenses were infinitely more serious, and which would probably have intervened by force if Great Britain had not prevented it, is seldom mentioned in connection with the American Civil War.

³ The name Dominion was adopted rather than Kingdom in order to avoid offending American opinion. Such Americans as Sumner, Chandler, and Seward were strongly

Canada—an event that ended, apparently forever, the possibility of the political union of these two North American nations. In fact, the effect of the American Civil War in its influence on the federation of the Canadian colonies could readily be developed into one of the major themes in Canadian-American relations. Its importance is seldom adequately recognized. The United States emerged from the Civil War, temporarily at least, the greatest military power in the world. Expansion westward was greatly stimulated by the Homestead Act of 1862. To preserve a separate British North American state, union was necessary, as it was to secure for Canada her own West.

Modern historical investigation has served to correct many of the earlier misapprehensions in regard to the attitude of Great Britain toward the American Civil War. It has been shown that English society at that period cannot be treated as a homogeneous whole—that there were at least three widely divergent views of the American struggle. Some Englishmen saw in the revolt of the South the attempt of a new "nation" to gain its independence. Being accustomed to think of Britain as the friend of oppressed national groups, they found it easy to sympathize with the Southern cause. But two other points of view were more generally held. While the aristocratic Tories were expressing their disdain for the North and sneering at the complete renunciation of the principles of 1776 which the policy of Lincoln seemed to entail, the textile operators of Lancashire and the northern counties were cheerfully enduring unemployment and its concomitant ills, inspired by the messages of Henry Ward Beecher and other apostles of abolition, who portrayed the struggle, not as a contest between free trade and protection, not as a forceful denunciation of the liberties of sovereign states, but as a crusade against that most vicious of institutions, human slavery. John Bright and Richard Cobden did much to sustain the faith of the English

---

opposed to Canadian federation, and this opposition so frightened Lord Derby that he refused to allow the use of the stronger term—an event that definitely retarded the growth of Canadian self-government. John A. Macdonald was a strong advocate of the title Kingdom.

working man in the belief that the Civil War involved a moral principle, and that principle was the true Northern cause. This was accepted by many Englishmen, in spite of Lincoln's repeated assertions that slavery was not the issue; that *union* was the principle at stake.

A very similar social alignment had taken place in Canada. The Tory classes were as hostile to America as ever, and openly rejoiced at the apparent disruption of the Union. On the other hand, the majority of Canadians, looking beyond the expressed cause of the war, could see the inevitable effect that a Northern victory would have upon the hated institution of slavery. It was this class that, while not animated by any strong friendship for the North, was generally favorable to the cause of emancipation. It was from this class also that the thousands of Canadians who enlisted in the Union armies were drawn. It is estimated that approximately twenty Canadians enlisted in the Northern forces for every one that joined the Confederacy. Of course, propinquity and the close family relationships that existed among the residents of the Northern states and the Canadian colonists explained much of this disparity. It also was related to the "bounty system" of the Northern conscription laws. But there was more to it than that. Such causes alone would not have induced forty thousand Canadians to enroll in the Northern armies. There can be little doubt that most of the Canadian people were at bottom convinced that the North was fighting for a cause that was just and humane.

But in spite of this evidence of sympathy for the Northern cause, the attitude assumed by many citizens of Canada was well summarized by the Montreal editor who wrote: "The Canadian people, heartily as they are opposed to slavery, have not seen, cannot yet see, why they should be friends with a people who have taken such pains to proclaim themselves our enemies; and to pander to every anti-British prejudice, every action of their own people most imbued with such prejudice or hatred."

That many of the Canadian people were thus affected toward the United States cannot be a cause of wonder to one who has followed the course of American political activities after the immense influx of German and, particularly, Irish immigrants after 1848. The manipulation of this great foreign vote could most easily be accomplished by an appeal to their native prejudices, and as a result many American political leaders allowed themselves to be drawn into a contest of vilification, with Great Britain as the object of assault. The Canadian reaction to these attacks, naturally, was not favorable. In August 1861 Canada's leading newspaper, the Toronto *Globe*, said: "The insolent bravado of the Northern press towards Great Britain and the insulting tone assumed towards these Provinces have unquestionably produced a marked change in the feelings of our people. . . . People have lost sight of the character of the struggle in the exasperation excited by the injustice and abuse showered upon us by the party with which we sympathized."

B. *Canada and the War.* Canadian hostility, however, was soon mingled with something of distrust and fear. In 1865 the United States had at its command the largest military establishment in the world. The presence of some million soldiers imbued with a resentful and retaliatory spirit, just south of the international border, caused no little anxiety in Canada. The memory of the Texas War was frequently recalled. "Even were the American government noted for its conciliatory foreign policy, and free from mob dictation," wrote an aristocratic Canadian editor, "and were we stronger in numbers and position—the absence of all defensive preparations might well be thought perilous." And these fears seemed fully justified, for the American people, flushed with victory, and deeply conscious of the real and also the imaginary wrongs inflicted upon them by the other branches of the English-speaking peoples, were in a mood that seemed to foreshadow vigorous action.

The Northern states, in particular, had special grievances against Canada—grievances based on raids into Northern territory undertaken by Confederate soldiers acting from a Canadian base. The first plot of this sort was directed against Johnson's Island in Sandusky Bay, and was forestalled by a warning sent out from the British Embassy at Washington. This was followed, however, by a much more important event—the Confederate raid on St. Albans, Vermont.

"President" Jefferson Davis had commissioned a certain Jacob Thompson to proceed to Canada and there to carry on such operations as "shall seem most likely to conduce to the furtherance of the interests of the Confederate States of America." The first plan of Mr. Thompson and his confederates was to capture the steamer *Michigan,* the only armed American vessel on the Great Lakes. This project failed, though two smaller boats were captured, and later lost. Turning then to land operations, Confederates planned the attack on St. Albans. On 19 October 1864 Bennett H. Young, a lieutenant in the Confederate army, with a party of about twenty-five Southern soldiers—armed but not in uniform—descended on the little town of St. Albans, situated about fifteeen miles from the Canadian border. After wounding two citizens and setting fire to a portion of the town, the detachment seized all of the money in the local banks, amounting to about $200,000, and left for their secret base in Canada. Pursued across the Canadian line, they were captured with the aid of the Canadian authorities, and about $75,000 was immediately recovered. The raiders were placed in a Canadian jail.

There is no evidence that the Canadian authorities had any foreknowledge of this raid. After the capture of the raiders a body of militia was placed along the border, and every precaution taken to prevent a repetition of such an event. Nevertheless, the whole Northern part of the United States was thrown into something of a panic; Canada was harshly criticized, and Seward gave six months' notice of the abrogation of the Rush-Bagot convention. Fortunately this last threat was never carried into execution, the notice being withdrawn in March 1865. One other raid was planned by Confederates working in Canada, but the activity of American officials in Chicago brought about the arrest of the raiders, who had left Canada separately and in disguise. The object of this attack was Camp Douglas, in northern Illinois.

The St. Albans raid was undoubtedly an outrageous act, justified neither by the laws of war nor by common sense. It was roundly condemned by Lord John Russell, by the London *Times*, and by the Canadian press. Although it is the consensus of instructed opinion that the Canadian government was not at fault in the matter, due to the secrecy of the preparations, and the immense length of the line to be guarded, nevertheless the raid did produce a sharp and bellicose reaction in the United States—an irritation that did not soon subside.

These events constituted the direct and overt acts upon which much of the American hostility to Canada was based. The bitter animosity against the United States which again flared up in Canada after the Civil War was due more particularly to events which occurred *at the conclusion* of that epoch-making struggle. These events were the Fenian raids.

c. *The Fenian Movement.* The Fenian movement was a by-product of the agitation that for centuries has marred the relations of the English and the Irish peoples. The peculiar character of the conflict with England, combined with the national characteristics of the Irish people, have made Ireland a conservatory in which secret orders have flourished in profusion. Many of the objectives for which they fought and schemed were laudable and just, but revolution, assassination, and graft have been the outward manifestations of the existence of some of these societies.

Emigration from Ireland to the United States had been in progress since before the American Revolution. It was not, however, until the period of the potato famines in 1845–8, and the disasterous revolutionary movement of the latter year, that this migration assumed truly important dimensions. During these and later years the Eastern states were inundated by a steady stream of immigrants, until at the present time the Irish-American population far exceeds in numbers and in wealth the population of the homeland. To the revolutionary leaders who, in spite of their defeat in 1848, had remained in Ireland, the possibility of using the wealth and personal services of this American community was an opportunity not to be passed by. Already imbued with a fanatical hostility toward England, the Irish-American immigrants needed only direction and inspiration to become a vital factor in British-American relations. To this end James Stephens, leader of the Irish Republican Brotherhood, or Phœnix Society, dispatched John O'Mahony to the United States for the purposes of organizing the Irish migrants. O'Mahony arrived in New York in 1853, and after conversations with leaders of the Irish already there, the Fenian Brotherhood was organized. By 1857 the organization was complete and O'Mahony was elected as its first national president. The members of the order bound themselves by an oath of "allegiance to the Irish Republic now virtually established" and further swore to "obey implicitly the commands of their superior officers" and to take up arms against Great Britain when so ordered. Although condemned by the Pope and his American subordinates, the society flourished and increased in numbers and influence. The Fenians enlisted in large numbers during the Civil War, and when James Stephens himself visited the United States in 1864, he was received with marked cordiality by American civil and military officials. It has been stated, and by a discriminating authority, that certain American political leaders at this time assured the Fenian Brotherhood of "material aid in the struggle they proposed to open with England." Canada was the obviously indicated point of attack, and from 1864 on, the Canadians resident along the border were periodically alarmed by rumors of Fenian raids.

At a great convention held in Chicago in 1863, the Irish Republic was formally proclaimed. A president was elected, senate and house of delegates organized, bonds and notes issued in the name of the Republic; an army was constituted, uniforms and flags were provided, and drilling soon commenced in various parts of the Union, without concealment and virtually without interference.

With the ending of the Civil War in 1865, still greater impetus was given to the movement. On the disbanding of the armies thousands of Irish-Americans—for the most part of the independent and adventurous immigrant type—were turned back into civilian life. The majority of them were unlearned in any trade or profession and did not fit readily into the new life. Having received a good military training and having had many of their old contacts and old habits broken and interrupted by four years of warfare, they proved excellent tinder, ready for the spark of the demagogue. Now when the call of their national tradition was accentuated by the love of adventure so lately stimulated, few there were who could withstand it. An attack on Canada, which many believed would prove completely and easily successful, would gratify at once their longing for excitement, their hatred of Great Britain, and their ideals of freedom. As a marching song expressed it:

We are the Fenian Brotherhood, skilled in the art of war,
And we're going to fight for Ireland, the land that we
adore.

Many battles we have won along with the boys in blue,
And we'll go and capture Canada, for we've nothing else
to do.

In the spring of 1866 Major T. W. Sweeney, late of the Union Army, became Secretary of War in the Fenian cabinet, and definite plans for the invasion of Canada were announced from Fenian headquarters. Arms and ammunition were collected at many places along the border, and in Buffalo and other Northern cities troops were drilled daily, in Fenian uniforms and carrying the Fenian flag. In Cincinnati committees had been appointed to visit all citizens "for the purpose of raising funds for the purchase of rifles to be used by the Irish army."

On 14 March the British Ambassador at Washington brought these events to the attention of the American Secretary of State and pointed out that American army officers were participating in them. There can be no reasonable doubt that the American officials already knew of the Fenian activities, and in failing to take more strenuous action to prevent the raids they were guilty of an offense against a peaceful neighbor, as well as a violation of the law of nations. Many prominent Americans, indeed, had openly encouraged the Irish leaders. In 1864 an Irish National Fair had been held in Chicago for the purpose of raising funds to finance the attack on Canada and the rebellion in Ireland that was to follow. To the directors of this fair Postmaster General Blair, a member of Lincoln's Cabinet, wrote: "I rejoice in the conviction that the days of Ireland's oppressor . . . are numbered. Let us conquer in this struggle and there will soon be an end put to the sway of the oppressors of Ireland." To hasten this victory he enclosed twenty-five dollars. Three American generals, two state governors, the Speaker of the House, and numerous Senators and Representatives sent letters of commendation, many of them following Blair's example and enclosing checks. The 19th Illinois Regiment prayed "to be in at the finish" with England, and enclosed $507. Another regiment desired "to flesh their bayonets in the corpulent Mr. Bull."

All Americans, however, were not engaged in egging on the Fenian battalions. The majority of them in all probability looked upon the whole thing as being a bit unreal and fantastic. Many of the better class of American citizens were definitely opposed to the whole movement. There was a widespread antipathy to Great Britain and the Empire, however, and many Americans would probably have agreed with the Buffalo editor who wrote: "Looking back two or three years to the time when Buffalonians were in hourly expectation of Confederate soldiers from Canada we can 'phancy the phelinks' of Victoria's loyal subjects. We don't wish them any ill but a little healthy scaring won't do them any harm." This feeling was even more clearly expressed by the editor of the New York *Citizen:*

"All American citizens who are not enamored with the course of England and Canada toward the United States during the late rebellion . . . [find in the Fenian activities] . . . an opportunity to have avenged the wrongs of British pirate vessels without costing the American government one dollar. Here the Canadians might have been allowed to realize the scoundrelism of their conduct in

121

sheltering the raiders of St. Albans and the yellow fever and assassination conspirators. What Mr. Seward may think about it we do not know, but are well satisfied a majority of the American people regret that the Fenian flag is not today floating over the steeples of a captured Montreal."

The explanation of the failure of American officials to put a stop to the whole movement is usually ascribed to the size and unity of the Irish vote. Hostility to Britain, moreover, was just as prevalent among the officials as among the common people.

Originally there had been a good deal of sympathy for the Irish cause among the radical groups in Canada. When first organized, the Fenian Brotherhood had actually enrolled members in Toronto and Montreal. When the Fenians began to plan the invasion and conquest of Canada, however, they lost the sympathy hitherto felt for their cause.

As time went on and the news of Fenian activities accumulated, the populace of Upper Canada in particular became more and more hostile. It also became nervous. The most grotesque and lurid rumors were given credence, and the Canadian militia was kept constantly on the alert from Manitoba to New Brunswick. Trade through the Welland Canal, and even on the Great Lakes, was interrupted during May 1866, and the Canadian government began to make active preparations for defense.

D. *The Raids.* The first raid against Canada was launched on 1 June 1866. In view of the time and energy spent in preparation, the whole affair was incredibly mismanaged. It had been intended to thrust across the border at a number of points simultaneously; but only one attack actually materialized at the appointed time. A party some eight hundred strong, under the leadership of a certain John O'Neill, whose record included charges of graft, arson, and murder, had concentrated at Buffalo. On the night of 31 May they moved without interference to Black Rock, and in the morning, having crossed the Niagara River, they captured the moss-grown Fort Erie. The Canadian authorities had, of course, known of the coming attack, and on

31 May the Adjutant-General had issued a call for 14,000 volunteers. This appeal was responded to enthusiastically, and by 3 June the province had more than 20,000 men under arms. The Canadian troops, however, had little save their enthusiasm, and as a result of poor equipment and bad leadership the party that tried to stop the raiders at Ridgeway was forced to retire. But this was the limit of Fenian success. Including reinforcements, it is probable that O'Neill's force did not at any time exceed 1,200 men, while the Canadians were concentrating ten times that number. In spite of their grandiloquent proclamation, which offered freedom to the Canadian people, the Fenians gained little or no support from the local inhabitants, and by 3 June they were in full retreat. On their way back to Buffalo, O'Neill and many of his followers were arrested by the commander of the United States gunboat *Michigan*, which had been patrolling the Niagara River. In a few days, however, they were released and their arms were returned to them.

On 4 June a second incursion into Canadian territory took place on the Vermont border. With a peculiar fitness St. Albans had been selected as one of the Fenian concentration centers, and three days after O'Neill's attack at Fort Erie, 1,800 Irish-Americans crossed into Lower Canada. Headquarters were established at Pidgeon Hill, but the invaders finally retired without giving battle to the Canadian troops who were advancing against them.

During these raids some eighty Fenians were captured by the Canadian authorities, and a number of these were condemned to death. The sentences were later commuted. On 6 June President Johnson, urged on by the British Ambassador, issued a proclamation ordering the strict enforcement of the neutrality laws. This tardy action led Governor-General Monck to write to Secretary of State Seward stating that the United States government "is entitled to my thanks, which I beg that you will convey to them for vigorously and faithfully putting their laws into force against the Fenians after the invasion of Canada had actually taken place." Sarcasm is not usually a characteristic of diplomatic correspondence, and its presence here is significant of the anger felt by Canadians in regard to what they considered to be the criminal negligence of the American officials. Once taken, however, the action of the American government was temporarily effective, and for this the British Minister made suitable and even cordial acknowledgment. The Fenian leaders were enraged at this hampering of their activities, and asserted that they had been cheated by the American government, which "had given them to understand that it would not interfere."

In September 1866, three months after this first assault on Canada, a Fenian convention was held, and at this meeting announcement was made of preparations for another invasion of the British Dominion. To raise funds for this enterprise, balls, picnics, and meetings were held; Irish bonds were sold, and contributions were accepted from American sympathizers. Military displays were arranged, until the Fenian uniform became a well-known sight in all Northern cities. In the fall of the same year Speaker Colfax of the House of Representatives announced at a Fenian picnic that he "was humiliated when our army was sent to do the dirty work of spies and detectives against the Fenians." At the same meeting Governor Oglesby and General Logan made fiery addresses. General Barry, who had punished some of his soldiers for assisting the Fenians, was dismissed from his command and the soldiers were pardoned. The Fenian headquarters stated publicly that they had assurance on "highest authority" that federal aid would appear but "slowly" if requested by state authorities for the purpose of checking the Fenians.

In December 1867 John O'Neill became president of the Fenian Brotherhood, and at a great convention held in Philadelphia early the following year more than 6,000 Fenian soldiers, in uniform and carrying the Fenian flag, paraded the streets on several successive days. It was two years later, however, before all of the arrangements for the invasion of Canada were completed; the delay was due to internal strife between various factions of the brotherhood. The money chests again were the cause of fratricidal strife. The raid finally took place in May 1870, but it was an even more dismal failure than the first attempt. The Canadian authorities had full information regarding the contemplated attack, at a number of points the American officials intervened, and the Fenians, disorganized and disheartened, were easily defeated. President Grant ordered the arrest of O'Neill, who was accordingly taken, "as he had been in 1866, to be again tried, convicted, and again pardoned unconditionally."

After his second release O'Neill was still enthusiastic and determined. He now turned his attention to what was then the Far West—the Minnesota-Manitoba district. In Manitoba, British authority was represented by a mere handful of soldiers and fewer officials. The Anglo-Saxon population was just beginning to enter the province, and the half-breed métis were already suspicious of their designs. O'Neill planned to take advantage of the unsettled situation in western Canada and turn it to his own uses. An expedition of about forty men was organized in Minnesota, crossed the border on 5 October 1871, and captured the Hudson's Bay Company's fort at Pembina. They had been followed, however, by a squad of American troops, who arrested and marched them back to the United States. The expected rising of the métis did not take place. The attack ended as a farce.

This ended the activities of the Fenian Brotherhood against Canada, and their real importance is to be found, not in the raids themselves, but in the way in which they renewed the old Canadian hostility toward the United States, and in their influence in helping on the cause of federation. The general feeling in Canada was that American newspapers had urged on the Irish bands; that minor officials had assisted them; and that the leaders of the country had failed to display reasonable care in guarding against violations of Canadian territory. Canada's anger was later enhanced by the refusal of the American government to consider Canadian claims for damages arising from the Fenian raids, at the time of the *Alabama* arbitrations in 1871. Canadians felt that the new principle of "due dilligence," first enunciated there, applied with particular nicety to this problem. In their reaction upon Canadian life, however, and in particular upon the problem of federation, the Fenian raids had a distinctly unique importance. This threat from the outside consolidated Canadian unity and made the formation of a federal union of British North America seem a necessary bulwark of independence and survival. As one student of Canadian affairs has well written, the raids "transmitted much more rapidly than was in any other way possible, into a steady Canadian spirit, the various opposing elements of the West and the East."

In the United States the raids have long since been forgotten, even by historians. The majority of Canadians also have now come to realize that these raids were but the natural outcome of conditions in the United States of the period. National hostility to Great Britain as a result of the real and imagined wrongs of the Civil War period, the ambitions of selfish and dishonest politicians, and the unsettled conditions arising from demobilization, all contributed to make the raids possible. Irish enthusiasm and hatred of England made them inevitable. As a formative factor in the growth of Canadian nationalism, the raids may well be remembered, but as unpleasant episodes between neighboring nations, each of which was in a state of considerable excitement, they may well be relegated to the realm of unremembered facts.

6. *British Columbia—Annexation or Confederation?*

By the treaty that settled the Oregon boundary in 1846, the Pacific coast of North America between 49° and 54° 40′ north latitude, and including Vancouver Island, was definitely declared to be part of the British domain. In all of the standard and conventional histories of the continent the struggles, intrigues, and arguments that preceded the signing of this treaty are considered at length, and the justice of the ultimate compromise is discussed. Yet most of these histories pass over in silence a period some twenty lears later when the destiny of the same region again became uncertain. In 1846 there was but a slight possibility of the surrender of this district by Great Britain; in 1868 it was highly questionable whether the Crown either desired or would be able to retain it.

Owing to a multiplicity of circumstances in the years before confederation, the annexation of British Columbia to the United States appeared to be the almost inevitable solution of what was, from the British point of view, a very unfortunate situation. An insignificant incident might easily have altered the whole course of Western history and have given the status of American territory to a region that is today one of the wealthiest and most productive areas of Canada. Had this event occurred, Canada would in the twentieth century have been barred from the Pacific, her development would have been delayed, her future growth retarded. Vancouver, one of the most important seaports on the continent, would now be on American soil, and Canadian trade with the Orient would be practically nonexistent. On the other hand, the United States would have gained a territory rich in timber, minerals, and fish; a region of almost unlimited water power, and of scenic beauty unsurpassed. All this was at stake in the crucial years between 1866 and 1870, yet little interest was displayed at the time, and historians have largely ignored it since.

Eliminating the anthropological and ethnographical significance of the Pacific coast Indians, the early history of British Columbia is synonymous with that of the various fur-trading companies. The fur business was a thriving industry, and save for an occasional traveler or explorer the officers of the North West Company or the Hudson's Bay Company were the only Europeans in the region. Gradually, however, settlers appeared and in 1849 the colony of Vancouver Island was founded, with Richard Blanshard as Governor. He was shortly succeeded by the famous James Douglas, chief factor of the Hudson's Bay Company.

The fur trade remained the economic backbone of the colony,

however, until, in 1858, gold was discovered on the Fraser River, and in 1860 in the Cariboo. Immediately the character of the colony changed, and Victoria, being the only settlement of any size, became the headquarters of adventurers and prospectors of every type. It is estimated that in three months twenty thousand immigrants entered through this port. The vast majority of these men were Americans, mainly from the deteriorating mines of California. There were many, however, from the Eastern states and from England, and Victoria shortly achieved a distinctly cosmopolitan aspect.

The newcomers were an extraordinary aggregation of men, the majority of them hardy, courageous, enterprising, and self-reliant. With these virtues, however, was coupled an unusual proficiency in the vices common to such men in such an environment. The quiet villages of Victoria and New Westminster were soon following the lead of godless San Francisco.

The economic and social results of this sudden influx caused a great increase in the difficulties of government, and Douglas soon found it necessary to exceed his powers in order to control the situation that developed on the mainland. Realizing the need of action, in August 1858 the imperial government passed an "Act to provide for the government of British Columbia," which formed the mainland region into an imperial colony, and here also Douglas was appointed Governor. Vancouver Island was allowed to remain a separate colony, but the two could unite at the will of the colonial legislators and on the acquiescence of the Queen.

At first it appeared as though the American immigrants would soon outnumber the British to such an extent that the colonies would of necessity become a part of the American Union. As the initial excitement died down, and as many of the miners, disappointed in their hopes of midatic wealth, left the colony, the balance became restored, and in 1862 an increased British immigration tightened the imperial bonds. But with the working-out of the placer mines and the practical collapse of the "rush," the two Pacific colonies became involved in ever increasing difficul-

128

ties. The imperial government was prodigal of advice, but did little in the way of offering the financial assistance the colonies so badly needed. In an effort to improve conditions Vancouver Island and British Columbia united in 1866, pooling resources and debts and endeavoring by the reduction of administrative offices to alleviate the economic stringency.

Although the population of the new colony of British Columbia totaled only 10,000 souls, the public debt in 1866 was $1,300,-000, and one quarter of the annual income was needed to meet the interest charges. To understand fully the deplorable situation that now faced the colony, it is necessary to appreciate its complete isolation from other parts of the British realm. The inhabited regions of Canada were two thousand miles away and separated from British Columbia by almost impassable mountains, by desolate prairies, and the barren northern shores of the rock-bound Lake Superior. A boat to England must round Cape Horn, or at best the passengers must cross the Isthmus of Darien and embark again upon the Atlantic. The only foreign intercourse easily available was with the American settlers in Washington, Oregon, and California, and on these British Columbia depended for supplies of every description. Even here there was no proper system of postal communication, and letters to Portland or San Francisco had to be prepaid in cash or else bear the American stamps that were sold in the post offices of New Westminster and Victoria. There was little industrial life in the colony, and the products of agriculture were insufficient to supply the local demand. The residents of the colony, moreover, naturally contrasted their isolation with the position of the residents in the Western American states. The fact that the transcontinental railway tie was established in the United States nearly twenty years earlier than it was in Canada had a close bearing on the attitude of the British Columbians.

The physical barriers, however, were not the only obstacles to a firm union between the colony and the mother country. English opinion was far from unanimous as to the value or expediency of giving further support to the outposts of empire. The *Times* did

129

no more than express the common opinion in the following editorial comments:

> "British Columbia is a long way off. . . . With the exception of a limited official class it receives few immigrants from England, and a large proportion of its inhabitants consists of citizens of the United States who have entered it from the south. Suppose that the colonists met together and came to the conclusion that every natural motive of contiguity, similarity of interests, and facility of administration induced them to think it more convenient to slip into the Union than into the Dominion. . . . We all know that we should not attempt to withstand them."

Lord Granville, Secretary of State for the Colonies, went even further and "expressed a wish that the British possessions in North America 'would propose to be independent and annex themselves.' "

Here English colonizing spirit is seen at a low ebb. The Whigs, immersed in the philosophy of Richard Cobden, had grave doubts concerning the ethical and the pragmatic value of a strong colonial policy. The Tories, prevented from exploiting the colonies for the good of the mother country, were inclined to cast them off as a hindrance and an expense. On the whole, English opinion was adverse rather than favorable to any strong effort to retain British Columbia, and no very grave obstacles would have been opposed to a peaceful transfer to the United States, had this been urged by the colonials themselves.

Many considerations of local pride and immediate advantage urged British Columbia toward American annexation. Local autonomy could be more fully exercised as a state of the Union than as a province of the newly formed Dominion of Canada. With the elimination of all trade barriers between British Columbia and the United States, the necessities of life could be obtained more cheaply, trade would be stimulated, and intercourse facilitated. With a population almost equally divided between Americans and British; with Canada far off and little known;

with the English homeland unresponsive and apathetic; with a tremendous financial burden and inadequate political institutions; in a physical situation impossible of defense and isolated from the British world—with all these factors urging her forward, the logical solution of the difficulties of British Columbia appeared to be found in annexation with her only neighbors, the Western states of the American Union.

It should be noted here that while Vancouver Island tended to favor annexation, the mainland was practically unanimous in support of federation with the Dominion of Canada. This situation was the result of a number of factors, outstanding among them being the fact that in the Union of 1866 the "Islanders" felt that they had been somewhat unfairly treated. They had been forced to accept the tariff laws of the mainland, and even the seat of government was for some time removed from Victoria to New Westminster.

That many Americans fully expected annexation to result from the situation on the North Pacific coast is amply verified by a study of the legislative debates, forensic utterances, and editorial comments of the period. The New York *News* anathematized the Whig Party which during Polk's administration had lost to the United States "a territory more valuable than all the wealth of all the Indies," but added that the existing conditions pointed to an early annexation of British Columbia. On 2 July 1866 one amiable but rather optimistic individual even went so far as to introduce in the House of Representatives a bill "for the admission of the States of New Brunswick, Nova Scotia, Canada East and Canada West, and for the organization of the territories of Selkirk, Saskatchewan and Columbia." Another suggestion was that British Columbia should be accepted in liquidation of the *Alabama* claims. As early as 1858 *Harper's Weekly* had declared that "many months cannot elapse before the Stars and Stripes float over the Fort [Victoria]."

At the close of the Civil War, the "manifest destiny" convictions of the American people were held with peculiar intensity, and *any* destiny that involved the taking over of British territory was viewed with particular satisfaction. Few expositions of this visualization of the American people as the chosen race have the clarity and directness of the following portion of an address on the subject of British Columbia, delivered before a Washington state society by Elwood Evans in 1870. (The sentiment expressed was not unique, but was held by the speaker in common with many Americans; the grammar, however, was peculiarly his own.)

"That it is the destiny of the United States to possess the whole of the northern continent I fully believe. . . . Our destiny, which must not, cannot be altered—a fiat which has the potency of irrevocable law—the forward march of Americanization until the whole continent shall be but one nation, with one sovereign government, one flag, one people."

Great Britain had won British Columbia at the time of the Oregon boundary dispute by graft, chicanery, and deceit; therefore it is

"commendable patriotic pride,—not covetousness, or ambition for territorial expansion nor lust for power which justifies—commands the effort [to regain it]."

Not all of the settlers in British Columbia, however, were willing to forego their British allegiance, and many preferred union with the Canadian Dominion—if suitable terms could be arranged. "No union on account of love need be looked for," wrote one British Columbian. "The only bond of union . . . will be the material advantage of the country, and the pecuniary benefits of the inhabitants. Love for Canada has to be acquired by the prosperity of the country and from our children." In other words, many of the colonists were willing to remain, or desirous of remaining, within the Empire if some solution could be found for their economic and political problems. It is an interesting fact that throughout this period the strongest advocates of confederation were also the most sturdy opponents of the existing government in British Columbia. Discontent was rampant in the colony. It was felt that England had given little but advice, that the government was arbitrary and wasteful, and that prosperity could not return while the colony remained in the Empire—unless connection by road and rail were formed with Canada.

In 1867 a petition had been sent to the home government by a group of citizens of Victoria asking that in view of the exigencies of the situation the colony be allowed to join the United States. Although this plea was heartily denounced by many other British Columbians, a second petition was circulated in 1869. On this occasion the document was addressed to President Grant and requested him to intercede with the British government and to arrange for the transfer of the colony to the United States. A report that the leaders in this movement were to be arrested led the Olympia *Tribune* to publish the following statement, which gives an incidental sidelight on conditions in the Washington territory:

> "We understand that the ruling powers of British Columbia . . . will arrest and punish the leaders of the annexation movement if it cannot be otherwise suppressed. We warn the rulers against such folly. The incarceration of a few men longing for American citizenship would fan into flame a fire long smouldering in our midst, and bring upon the people of that country a force of filibusterers who under the pretext of releasing the prisoners would really seek the overthrow of the British Dominion upon this coast."

To this the Victoria *Colonist* aptly replied that at the time the abortive movement was abandoned the document bore considerably less than fifty signatures. Whatever the number of signatures, President Grant ignored the petition, and its only effects were to assist in crystallizing opinion in British Columbia and in providing an argument for American expansionist orators. The petition did, however, reach the United States Senate, and the Committee on Pacific Railways quoted from it in its report in

1869. The committee at that time felt that the construction of an American line to the North Pacific would almost inevitably result in the annexation of British Columbia.

In January 1868 a great meeting had been held in Victoria at which Amor de Cosmos, one of the most picturesque figures in Canadian history, argued eloquently in favor of confederation and in opposition to union with the United States.[4] As a result of his efforts a committee was selected to urge upon Governor Seymour and upon the Dominion government the desirability of uniting the Dominion and the colony. On 25 March Ottawa replied to the representatives of this committee in the following terms: "The Canadian Government desires union with British Columbia and has opened communication with the Imperial government on the subject of the resolutions, and suggests immediate action by your legislature and passage of an address to Her Majesty regarding union with Canada. Keep us advised of Progress." The Legislative Council of British Columbia, however, was controlled by the annexationists, and the supine Governor was too weak to support either cause.

In May 1868 the Confederation League was organized. As expressed in its title, the object of this body was to secure the entry of British Columbia into the Dominion of Canada. On 14 September a convention was held at Yale—the head of navigation on the Fraser River—at which the Governor and the Legislative Council were severely criticized for their failure to forward the case of confederation, and for misgovernment in general. But in spite of the interest aroused by the League, the elections of December 1868 went against its leaders, and the Legislative Council by a vote of eleven to five condemned the taking of any action at that time.

During the summer of 1869 one of the great obstacles to confederation was removed when the Dominion government took

---

[4] This interesting figure was born at Windsor, N. S., with the prosaic name of William Alexander Smith. He emigrated to California, changed his name, came to Victoria in the gold rush of 1858, and established the *British Colonist*. Later he became Prime Minister of British Columbia, and then member of the Dominion House. He died from the effects of an overlong oration (himself the orator).

over the rights of the Hudson's Bay Company to the territory between British Columbia and Canada proper. Thus the way for the transcontinental railway was opened and this railroad was the *sine qua non* of all schemes of confederation. This cannot be too strongly emphasized. Without the prospect of railroad communication with Canada, British Columbia would certainly have joined the American Union. The patriotic *British Colonist* warned the Canadian government that if the enterprise stopped east of the Rockies, "it may stop there for good as far as British Columbia is concerned. Whatever may be the pecuniary interests and necessities of Canada, we know ours to demand immediate consolidation by the only bond strong enough to retain British Columbia." The same paper again said that "of all the conditions usually attached to a union of this colony with Canada, that of early establishment of railroad communication from sea to sea is the most important. If the railroad scheme is utopian, so is confederation. The two must stand or fall together."

Governor Seymour died in May 1869—an event of great good fortune for the Loyalists of the colony. At a time when British Columbia had needed a leader, it had been ruled by a man whose strongest attitude was a tentative negation.

The imperial government was now enabled to appoint Anthony Musgrave, whose energetic personality was the precise antithesis of that of the willowy Seymour. The processes of government, however, were slow, and because of an accident the new Governor was not able at once to attend to the vital problem of annexation or confederation. As a result, during the winter of 1869–70 a resurgence of annexationist sentiment was evident. "Annexation may now be said to be rampant in this community," wrote the editor of the *Colonist*. "It no longer lurks in secret places and shuns publicity. It may be said, and doubtless with much truth, that the Annexationists are for the most part American citizens who, having adopted this colony as their home, are naturally anxious that the institutions and the flag of the Fatherland should extend over it. But the party is not solely composed of such." Two of the Victoria papers vigorously supported annexation, and it was obvious that a crisis was approaching. The American people were again interested in the question by the introduction of the Corbett Resolution in the Senate. This resolution contained instructions to the Secretary of State to "inquire into expediency of . . . the transfer of British Columbia to the United States." It was not, however, acted upon.

The crisis came in British Columbia with the meeting of the Council in February 1870. Governor Musgrave had prepared for this meeting a statement urging immediate consideration of terms of confederation. The insistent character of the Governor's demand bore down the opposition, and in spite of the protests of Dr. Helmcken and a few other staunch annexationists, the desired resolution was passed. This was the turning-point of the contest, and when on 13 April a mass meeting was held in Victoria, the *Colonist* was able to report that "the most ardent advocate of confederation with responsible government must have felt satisfied with the result. The most intense enthusiasm pervaded the assemblage. The most vague hint in the direction of annexation was met with a howl of execration." Thus rapidly did conditions change under the hand of an adroit and determined leader.

All that then remained was to decide on the terms of union, and this was done with mutual satisfaction. On 20 July 1871 British Columbia became an integral part of the Dominion.

In the carrying out of the terms of the union, the railroad agreement was the first in importance, and the long delays in construction resulted in much ill feeling in British Columbia. The union had not been born primarily of love, and any failure on the part of the Dominion government might easily have resulted in the withdrawal of the western province. In 1878 the British Columbia legislature went so far as to threaten separation, but a change of ministry at Ottawa and a more energetic railway policy soon cleared the atmosphere. With the completion of the Canadian Pacific Railway in 1885, "manifest destiny" was finally defeated in British Columbia.

5

Major Boundary Disputes

1. *Introduction*

The British and American negotiators who wrote the Treaty of Paris (1783) left to their descendants a legacy of ambiguous phrases. In attempting to decide the boundaries that should divide the new nation from the remnants of the old Empire, these diplomats undertook the task of defining in exact language geographical boundaries of which they had a very inexact knowledge. As a result the treaty became a very Pandora's box, whence issued problems and perplexities that more than once led Britain and America to the verge of war and were for many years a constant source of irritation to the peoples of the United States and Canada.

The Treaty of Paris, however, was not alone as a cause of boundary disputes. As the American and the British settlers pushed westward over the continent, it became necessary to settle again and again the old question of division and demarcation. The Great Lakes, the Lake of the Woods, the central plains, the Oregon Territory, and finally, turning north, the deeply wooded coast of Alaska—each provided a new problem for dispute and disagreement.

Three of the controversies that strained the peaceful relations of the claimant countries may well be classified as of major importance in the history of British-American relations on the continent of North America. Maine, Oregon, and Alaska were on different occasions words potent in their threat of war. Now finally settled, they may be discussed with a candor and an understanding that was not possible during the heat of the struggle, while bitter passions still endured.

2. *The Northeastern Boundary*

A. *The Significance of This Dispute.* The most persistent Canadian criticism of British diplomacy has, for three quarters of a century, centered on the imperial conduct of Canadian–United States boundary disputes—and particularly on the negotiation of the clauses of the Webster-Ashburton Treaty dealing with the Maine–New Brunswick line. The burden of this complaint has been that British statesmen sacrificed Canadian interests in order to advance the cause of Anglo-American friendship. That there has been some general justification of this dissatisfaction can hardly be denied, but to an objective observer the Canadian case appears weakest just where it has been most strongly urged—that is, in the case of the Ashburton negotiations. The fact that the American Senate and the legislature of Maine each had to be intimidated by Webster's threat of disclosing concealed information favorable to Canada before these two bodies would agree to the Treaty of 1842 proves that Americans did not feel that Lord Ashburton had unduly favored their case. Nevertheless, Canadian public opinion was persistent in the belief that British complacency and American sharp practice resulted in 1842 in a surrender of Canadian rights.

The explanation of this long-continued feeling of dissatisfaction is found in the vital importance that the northern portion of the territory in dispute possessed from a Canadian standpoint. Direct railroad connection between Canada proper and the Maritime Provinces was a necessity, and such a connection, under the settlement of 1842, has necessarily to pass through Maine. Thus every Canadian who travels by rail from Montreal to Halifax [1] is reminded of the treaty in which "Canadian rights" were "sacrificed" on the altar of Anglo-American friendship. More than once Canada has been described as the "shuttlecock" of Anglo-American relations.

The actual territory involved in this controversy was not of prime importance; as compared with the Oregon region, for example, it was practically valueless. In 1840, however, northern Maine seemed more important and Oregon infinitely less important than today. From the Canadian point of view, the retention of this territory by the United States was an annoyance because it cut across the direct route to the Atlantic coast. Its commercial value was more highly appraised than it is today, but, above all, the contestants in 1842 were actuated by a sentimental antipathy to any derogation of their sovereign rights; and in this they were not unique, for exactly similar emotions would be aroused today by any suggestion that Canada be allowed to purchase northern Maine, or that the United States arrange for the annexation of the Maritime Provinces.

B. *History of the Dispute.* The difficulty over the northeastern boundary was a product of the American Revolution and the Treaty of 1783. Even before that time, however, the problem had been recognized, and Great Britain and France had been struggling for the possession of this very territory. The boundary between New England and Acadia had ever been in dispute, and this uncertainty was particularly acute between 1713 and the final defeat of the French in 1763. After the Treaty of Paris, with the whole Atlantic coast under the British Crown, the boundary was rather vaguely located as the southern watershed of the St. Lawrence River, and on the east as a line drawn due north from the source of the St. Croix River.

[1] The main line of the Canadian Pacific Railway runs through the state of Maine; that of the Canadian National swings north in order to stay on Canadian soil.

The American representatives in Paris during the negotiation of the Treaty of 1783 were among the most brilliant men of their day, but unfortunately their knowledge of geography was inadequate for the successful completion of the task to which they were assigned: the definition of the boundaries of the United States and the British dominions in North America. Moreover, the maps of the period were faulty, and place-names varied at the whim of the cartographer. The British commissioners in Paris were unwilling to accept the New England–Nova Scotia boundary as the international line of the future, and advanced claims to territory west of the St. Croix as far as the Piscataqua—claims that were subsequently reduced by successive steps to the Kennebec, the Penobscot, and finally the St. Croix itself. The claims were based on old French pretensions that Great Britain had heretofore combated. It is interesting to note that France still supported this view as late as 1778, in spite of her close relations with the revolting colonies. The Americans, on their part, at first contended for the St. John, but agreement was finally reached in a return to the St. Croix. Regardless of the method by which the agreement was reached, and without attempting to evaluate the personal or national motives involved or the relative dexterity of the British and American commissioners, the fact remains that a decision was made, and that it then became the foundation upon which all subsequent argument was based. The agreement was expressed in the Treaty of 1783, as follows:

> "From the northwest angle of Nova Scotia, viz., that angle which is formed by a line drawn due north from the source of the St. Croix River to the Highlands; along the Highlands which divide those rivers that empty themselves into the River St. Lawrence, from those which fall into the Atlantic Ocean, to the northwesternmost head of the Connecticut River. . . . East, by a line to be drawn along the middle of the River St. Croix, from its mouth in the Bay

of Fundy to its source, and from its source directly north to the aforesaid Highlands."

The treaty further provided that any islands which had heretofore been included in Nova Scotia should so remain.

Almost at once difficulties arose, and the first of these was in regard to the identity of the St. Croix River. On the map used by Oswald, Franklin, and their compatriots at Paris, two rivers were shown as emptying into Passamaquoddy Bay, and the most easterly of these was agreed upon as the boundary river. In reality, three rivers reached the sea in this bay, the third being to the west of those known to the negotiators, and all three rivers were sometimes known as St. Croix, according to the whim of individual cartographers. The difficulty was further accentuated by the fact that the true situation of the boundary river (the present Magaquadavic) was not as it was depicted on Mitchell's map. Canadian settlers in the newly formed province of New Brunswick thus had an excuse to push on and to proclaim the more westerly river the true St. Croix. Jay said that the fault in Mitchell's map had been discussed in the Paris negotiations, and that the decision had been made with this mistake in mind, but Adams declared that the negotiators knew nothing of the ambiguity. Jay and Adams agreed, however, that the Magaquadavic was the river selected. Investigations and surveys were made by individuals and by the Massachusetts and federal governments. After some years of uncertainty, the Jay Treaty of 1794 made a temporary and partial settlement. (As John Bassett Moore has pointed out, this treaty was the result of the first modern recourse to arbitration, a procedure known in classical times and then forgotten for fifteen centuries.) The commissioners were agreed that the river claimed as the St. Croix by the Americans should be accepted, and not the more westerly stream designated on Mitchell's map. Thus in a contest between the validity of a faulty map and a questionable local appellation, the name rather than the cartographical definition was accepted.

Under the Treaty of 1794 a commission was appointed to discover the "source" of the St. Croix, and here Great Britain lost its contention. The more northerly branch was chosen, and at its headwaters was erected a monument. This solution was agreed to in 1798.

With the boundary agreed upon to this point, the real difficulty then became apparent. How far north should the "due north" line extend? The line was to run as far as "the Highlands . . . which divide those rivers that empty themselves into the River St. Lawrence, from those which fall into the Atlantic Ocean." Now, the St. John River empties into the Bay of Fundy, and the United States insisted that this was in fact emptying into the "Atlantic Ocean." Great Britain disputed this, insisting that the words "Atlantic Ocean" had been intended in a strictly literal sense, and the St. John did not fulfil the requirements. The importance of the controversy arose from the fact that the highlands that separate the headwaters of the St. John from the headwaters of the St. Lawrence tributaries are very near the great river itself; while the highlands separating the Maine rivers (which surely emptied into the ocean) from the tributaries of the St. Lawrence would be crossed at Mar's Hill, only forty miles "due north" of the monument erected on the St. Croix. Great Britain insisted that the intention had been to divide the river basins, and that the words "Atlantic Ocean" had been used to assure the St. John Valley to the British domain. The Americans replied that the intention had been to define the southern boundary of Quebec as it had been proclaimed in 1763; and in that proclamation the highlands had been mentioned as running to the Bay of Chaleur —undoubtedly the northern range. The fact that an old French grant, known as Madawaska, was situated in the middle of the territory claimed by the United States, and that the United States had never exercised jurisdiction over this district, seemed to support the British contention. So also did various French maps, though Great Britain had previously contended against the French for the very region she now attempted to retain. The testimony of the maps, however, was inconsequential, for ample cartographical proof could have been adduced to support almost any claim by either side. In general, the French and English maps were opposed to those produced by the United States. Each state could find scientists to support its politicians.

The War of 1812 demonstrated very forcibly the necessity of a direct and uninterrupted line of communication between Canada and the Maritime Provinces. The result was an added insistence from the side of Great Britain on the valadity of her claim.

The Treaty of Ghent, 24 December 1814, provided for a number of joint commissions to settle various boundary problems. The first of these, that to decide the ownership of certain islands in Passamaquoddy Bay, reported an equitable settlement on 14 November 1817. The commission on the main problems connected with the northeast boundary continued its deliberations until April 1822, when the two sides drew up *ex parte* reports, and the arbitration broke down.

In 1820 Maine separated from Massachusetts and was admitted to the Union as a sovereign state. From that time on, the contest bore a more threatening aspect, for the legislature of Maine was more vitally interested in a successful solution than Massachusetts had been, and violent measures appeared more excusable to those who felt more deeply.

In January 1825 Maine protested that Canadians were trespassing on American soil and cutting timber in the forests of that state. Great Britain, in reply, pointed out that the Madawaska and Aroostook settlements had been founded many years before, and that heretofore the United States had registered no objection. The British government further declared that certain American officials had been attempting to exert their jurisdiction in these regions, and the United States in reply asked that Maine and New Brunswick display a mutual forbearance until some definitive agreement could be reached. Such an arrangement was made, but frequent clashes of state and provincial representatives continued to take place.

In 1826 Albert Gallatin was sent to England to attempt to effect a settlement. Great Britain insisted on neutral arbitration, for joint commissions had already proved a failure, and to this Gallatin was finally forced to accede. An agreement to this effect was drawn up, and with the consent of the American Senate and the signature of the President it became operative. The King of the Netherlands was agreed upon as arbiter. For his use and assistance a general map of the region was jointly prepared, and this was submitted together with the British and American arguments.

The difficulty encountered in the ensuing arbitration was the difficulty invariably attending international discussions. Each nation, through its accredited representatives, had made a claim; the people, therefore, accepted this as their own and became insistent upon receiving "justice"; the diplomats were driven by the pressure of public opinion to defend and win their case (defeat might mean the unhonored end of a public career). To the aid of the diplomats were called the scientists, who prostituted their learning in the support of a diplomatic brief. Thus the case was prepared, and it was presented with an accompaniment of forensic eloquence that tended further to obscure the truth. No attempt was made to do justice; no search was prosecuted to discover the truth. Public opinion, diplomats, scientists, and orators joined to advance the cause of the nation, and truth, justice, and sincerity were lost in the excitement of winning the case.

Gallatin prefaced the American case, simply restating at great length, and with careful attention to every detail, the claim outlined above.

There can now be little doubt that the American claim was justified by the intentions of the commissioners of 1783. It is morally certain that the intention then was to re-enact the boundary line of the Proclamation of 1763, and that the British argument based on the difference between the Bay of Fundy and the Atlantic Ocean was simply an ingenious quibble. Unfortunately, the Treaty of 1783 was so badly worded that it could not be translated into a practical topographical boundary. The British case was not a sound one, and a decision based solely upon justice would, in all probability, have given Maine more than was ultimately received.

The King of the Netherlands was so impressed by the topographical difficulties that obstructed the running of a boundary line in accordance with the wording of the treaty that he entirely gave up the attempt. On 20 January 1831 he declared that the treaty was "inexplicable and impracticable," and he designated an arbitrary compromise line as the most feasible solution. This decision gave 7,908 square miles to the United States, and 4,119 square miles to Great Britain. It was based largely on the line of the St. John, as the United States had desired, but met the British claim in regard to certain other details. The state of Maine violently protested against acceptance of such a decision, and although President Jackson was ready to join the British government in assenting to the award, the Senate refused to give its consent. The President was forced to acquiesce.

American feeling against the King's award was crystallized and made vocal largely through the efforts of W. P. Preble, American Minister to The Hague, and himself a citizen of Maine. He returned to the United States and wrote and spoke against acceptance with intensity and vigor.

The King's decision was not in accordance with the terms on which the problem had been submitted to him. He had been asked for a judicial decision: he had replied with a political compromise. Yet from both a practical and an ethical standpoint it would have been better if the United States had accepted his decision. To refuse was to give the impression, however unjustified, of bad sportsmanship. President Jackson later recognized this, and wrote in reference to this event: "The only occasion of importance in my life, in which I allowed myself to be overruled by my friends, was the one of all others in which I ought to have adhered to my own opinions." The arbitration agreement had invited the arbiter to "make a decision on the points of difference," and this was to be final and conclusive. From the practical standpoint, the failure to agree to this award ultimately cost the

United States 900 square miles of the territory in dispute. The award was unjust, but it should have been accepted.

Between 1831 and 1841 the portfolio of Foreign Affairs in the British Cabinet was held, with one short interruption, by Lord Palmerston, and his far from subtle diplomacy produced a reaction in the United States that did not promote a peaceful settlement of the outstanding differences at issue between the two governments. Throughout the period popular feeling in the United States, as well as in Nova Scotia and New Brunswick, was gradually intensifying, and on several occasions war appeared to offer the most probable solution. Overt acts on the part of nationals of one country or the other were of frequent occurrence. In 1831 the New Brunswick authorities arrested, tried, and convicted certain officers of Maine for attempting to hold an American election in the Madawaska district. In 1836 a Canadian justice was arrested for executing process on American soil. In 1837 a certain Greeley was arrested with some others for attempting to take a census in Madawaska for the American government, and in the same year British engineers began survey operations on a proposed railway, designed to pass through the disputed region.

On 28 December 1835 the British also withdrew their acceptance of the Dutch award, and they then offered another compromise boundary, which the United States refused. In return the President offered to request Maine to accept the line of the St. John River from its source to its mouth as the boundary, but this Great Britain, in its turn, refused. In March 1838 Maine again entered the controversy, demanded that a survey be made in accordance with the American interpretation, and insisted on the enforcement of this boundary. The federal government refused to accede to these requests, but it did authorize a survey of the region with a view to erecting fortifications.

Throughout this period the population was growing in both Maine and New Brunswick, and the disputed area was constantly increasing in value. The people of the Maritime Provinces were largely Loyalist in derivation, and their natural anti-American sentiment was accentuated by every hostile act and word in Maine or the United States.

In 1838 the legislature of Maine gave Governor Fairfield $800,000 for military defense, and, thus supported, the Governor called out the militia and took forcible possession of the greater part of the disputed area. Forts were erected throughout the region to prevent a successful counteraction. At the same time Congress authorized the President to call out the militia for a six months' term and placed at his disposal the sum of $10,-000,000. The province of New Brunswick was now thoroughly aroused, and the bellicose attitude of Governor Fairfield seemed to presage further difficulties. It began to look as though the so-called Aroostook War might develop into a real conflagration. Nova Scotia, aroused for the safety of her sister province and actuated by the same Loyalist antipathy toward the Americans, called a special session of its legislature, voted $100,000 for the immediate support of New Brunswick, and amid scenes of great popular enthusiasm promised to place at the disposal of the junior province every dollar and every man in Nova Scotia, should war become an actuality. War appeared to be not only a possible, but even a probable result.

In an attempt to avert such a calamity, General Winfield Scott was dispatched to Maine, where he succeeded in persuading Governor Fairfield to withdraw his troops and await the outcome of the newly resumed diplomatic negotiations. New surveys were made by each country and negotiations continued through 1840 and 1841. In the latter year Lord Palmerston was succeeded as Secretary of State for Foreign Affairs by Lord Aberdeen, and Anglo-American relations at once took a more favorable course. Aberdeen, apparently, believed in the justice of the British contentions regarding the northeastern boundary, but he also realized that the Americans were equally convinced of the validity of their case, and consequently he decided that a compromise was the only possible solution. He realized, moreover, that an early decision was imperative if war was to be avoided. Neither Great Britain nor the United States really wanted war: indeed, such a struggle would have been commercially disastrous for both countries.

In March 1841 Daniel Webster became American Secretary of State, and he too was desirous of finding a "shorter way" to the settlement of this old and serious conflict. As a result of Webster's expressed willingness to accept a decision by direct negotiation, and to agree if necessary to a compromise boundary, Lord Aberdeen, passing over certain senior but die-hard diplomats, commissioned Lord Ashburton to proceed to America, at the same time investing him with full powers to arrange a definitive settlement.

The appointment of Lord Ashburton was a real concession to the United States. In 1808, as Alexander Baring, he had vigorously attacked the British Orders in Council, and in 1816 he had told John Quincy Adams that he wished Great Britain would give all Canada to the United States immediately. Ashburton's wife was an American, and he was well and favorably known in the United States. This, then, was the man who arrived in Washington "authorized to treat for a conventional line, or line by agreement, on such terms and conditions, and with such mutual consideration and equivalents as might be thought just and equitable."

After a great deal of persuasion, Webster succeeded in getting Maine to appoint delegates equipped with full powers to negotiate a final agreement. Massachusetts was also included. Lord Ashburton formally opened the discussions on 13 June 1842. The arbiters at once concurred "in the opinion that no advantage would be gained by reverting to the interminable discussions on the general grounds on which each party considers their claims respectively to rest." These claims had been thoroughly canvassed with no prospect of an agreement.

Lord Ashburton began by asserting the British right to the whole territory, but indicated his willingness to compromise on a line that would give Great Britain some two thirds of the territory in dispute. This proposal so enraged the Maine delegation that their leader (the ubiquitous Preble) advocated an immediate adjournment. On Webster's insistence, however, this plan was abandoned, and on 29 June the Maine commissioners offered a counterproposal, which Ashburton in turn declared impossible of acceptance. Personal conferences between Ashburton and Webster were initiated by the former on 13 July, and by 15 July tentative terms were arranged and submitted to the state representatives for approval. Without covering the intricate details, suffice it to say that the United States received seven twelfths of the disputed territory, the right to navigate the St. John River, and, according to Webster, four fifths of the value at stake. Great Britain further agreed to allow the United States to retain the land at Rouse's Point, Lake Champlain, upon which, because of a faulty drawing of the 45th parallel, an American fort had been erected. This was a unique event in the history of international negotiations. Webster gained further concessions in Lake Huron and in the Lake of the Woods. On 22 July the Maine delegation with protests and lamentations agreed to this boundary, and Preble departed "as sulky as a bear." On 9 August the treaty was signed by Ashburton and Webster, and on the 11th of the same month it was communicated to the Senate.

A recital of the events leading to the ratification of this treaty would be far from complete without mention of the part played by the famous "red-line map." This map was discovered in the Paris Archives by Jared Sparks, who was carrying on an investigation there to obtain material in support of the American case. It was supposed to be the map used by Franklin, on which that astute diplomat had drawn a red line designating the boundary substantially in accordance with the claims of Great Britain as later presented. Webster, realizing the damaging nature of this evidence, at once impounded the map and ordered the search discontinued. The true significance of this document appears in its later use by the Secretary of State. Using the threat of publication as a club, he was able to force the legislature of Maine and the United States Senate to agree to the Webster-Ashburton Treaty. Webster was subsequently assailed by American, British, and Canadian opponents with the charge of dishonesty because he failed to make public the map during the negotiations. But, wrote Webster in reply, "I did not think it a very urgent duty to go to Lord Ashburton and tell him that I had found a bit of doubtful evidence in Paris." That Webster's action was not contrary to the "rules of the game" was verified by Lord Ashburton, who said: "My own opinion is that in this respect no reproach can fairly be made." Great Britain, moreover, was involved in a very similar transaction, for with the opening of negotiations the Foreign Office went to the trouble of concealing the famous Mitchell's map, which tended to support the American case. Even Ashburton was not apprised of its existence until it was produced in Parliament to silence the violent criticism leveled against the treaty by Lord Palmerston and his irate friends.

The Webster-Ashburton Treaty was ratified by the Senate on 20 August 1842. In homage to clarity it may be summarized thus:

Maine and Massachusetts surrendered five twelfths of their territorial claim, and received in return the privilege of navigating the St. John River, and $300,000 as general compensation.

Great Britain surrendered seven twelfths of its territorial claim, made various concessions at other doubtful points on the international boundary, and received approximately 5,000 square miles of the disputed region.

The United States received the right of navigation on the St. John; 40 square miles at Rouse's Point, where an American fort had been raised; 40 square miles at the head of the Connecticut River, and an island of about the same size between Lakes Huron and Superior; 7,000 square miles of the disputed territory; and in return abandoned a weak claim to 6,000 square miles on the west of Lake Superior, and the 5,000 square miles on the Maine–New Brunswick border.

c. *The Reception of the Treaty.* Mingled sentiments greeted the treaty when its terms were made public in Great Britain. The Tories under Lord Palmerston denounced the "Ashburton Capitulations," and a series of scathing articles by Palmerston was published in a London paper and did much to arouse popular dissatisfaction. On the other hand, the government leaders greeted the solution with satisfaction, and in Parliament Peel, Brougham, Aberdeen, Hume, Douglas, and even Disraeli joined in the defense and praise of Lord Ashburton. Great Britain, after all, was not vitally interested, and popular feeling soon died down with a growing appreciation of the peace that followed the settlement. Lord Ashburton, writing on the subject, wisely declared:

> "It is a subject upon which little enthusiasm can be expected. The truth is that our cousin Jonathan is an aggressive, arrogant fellow in his manner . . . by nearly all our people he is therefore hated and a treaty of conciliation with such a fellow, however considered by prudence or policy to be necessary, can in no case be very popular with the multitude. Even my own friends and masters who employed me are somewhat afraid of showing too much satisfaction with what they do not hesitate to approve."

In the United States a feeling of gratitude was generally expressed at the termination of this long and profitless struggle. Maine and Massachusetts grumbled, but the financial compensation proved an excellent sedative. The country as a whole rapidly forgot the incident, and this in spite of the fact that the United States was the country with the most right to complain, for, as has now been generally admitted by historians, the American case was founded upon a much surer basis than that of Great Britain, and pure justice would have given to the United States an even larger percentage of the territory in dispute.

Far different was the reception of the treaty in Canada. The old Loyalist sentiment was still strong, and to the men holding it the attempt of the United States to seize a portion of New Brunswick was simply another act in a long series of hostile operations, which included the expedition of 1775, the War of 1812, the overt incidents during the Canadian rebellion of 1837, and the generally antagonistic, threatening, and bombastic attitude of the American press and people. Now, with the supine assent of Great Britain, the United States had succeeded in driving a wedge between Canada and the British possessions in the Maritime Provinces. Canadian interests had been "sacrificed" to feed the insatiable appetite of American imperialism, and Britain had not defended her own. The legend of "the sacrifice of Canadian interests" here had its start, and it has been propagated in school texts, in serious histories, on the platform, and in the press ever since. An older popular Canadian historian who is still read in some circles speaks of Lord Ashburton as one "whose name to this day is never uttered in Canada without contempt and shame." Unjust as such accusations are, it is nevertheless a fact that many Canadians still consider the Ashburton Treaty of 1842 to be the first and most important instance of the loss of Canadian rights due to the complacency of Great Britain and the crooked diplomacy of the United States. And in this way the Maine–New Brunswick boundary dispute has held in Canada an importance that would be totally inexplicable judged solely by the value of the geographical prize involved.

3. The Oregon Boundary

A. *The Point at Issue.* On the continent of North America the nineteenth century was a period of political and military expansion, and with the United States, Russia, Spain, and Britain all taking part in this movement, a conflict of interests became inevitable. Of the many territorial disputes which thus arose, that concerning the "Oregon" boundary involved the largest and incomparably the richest domain. The territory in dispute included not only the modern and beautiful state of Oregon, but Washington, the lower portion of British Columbia, and all that section of the United States north of the 42nd parallel of north latitude and west of the Rocky Mountain divide. In short, the Oregon Territory was bounded by 42° and 54° 40′ north latitude, on the east by the crest of the Rockies, and on the west by the Pacific Ocean. An approximate width of 550 miles, and a length of 650 miles, made the total area some 360,000 square miles: no mean prize, even on this most bountiful of continents. When the respective territorial rights of the United States and Great Britain in this region were defined, the long boundary that began in the waters of the Atlantic reached its destination on the shores of the Pacific. The partition that began in 1783 was then complete.

Not only was the Oregon Territory extensive geographically, but it contained immensely rich resources in timber, fisheries, and minerals. When to these advantages are added the excellent agricultural, ranching, and fruit lands of the interior valleys, the fur trade of British Columbia, the admirable harbors of Prince Rupert, Vancouver, and Seattle, and finally (on the coast at least), a delightful climate, some idea is obtained of the reward for which diplomatic battles were waged in the first half of the nineteenth century. Fortunately, the true value of the region was not suspected in 1845, for, had the governments of the day fully realized the worth of the prize for which they were contending, "54° 40' or Fight" might well have become more than an election cry, and Great Britain would have maintained with more determination her claim to the territory lying between the 49th parallel and the Columbia River. The common attitude of the day, however, was well expressed in the scornful words of a British author, who mentions "Vancouver's Island, which, if we are absurd enough to plant a colony in the Northern Pacific, is the least objectionable seat." Until a few years before the final settlement of the dispute, Oregon was thought of—in England, at least—only as the home of the fur trader and his prey, a region to be visited by the adventurous; to be fought for if "national honor" demanded it, but of no real importance. Even the closer view obtained from the United States failed to indicate the potentialities so obvious today.

Spain and Russia as well as the United States and Great Britain were involved in the contest for this last and greatest of the frontier regions. In the earliest days of Pacific exploration Spanish and British seamen had fought for gold and glory; in later years the chancelleries of Great Britain and America strove for territory and power. As the days of treasure ships and authorized piracy passed away, the contest changed its nature, and British, American, and Russian fur companies carried on an economic and political as well as semimilitary battle for control. Even this unacknowledged warfare did not force a solution of the problem, and it was not until farmers began to force their way across the mountain barriers and to settle in the fertile valleys of the coast that the logic and the dangers of the situation became sufficiently powerful to force a compromise, in 1846.

B. *Discovery and Occupation.* As rights of sovereignty, gained by discovery, were claimed by both Great Britain and the United States, some knowledge of the history of the exploration of the Pacific coast is a prerequisite to a just appreciation of their conflicting claims. Yet an accurate knowledge of the history of Pacific exploration did not exist in 1846, and indeed, even at the present time, the name of the first European to visit the western coast of North America cannot be stated with assurance. It is known that, within thirty years of the discovery of the Pacific Ocean, Spanish captains were sailing on its waters, and it is generally supposed that one Fenelo was the first to follow the coast to a point above the 42nd parallel of north latitude. This trip was made in 1543, and apparently it was not until 1602 that another Spaniard reached the region that was to become the Oregon Territory. In that year Aguilar, a lieutenant of Vizcaíno, sailed as far as the 43rd parallel, discovering and naming Cape Blanco. In 1774 Pérez and Martínez sailed as far north as 55°, and on their return anchored off Point Esteven, taking possession in the name of the Viceroy of Mexico, whose commission they bore. In the following year three adventurers—Hecata, Ayala, and Quadra—explored the coast from the 27th to the 58th parallels, the first entering and naming the San Roque (Columbia) River.

The earliest British claim was based on the voyage of Sir

Francis Drake (1580), but the latitude reached by this piratical adventurer has never been accurately determined, though most authorities agree that he at least reached 43° north latitude, and some even insist on 48°. In 1778 the famous Captain Cook, who shortly afterwards lost his life on the Sandwich Islands, explored the coast from the 44th to the 59th parallels, and proceeded even farther north.

Captain Robert Gray, a New England trader, was the first American to reach the Oregon coast, and the record of his trips, from 1787 on, formed the foundation on which the American claim to discovery principally rested. He claimed to have first discovered, and certainly he named, the Columbia River, but in view of the well-authenticated record of Hecata's trip, Gray's claim cannot be substantiated.

Starting in 1788, Captain Meares, an Englishman, made frequent trading voyages to the west coast, using Nootka as a base. Many, if not all, of these trips were made under the Portuguese flag because of the existing British monopoly regulations. In the same year that Meares made his first trip, Martínez and López, two Spanish captains, explored the whole coast even as far as the Aleutian Islands.

The first man actually known to have crossed the continent from the Atlantic to the Pacific was Alexander Mackenzie, a partner in the North-West Company. In 1793 he crossed the Rockies at about 54° north latitude, descended the Fraser to 52° 20', and thence, passing the Coast Range, ultimately reached the ocean. In 1805 the famous Lewis and Clark expedition passed the mountain barriers, reached the Columbia, and followed it to the sea. The following year Simon Fraser, another officer of the North-West Company, reached the Pacific by way of the river that now bears his name.

From this time forward visits to the Pacific coast were of frequent occurrence, both by land and by sea, and trading posts of the American, British, and Russian fur companies were soon established in the territory. The Hudson's Bay Company rapidly outdistanced or absorbed all its competitors, and only the American Trading Company was able to maintain any serious opposition.[2]

These exploring and trading expeditions were not always attended by peace. Captain Meares, after 1788, had made Nootka a semipermanent base—a proceeding to which Spain voiced strenuous opposition. Without waiting for the end of the negotiations that were in progress, the Viceroy of Mexico outfitted an expedition under Captain Martínez, who proceeded to Nootka, captured most of Meares's ships, destroyed his buildings, and drove him out. The Spaniards took formal possession of Nootka on 24 June 1789. The Spanish King again laid claim to the whole of the Oregon Territory, and the Count de Florida attempted to justify this claim when he wrote that "although Spain may not have establishments or colonies planted upon the coasts, or in the ports in dispute, it does not follow that such coasts or ports do not belong to her." To this Great Britain replied that "British subjects had an indisputable right to the enjoyment of a free and uninterrupted navigation, commerce, and fishing; and to the possession of such establishments as they should form with the consent of the natives of the country not previously *occupied* by any European nation." The capture of Nootka nearly precipitated a war, but Spain was deserted by her ally, France, and could not undertake such a conflict alone. As a result she agreed to pay an indemnity, and to allow British subjects equal rights of trade and settlement north of the 38th parallel of north latitude. South of that parallel, Spain claimed exclusive jurisdiction. This Nootka Convention was the first public withdrawal by Spain from her long-established attitude—that of the possessor of exclusive sovereignty over the American shores of the Pacific Ocean south of Alaska. The Nootka controversy marked the first occasion that the United States had to consider the problems attendant on a neutral position. Because Spain and Great Britain arrived at a diplomatic adjustment no actual decision was necessary for

[2] In 1811 John Jacob Astor and his associates founded Astoria. Six of the original partners were British.

the United States, but the problem posed in 1790 had to be met a few years later.

After the outbreak of the War of 1812 Astoria, the American trading post on the Columbia River, was sold by the Pacific Fur Company to the British North-West Company to prevent its falling into the hands of the British as a prize of war. A month later a royal man-of-war appeared, and its captain took formal possession in the name of King George. But the Treaty of Ghent (1814) authorized a return to the *status quo ante,* and the American government demanded the restitution of Astoria. Great Britain insisted, naturally, that the post had been purchased and was not included in the spoils of war. The difficulty was settled and the United States was again given possession in 1818. In the convention of that year, a *modus vivendi* covering the whole "Oregon Question" was agreed to, and this compact remained legally in force until 1846, though primarily signed for only ten years. By this convention the two nations agreed:

> "that any country that may be claimed by either party on the north-west coast of America, westward of the Stony Mountains, shall, together with its harbors, bays and creeks, and the navigation of all rivers within the same, be free and open for the term of ten years from the date of the signature of the present Convention, to the vessels, citizens and subjects of the two powers; it being well understood that this agreement is not to be construed to the prejudice of any claim which either of the two high contracting parties may have to any part of the said country, nor shall it be taken to affect the claims of any other power or state."

The following year a treaty was signed by Spain and the United States, in which the Spanish King "ceded to the said United States all his rights, claims and pretentions to any territory east and north of the said line [the 42nd parallel], and . . . renounces all claim to the said territory forever." Thus the United States became heir to the Spanish claims, which, so far as discovery was concerned, were unimpeachable. Spain, however, had agreed to Britain's assertion of equal rights to commerce and settlement. There was, moreover, great doubt of the validity of the Spanish claim because occupation had failed to follow discovery within a reasonable time. This lack was in part supplied by the priority of the establishment of Astoria, which, as has been said, was founded by the American Fur Company in 1811.

In 1821 another complication arose. By an imperial ukase of that year, the Czar of Russia claimed the whole of the west coast of North America from the Aleutian Islands to the 51st parallel. The United States and Great Britain immediately protested (this Russian threat was one of the major factors leading to the promulgation of the Monroe Doctrine), and the result is seen in the Treaty of 1824 with the United States, and the Treaty of 1825 with Britain, in which Russia agreed to 54° 40′ as the southern boundary of her North American domains.

In 1824 Fort Vancouver was established on the north bank of the Columbia River, not far from its mouth, by the Hudson's Bay Company (which had absorbed the North-West Company in 1821). Here, according to Morison, "a Scots factor, Dr. John McLaughlin, ruled the community with wisdom and humanity, preserved the peace between whites and Indians, upheld civilized standards of social life, and later received American missionaries so hospitably that the school children of the American North-West today are taught to regard him as 'the Father of Oregon.'"

In 1818, 1824, and again in 1826 attempts were made by the British and American governments to find a mutually acceptable line of division. As Britain, however, insisted on the line of the Columbia, and as the United States refused to consider any division south of the 49th parallel, these attempts were doomed to failure. In 1826 Great Britain disclaimed any pretensions to an exclusive title, merely insisting that her title was good as against the United States. The American government, on the contrary, asserted an exclusive sovereignty from the 42nd to the 52nd parallels—this being the territory drained by the Columbia—and also claimed the whole Oregon Territory by right of discovery and occupation. The greatest concession that the Americans would make was outlined in a letter from Clay to Gallatin:

> "As by the Convention of 1818 the 49th parallel of north latitude has been agreed to as the line of boundary between the United States and Great Britain east of the Stony Mountains, there would seem to arise . . . a strong consideration for the extension of the line along the same parallel west of them to the Pacific Ocean. . . . This is our ultimatum. . . . We can consent to no other line more favorable to Great Britain."

This offer was refused by the British, who in turn proposed the Columbia River, guaranteeing freedom of navigation to American citizens. On 6 August 1827 the Convention of 1818, as regards the Oregon Territory, was indefinitely renewed, subject to denunciation by either nation on one year's notice. It remained in force until 1846.

From 1827 to 1838 little interest was manifested in the Oregon Territory, except by those engaged in trading or missionary enterprises. The Hudson's Bay Company had rapidly gained control, and in 1838 John Henry Pelly of that company was able to report as follows: "We have compelled the American adventurers, one by one, to withdraw from the contest, and are now pursuing the Russian Fur Company so closely that we hope at no very distant period to confine them to their own proper territory." The Hudson's Bay Company officials not only acted as commercial agents, but filled the offices of legislator, executive, and judiciary throughout the whole region. In 1821 they had absorbed their ancient rival, the North-West Company, and by 1845 they had eight permanent posts on the Columbia, six on the Fraser, and a great number of smaller stations scattered throughout the territory—many of them in the disputed region between the 49th parallel and the Columbia River. Communication was almost entirely by company vessels, and Indians and settlers alike depended on the company for supplies. Greenhow, who compiled the official case for the American government in

1846, said that "from 1813 to 1823 few if any American citizens were employed in the country west of the Rocky Mountains; and ten years more elapsed before any settlement was formed or even attempted by them in that part of the world. The Americans had no settlements of any kind and their government exercised no jurisdiction west of the Rockies." Thus until 1823 at the earliest the United States could advance little claim to sovereignty in Oregon based on occupation, and even in 1839 it was estimated that there were only one hundred and fifty-one citizens of the United States in the territory. In that year it was reported to Congress that:

> "A few years will make the country west of the Rockies as completely English as they can desire. Already the Americans are unknown as a nation, and as individuals their power is despised by the natives of the land. A population is growing out of the occupancy of the country whose prejudices are not with us, and before many years they shall decide to whom the country shall belong, unless in the meantime the American government make their powers felt and seen to a greater degree than has yet been the case."

The Oregon Provisional Emigration Society was founded in 1838, and due to its endeavors and the energy of certain pioneer settlers, a considerable increase in population occurred after 1840. Time was on the side of the Americans, for the fur trade in the Columbia Valley was gradually waning in importance, while hard times among Eastern farmers were making the fertile fields of Oregon seem more and more attractive.

The Maine–New Brunswick boundary dispute was ended by the Ashburton Treaty of 1842. This being out of the way, Fox suggested to Secretary of State Webster that an early and final settlement of the Oregon Question would still further cement the international friendship they both desired. To this Webster heartily consented. Conversations then started, which, continuing to 1846, resulted in a definite resolution of the difficulty. Before tracing this development, however, it might be well to examine the bases upon which the two nations founded their claims to possession.

c. *The American Case.* By the Treaty of 1819 Spain had ceded to the United States all her title to the Oregon Territory. What legal title, then, did Spain enjoy? Sovereignty may be obtained over unoccupied territory, according to the law of nations, by *discovery, occupation, treaty, prescription,* or *contiguity.* Spain's claims were based on discovery, treaty, and a Papal decree. The fact that Spanish officers, duly commissioned by the Spanish government, had been the first to discover the Oregon Territory cannot be contradicted. But a summary of opinion shows that international law does not give a clear title to sovereignty based on discovery alone; to make such a title valid, occupation must follow within "a reasonable time." Grotius, the father of international law, said that "in order to enjoy the domain there should be a corporeal possession." Puffendorf was more explicit: "The title to the territory shall rest in him who is first to occupy it, and not in him who happens first to come in sight of it." Burlamaqui wrote that "the dominion over vacant countries is to be acquired by taking possession of them," while Vattel, the greatest lawyer of his day, said: "All mankind have an equal right to the things that have not yet fallen into the separate possession of anyone; such things belong to the first occupant." The same author again states that any nation can claim a territory "in which it has formed some settlement, or of which it makes some actual use." Sovereignty is given "by occupation, not by mere discovery," wrote a more modern lawyer. At best, discovery alone could give only an inchoate title, or, as Gallatin himself admitted, "Discovery gives an *incipient* claim." Again, this American diplomat declared: "Prior discovery gives a right to occupy, provided that occupancy takes place within a reasonable time, and is followed by permanent settlements, and by cultivation of the soil." As was to be expected, Great Britain also took this view, and Rush reported to Adams that "Great Britain could never admit that the mere fact of Spanish navigators having first seen the coast at a particular point . . . without any subsequent or efficient acts of sovereignty or settlement following on the part of Spain, was sufficient to exclude all other nations from that portion of the globe." Therefore it appears that although Spain had gained an incipient or tentative title to Oregon by discovery, the fact that no attempts at settlement or occupation were made during the 275 years between 1543 and 1819 rendered the Spanish title invalid.

By the Nootka Convention of 1790, Spain and Great Britain were declared to enjoy equal rights on the Pacific coast, and thus the Spanish title to exclusive possession was again invalidated.

The only other basis of the Spanish claim was that founded on the bull of Pope Alexander VI in which the New World was divided between the monarchs of Portugal and Spain. This claim was not seriously considered by either Spain or Great Britain after the first few years of westward expansion, but Secretary Buchanan later went so far as again to introduce it, as he "had never seen [it] seriously questioned by any European nation." Gallatin, however, treated this argument in a summary fashion when he wrote: "The claim of the United States to absolute sovereignty over the whole Oregon Territory, in virtue of the ancient exclusive Spanish claim, is wholly unfounded."

Thus the Spanish title, based on discovery or treaty or Papal decree, in reality amounted only to a right of joint occupation shared in its entirety with Great Britain. The rights and pretensions ceded to the United States in 1819 were practically worthless, for the United States gained nothing that she did not already possess by the Convention of 1818. Nevertheless, many American lawyers contended that the Spanish right by discovery, combined with the American right by settlement, gave the American government a just title to exclusive control. Considering, however, that it was not until 1840 (three hundred years after the discovery) that occupation on any measurable scale occurred, this contention is not particularly convincing.

The American case, however, did not rest solely on the rights derived from Spain. On the basis of discovery, occupation, treaty rights, and contiguity, Washington asserted its own claim.

The trips of Captain Robert Gray, who, it was asserted, discovered the Columbia River, and the overland explorations of Lewis and Clark, formed the foundation of the American claim based on discovery. The United States also advanced a peculiar claim to the basin of the Columbia. "The rights of the United States to the Columbia River," wrote Secretary Adams to Rush, "rest upon its discovery from the sea and nomination by a citizen of the United States; upon its exploration to the sea by Captains Lewis and Clark." And as further amplified by Calhoun this claim included the whole valley of the Columbia and its tributaries, extending from the 42nd to the 52nd parallels. This interpretation of international law was, of course, combated by Great Britain, and the British argument, moreover, questioned the right of Gray, a private commercial adventurer, to give any claim whatever. He had not been officially commissioned by the American government, and that government could not rely on any title derived from his travels; this view was upheld by the international lawyers of the day. Lewis and Clark were properly commissioned and, had they been the first to discover Oregon, the "incipient" rights thus attained would then have been impregnable. Both Drake and Cook, however, had antedated Captain Gray. To have had any validity whatever, the explorations of Gray and of Lewis and Clark should have been followed within a reasonable time by occupation or settlement, and this, according to the American government, had actually occurred. Astoria was founded in 1811, and was restored to the United States at the close of the War of 1812, at which time an American garrison had taken formal possession of the post. This was the only official act performed in the Oregon Territory by the United States government. But Astoria had been shortly afterwards abandoned, and was subsequently sold to and occupied by the North-West Company. Between 1818 and 1839 almost the only Americans living in Oregon were the missionaries, and though after 1840 a large number of settlers did come in, they did so simply as private individuals and were not authorized or assisted by the federal government. Consequently, they could give no valid claim to sovereignty, though their presence did undoubtedly affect the decisions of the political negotiators who ultimately settled the dispute. Finally, these migrations took place after the signing of the Convention of 1818, and according to the terms of agreement the question of sovereignty was left in abeyance, and no act performed while it was in operation could affect the respective claims of Britain or America.

Thus by discovery and by occupation the American title was dubious at best, and certainly could not support any pretensions to complete and exclusive control.

The treaties affecting the validity of the American case were the Treaty of Ghent, by which Astoria was handed back; the Convention of 1818, authorizing joint occupation with Great Britain; the Treaty of 1819, by which Spain's claims were transferred to the United States; and the Treaty of 1824, in which Russia agreed to remain north of 54° 40'. By no interpretation could these treaties be logically considered a basis on which to build an exclusive American right to the sovereignty of Oregon.

Prescriptive rights, obviously, could not apply to a region so recently discovered.

Only the claim based on contiguity remains. As a result of the Louisiana Purchase and the Convention of 1818, the territory of the United States was contiguous with that of Oregon between the 42nd and the 49th parallels. Viewed from an objective standpoint, this appears to be the only truly valid claim that could be advanced in support of the American case.

To sum up, even accepting Gallatin's unification of the Spanish claim by discovery with the American claim by occupation (a questionable procedure, for the Spanish claim, apart from its inherent weakness, was not acquired until after the Convention of 1818, which left the question of sovereignty in abeyance), the argument of the United States does not appear valid. A very long time elapsed after discovery before any attempt was made at colonization, and when settlers did arrive, they were unsupported and unauthorized by the government at Washington. By treaty and by prescription the United States enjoyed no right that was not shared with Great Britain, and the slight though valid claim by contiguity applied only to that section of Oregon south of 49°.

But however weak the American case might be in law, it was strong in substance. The fact was that in 1846 the area was widely though thinly settled by farm families, almost all of whom looked upon themselves as Americans. In the year 1843 alone over 900 such settlers arrived. They were soon acknowledging allegiance to a provisional government, and in 1845 they elected a Governor. Against this influx the British claims were sustained by only an occasional fur-trader. In contests between frontier communities based on agriculture and on fur the former has inevitably and invariably survived.

D. *The British Case.* The British government, differing from that of the United States, made no claim to exclusive sovereignty over the whole of the Oregon Territory. What Great Britain did claim was a title as valid as that of the United States, and a better title to the region north of the Columbia River. The British case was based on the following arguments:

1. *Discovery.* The voyages of both Drake and Cook had antedated those of Gray, and each of these adventurers had been a duly commissioned representative of the British Crown. Meares, Vancouver, Mackenzie, Fraser, and Thompson had all carried on this work, and Vancouver in particular had made a very careful survey of the west coast, even sending a cutter one hundred miles up the Columbia River. The English claim is vitiated, however, by the fact that only Drake, Cook, and Vancouver had been commissioned, and by the fact that Spanish explorers had preceded them all.

2. *Occupation.* The first attempt to found anything in the nature of a permanent settlement in Oregon was the establishment of Meares at Nootka Sound. This post, started in 1788, was considered so important by the Spanish Viceroy in Mexico that he sent an expedition to destroy it—an act for which Spain was forced to make compensation, at the same time admitting Britain's right to the enjoyment of all privileges on the west coast.

The first official act of occupation in the Oregon Territory was performed by a British officer in the War of 1812, when he took command of Fort George (Astoria). This settlement, however, was later returned to the United States and finally passed to the North-West Company. Consequently, neither country could use its connection with Astoria as a basis of a legal claim. The North-West Company and the Hudson's Bay Company each made many small settlements, but these were of a temporary character only and were not the official colonizing action of a sovereign state. Thus the British claim to jurisdiction based on exploration followed by occupation was quite as untenable as that of the United States.

3. *Treaties.* The Nootka Convention of 1790 gave Britain equal rights with Spain to carry on trade or colonization; the Convention of 1818 was a similar agreement with the United States; and in 1825 Russia agreed to refrain from disputing Britain's title south of 54° 40'. Thus Great Britain gained by treaty only the privileges of trade and settlement—privileges also held under similar conventions by the United States.

4. *Contiguity.* The Convention of 1818 extended the British-American boundary from the Lake of the Woods to the crest of the Rocky Mountains, along the 49th parallel. All to the north of this line and east of the Rocky Mountains was British territory, and thus by contiguity Great Britain had a claim to Oregon north of 49°, just as valid as that of the United States from 42° to 49°.

It may thus be seen that neither nation had a perfect or even a strong legal case. The United States through the Spanish cession (even if Spain had not forfeited her rights by nonuse) gained only an incipient right, which her failure to colonize rendered nugatory. Britain's title by discovery and occupation was equally invalid. No exclusive right was given either nation by treaty, and no right at all could be urged by prescription. The only possible claim either nation could justly advance was that gained by contiguity, and this favored the United States below 49° and Great Britain above that parallel.

E. *Negotiating the Treaty.* An involved dispute in which neither litigant can prove his case easily leads to grave excesses of partisan exaggeration. The very weakness of a national cause is sometimes responsible for the most violent outbursts in its defense. In the matter of Oregon this condition was particularly true of the United States, for the American people had a better appreciation of the value of the prize for which their government was contending. To the average Englishman, Oregon appeared to be "a costly, unprofitable encumbrance," but, being involved in the dispute, he had the natural and human dislike of admitting defeat. To the Americans, with a better knowledge of the country and imaginations heated by the contest, Oregon appeared to be "our land of promise—and England must and will take herself off." A further incentive to American interest was the "isolation complex" that had been created by Monroe's enunciation of his famous doctrine. Thus in 1840 it seemed to be "the true policy of the United States by all lawful means to resist the inclusion of European dominion in America and to confine its limits and abridge its duration wherever it may actually exist." This constituted an interesting expansion of the original doctrine, which, of course, was essentially a self-denying ordinance. By a neat twist President Polk had made it into an instrument of expansion. This attitude has been generally overlooked in appraising the forces at work in the Oregon Question. Yet it was stated with crystal clearness by the President himself—to whom, incidentally, much of the bitterness of the controversy was due. "The fixed policy of the American Government," he wrote, "should be not to permit Great Britain or any foreign power to plant a colony or hold dominion over any portion of the people or territory . . . of Oregon." General Cass was even less diplomatic. "We must have no red lines traversing Oregon—the whole is ours and we must have it." Oregon was also an area where the maritime and commercial interests of the Eastern section of the United States felt they had a stake. It was a window upon the Pacific Ocean, and an outpost for trade with the Orient.

Fox and Webster reopened the discussion of the Oregon Question in November 1842. Increasing difficulties in the territory, where the new settlers were beginning to object to the rule of the Hudson's Bay Company, made both parties anxious for a settlement. No diplomatic solution of the Oregon Question was possible, however, in 1842, and the whole problem became entangled in the expansionist tendencies of national policy in a presidential year.

In the campaign of 1844 the Oregon controversy played an important part. James K. Polk, floating the vessel of his political ambitions on the high tide of expansionist sentiment, stirred his fellow Americans to enthusiasm with his insistence on "the Reoccupation of Oregon and the Reannexation of Texas." This was the day when "Fifty-four forty or Fight" expressed the temper of the people. President Polk was himself a sincere expansionist, though he was willing to settle for much less than 54° 40'.

On 15 January 1845 Sir Richard Pakenham, the British Minister at Washington, suggested arbitration, but Calhoun refused to consider this so long as any possibility of reaching a decision by direct negotiation remained.

In his inaugural address President Polk reiterated his campaign pledges in regard to Oregon, and again declared that the American "title to the whole of Oregon is clear and unquestionable." The new President's actions, however, were not so extreme as his words. He had hardly recovered from the trials of the inauguration ceremony when he offered, through Secretary of State Buchanan, to compromise the dispute at the 49th parallel. This proposal was addressed to Sir Richard Pakenham, and that official refused the offer without even referring it to London. This forced Polk to take more strenuous measures, and he asked Congress to give the required notice to terminate the joint occupation of Oregon, to extend the laws of the United States over that territory, and to erect forts there. He again asserted the rights of the United States to the whole region, and still later declared "that the British contentions of title could not be entertained to any portion of the Oregon Territory." On 27 December the British proposed arbitration, but by this time American feeling had risen too high for such pacific measures, and the proposal was refused.

President Polk's campaign had aroused a real interest in Oregon among the American people—an interest that had been prepared for by the migrations into the territory during the early forties. Countless pamphlets and scores of books were written and published in support of the American claims, and extraordinary productions some of them were. The President's remark about "looking John Bull in the eye" brought an enthusiastic response. Voices were not lacking, however, to proclaim the idiocy of a war over this question, and to remind the legislators of the bad light such a war would cast on the United States, in view of her refusal to arbitrate. The popular and perfectly safe sport of "twisting the Lion's tail" was carried to such an extreme by some Congressmen that Senator Haywood of North Carolina was led to quote from George Washington that "the nation which indulges toward another habitual hatred, is, in some degree, a slave."

Neither country, however, actually wanted war. Britain was not vitally interested in Oregon, and few Canadians were thinking of the Pacific. Attention in Canada was concentrated, not on a doubtful boundary of a distant and probably worthless wilderness in the mountains of the West, but on the struggle for constitutional reform in Upper and Lower Canada.

The British Foreign Office, with Aberdeen in place of Palmerston, was no longer obsessed by the idea that the Columbia River was another St. Lawrence or Mississippi and a vital link in the trade route with China.[3] In Britain, moreover, the influence of the Manchester economists was becoming every day more powerful, and the temptation to engage in military adventures overseas was losing much of its popular allure. Britain wanted peace and freedom—above all, freedom for trade. If this desire led to a relaxation of the bonds of empire, that was regrettable but not, in itself, a matter of the first significance. In addition

---

[3] It is possible that when its unequaled power resources are fully exploited, the Columbia may, in fact, exceed either of the eastern rivers in its national importance.

Great Britain was more ready to compromise because the Hudson's Bay Company had now withdrawn, or was preparing to withdraw, from Fort Vancouver on the Columbia, and had established its headquarters at Fort Victoria, on the southern point of Vancouver Island. The fur trade in the Columbia Valley was dying out. The British, finally, were involved in an exceptionally acute domestic problem as a result of the crop failures of 1845. In Scotland and Ireland a large percentage of the population was threatened with starvation, and in the Houses of Parliament the repeal of the Corn Laws was absorbing the attention of all the party leaders.

In the United States, on the other hand, the struggle over slavery was already casting its ominous shadows over the land, and President Polk, having succeeded in annexing Texas, was now preparing for war with Mexico. The whole expansionist tendency of his administration was in part a reflection of the self-confident and aggressive spirit of the nation just entering on a period of industrial and commercial development. It was also in part, consciously or unconsciously, an effort to distract attention from the apparitions of conflict at home by concentrating on the safer forms of controversy abroad. But the latter did not include the serious prospect of a shooting war with Great Britain. It was quite evident that the responsible officials both in Washington and in London would support a sensible compromise proposal. Britain certainly did not want a war, and the United States, although it would not have surrendered any territory south of the 49th parallel, equally certainly was not prepared to fight for 54° 40'. This was now realized by Great Britain.

On 18 May 1846 Lord Aberdeen initiated the conversations that ultimately led to a settlement of the question at issue. On that date he wrote to Pakenham: "You will . . . propose to the American Secretary of State that the line of demarcation should be continued along the 49th parallel from the Rocky Mountains to the sea-coast, and thence in a southerly direction through King George's Channel and the Straits of Fuca to the Pacific Ocean, leaving the whole of Vancouver's Island with its ports and harbors in the possession of Great Britain." This was the line for which the United States had in reality been contending, and, in spite of the opposition of Buchanan, the proposal was submitted to the Senate by President Polk, and the consent of that body was quickly obtained. The treaty was signed on 15 June 1846. It drew the line of division along the 49th parallel "to the middle of the channel which separates the continent from Vancouver's Island, and then southerly through the middle of the said channel, and of Fuca's Straits, to the Pacific Ocean." Provision was also made for free navigation of the Columbia River, and for the confirmation of the possessory rights in the Columbia country of the Hudson's Bay Company and the Puget Sound Agricultural Company.

The treaty, under the existing conditions, was just and equitable. *Neither nation had a clear legal title to any of the territory,* and the result was practically an equal division. Great Britain was given the better harbors, and greater resources in minerals, timber, and fish; the United States received much more agricultural land, and a district that has, on the whole, a better climate. This decision, moreover, is almost unique among the solutions of American boundary troubles, in that it has been accepted with reasonable satisfaction by both nations. A better proof of its justice could hardly be demanded.

4. The Alaskan Boundary

A. *The History of the Problem.* Although the dispute over the Alaskan boundary did not become serious until after the discovery of gold in the Yukon in 1897, and was not permanently settled until 1903, it is necessary to go back almost one hundred years in order to understand the facts on which Canada and the United States based their respective contentions.

During the early years of the nineteenth century the ownership of the northwestern corner of the continent was in dispute. Explorers, fur traders, and merchants of Russia, the United States, and Great Britain were all pursuing their vocations by sea or land along the island-sheltered coasts of the Alaskan peninsula. Under the circumstances it was inevitable that conflicts should arise, and the vigorous policy of Russia in particular aroused some anxiety in the United States. By a ukase of 1821, Russia asserted her exclusive sovereignty as far south as the 51st parallel of north latitude. This claim was at once combated by Washington and London. It is now generally recognized that the fear of Russian aggression in Alaska played a large part in convincing Adams and Monroe of the necessity of stating and defending the policy that was soon enunciated in a presidential message, and has since been known as the Monroe Doctrine.

The threat of force as implied in the Monroe Doctrine was not an altogether satisfactory solution of the Alaskan problem, and negotiations between the American and Russian governments were instituted, to culminate in the Convention of 1824. Under the terms of this convention the United States agreed to establish no posts north of 54° 40′, and in return was assured of unrestricted opportunities in the fishing industry, and of permission to trade for ten years in the interior seas, gulfs, harbors, and creeks of the Alexander Archipelago, as the whole coastal region north of the 54th parallel was known.

Meanwhile Great Britain was not idle. After some delay, Canning succeeded in negotiating a similar treaty, which was signed on 28 February 1825. It was on the wording of this Anglo-Russian Treaty that all the subsequent debate over the exact boundary of Alaska was based. Articles III and IV contain the passages that were so variously interpreted. Their importance justifies quotation in full:

"*Article III.* Commencing from the southernmost part of the Island called Prince of Wales Island, which point lies in the parallel 54° 40′, and between the 131st and 133rd degrees of west longitude (meridian of Greenwich) the said

line shall ascend to the north along the channel called Portland Channel, as far as the point of the continent where it
strikes the 56th degree of north latitude. From this last
mentioned point the line of demarcation shall follow the
summit of the mountains situated parallel to the coast as
far as the point of intersection of the 141st degree of west
longitude (of the same meridian), and, finally, from the
said point of intersection, the said meridian line of the 141st
degree in its prolongation as far as the Frozen Ocean, shall
form the limit between the Russian and British possessions
on the continent of America to the North-west.

Article IV. With reference to the line of demarcation laid
down in the previous article it is understood: *1st*. That the
Island called Prince of Wales Island shall belong wholly
to Russia. *2nd*. That whenever the summit of the mountains
which extend in the direction parallel to the coast from the
56th degree of north latitude to the point of intersection of
the 141st degree of west longitude shall prove to be at a
distance of more than 10 marine leagues from the ocean the
limit between the British possessions and the line of the
coast which is to belong to Russia, as above mentioned shall
be formed by a line parallel to the windings of the coast,
and shall never exceed the distance of ten marine leagues
therefrom."

In these two articles are found the definitions which, by partisan interpretation, became the basis of the Alaskan boundary
controversy. Article III was written under the supposition that
an orderly range of mountains paralleled the north Pacific coast
—a supposition later proved altogether erroneous. Mountains
there were in great profusion; but of order there was none. To
one who has traveled through the famous "inside passage" of the
British Columbian and Alaskan coast the utter impossibility of
drawing "a line parallel to the windings of the coast" is at once
evident.

Owing to a meager knowledge of the country, and to a general lack of interest, no disputes arose concerning this boundary between 1825 and 1867, with the single exception of a trivial altercation over the right of navigation on the Stikine River. In the year 1867, however, the Dominion of Canada was formed, and the United States purchased Alaska from the Czar. Four years later British Columbia entered the Dominion. Thus the stage was prepared.

The Lieutenant-Governor of the new Canadian province soon requested the federal authorities to take steps to bring about a final and definitive elucidation and settlement of the national rights in northwestern America. On 11 July 1872 Canada requested the British Foreign Office to approach the United States on this subject. As a result of the efforts of Edward Thornton, British Ambassador at Washington, the President, on 2 December 1872, recommended to Congress the appointment of a joint commission "to determine the line between the territory of Alaska and the co-terminous possessions of Great Britain." Unfortunately for the future good relations of the two countries, this suggestion was not well received. Hamilton Fish, Secretary of State, announced publicly that such a commission would take ten years to do the work and would cost a million and half dollars. This expense the United States was unwilling to bear.

Matters soon became more complicated. American and Canadian settlers and trappers in the region of the Stikine River were in a constant state of commotion. In 1877 the case of Peter Martin, an American citizen, arrested and convicted by Canadian officials for an offense committed on disputed territory, aroused international interest. In the same year the Dominion government sent Joseph Hunter to the Stikine to determine, if possible, the line of demarcation. Hunter's instructions from the office of the Surveyor-General were to locate the line at a distance of ten marine leagues from the coast, "on a course at right angles *to the general bearing* thereof, opposite."

Thus Canada stated her belief that "the line of the Coast" should be taken to mean the "general bearing" or "general trend" of the coast, an interpretation that the United States was later to reject indignantly, for a settlement based on such a premise would give Canada a number of the better harbors in Alaska. Twice during 1877 Thornton pressed on Secretary Evarts the desirability of an early agreement, but a *modus vivendi* by which Hunter's line on the Stikine would be temporarily recognized was the most that Washington would do. This temporary acceptance was to be "without prejudice to the rights of the parties when the permanent boundary came to be fixed."

On 24 April 1884 William H. Dall, of the United States Survey, wrote to George M. Dawson, of the Division of Geological Survey of Canada, stating that the line of the Treaty of 1825 was impossible of location, as there was "no natural boundary, and the continuous range of mountains, parallel to the Coast, shown on Vancouver's charts, having no existence as such, the United States would undoubtedly wish to fall back upon the line parallel to the windings of the coast. It would, of course, be impracticable to trace any such winding line over the sea of mountains." Secretary Bayard wrote to Lord Salisbury that, in view of the erroneous ideas of those who drew up the treaty, the document "really gave no boundary at all"—a statement that was completely and obviously true. This presented an ideal opening for the discussion of a compromise line, but no steps were taken to that end. During 1887–8 Dall and Dawson continued their discussions at Washington and the divergent views became ever more pronounced. Was the boundary to cross over inlets that projected 40, 50 or even 100 miles into the interior, or was the American *lisière* to remain intact? Each of these eminent scientists decided in favor of the contentions of his own country, and no agreement could be reached.

In 1897 gold was found in the Yukon and Alaska, and the boundary question immediately took on a new importance. Sir Julian Pauncefote suggested that a commission of three, one American, one Briton, and one neutral, be selected to adjust the difficulty, and that in the meantime an arbitrary line should be agreed upon. This suggestion was not accepted by the United States, but in June 1898 a joint commission met at Quebec to discuss a number of international difficulties. Canada made two proposals to this body in relation to the Alaskan boundary: (1) that a conventional line be drawn giving the Dominion Pyramid Harbor on Lynn Canal, and ceding the remainder to the United States; or (2) that the whole matter be left to arbitration in accordance with the terms of the Venezuelan arbitration. Both of these plans were rejected by the United States. The American commissioners in turn offered their suggestion: namely, that a judicial body of three eminent jurists from each country be convened and instructed to interpret the treaty. This scheme was vetoed by Great Britain. The matter was then referred back to the national governments for further discussion through diplomatic channels.

The turn of the nineteenth century and the beginning of the twentieth was a period of tension and of creation in Anglo-American relations. Great Britain, engaged in the Boer War, was aware of a hostile public opinion in the United States, at a time when the government of the United States was pressing for a revision of the Clayton-Bulwer Treaty (1850). The Spanish-American War had revealed the necessity of a transisthmian canal to enable the United States Pacific and Atlantic fleets to maintain full co-operation. The Clayton-Bulwer Treaty stood in the way of the United States building the canal alone, and the United States was bringing pressure to bear on Great Britain to agree to a revision that would allow Washington to go ahead with the project. In the Far East, Great Britain was anxious to act in conjunction with the United States to prevent what appeared to be the imminent partition of the Empire of China among the great powers. At the same time the British position, in a naval sense, was being threatened by the rise of German naval power.

In a situation as grave as this, British statesmen were painfully aware that their cherished "splendid isolation" was something less than adequate. Decisions of profound importance for the next half century were taken by Great Britain in these years. Support for British policy in the Far East was sought through co-operation with the United States in the Open Door policy and with Japan in the Anglo-Japanese Alliance (1902). In the New World, United States good will was sought through British agreement in the Hay-Pauncefote Treaty (1901), by which the United States was given virtually a free hand to go ahead alone with a transisthmian canal.

Thus Great Britain moved to consolidate a strong friendship with the United States. This policy was highlighted by British concessions during the Venezuela dispute in 1895, by acceptance of American wishes in the Hay-Pauncefote Treaty and above all by British friendship toward the United States during the Spanish-American War, at a time when almost every other country in the world was opposed to the policy of the United States. This whole situation had a most important bearing on the solution of the Alaska boundary problem. Many Canadians felt that the concessions made by Great Britain in the transisthmian negotiation ought to have been counterbalanced by American concessions on the Alaska boundary. This would have been to secure by diplomacy what it was most unlikely that Canada could secure through the judicial process. Canada sacrificed her national interest in 1901, however, by not pressing for *quid pro quo*, in order to further the world policy of the British Empire.

The United States had insisted on a juridical solution of the Alaska boundary question, rejecting both diplomacy and arbitration. This put her case on strong ground because by a legal interpretation of the Anglo-Russian Treaty of 1825, as it is generally agreed today, the United States had the stronger case. In line with the now settled policy of Great Britain to nourish Anglo-American friendship, the Hay-Herbert Convention (24 January 1903) was concluded. By this convention the United States and Great Britain agreed to the formation of a joint tribunal, composed of three "impartial jurists of repute" from each nation. The duties of this body were to adjudicate on the provisions of the treaty. It was not an arbitral commission; it was a judicial board. It was appointed, not to arrange a practical and reasonable solution of the difficulty, but to interpret legally a document that was geographically absurd.

B. *The Members of the Tribunal.* The composition of this judicial body was of great moment, for only as the people of the two countries were assured of the impartiality of the judges would they be satisfied with the results. The British government in response to the demand of Canadian sentiment nominated Louis A. Jette and Allen B. Aylesworth, two eminent members of the Canadian bar. The third member nominated by Great Britain was Lord Alverstone, who held the highest position in the judiciary of the United Kingdom. Few exceptions were taken to these appointments by the American press or people. Amerians in general, however, felt that Canada was engaged in "trying to put something over" on the United States. From the President down, it was believed that the Dominion had trumped up a spurious claim only after the territory had been suddenly and unexpectedly proved of value. This criticism was not entirely just, as an examination of the previous negotiations will prove, but it is of course true that the Canadian claim was urged much more vigorously after 1897 than before, and that many of the Canadian arguments were exceedingly feeble. The appointments made by Great Britain were announced after the appointments made by President Roosevelt.

On 18 February 1903 President Roosevelt made public the names of the American nominees: Secretary of War Root, Senator Lodge of Massachusetts, and Senator Turner of Washington. A storm of protest swept over Canada, and the Dominion government took the unusual step of formally objecting to the appointment of the two Senators. Elihu Root had the confidence and respect of the whole English-speaking world. He was a man of the most scrupulous honesty: honorable, able, and conscientious. Senator Turner was little known even in his own country —but was a politician from Washington, the state most vitally interested in the retention of Alaska. The political career of Henry Cabot Lodge, on the other hand, had been characterized by an excessive devotion to partisan and nationalistic ends. It is not too much to say that for a quarter of a century he had been recognized as a mischievous force in international relations, and that in relation to things British in particular he had displayed a complete lack of objectivity. He had been the incarnation of bigoted nationalism and jingoistic imperialism, and his nomination as an "impartial jurist of repute" was bitterly resented in Canada.

Whatever may be said of the final decisions of the tribunal (and they were probably quite justified), it must be agreed that "in making these selections the United States Government dishonored its own Treaty." Every member of the trio was a politician, and while Root might have been willing to sacrifice his political future in order to deal fairly in the matter of the Alaskan boundary, yet he must be regarded as a party to the dispute in that he was a member of Roosevelt's Cabinet. No such illusions could be held in regard to Senators Lodge and Turner. The former, moreover, had already committed himself in regard to the matter to be settled. In a speech at Northampton, Massachusetts, delivered on 16 October 1902, Senator Lodge had said that "no nation with any self-respect could have admitted" the Canadian claims, and went on to link the "national honor" with the American contentions regarding the Alaskan boundary.

With the announcement of the choice of American delegates public opinion in Canada at once became pessimistic. If Lodge and Turner were to represent the United States, declared the Toronto *Globe*, "it makes little difference how ably the Canadian case is presented." The Montreal *Gazette* agreed that "the representatives of the United States were hardly open to conviction," while the Toronto *News* summed it up thus: "Mr. Root is a lawyer of real eminence. Senator Lodge is a well-known jingo. Senator Turner comes from the State in which Seattle is situated."

But the Canadian papers were not alone in recognizing the inappropriateness of President Roosevelt's selections. The famous Springfield *Republican* (an American journal which for liberal independence deserved to be linked with the Manchester *Guardian* in Great Britain or the Manitoba *Free Press* in Canada) stated editorially:

"If the President were to seek the country over for men who were entirely without the judicial quality on this question, he could not find persons whose minds are more set than Messrs. Lodge, Turner and Root. Their selection cannot be interpreted in any other way than that the President intends to block the slightest chance of a decision in the least favorable to Canada."

Unfortunately, however, the famous Massachusetts paper did not express the sentiments of a majority of Americans. The Seattle *Post-Intelligencer*, having previously argued that "there was nothing to arbitrate," now relied upon and was proud of the fact that "none of the American commissioners will yield a single point." The state House of Representatives at Olympia passed a resolution denouncing England in violent terms and demanding of the American representatives a firm adherence to every American claim.

Placed on the defensive as a result of his appointments, President Roosevelt wrote to Justice Holmes of the Supreme Court explaining his choice by the statement that "no three men fit for the position could be found in all the United States who had not already come to some conclusion" on this subject, and that the American delegates were "anxious to do justice to the British claim on all points." The first statement of the President was probably true, but the inference was absurd. Had Roosevelt appointed three justices of the United States Supreme Court, there could have been no possible occasion for Canadian objection; but in order to pacify the Senate, to assure himself of its support, and because he honestly felt that Canada was making a consciously unjust claim to American territory, he had appointed the men named. This, of course, is an explanation, not an excuse. There can, furthermore, be no possible justification for the President's bombastic method of informing Britain (through Justice Holmes) "that if there is any disagreement—not only will there be no arbitration of the matter but in my message to Congress I shall take a position which will prevent any possibility of arbitration hereafter . . . and which will give me the authority to run the line as we claim it without any further regard to the attitude of England and Canada." His letter to Justice Holmes demonstrated the great failing of President Roosevelt: his complete inability to see more than one side of any given question; but it also shows the existing attitude of the United States. Americans generally felt that Canada was trumping up an unjustifiable claim. It was this sentiment, as well as the real need for greater police protection, that led the President to dispatch a body of troops to Alaska at this time, and few people who understood his attitude could doubt that he fully intended to use them in case the tribunal decided against the American claims. Here was "shirt-sleeve" diplomacy in its crudest form.

Apologists for President Roosevelt have since argued that he agreed to the proposal of judicial determination simply to give Great Britain an easy way out of a difficult situation. He was fully satisfied that there was no shred of justification for the Canadian claims and was certain that any jury would so decide. Therefore the appointments were merely a form and the personalities did not count.

The answer to this argument is, of course, that if the President was really convinced of the inevitable victory of his cause, he could have afforded to carry out his promise to appoint "jurists of repute." He could have avoided the dishonesty of his selections and still have won his case. The fact that President Roosevelt was in general disposed to be friendly in his attitude toward Canada and Great Britain is no argument against the condemnation that his action in this case rightly invoked. Nor is the fact that he was personally convinced of the justice of his case. President Roosevelt was always personally convinced of the righteousness of every cause he espoused. Moreover, a conviction is no justification for these dubious proceedings; even in international affairs the end does not justify the means.

It was distinctly creditable to the Canadian people that they did not demand at this time that the King appoint "impartial jurists" of the same type as those representing the United States.

Though realizing that the decision of the tribunal would probably be against them, and that it could not be for them, the Canadian authorities carried out the treaty stipulations in spirit and in letter.

c. *The Problems before the Tribunal.* In summary, the questions before the tribunal, which met in London on 3 September 1903, may be stated as follows:

1. *The Point of Commencement of the Boundary.* On this particular matter there was little discussion. At first the American counsel argued that Wales Island (considerably south of the island now known as Prince of Wales Island) was the one intended in the definition. Inasmuch as this island was not named until long after 1825, the contention was dropped, and Cape Muzon was declared to be the correct point of departure.

2. *What was Meant by Portland Channel?* The only inlet of that name was discovered, named, and charted by Captain Vancouver. The difficulty arose from the fact that the channel divided in its upper reaches and where united, it was studded with islands, making many small channels. The two great inland branches of Portland Channel were known as Portland Canal and Observatory Inlet. Both sides agreed that Portland Canal was the branch mentioned in the treaty, but the difficulty arose in drawing the line through Portland Channel itself. Did the name Observatory Inlet include that part of Portland Channel between the 55th degree of north latitude and the ocean, to the south of the larger islands? The British claimed that the line should follow the northern bank, leaving all the islands to Canada; that Observatory Inlet extended all the way to the ocean and that "Portland Channel" was the passage between the islands and the northern coast. The Americans claimed that the line, on emerging from Portland Canal, should cross to the Observatory Inlet side of Portland Channel, and thus to the ocean. By this method the United States would take all four islands. The American counsel pointed out that the lower part of Observatory Inlet had usually been mentioned as Portland Channel, while the British attempted by quoting Vancouver to

prove that Portland Channel *did not* include the lower part of the inlet.

3. *The Line from "the southermost point of Prince of Wales Island to Portland Channel."* This depended on the decision in the second problem, and was adjusted in accordance with that award.

4. *The Line from Portland Canal to the 56th Parallel.* The United States claimed that the line should be drawn straight, entirely disregarding the contour of the coast.

5. *The Width of the* Lisière. This was the real problem. The British claimed that the words "coast" and "ocean" had been used indiscriminately and with identical meaning, but the Americans replied that the treaty specifically stated that the line should be drawn parallel to the sinuosities of the coast. It being impracticable to draw a line parallel to such a coast in such a country, the Americans claimed that it should be laid out at a distance of ten marine leagues from a line following the general trend of the headwaters of the many inlets. Britain claimed that the boundary should parallel a line joining the headlands of the coast—the outlets of the fiords. Under this interpretation Britain would have access to the headwaters of certain inlets, for many of these narrow lanes extended more than thirty miles inland. Equally authentic maps were produced to support each case.

6. *How the* Lisière *Should be Measured.* This was the same as question five. There were three possible alternatives. The boundary might be drawn (a) parallel to the general direction of the mainland coast, as the British contended; (b) parallel to the line separating Russian territorial waters from the ocean; (c) parallel to a line joining the heads of the inlets, as the Americans desired.

7. *Did Mountain Ranges Exist?* The United States claimed that no ranges upon which measurements could be based existed; Great Britain maintained that individual mountains joined by imaginary lines might be considered a range. This contention was not strongly urged, and thus Article III of the Treaty of 1825 was declared inapplicable.

D. *The Decision of the Tribunal.* The difficulties that confronted the tribunal arose, primarily, from the fact that the boundary definition which these judges were to interpret was written by men who had but a scant knowledge of the physiographic conditions of the country they were dividing. Thus it was necessary to go behind the phraseology and find the motives of the negotiators of a treaty signed almost one hundred years before. The objects that the Russian and British diplomats of 1825 had attempted to accomplish had to be explored, and to be interpreted in the light of a scientific knowledge of the geographic conditions.

The tribunal met in London on 3 September, and on 20 October the results of its deliberation were announced.

From the first, Canadians had feared that Lord Alverstone would be influenced by the exigencies of British foreign policy —the policy which was primarily directed toward the establishment of better relations with the United States. This feeling was widely shared in London, where the *Saturday Review*, for example, said: "The directors of our policy are throwing our premier colony to the able diplomacy of the United States as a small pledge of our determination to be friends at all hazards." It has since been clearly shown that Alverstone was so influenced, chiefly by Lansdowne and Balfour. In the event, on every issue of importance he voted with the American representatives, and thus, by a vote of four to two, the contentions of the United States were upheld. The Americans, of course, did have the better case.

The point of departure of the boundary line was, as stated above, decided by agreement and with little discussion.

The question of how the boundary should be drawn through Portland Channel was one of the most difficult tasks before the tribunal, and, by Canadian authors, the decision in this instance is considered positive proof of the potency of political considerations over the actions of the tribunal. In truth, no other explanation seems adequate; there can be little doubt that the tribunal in this instance accepted a compromise, which, however justified by the political considerations involved, was a direct violation of the judicial character of the court. Instead of accepting either the American or the British claim *in toto*, the line was drawn through Tongas Passage, thus giving each country a portion of its claim, but entirely disregarding the real problem involved. The original negotiators might, logically, have intended the line to be drawn either as the British claimed or as the Americans claimed; certainly they had no intention of dividing the channel islands between the two. Alverstone urged that "Vancouver may have intended to include Tongas Passage in that name [Portland Channel] and . . . I think that the negotiators may well have thought that Portland Channel . . . issued into the sea by the two passages." But this was a direct contradiction of Alverstone's own words on a previous occasion, when he had stated the Canadian contention to be "absolutely unanswerable." Moreover, this compromise was not suggested until a deadlock seemed imminent. There can be scarcely any doubt that Lord Alverstone's final pronouncement was merely an attempt to rationalize a political expedient, and that Aylesworth spoke the truth when he said: "There is not the slightest evidence anywhere . . . that either Vancouver or any subsequent explorer ever considered or so much as spoke of Portland Channel having two entrances to the Ocean or as including the Passage through which this Boundary line is now made to run." Roosevelt himself regarded the Canadian claim as strong on this point, and was prepared to accept an award that gave all four islands to Canada. Lodge was more intransigent than even the President on this point.

This particular decision cannot be viewed except as an immense mistake, for it cast doubt upon the judicial quality of the whole award. Such doubts do not seem justified by the other decisions, which all have ample basis in the arguments presented.

The third problem, regarding the course of the line from Cape Muzon to Portland Channel, was dependent on the second, and the decision was made to accord with the boundary in the channel.

The fourth question was settled when the line was drawn directly from the head of the Portland Canal to the 56th parallel, disregarding the coast entirely, and thus favoring the American contention.

The fifth and sixth points were so closely allied that they may be treated as one. This was the most important of all the problems before the tribunal, and here again the American case won by a vote of four to two. A careful study of the documents on either side seems to confirm the justice of this conclusion. The American counsel claimed that in the negotiation of the Treaty of 1825 the Russian diplomats had intended "to create an unbroken barrier along the entire waterfront of the continent." Thus the boundary must be drawn parallel to a line joining the headwaters of all the larger inlets, for otherwise this *lisière* would not be intact. This view seems to be supported by a perusal of the records of the negotiations of 1824–5.

The British claim that individual mountains might be joined to form a chain was so weak that it easily succumbed to argument.

These, in summary, are the decisions of the tribunal. In all but one case they seem justified by the facts, and yet that one case of political compromise tarnished the whole award. The two Canadian judges took the almost unprecedented and unfortunate action of refusing to sign the award. This did not affect the validity of the findings, but it did crystallize public sentiment in Canada against the "political agreement." Sir Louis Jette and Mr. Aylesworth issued a minority report in which they stated that they had refused to sign the award because they could "not consider the finding of the tribunal as to the islands, entrance to Portland Channel, or as to the mountain line, a judicial one."

E. *Effect of the Decisions.* As was to be expected, the decisions of the tribunal were received with rejoicing in the United States. Lord Alverstone was praised for his impartiality, evidenced in voting against his country, and the whole adjudication was looked upon as a triumph of American diplomacy.

In Canada the award was almost universally condemned. This censure was directed not so much against the details of the award itself as against the methods employed in reaching these decisions. Two main lines of criticism were evidenced in the national press: first, the betrayal of Canadian interests by the mother country, for political reasons; and second, the American disregard of the convention stipulations in the selection of jurists.

With reference to the first point, the Vancouver *Province,* one of Canada's leading journals, but published on the Pacific coast, where feeling was most intense, declared: "It shows that we cannot depend upon the Mother Country to protect our interests; it shows that we cannot depend on her to see common justice done us, when, by sacrificing us, she has an opportunity of catering to a sentiment which does her much less credit than she imagines." The Victoria *Colonist* summarized the Canadian feeling thus: "About the decision we do not care. Our main consideration is the means by which it was arrived at. . . . The prevailing tone of the British Press has not been the necessity of maintaining Imperial rights, but the necessity of cultivating the friendship of the United States." *Le Journal,* an influential French paper of Montreal, stated that "we find ourselves contemplating, not the decisions of an Arbitration Commission, but a diplomatic arrangement." In a bitter mood the Rossland *Miner* exclaimed: "Perhaps we should be thankful that there is no territory left which grasping Americans can reach for, and complaisant British Commissioners give away." This sentiment was again voiced as follows: "This is not the first time that British diplomacy has proven costly to Canada. Canada, however, accepted a 'loaded' Tribunal as a means of effecting settlements. The negotiations have gone against us and it is our duty to submit. . . . What Canada should do to protect herself in the future is a question which deserves and will undoubtedly receive deep consideration."

Perhaps the most exact summary of the Canadian viewpoint is to be found in the editorial of the Manitoba *Free Press,* from which the following is quoted:

> "We recognize, of course, that the Canadian case may have been the weaker of the two. If this were the case it is

doubly unfortunate that the decision should have been reached by means that have left one of the parties to the dispute convinced that it has not been justly dealt with. . . . The merits of the case, to the satisfaction of one of the parties, can never be decided now. If Canada was right, the decision was lamentable; if she was wrong, it is calamitous that an impartial tribunal could not have made this clear. As it is, the damage is irreparable. Canadians, with very few exceptions, will accept without question the statements of their representatives that their interests were sacrificed; and the resulting resentment is certain to affect the attitude of Canada towards the United States, and, in a still greater degree, towards the Motherland."

Such, unfortunately, was the reaction of Canada to the award of the Alaskan boundary tribunal. Had the United States been willing to submit her case to The Hague, or to an impartial juridical body, as Canada had desired, the result would have been, in all probability, substantially the same, except that Canadians could not feel that they had been unfairly treated. The United States had the better case, and it is unfortunate that President Roosevelt should have taken such means to assure himself of victory. Had justices of the United States Supreme Court been appointed in the place of the two Senators, Canadian criticism of the award would not have been audible. Under the circumstances, when faced with what they considered to be a "loaded" bench; when they saw what appeared to be incontrovertible proofs of political influence being used against their case; and when every decision of importance was decided against them, the chagrin of the Canadian people can be readily understood and appreciated.

That justice was done under the circumstances cannot but be regarded as a fortuitous circumstance; for once, right was on the side of might. The United States gained her just deserts, but by means of which she cannot be proud; while many Canadians do not yet feel that a case supported in such a manner could have been sound.

The decision is still a matter of heated comment in certain parts of the Dominion, particularly in British Columbia and the Yukon, for the American *lisière* adds considerably to the difficulty of communication and shipment between British Columbia ports and Yukon mines. Unless, however, the Yukon experiences a very great revival of industry and trade, it is probable that this matter will gradually sink into the oblivion of the forgotten past.[4]

The chief continuing significance of the Alaska boundary decision, and particularly the way in which it was effected, came some years later. The anti-American hostility aroused in 1903 greatly influenced the votes of 1911. The ease with which sentiment against the United States was worked up by the anti-reciprocity forces was clearly connected with the events of a decade earlier.

But more important still was the impetus given by the Alaska boundary award to the demand for Canadian control of Canadian foreign policy. From this time on, it was difficult for an average Canadian to argue against the assertion that Canada had been sacrificed by British diplomats for British reasons. The fact that Canada was in the wrong in the argument in 1903 is, in this matter, unimportant. Canadians were convinced that they were sold for British profit. The logical conclusion was that Canada should control her own destiny in foreign as in domestic matters. The Alaska boundary award may, in this sense, be directly related to the Statute of Westminster.

[4] It is of interest to note that because of the rapid recession of the glaciers that filled the upper ends of some of the fiords, open water is now reaching into Canadian territory! If President Roosevelt were alive today, he would certainly have something to say about a Providence that could thus challenge the decision of his packed tribunal.

6

Minor Boundary Disputes

1. Introduction

Although the problems of Maine, Oregon, and Alaska were the most important boundary questions to arise between the United States and Canada, they were not the only difficulties that developed in the demarcation of the territorial possessions of the two nations. The San Juan boundary dispute resulted from the carelessness or the lack of geographical knowledge of the negotiators of the Oregon treaty. The Lake of the Woods boundary was of very slight importance, but the question of jurisdiction over Bering Sea, and the seal herds that frequented it, was of a more vital import. This problem, though dealing with more than boundary definitions, has been included in this chapter for the sake of convenience.

2. The San Juan Boundary

A. *The Genesis of the Question.* The Treaty of 1846 settled the Oregon boundary question in its major details. The treaty was not, however, specific and exact in its delineations of the respective rights of the United States and Great Britain in regard to the islands situated between Vancouver Island and the mainland. Whether this lack of detailed specification was due to carelessness on the part of the negotiators, or was simply a result of the meager knowledge of the geography of the Pacific coast current at the time, is immaterial. Article I of the treaty traces the boundary along the 49th parallel of north latitude "to the middle of the channel which separates the continent from Vancouver's Island, and thence southerly through the middle of the said channel, and of Fuca's straits to the Pacific Ocean: provided, however, that the navigation of the whole of the said channel and straits south of the 49th parallel of north latitude remain free and open to both parties."

Had there been one obvious and coherent channel separating Vancouver Island from the mainland, this definition would have served the purpose intended. Owing, however, to the presence of a cluster of islands in the southern portion of the Gulf of Georgia, a number of possible channels made difficult the task of the surveyor. Two passages through these islands were in common use: Rosario Strait, between the major islands and the continent; and the Canal de Haro, the waters of which touched the shores of Vancouver Island. Each nation claimed the islands,[1] the United States asserting that the boundary should pass through the Canal de Haro, and Great Britain insisting on Rosario Strait. Since the introduction of the steamship the Canal de Haro has been more frequently used by coast and ocean shipping, but in the days of the sailing ship Rosario Strait was the more popular route—a fact that gave color to the British claim that this passage should be considered the main channel.

San Juan, the largest island, and the one that has given its name to the whole controversy, is fourteen miles long by four and one-half in width. Until 1850 only Indians had used the island, except for some herds of cattle belonging to the Hudson's

---

[1] These consisted of San Juan, Orcas, Lopez, Waldron, Blakely, Decatur, Shaw, and a number of smaller islets; taken together, they comprise about 170 square miles. Howay and Schofield: *History of British Columbia* (Vancouver), Vol. I, p. 301.

Bay Company, and the herdsmen. But in that year the company established a salmon-canning plant, and in the following year a post was located there.

In 1852 the Oregon legislature included San Juan in Island County, and when Washington Territory was created in 1853, the island became a part of Whatcom County. When the company refused to pay the American taxes, the sheriff of the county appeared on the island in 1854, seized a number of sheep, and sold them at auction. He was driven off and pursued by company officials in the S.S. *Beaver* (the first steamer on the North Pacific Ocean), but escaped. Governor Douglas of Vancouver Island immediately sent a letter of harsh protest to Governor Stevens of Washington Territory, stating that he had orders from the home government "to treat those islands as part of the British Dominions."

Relations became so unpleasant that in 1856 the American and British governments appointed commissioners in an attempt to solve the difficulty in a mutually satisfactory manner. Archibald Campbell on behalf of the United States, and Captain James C. Prevost for Great Britain, met at Esquimalt on 27 June 1857. After a careful study of the treaty and a survey of the hydrographic conditions, Prevost decided that Rosario Strait was the one intended by the negotiators of the Treaty of 1846; after an equally careful investigation, Campbell decided in favor of the Canal de Haro. From these conclusions neither commissioner would move. Crampton, British Ambassador at Washington, suggested to President Pierce that a compromise line be selected, but this request was refused, as was also the proposal that the decision be left to the arbitration of representatives of Belgium, Switzerland, and Denmark.

Pending a solution of the difficulty, matters had become peaceful on the island, when suddenly, on 27 June 1859, Captain George Pickett, acting under the orders of Brigadier-General Harney, commandant of the Oregon Department, descended on the island with D Company of the 9th Infantry. Harney had taken this action on his own initiative for the purpose of protecting American settlers from Indian attacks, and "to resist all attempts at interference by the British authorities." The entire control of the island was vested in Pickett's force. This action was a breach of faith, and although applauded by the citizens of Washington, Harney was a source of considerable anxiety to his home government. Governor Douglas was ready to plunge the two great nations into war, but fortunately Admiral Baynes, in charge at Esquimalt, was a man of cooler mind, and he vetoed any precipitate action. The American Secretary of War sent General Winfield Scott to take temporary control in Oregon—an admirable appointment, as General Scott was a man of clear understanding and excellent judgment. He removed the American troops from San Juan; arranged with Admiral Baynes for a joint occupation to commence on 30 March 1860; and tried (though in this he was unsuccessful) to persuade General Harney to accept a command in another field.

Matters having been thus temporarily settled, General Scott departed for the East. Scarcely had he left the Territory when General Harney again proclaimed San Juan Island a part of Washington. Thereupon he was recalled to Washington and lightly reprimanded; the legislature of the territory at the same time passed a resolution of praise and gratitude and nominated General Harney for the Presidency of the Union.[2]

The people of Washington and Oregon Territories were, moreover, deeply enraged against General Scott. Writing a short time after this, a Western editor declared: "When the result of General Scott's negotiations with the British authorities in regard to the island of San Juan became known to the people of the Pacific Coast there was an almost universal surprise and indignation in regard to it. There were none to defend the action of the American commissioner; [an action] so disgraceful to the flag of his country and so unworthy the commission he bore."

During the Civil War the question of San Juan was forgotten

---

[2] Scott wondered "Whether it is safe in respect to our foreign relations, or just to the gallant officers and men of the Oregon Department, to leave them longer at so great a distance subject to the ignorance, passion and caprice of the headquarters of that department." *American State Papers: Executive Documents*, no. 65, pp. 190–1.

and it was not until 1871 that final action was taken to effect a settlement. By the Treaty of Washington of that year, Great Britain and the United States mutually agreed to leave the question to the decision of the Emperor of Germany.

B. *The Claims.* The British case rested on a very literal interpretation of the wording of the treaty. The channel that "separates the continent from Vancouver's Island," according to the proponents of the imperial view, could apply only to Rosario Strait, the strait nearest to the mainland. The Canal de Haro did not divide "the continent from Vancouver's Island," because it was already separated to the east by Rosario Strait. Again, the Canal de Haro in part of its course took a westerly direction, while Rosario Strait bore "southerly" in accordance with the treaty terms. A more potent argument for the British claim was found in the fact that Rosario Strait was used almost invariably by the mariners of the time. This strait, moreover, was the one marked on Vancouver's maps, and certain official American charts showed the boundary passing through Rosario Strait.

The most valid claim of the United States was founded upon the acknowledged fact that the only reason which led the negotiators of the Oregon Treaty to depart from the 49th parallel was to give all of Vancouver Island to Great Britain. The greater width and depth of the Canal de Haro was also urged in an attempt to prove it the logical channel, and evidence seemed to indicate that some, at least, of the original negotiators had the Canal de Haro in mind. Mr. McLane, American minister in London, had, in 1846, reported to his home government the outline of a proposal about to be made by the British government, in which the Canal de Haro was specifically mentioned. In an address to the Senate, Benton spoke of the line passing through this channel—a statement to which the British authorities took no exception. In refutation of the arguments favoring Rosario Strait, the American case enumerated maps of both countries in which the boundary was drawn through the Canal de Haro. Bancroft contended that "southerly" was intended only in contradistinction to "northerly"; and he further pointed out that the Canal de Haro had been surveyed and used by the Spanish and the Americans.

It is probable that the truth of the case was most clearly expressed by Ambassador Pakenham when he said: "It is my belief that neither Lord Aberdeen nor Mr. McLane nor Mr. Buchanan possessed at that time a sufficiently accurate knowledge of the geography or hydrography of the region in question to enable them to define more accurately what was the intended line of boundary than is expressed in the words of the treaty." He added further that neither of the lines suggested could "exactly fulfill the conditions of the treaty which, according to their literal tenor, would require the line to be traced along the middle of the channel (meaning the whole intervening space) which separates the continent from Vancouver's Island." Finally, a modern scholar has summarized the matter thus: "If the British diplomats had in mind the Rosario channel along which Vancouver had sailed, as traced on his chart, they kept it securely secret: and if the Americans had Haro Strait in mind they refrained from saying so. The terms of the treaty fitted either strait, or perhaps it would be more nearly correct to say, fitted neither strait." [3]

c. *The Decision.* The United States was fortunate in having as Ambassador to Berlin a gentleman of the reputation and wide learning of George Bancroft. When the problem of San Juan was left to the arbitration of the German Emperor, Bancroft prepared and presented the American case. Admiral Prevost, who as Captain Prevost had negotiated with Archibald Campbell some twelve years before, presented the British argument. At the insistence of the United States, the Emperor was requested to deliver a decision designating either the Canal de Haro or the Rosario Strait—no compromise was admissible.

On 21 October 1872 Emperor William delivered his verdict in the following terms:

"The claim of the Government of the United States,— viz., that the line of boundary between the dominions of

[3] Howay and Schofield, op. cit., Vol. I, p. 324.

His Britannic Majesty and the United States should be through the Canal de Haro—is most in accordance with the true interpretation of the Treaty concluded between the Government of His Britannic Majesty and that of the United States of America, dated at Washington, June 15, 1846.

WILLIAM."

Thus was finally settled as fairly and satisfactorily as might be, the final westward link of the boundary between the United States and the British Dominions on the continent of North America. The islands have proved of only modest value, and the memory of the contest for sovereignty is fast fading. Residents of the city of Victoria may still sigh as they view San Juan Island lying almost at their doors, but even they are resigned and the rest of Canada has forgotten.

The San Juan dispute ended in victory for the United States, as the Maine–New Brunswick controversy had, on the whole, been a victory for the British. Both were victories for peace.

3. The Lake of the Woods Boundary

The Treaty of 1783, which ended the American War of Independence, outlined the boundary that was to separate the revolted colonies from British North America, but, as has been pointed out before, this treaty was drawn up by men who possessed only the most elementary and inadequate knowledge of the geographical conditions with which they dealt so confidently. The result was a long succession of disputes, which for many years endangered the peace and disturbed the relations of Britain and America. One of the smallest and least momentous of these disputes was that connected with the Lake of the Woods.

A glance at a map of the boundary between Minnesota and

Manitoba shows the line running due east along the 49th parallel of north latitude well into the center of the Lake of the Woods. It then takes a sharp turn to the north, crossing a broad peninsula to meet a narrow inlet of the lake on the northern side. Thence it proceeds through the center of the lake in a southerly direction to the head of Rainy River. Thus, the line seems to take an excursion northward simply for the purpose of cutting off from Manitoba this wide peninsula. The explanation of this seemingly unaccountable divergence from the straight line is to be found in the inadequate geographical knowledge of British and American diplomats of the last two decades of the eighteenth and the early years of the nineteenth centuries.

Article II of the Treaty of 1783, after tracing the boundary from the Atlantic Ocean to the Lake of the Woods, proceeded, "through the said Lake to the northwestern point thereof, and from thence on a due west course to the River Mississippi." Doubts shortly arose as to the possibility of meeting the Mississippi by drawing a line due west from the point thus designated. Consequently, in the Treaty of Amity and Commerce (Jay Treaty) of 1794, it was agreed that if, as a result of a joint survey of the headwaters of the Mississippi, it was proved that no such line could be drawn, then "the two parties will proceed by amicable negotiation to regulate the boundary line in that quarter . . . according to justice and material convenience, and in conformity with the intent of the said Treaty."

It having been agreed after the War of 1812–15 that the boundary between Canada and the United States should follow the 49th parallel of north latitude from the Lake of the Woods to the summit of the Stony Mountains, the following article was approved in the Convention of 1818 between Great Britain and the United States:

"It is agreed that a line drawn from the most northwestern point of the Lake of the Woods along the 49th parallel of the north latitude, or, if the said point shall not be in the 49th parallel, then that a line drawn from the said point due

197

north or south as the case may be until the said line shall intersect the said parallel of north latitude, and from the point of such intersection due west along and with the said parallel, shall be the line of demarkation between the territories of the United States and those of His Britannic Majesty."

It was the wording of this article that ultimately caused the idiosyncrasy of the modern boundary.

In the same year a joint boundary commission was appointed and by 1826 the line had been traced through the Great Lakes, and the "most northwestern" corner of the Lake of the Woods had been decided upon and marked.

It was not until April 1870 that difficulties arose over the boundary defined in 1818. In that month, however, a party of American engineers reported that a Hudson's Bay Company's post to the north of Pembina was, in fact, on American soil. This report led President Grant to insert in his annual message a plea for the final settlement and demarcation of this part of the international boundary. Congress and the British government having agreed, a joint commission was appointed. Archibald Campbell, who had represented the United States in the San Juan boundary dispute, was the American commissioner, and Captain D. R. Cameron, R.A., was associated with him on behalf of Great Britain.

The first meeting was held on 16 September 1871 at Pembina, and here the methods of procedure were agreed upon. After a careful search the monument raised in 1826 to mark the northwestern point of the Lake of the Woods was discovered, and though the British commissioner at first refused to agree, this point was ultimately accepted as correct. The temporary refusal of Captain Cameron was made in the hope that the home governments might make some political arrangement by which Canada could retain the peninsula that jutted out into the lake just south of the "most northwestern" point. On this peninsula the Canadians already had a primitive post, and a wagon road joining it to Fort Garry—afterwards Winnipeg. As the home governments could not reach any agreement, Captain Cameron complied with his instructions and agreed to the American contention.

This matter settled, the remainder of the problem was purely scientific, and on 29 May 1876 the reports were certified and duly attested in London.

Although comparatively unimportant, the final demarcation of this section of the boundary was unnecessarily exact, and the peninsula in dispute might well have been surrendered by the United States. The result would have been a minute financial and territorial loss, and in view of the Canadian post established on the peninsula, such an action would have been very well received in the Dominion. Legally, however, the United States was only maintaining her rights, and the territory was properly allotted.

4. The Bering Sea Arbitration

A. *The Problem.* By an imperial ukase issued on 7 September 1821, Alexander I, Emperor of Russia, granted to the Russian-American Company exclusive rights in commerce and fishing on the west coast of North America above the 51st degree of north latitude. He further asserted the sole jurisdiction of Russia over Bering Sea to a distance of one hundred Italian miles from the coast. Foreign vessels violating this edict would be liable to capture and confiscation. John Quincy Adams, American Secretary of State, joined with the British government in a strong protest against these pretensions, and as a result, in the Treaties of 1824 and 1825, negotiated respectively with the United States and Great Britain, Russia formally agreed to restrict her claim of exclusive jurisdiction "to the reach of a cannon-shot from shore."

The Emperor of Russia, in a convention signed at Washington on 30 March 1867, transferred to the United States the Russian title to "all the territory and dominion now possessed on the continent of North America and in the adjacent islands." The eastern boundary of the territory thus ceded was defined in the Treaty of 1825 with Great Britain. The western boundary, commencing in Bering Straits, proceeded "due north without limitation." South of the straits the line ran through Bering Sea "to the meridian of 172° west longitude: thence from the intersection of that meridian in a southwesterly direction . . . to the meridian of 193° west longitude so as to include in the territory conveyed the whole of the Aleutian Islands east of that meridian."

The particular value of Alaska at this time was due to the abundance of fur-bearing animals and the presence of the extensive seal-fisheries that were centered on the Pribilof Islands. The sealing industry had commenced as early as 1706 when the Russian ship *Vladimir* had taken two thousand pelts to an Asiatic port. The business as carried on by the Russian-American Company was purely a land enterprise, and it was not until 1866 that a certain Captain Hugh McKay perceived the possibilities of pelagic sealing. This gentleman was a British sailing master using Victoria as his base, and by 1890 that picturesque port had become the center of a considerable sealing industry. At its height, more than fifty ships were employed annually in the sealing business for Canadian firms.

So successful were the efforts of these companies that the number of seals annually reaching the breeding-grounds on the Pribilof Islands rapidly decreased, and the danger of total extermination became serious. The American firm of Hutchinson, Kobel and Company had leased the Pribilof rookeries from the United States government in 1869, but their lease was shortly transferred to the Alaska Commercial Company. This company, like its predecessors, confined its activities to the capture of the seals during the breeding season when the animals were helpless on the rocks of St. Paul, St. George, and other islands. The profits of the company soon began to suffer serious depreciation, due to the diminished size of the herds, which in turn resulted largely from the pelagic activities of Canadian ships (a few Americans,

Russians, and Japanese also engaged in this business), and to the reduced price received in the world markets as a result of this competition.

A number of regulatory statutes were enacted by the American government with a view to the conservation of the seal herds, but it was not until 1881 that, as a result of repeated solicitations made by the Alaska Company, any drastic action was taken. In that year a United States Treasury order was issued which, inferentially at least, proclaimed the greater portion of Bering Sea as a *mare clausum*. This ruling was confirmed in 1886 by Daniel Manning, then Secretary of the Treasury, and in August of that year three Canadian vessels were seized in Bering Sea. Although these vessels had been captured at a distance of over sixty miles from the nearest land, they were confiscated, condemned, and sold; their masters were found guilty of killing seals "within the limits of the Alaska Territory or the waters thereof," and were fined. Judge Dawson, of Sitka, in condemning these vessels, had acted under direct instructions from the Attorney General of the United States, and there could be no mistaking the issue, although Secretary Blaine later denied that a claim to Bering Sea as a *mare clausum* had ever been made. At that time he declared that the Canadians were arrested because engaged in a traffic that was *contra bonos mores*. The British government entered an immediate and formal protest. In the following year five more Canadian vessels were captured, and the British government, actuated by the intense feeling aroused in the Dominion, again vigorously protested. During 1888 Secretary Bayard attempted to arrange an international conference, but at the request of the Canadian government, which was preparing a monograph on the problem, Great Britain withdrew and the projected conference was never convened.

Throughout this period popular resentment had been rising in Canada against what were considered to be the arbitrary actions of the American authorities. The sealing industry in Victoria was threatened with disaster. "It is monstrous," wrote the editor of the Ottawa *Journal*, "that a vessel should be seized on the open sea, its contents rifled, itself confiscated, mayhap its owners jailed, all on the strength of a single nation's self-authorized legislation." The Victoria *Colonist* was no less emphatic: "The idea of cutting off a part of the ocean by a line in great part purely imaginary, and then calling the part so cut off a closed sea, is an act for which there is neither law nor reason." The same paper expressed its opinion of the motives actuating the Washington government when it stated that "the cruiser *Rush* was the Alaska Fur Company's scarecrow—nothing else." The matter aroused in Canada a feeling decidedly hostile to the United States, but it must be recognized that the Canadian methods of sealing were rapidly destroying the herds and that a few years more would have ended the industry entirely. The methods employed and arguments used by the United States were unfortunate, but some serious action was necessary.

During the years 1888 and 1889 the problem of the Bering Sea fisheries was canvassed in all of its phases by American legislators and press. In the latter year five more Canadian ships were seized, while three others were warned to leave the sea. As one American historian has phrased it, "in Great Britain public opinion became much aroused, and in Canada it was still more excited. In the United States Republicans and Democrats vied with each other in 'twisting the Lion's tail.' " [4] Nor was international friendship increased by the imperious tones of Lord Salisbury, or the crude and prejudiced bluntness of Secretary Blaine. Ultimately, however, the practical common sense of the two nations prevailed, a *modus vivendi* was agreed upon as a temporary expedient, and after many fruitless attempts the diplomatic obstructions were overcome and a treaty of arbitration was signed on 29 February 1892. By this treaty the signatory powers agreed to refer the problem for settlement to a judicial tribunal composed as follows: two members were to be appointed by the President of the United States; two by the Queen of Great Britain; and one each by the President of the French Republic,

[4] Willis F. Johnson: *America's Foreign Relations* (New York, 1916), Vol. I, p. 102.

the King of Italy, and the King of Sweden. The gentlemen appointed were required to be "jurists of distinguished reputation in their respective countries," and the fourteenth article provided that "the high contracting parties agree to consider the result of the proceedings of the Tribunal of Arbitration as a full, perfect, and final settlement of all the questions referred to it by the arbitrators."

B. *The Tribunal and the Five Points.* The first session of the tribunal was held in Paris on 23 February 1893. The judges appointed by the President of the United States were John M. Harlan, of the Supreme Court, and Senator John T. Morgan. Lord Hannen, of the High Court of Appeal, and Sir John Thompson, Minister of Justice and Attorney General of Canada, were appointed by the British Crown. The neutral arbitrators were: Baron Alphonse de Courcel of France; the Marquis Emilio Visconti Venosta of Italy; and Mr. Gregers Gram, a minister of state of Norway and Sweden.

The questions to be decided were summarized in five articles, as follows:

"I. What exclusive jurisdiction in the sea now known as the Bering's Sea, and what exclusive rights in the seal fisheries therein, did Russia assert, and exercise prior and up to the time of the transfer of Alaska to the United States?

"II. How far were these claims of jurisdiction as to the seal fisheries recognized and conceded by Great Britain?

"III. Was the body of water now known as the Bering's Sea included in the phrase 'Pacific Ocean,' as used in the Treaty of 1825 between Great Britain and Russia; and what rights, if any, in the Bering's Sea were held and exclusively exercised by Russia after the said Treaty?

"IV. Did not all the rights of Russia as to jurisdiction, and as to the seal fisheries in Bering Sea east of the water boundary in the Treaty between the United States and Russia of the 30th of March, 1867, pass unimpaired to the United States under that Treaty?

"V. Has the United States any right, and, if so, what right, of protection of property in the fur seals frequenting the Islands of the United States in Bering Sea, when such seals are found outside the ordinary three-mile limit?"

The two nations further agreed that if the foregoing questions were settled in such a way that "the concurrence of Great Britain is necessary to the establishment of regulations for the proper protection and preservation of the fur seal . . . the Arbitrators shall then determine what concurrent regulations . . . are necessary." Provision was also made for the determination of an indemnity if the tribunal found that the United States had exceeded its legal right in confiscating Canadian vessels.

c. *The American Case.* The case of the United States goverment was carefully prepared, and was presented by attorneys of outstanding ability. Although Secretary Blaine had distinctly stated that the United States did not regard Bering Sea as a *mare clausum*, it seems impossible to interpret otherwise the claims of the American case. In the argument the United States declared that Russia had acquired a proscriptive right to sovereignty in Bering Sea through immemorial use. Alexander I had claimed this right in the ukase of 1821, and Russia had enjoyed it undisturbed until 1867, when it was transferred inviolate to the government of the United States. The case declared emphatically that Russia had ceded all her rights to land and sea in North America to the United States in 1867. In support of this claim the American case cited the various acts of Congress, the letters of the Treasury Department, and the judicial decisions in connection with the confiscated vessels. It was further argued that the term "Pacific Ocean," as used in the treaties of 1824 and 1825, did not apply to Bering Sea, and that various actions taken by Russia between 1825 and 1867 confirmed her title to undisputed sovereignty in Bering Sea.

On the fifth question before the tribunal the American contention was susceptible of more logical and more plausible support. The United States claimed "a right of protection and property in the fur seals frequenting the Pribiloff Islands when found outside the ordinary three mile limit, based upon the established principles of the common and the civil law, upon the practice of nations, upon the laws of natural history, and upon the common interests of mankind." A long description of the life and habits of the fur seal was detailed, and the fact that the seal herds regularly resorted to the Pribilof Islands was stressed. The herds spent every breeding season on this American territory, they left only in search of food, and they were, in fact, domestic animals in which the United States claimed an exclusive property right. Argument by analogy in support of the claim to supervision and protection beyond the three-mile limit was based on the British defense of the Irish oyster fisheries, the Scotch herring fisheries, and the pearl beds of Australia and Ceylon. Finally, the case demonstrated that if pelagic sealing continued without restriction, in a very few years the whole seal herd would be exterminated, resulting in an irreparable loss to mankind as a whole.

D. *The British Case.* Having pointed out that Bering Sea was the common highway to and from the Arctic Ocean, the northern part of the Yukon territory, and the Mackenzie River, the British case maintained that it must be "an open sea in which all nations of the world have a right to navigate and fish." The British case demonstrated by a series of historical notes that Russia had never before 1821 "asserted or exercised" any rights in the North Pacific to the exclusion of other nations. This claim was supported by an overwhelming mass of historical data including the works of almost every noted authority on the region. The imperial ukase of 1821 was the only attempt on the part of Russia to claim sovereign rights in Bering Sea, and this claim "was made the subject of immediate and emphatic protest by Great Britain and the United States of America." Russia then "unequivocally withdrew her claims." The Treaties of 1824 and 1825 declared and recognized the rights of subjects of the United States and Great Britain to navigate and fish in all parts of the sea beyond the territorial limit of three statute miles. Between 1825 and 1867 these rights were freely exercised by the vessels of many

parallel of north latitude there was to be a closed season each year from 1 May to 31 July. Only sailing vessels bearing special licenses could engage in the industry. Indians hunting for their personal benefit were exempt, but all others engaged in sealing were to be subject to supervision by either government. No use was to be made of firearms, nets, or explosives. These regulations were to remain in force for five years, but could be abolished or modified by common agreement. They were to be examined every five years with a view to revision.

The tribunal further urged: (1) the desirability of supplementary legislation by the governments of Canada and the United States; (2) a closed season everywhere for two years; and (3) the enactment of municipal measures to give effect to the regulations determined upon by the tribunal.

As the seizures of Canadian vessels had been declared illegal, the question of a financial indemnity now arose. The British claims amounted to $542,169.26 with interest at seven per cent. On 21 August 1894, Walter Q. Gresham, then Secretary of State, offered a lump sum of $425,000 in full payment—an offer at once accepted by Great Britain. But the American Congress was at that moment in an uncompromising mood and refused to pass the appropriation. Thereupon a joint commission was appointed by the two governments, and after discussions lasting until December 1897, Great Britain was awarded the sum of $473,151.26 —the money being duly voted by Congress.

There can be no reasonable doubt that, on questions of international law, the contentions of the United States were ill founded. The arguments presented by the counsel, and the dissenting opinions of the American members of the tribunal, do not carry conviction, and in the opinion of all modern and reputable authorities the American case was not legally tenable. It was unfortunate that America, who had ever prided herself upon being the foremost nation in declaring the inviolability of property at sea, should thus flagrantly and illegally violate the very principles for which she had so long and bravely contended.

F. *The Reception of the Award and Further Developments.* Public opinion in Canada was gratified by the legal justification of the British case. But this gratification was tempered with doubt in regard to the probable effect that the regulations would exert upon the Canadian sealing industry. The Ottawa *Citizen* stated that "while the Arbitrators had solemnly recorded their judgment that the United States' contentions were untenable, they had, nevertheless, adopted provisions for the future government of the industry which practically handed it over to the Americans." The editor of the Victoria *Colonist* wrote: "These Regulations as effectively close the sea as if there had been an actual recognition of the claims of the Americans to jurisdiction." These typical quotations fairly voice the opinion of the majority of the Canadian people, who, being unaware of, or refusing to credit, the terrible destruction consequent upon pelagic sealing, could not appreciate the imperative necessity of such strict control. Although not always accepted with the best of grace, the regulations were, in almost every case, scrupulously obeyed.

In the United States the award was viewed in a different light. Chagrined at the summary treatment meted out to the American case, the people of the United States, nevertheless, soon realized that in securing the regulations they had in fact won their case. "The decision," said the New York *World*, "seems to be against the United States. Really it gives the government and its lessee, the fur company, all that was rightly asked." Edward J. Phelps, one of the American counsel before the tribunal of arbitration, declared that "the stringent regulations propounded on the restriction of pelagic sealing will amount . . . to a substantial prohibition of it, and give the United States all the fruits they would have obtained by a decree in favor of the claim of right."

At the end of the five-year period during which the regulations were to be operative, matters tended to return to their previous lawless state—a condition that was intensified by the growing competition of Japanese sealing vessels. Although the United States forbade its citizens to engage in pelagic sealing, the Canadian government took no such action, and general dissatisfaction was expressed in the United States. After a great deal of discussion the matter was referred, with many other Canadian-American problems, to a joint tribunal composed of six representatives of each country. This tribunal began its sessions at Quebec on 23 August 1898, but, owing to trouble over the Alaskan boundary question, it dissolved with nothing material accomplished. In 1897 a provisional treaty was signed by Russia, Japan, and the United States, but as the British government refused to acquiesce in its terms, it was never enforced.

After more than a decade of futile attempts at agreement and regulation, a fifteen-year agreement was signed by Russia, Japan, Canada, and the United States. By this agreement of 7 July 1912, there was to be no pelagic sealing north of the 35th parallel of north latitude. The United States was to divide its catch as follows: 70% for herself; 15% to Canada; 15% to Japan. Japan was to give Canada 10% of her total catch, and the same amount to Russia and the United States. Finally, Russia was to divide 30% of her catch equally between Canada and Japan. By these terms the United States received a practical monopoly, but agreed to apportion her gains among those who had been her competitors. By 1912 the annual catch of Canada, Russia, and Japan was quite insignificant.

The award of the Paris Tribunal ended the halcyon days of the Canadian sealing fleet, but had the indiscriminate slaughter of pregnant and nursing animals continued, as in the years from 1865 to 1890, the whole herd would shortly have been exterminated. Under the new conditions the permanence of the sealing industry was assured and the whole problem disappeared from the realm of international contention. The decision in this case, moreover, provided a precedent that may well prove of the greatest value in solving problems associated with salmon and halibut fisheries on the high seas in the same geographical region.

7

The Fisheries Controversy

1. A Century of Contention

The fishing banks of Newfoundland and Labrador provided the incentive for the first industrial activity undertaken by Europeans on the continent of North America. The Breton sailors who followed Jacques Cartier developed a flourishing and dependable trade based on the unlimited supply of marine food discovered in the northwestern Atlantic. So productive did this undertaking become that other nations soon turned covetous eyes upon the shores of Newfoundland, and English fishermen began to invade the waters hitherto monopolized by France. By virtue of the voyage of Sir Humphrey Gilbert, England claimed the island as her own—an assertion of title vigorously opposed by the French. After many years of strife France gave up the battle and, in the disastrous Treaty of Utrecht (1713), admitted the sovereignty of Great Britain, and received in return certain carefully restricted privileges pertaining to the fisheries that her citizens had so largely developed.

With France practically eliminated, sixty years passed in an uneventful manner, but with the success of the American Revolution the controversy again started, involving not alone the right of fishing in the waters of Newfoundland and Labrador, but certain vested interests in the Gulf of St. Lawrence, the

Atlantic coast of Nova Scotia, and the Bay of Fundy. The whole problem became known as the North Atlantic Coast Fisheries Dispute, and down to the present day it has been an almost constant, and a most irritating, factor in the international relations of the United States, Great Britain, Newfoundland, and Canada. Arbitrary actions by local authorities, disregard of essential restrictions by fishing vessels, and the completely divergent and contradictory claims of two great nations produced a series of exasperating incidents, which on a few occasions threatened serious consequences, and which always acted as a disturbing factor by the prevention of complete understanding and international harmony.

As with so many other problems on this continent, the fisheries dispute was a product of the American Revolution. Before 1776, British subjects in Boston, New York, or Charlestown had enjoyed precisely the same rights of participation in the Atlantic fisheries as had their fellow citizens in Halifax, Quebec, or London. They were equally subjects of the British Crown, in which reposed the title of ownership. With the enunciation of the Declaration of Independence, however, and in its subsequent recognition by Great Britain, the rights of the citizens of the United States in regard to the fisheries of Nova Scotia, Newfoundland, and the Gulf of St. Lawrence became obscured. During the negotiations in Paris that ended the Revolutionary War, a clear distinction became apparent between the "shore" fisheries and the "bank" fisheries. Great Britain had previously claimed the right to exclude foreign vessels not only from fishing within territorial waters, but even from fishing on the "banks," many of which were thirty or forty miles from the shore. This claim had been agreed to by both France and Spain. With the strange complacency that marked the British conduct during the Paris negotiations, it was shortly agreed that "the people of the United States shall *continue to enjoy* unmolested the right" to indulge in the bank fisheries, and that they should *"have the liberty* to take fish" in territorial or coast waters. Of this distinction in wording much was to be said later.

The American negotiators at Paris, especially Franklin, Jay, and above all Adams, adhered to the statement that prior to Independence the right of fishing was vested equally in the mother country and the colonies, and that when these separated, equal rights accrued to each. In later years the British government asserted that it had agreed to no such proposal, and the wording of Article III of the Treaty of 1783 at least gives room for doubt:

> "It is agreed that the people of the United States *shall continue to enjoy unmolested, the right to take fish of any kind on the Grand Bank and on all the other banks of Newfoundland:* also in the Gulf of St. Lawrence and at all other places in the sea where the inhabitants of both countries used at any time heretofore to fish: and also, that *they shall have the liberty to take fish of every kind on such part of the coast* of Newfoundland as British fishermen shall use, but not to dry or cure the same on that island: and also on the coasts, bays, and creeks of all other of His Britannic Majesty's dominions in America: and that the American fishermen shall have liberty to dry and cure fish in any of the unsettled bays, harbors, and creeks of Nova Scotia, Magdalen Islands and Labrador, so long as the same shall remain unsettled, and so soon as the same or either of them shall be settled it shall not be lawful for the said fishermen to dry or cure fish at such settlements without a previous agreement for that purpose with the inhabitants, proprietors or possessors of the ground."

The conflict of definitions embodied in the use of the words "right" and "liberty" formed the basis for all subsequent disputes in regard to the Atlantic fisheries. The United States claimed that its nationals enjoyed the advantages here enumerated as inalienable "rights" which could not be affected by any future decision of Great Britain, nor be abrogated by war. The British leaders, however, disputed this interpretation and, while admitting the right of Americans to take fish on the banks that

take, dry, and cure Fish on Certain Coasts, Bays, Harbors and Creeks of His Britannic Majesty's Dominions in America, it is agreed between the high contracting Parties, that the Inhabitants of the said United States shall have forever, in common with the subjects of His Britannic Majesty, the Liberty to take Fish of every kind on that part of the southern Coast of Newfoundland which extends from Cape Ray to the Ramean Islands, on the Western and Northern Coast of Newfoundland, from the said Cape Ray to the Guerpon Islands, on the shores of the Magdalen Islands, and also on the Coasts, Bays, Harbors and Creeks from Mt. Joly on the southern Coast of Labrador, to and through the straits of Belle Isle, and thence northwardly indefinitely along the Coast, without prejudice however, to any of the exclusive Rights of the Hudson Bay Company; and that the American Fisherman shall also have the liberty forever to dry and cure Fish in any of the unsettled Bays, Harbors and Creeks, of the southern part of the Coast of Newfoundland hereabove described, and of the Coast of Labrador; but, so soon as the same or any portion thereof shall be settled, it shall not be lawful for the said Fisherman to dry or cure Fish at such portion so settled, without previous agreement for such purpose with the Inhabitants, Proprietors, or Possessors of the ground, and the United States hereby denounces forever, any Liberty heretofore enjoyed or claimed by the Inhabitants thereof to take, dry or cure Fish, on, or within, three marine miles of any of the Coasts, Bays, Creeks or Harbors of His Britannic Majesty's Dominions in America not included within the above mentioned limits: provided, however, that the American Fishermen shall be admitted to enter such Bays or Harbours for the purpose of shelter and of repairing Damages therein, of purchasing wood, and of obtaining Water, and for no other purpose whatsoever. But they shall be under such restrictions as may be necessary to prevent their taking, drying or curing Fish therein, or in any other manner whatever abusing the Privileges hereby reserved to them."

216

The wording of this article apparently supported the British contention as regards the interpretation of the Treaty of 1783, for in regard to the privileges guaranteed to American fishermen the word "liberty" rather than "right" is again employed. The convention, moreover, gravely restricted the *liberty* to be enjoyed by the United States. In return for the privilege of drying and curing fish in certain uninhabited regions, the American commissioners specifically renounced all claim to the enjoyment of the fisheries outside the limits definitely prescribed. Although American vessels were permitted, under stress of weather or other circumstances, to enter any harbor or bay in the North Atlantic, they were in so doing to be subject to British supervision. The rights here acquired, or, as Gallatin and Rush claimed, reasserted, were given in perpetuity, and were not subject to abrogation by war. Thus viewed, the Convention of 1818 was a compromise; the United States gained certain perpetual rights, but Great Britain succeeded in greatly restricting the area over which any American claim could be asserted.

There were two outstanding defects in the convention as finally signed, and it was these two points that formed the basis of the dispute that later developed. According to this agreement, American fishermen were to have the liberty of taking fish "in common with the subjects of His Britannic Majesty." Now, did this signify that the Americans were to enjoy complete national autonomy in all places frequented by British fishermen (within the prescribed limits), or did the words "in common" mean that the American vessels and crews were to be subject to the same restrictions as their British competitors? In other words, were the fishing regulations imposed by Great Britain (later Canada and Newfoundland) to be binding upon American as well as British and colonial fishermen? The convention definitely stated that, when taking refuge in harbors and bays not included in the treaty coast, American vessels were to be subject to British regulations. Did the failure to include such a specific statement mean that on the treaty coast the British authorities could legislate only for their own nationals? The British contention was that the

Americans had equal rights on the treaty coast, and that they, like the British, were subject to the rules of the territorial authorities. The United States argued that the treaty would have included a specific statement to this effect if it had been intended. Under similar circumstances France had contended that "liberty" meant that they could keep out the British. The Americans claimed that the words "in common" had been inserted to prevent any such claim by the United States, but that they did not mean that the imperial authorities could impose their regulations upon American vessels.

The second point on which differences developed was found in the renunciatory clause. The United States gave up all rights to fish within three miles of "the coasts, bays, creeks or harbors of His Britannic Majesty's dominions in America" not included in the treaty coast. The problem arose in regard to the line from which the three-mile limit was to be measured. Should this line of demarcation follow the sinuosities of the coast, or should it parallel a line drawn from headland to headland across the openings of each harbor or bay? Was every expanse of water denominated a "bay" to be closed to American vessels, even though it might be twenty miles wide? This was the claim of Great Britain, while the United States demanded that the boundary parallel every twist or turn of the coast, thus opening to American vessels every bay whose mouth was over six miles (three miles from each shore being territorial water) in width.

These two issues were discussed and debated for more than eighty years by the leading statesmen, politicians, and lawyers of two great nations, and more than once the threat of war was brought into the argument. Ultimately, by a somewhat unusual coincidence, the management of the foreign affairs of the British Empire and of the United States fell at the same time into the hands of reasonable, pacific, and intelligent men. The major issues involved were then settled in a very few months.

Although the faults of the Convention of 1818 were evident and though the various methods of interpretation were obvious to all, the document was signed, and in the following year, by

Parliamentary enactment and by Orders in Council, Great Britain instructed the Governor of Newfoundland to carry out the new arrangement to the best of his ability.

For some little time after the signing of the Convention of 1818 no matters of great moment disturbed the international harmony. It is interesting to note, however, that in correspondence with France in regard to the claim of that nation to exclusive rights in certain fishing waters off the Newfoundland coast, the United States accepted and urged the British case.

In 1836 the government of Nova Scotia, aroused by undoubted infringements of the treaty stipulations by American fishermen, passed more stringent regulatory statutes calculated to end these violations. Between 1820 and 1830 a few seizures had been made, but the extended coastline of British North America had offered an alluring prospect to unscrupulous American fishermen and traders, and in consequence a great deal of illicit fishing and trading had been accomplished with very little danger of interruption. The law now passed by Nova Scotia, and later embodied in the imperial statute of 1919, permitted customs officers, members of the Import and Excise Service, sheriffs and magistrates, to board any suspicious vessel found within territorial waters and to seize and confiscate it upon failure to comply with an order to leave within twenty-four hours. A fine of $200 was to be collected from any person who attempted to hinder the officers of the Crown in carrying out this duty. A similar law was enacted in Prince Edward Island.

2. *The* Washington *Incident*

In 1843 a real issue developed. In that year the American ship *Washington* was seized in the Bay of Fundy, though at a distance of ten miles from the shore, and condemned in a Canadian court. This seizure was made under the British construction of the

Convention of 1818, by which all "bays," except on the treaty coast, were closed to American vessels. As a result of the excitement caused by this event, Edward Everett and Lord Aberdeen carried on a protracted correspondence, in which each set forth again and again their conflicting views as to the interpretation of the Convention of 1818 in regard to the meaning of "bays."

As was to be expected, the controversy over the *Washington* aroused no little feeling in the United States, particularly in the sections of New England which relied to a great extent upon the Atlantic fishing trade for their existence. This high tension was reflected in a letter sent to his Secretary of State by President Fillmore, in which he expressed the hope that there might be found "some line of proceeding that will allay the present excitement and prevent any bloodshed." The advisability of sending an American warship to protect the citizens of the United States engaged in the fishing trade was discussed, and Great Britain countered with the promise of a fleet of small armed patrol vessels to assist in guarding the colonial waters. A heated discussion was carried on in the United States Senate, during which it was plainly stated that the object of the British enforcement laws was to compel the United States to enter into a reciprocity agreement with the colonies. As time passed, feeling among the fishing population became more and more intense, and during 1853 many fishing vessels left Gloucester and Boston equipped with arms and ammunition for protection against any action by British vessels. The danger involved in such a proceeding was apparent, and William L. Marcy, who by that time was Secretary of State, sent a circular to all port directors warning them against all acts of hostility. At the same time an American naval force was dispatched to the fishing-grounds for the protection of the national rights.

The point at issue was settled, though the principle was not established, by the declaration of the British government that, so far as the Bay of Fundy was concerned, American vessels would be allowed to sail and fish therein without molestation, as an act of grace, though the United States could assert no legal right. It was immediately made evident that similar treatment was not to be accorded American vessels in other large bays. In 1852 Daniel Webster, American Secretary of State, had practically admitted that the British contention in this regard was justified by the Treaty of 1818. His statement, which was officially given to the press, declared in part:

"It would appear that by a strict and rigid construction of this Article [Article I, Convention of 1818] fishing vessels of the United States are precluded from entering into bays or harbors of the British Provinces. . . . A bay, as is usually understood, is an arm or recess of the sea, entering from the ocean between capes or headlands; and the term is applied equally to small and large tracts of water thus situated. . . . The British authorities insist that England has a right to draw a line from headland to headland, and to capture all American fishermen who may follow their pursuits inside that line. It was undoubtedly an oversight in the Convention of 1818 to make so large a concession to England."

Shortly after this Webster went further and admitted that Great Britain was "undoubtedly right"—a concession that was used with effect in the British case presented at The Hague in 1909.

The famous reciprocity treaty was signed on 5 June 1854. This treaty was to endure until destroyed by the bad feeling incidental to the American Civil War. The treaty gave to American fishermen the enjoyment of all the British fisheries in North America, the privilege of purchasing bait and supplies in Canadian and Newfoundland ports, and exemption from all taxes except lighthouse dues. In return, the United States granted to British fishermen the right to pursue their occupation in American waters north of 39° north latitude, and there was a mutual reduction in customs dues. The treaty could be abrogated by either party on one year's notice, and this was given by the United States on 17 March 1865.

In 1856 the last act in the drama of the *Washington* was

staged, when by a vote of two to one the arbitration tribunal organized for the purpose declared the owner's claim for damages to be valid. The tribunal decided that the Convention of 1818 gave Great Britain no right to exclude American vessels from the Bay of Fundy, and that the United States had never renounced their right to fish in that bay.

The reciprocity treaty terminated in 1866, and during the negotiations for its renewal American fishermen were issued licenses that assured them of the same privileges they had enjoyed under the treaty. On 1 July 1867 the Dominion of Canada was formed; and on 8 January 1870, all efforts at renewing the reciprocity treaty having failed because of the hostility of the United States, by an Order in Council the Dominion ended the system of issuing licenses to American fishing vessels, and provision was made to prevent illegal encroachments on Canadian waters.

On 9 June 1870 George S. Boutwell, then American Secretary of the Treasury, issued a circular of instructions that was important in its bearing on one of the main points later to be at issue between Great Britain and the United States. In this dispatch the Secretary said: "Fishermen of the United States are bound to respect the laws and regulations for the regulation and preservation of the Fisheries *to the same extent to which they are applicable to British* or Canadian fishermen."

This statement was frequently quoted in the subsequent controversy concerning the jurisdiction of the British legislative bodies over American fishermen.

3. The Treaty of Washington

The many-sided Treaty of Washington, concluded on 8 May 1871, dealt with the fisheries problem in Articles 18 to 25 inclusive. These articles provided for the annulment of all duties on fish; American citizens were given the right to participate in all Canadian sea fisheries; Canadians received similar concessions in American waters north of the 39th degree of north latitude; and, finally, provision was made for the establishment of an arbitration board to decide the justice of the British claim that in this treaty the Empire had surrendered more rights than it had received in return. The board met at Halifax in 1877 and, conceding the validity of Britain's claim, awarded damages in the sum of $5,500,000. This amount has generally been considered, and justly, to have been excessive.

The next incident of international importance occurred in 1878 at Fortune Bay, Newfoundland. The inhabitants of this, Great Britain's oldest colony, were noted then, as they are today, for a sincere and somewhat unusual interest in matters of religion. As a result of this characteristic, there was among the laws of the colony a statute forbidding the pursuit of the fishing industry on the Sabbath Day. There was also a law designating certain closed seasons for particular methods sometimes employed in herring fishing. Many of the New England fishermen had so far forgotten their Puritan heritage as to be greatly annoyed at this restriction on the seventh day, and in many cases completely ignored the regulation. Moreover, they did not see the necessity of obeying a law that fixed an arbitrary closed season at the very time they most desired to fish. Naturally, this attitude caused an unfavorable reaction among the subjects of the Queen in Newfoundland, and on a certain Sabbath morning in January 1878 a body of indignant citizens put off their habitual calm and, descending upon a party of American fishermen who were pursuing their vocation in Fortune Bay, drove them off, declaring that they had violated the laws cited above, and that they had also made an illegal use of a seine. Again a sharp discussion arose between the British and American governments respecting the amenability of the American fishermen to the laws of Newfoundland. Great Britain supported the claim of the colony that American fishermen were subject to local laws while in the territorial waters, but the Department of State replied that the

Treaty of Washington, and the Convention of 1818 before it, had given citizens of the United States full rights to regulate their own conduct while engaged in the North Atlantic fisheries. To settle the matter temporarily and to remove the danger inhering in the existing situation, Great Britain agreed to pay compensation for the occurrence at Fortune Bay, on the ground that the individual citizens of Newfoundland had no authorization to take matters of control into their own hands. The Foreign Office stated, however, that it had no intention of giving up its contention in regard to the applicability of colonial laws to American fishermen within territorial waters.

The strict regulations imposed by the colonial governments upon their own and American fishing vessels, and the far-reaching measures taken to prevent illicit trade, were a continual source of annoyance to the American fishermen. In December 1884, delegates from nearly every fishing center in New England met at Gloucester and passed a rather violent resolution urging the government of the United States to repudiate the fishery clauses of the Treaty of Washington and "restore to our fishermen the rights taken from them by the Treaty of 1818."

At this time the industries of the United States were shielded by a very high tariff (though not so high as the tariffs since that date), and the New England delegation to Congress was insistent in its demand that similar protection be given the important fishery interests of New England. As a result, in 1885 the American government terminated the application of the fishery clauses of the Treaty of Washington.

In 1886 Canada countered with a law that specifically forbade the purchase of bait by American fishermen in Canadian ports, and provided for the seizure of any foreign vessel entering Canadian waters "for any purpose not permitted by treaty or convention of the United Kingdom or Canada for the time being in force." Numerous seizures of American vessels charged with illegal fishing, smuggling or breaches of the regulations of the Convention of 1818, brought about an acrimonious discussion in legislature and press. Americans charged that Canada was trying to force the United States into renewing the reciprocity agreement of 1854–66. On the other hand, Canadians denounced the actions of the United States as an attempt of big business to break down Canadian tariff walls. There was, obviously, more truth than imagination in each of these charges. Feeling in the United States became so strong that a retaliatory statute was enacted by Congress, which forbade all Canadian and Newfoundland fishing vessels to use American ports except as a measure of safety. Fortunately, this law was never put into effect.

In the same and following years Newfoundland passed laws increasing the restrictions on the catch and sale of bait fishes, and demanding that all who wished to take part in this trade first acquire licenses. In 1893, by the Foreign Fishing Vessels Act, these regulations were strengthened and enlarged to include the prohibition of recruiting crews for American vessels within Newfoundland waters.

A treaty was concluded on 15 February 1888 that provided for a complete and just settlement of all the points in dispute, but owing to the political situation in the United States, the Senate refused its ratification. Pending such action, a *modus vivendi* was agreed upon between Canada and the United States, by which American fishermen who had purchased licenses were relieved of all other restrictions. This was originally intended to operate for two years only, but at the end of that time it was continued in force, under statutory authority, until 1 January 1924.

Although the feeling aroused in the United States by the renewal of the fisheries troubles was at first directed against Canada and Newfoundland, the incidence of this ill will was soon transferred to Great Britain because of the activities of the Irish and other American groups afflicted with Anglophobia. As a recent author has said, "every frictional episode was systematically exaggerated and the permanent diplomatic settlement of all the controversies prevented." The accession, at this time, of Salisbury to the British premiership was only exceeded as a calamity by the appointment of James G. Blaine to the office of Secretary of State at Washington. Salisbury was uncompromising in his blunt use of the imperative, while Blaine, in many of his actions, adequately represented the hyphenated Americans whose enthusiastic support he received. From such men alone no possible solution could be expected—unless it were war. In spite of these obstacles, however, comparative calm reigned over this field of controversy between 1886 and 1905. This was due to the policy of Newfoundland in issuing licenses, and the practical good sense of the American fishermen in accepting this method of regulation rather than in trying to force a hasty settlement more in accord with their desires.

In 1902 an effort had been made by Secretary Hay to negotiate with Newfoundland. The Bond-Hay agreement, which was then drawn up, gave reciprocal freedom from customs duties on certain articles, and permitted the American fishermen to purchase bait and supplies in Newfoundland. There was a good deal of opposition to this agreement in Canada, as it would have deprived the Dominion of the lever it had been using in its constant effort to force the United States to agree to reciprocity. This convention would have been an excellent arrangement for both Newfoundland and American fishermen, though it would have hurt the business of the big canning and fish-products concerns of New England, as Newfoundland competition would not be hindered by a protective tariff. Henry Cabot Lodge, Senator from Massachusetts, led the forces of opposition in the United States, and as an election was approaching and these fishing companies were expected to contribute heavily to the Republican cause, it was found impossible to gain a favorable vote in the Senate. In 1904 all hope of ratification of the Bond-Hay convention was abandoned. The measure was also vetoed by the Imperial Parliament at the insistence of Canada.

The conflict now was really three-sided rather than two-sided. Canada wanted free entry for her fish into American ports, and wished to gain a general reciprocity agreement, though the general prosperity that had increasingly marked Canadian conditions after 1896 had reduced the urgency that had previously marked the Canadian approach to this problem. In return for a broad agreement on trade Canada was prepared to allow American fishermen to have access to the disputed waters. Ottawa also hoped that the imbroglio might result in the union of Newfoundland with the Dominion.

Newfoundland was obtaining about $15,000 a year from license fees. The island colony realized that in its control of the supply of bait it had the strongest of all levers, and in return for freedom of purchase it demanded access to the American markets.

The United States was not greatly averse to the admission of Newfoundland fish, but did seriously object to the proposed admission of the immensely larger Canadian catch. This would have crippled the New England industry.

The whole triangular relationship between the United States, Canada, and Great Britain had gone through a marked modification during the years 1895–1904. The United States, having recovered from the effects of the Civil War and having completed the conquest of the frontier, had become a nation of tremendous industrial and commercial activity. This vitality was finding expression in a modern form of imperialistic expansion, as was illustrated by the quite unnecessary war with Spain and the accessions of territory and prestige with which it was concluded. It is significant that in this conflict the United States was almost universally condemned by other nations, with the important exception of Great Britain. Although there were many matters at issue between Washington and London during these years, the general trend was toward increasing amity and a real though far from formal entente.

During the same period Canadian growth in economic strength, in population, and in political independence was reflected also in a general confidence and national unity that made it possible for Canadian representatives to speak with increased assurance in Anglo-American debates on Canadian issues. The adoption by the Liberal Party of the main principles of Macdonald's National Policy, the completion of one national transcontinental railway and the initial steps toward the creation of two others, and, above all, the movement into Canada of increasing numbers of immigrants, many of them from the United States itself, changed the whole spirit of the Canadian nation.

It is only against this general background that the final developments in the fisheries controversy can be logically interpreted.

In 1905 the fishing industry was once more thrown into confusion. Newfoundland repealed the Foreign Fishing Vessels Act, and enacted a new law forbidding Americans to purchase or to recruit crews in Newfoundland waters. Proving ineffective, this law was also repealed, and in 1906 a new bill, forbidding American captains to hire Newfoundland crews, was drawn up. As a result of earnest diplomatic representations from the United States and Great Britain, however, this law never went into effect, and after a great deal of discussion the following rules were agreed to as a temporary expedient, until some final settlement could be arranged:

1. American fishermen were allowed the use of purse seines.
2. Newfoundland sailors could be hired outside the three-mile limit.
3. Americans agreed to refrain from fishing on Sundays.
4. Americans agreed to make entries at customhouses.
5. Americans agreed to pay lighthouse dues.
6. Statute of 1906 was not to become effective.

In the following year this agreement was amended to forbid the use of purse seines. In 1908, Canadian representatives appeared in Washington to discuss the possibility of a general treaty to regulate the whole fisheries situation as far as these two countries were concerned. A tentative agreement was prepared, but it was not signed.

By a coincidence as fortunate as the conjuncture of Salisbury and Blaine had been unfortunate, there were in Washington at this time two men of unusual intellectual attainments who were actuated by a sincere desire for international understanding. These men held the responsible positions of American Secretary of State and British Ambassador to the United States, and were, respectively, Elihu Root and James Bryce. A further excellent indication of the probability of an era of good will and accommodation was found in the person of the British Minister of Foreign Affairs, Sir Edward Grey. The results produced by these three men in the promotion of international amity are a striking proof of the ability of honest and intelligent men to use the prevailing methods of diplomacy to produce a salutary result.

On 14 April 1908, there was signed at Washington by Root and Bryce an arbitration convention under which these two great world powers agreed henceforth to submit to arbitration at The Hague those differences "of a legal nature or relating to the interpretation of treaties" which had arisen or which might in the future arise. It at once became obvious that the northeastern fisheries question came within the scope of this convention, and on 27 January 1909 the two powers agreed to submit the legal aspects of this problem to The Hague for final and definitive settlement. This agreement provided for the selection of a tribunal under Rule 45 of the Hague Conventions; it outlined the methods of presentation and argument to be adopted; agreed that the Hague decision was to be subject to revision by the two parties; and specifically stated the seven questions to be submitted for decision.

4. The Hague Tribunal

Article 45 of the Hague Conventions was used as the basis for selecting the panel of judges who were to adjudicate the matter at issue. It was agreed that there should be one American member of the tribunal and one subject of the King, and these offices were filled by Judge George Grey, of the United States Circuit Court of Appeals, and Sir Charles Fitzpatrick, Chief Justice of Canada. There were also three neutral members: A. F. de Savornin Lohman, Minister of State in the Netherlands; Luis María Drago, former Minister of Foreign Affairs in the Argentine Republic, and author of the famous "Drago Doctrine"; and

229

Dr. Heinrich Lammasch, Professor of International Law in the University of Vienna, and member of the Upper House of the Austrian Parliament. Dr. Lammasch was to act as umpire and to preside over the sessions of the tribunal. Both he and Dr. Lohman had had previous experience in important international arbitrations, and their selection was most satisfactory. In fact, the whole court was composed of men of the highest judicial character, and to this is due, in a large measure, the success of its work and the universally favorable reception everywhere accorded its decisions.

The proceedings of the court of arbitration in this matter have been collected and published in twelve large volumes. Necessarily, then, all that can be attempted here is a statement of the problems, a brief and condensed summary of the leading arguments of either side, and an outline of the decision of the court. As previously indicated, the points at issue were summarized in seven questions, and these will be separately considered.

The first question submitted to the tribunal, and also perhaps the most important, was as follows:

Can Great Britain impose reasonable regulations,
1. As to hours, days, and seasons when fish may be taken on the treaty coast without the consent of the United States?
2. as to the methods, means, and implements to be used in taking fish, or in carrying on fishing operations upon such coast, and
3. as to any other matters of similar character relating to the fishing industry?

The matter here at issue rested primarily on the interpretation of the words "liberty" and "in common" as used in the Convention of 1818. Great Britain insisted that the "liberty" accorded the United States by that document was simply a privilege— "equivalent merely to permission." In support of this the British lawyers pointed to the phraseology of the convention whereby

Great Britain acknowledged the "right" of the Americans to the bank fisheries (which were outside territorial waters), but used the word "liberty" in regard to the shore fisheries. The United States, however, argued that "liberty" and "right" were here used with the same meaning or intent. The American counsel further contended that the Convention of 1818 was simply a restatement of the inalienable rights which the United States had always claimed, and which had been acknowledged in the Treaty of 1783, except in so far as these rights were specifically renounced in the convention itself.

Again, Great Britain argued that the words "in common" definitely limited the American sailors to such rights as were possessed by their British rivals. "Now there can be no pretence that British fishermen are not subject to the sovereign power of His Majesty and these words show that American fishermen are to have the same liberty as British fishermen, but no more." And again, "It was merely permission to fish, in common with British fishermen, and was necessarily subject to the right of regulation by the government of the country." The American lawyers replied, however, that the words "in common" had been inserted for a particular purpose. In a previous argument between Britain and France, in which the former had granted fishing privileges to French vessels, the government at Paris had attempted to interpret this action as a transfer of exclusive rights. They had then refused to share the fisheries with the British. It was to obviate the possibility of the recurrence of such a situation that Great Britain had insisted on the insertion of the words "in common" in the Anglo-American convention. The United States insisted that it was on a parity with Newfoundland in so far as the right to formulate regulations was concerned. For reasons of expediency, the American government could not make these regulations, but it claimed the right to approve or disapprove laws enacted by the island authorities. The United States agreed that some form of control was necessary and reserved the right to decide whether or not the fishery statutes from time to time enacted by Canada and Newfoundland were reasonable. Regula-

231

tions might very easily be enforced which were discriminatory and unfair.

Great Britain replied that, since the United States admitted the necessity of regulations, since the Newfoundland government was the logical body to enact such rules, and since the Convention of 1818 did not hint at any restriction upon the right of Great Britain in this regard, American fishermen were obliged to obey such laws in common with those of Great Britain. The Americans insisted, however, that the Convention of 1818 had definitely limited British sovereignty by granting certain perpetual liberties to the United States, and further, "that the government of the United States fails to find in the treaty any grant of right to the makers of the colonial law to interfere at all, whether reasonably or unreasonably, with the exercise of the American rights of fishery."

Finally, Great Britain contended that the Convention of 1818 bestowed a new and unrelated liberty upon American citizens, that the circumstances surrounding the negotiation and the wording of the Treaty of 1783 no longer had any bearing on the problem of fishing rights. This the United States denied, arguing that the War of 1812 had not abrogated the inalienable rights resident in the American government, and that the Convention of 1818 confirmed in favor of the United States, as against Great Britain, an international servitude.

In view of the obvious and fundamental divergence of the two interpretations—a divergence that had apparently existed in the minds of the framers of the convention, as well as in those of the men who now sought to explain it—a decision in the nature of a compromise was to be expected. Such a decision was given. The award upheld the right of Great Britain to make laws without the consent of the United States—this being an inalienable attribute of sovereignty—but such laws were not to violate the convention; they must be appropriate or necessary for the protection of the fisheries, or desirable on the grounds of public morality, and must apply without discrimination to American and British alike. Furthermore, all laws relating to these matters must be published, two months before enforcement, in the London, Canada, and Newfoundland gazettes. If the United States should consider any such law to be unreasonable, it might appeal to a permanent mixed commission, which was to be composed of one national of each country and, if necessary, a neutral referee. Finally, in regard to anterior actions of the two states, the tribunal decided that they should be subject to review by a joint commission, which would decide upon a satisfactory settlement. The tribunal itself agreed to appoint the third member of such a commission. This decision was later revised by mutual agreement, and in accordance with the provisions of the Root-Bryce agreement.

The second problem proposed to the Hague Tribunal for arbitration was as follows:

"Have the inhabitants of the United States, while exercising the liberties referred to in the said Article, a right to employ, as members of the fishing crews of their vessels, persons not inhabitants of the United States?"

Here the issue was less involved than in the first question. Great Britain claimed that the convention meant exactly what it said—that liberty to fish on the treaty coast was given to "the inhabitants of the United States." The American government maintained, on the contrary, that the intent of the treaty was to confer this privilege upon American vessels, or vessels owned by Americans, and that the nationality of the crew was immaterial. The difficulty that necessitated the insertion of this question had arisen from the practice of certain American owners who had annually sent vessels north under a very small crew and had relied on the services of hired Newfoundlanders to fill their holds with fish. A long diplomatic correspondence had centered on this practice, but no solution had been achieved. The British argument was logical and clear. Vessels, as such, can have no right; the American negotiators of the Convention of 1818 had been interested in supplying occupation for New Englanders, not for the residents of Newfoundland; and, finally, Secretary Evarts had admitted these facts (17 May 1880) in regard to the similar Washington treaty. The American counsel denied that Rush and Gallatin had been actuated by such motives in 1818; they criticized the British interpretation of Secretary Evarts's report; and contended that the hiring of men to fish for American owners was, in reality, the same thing as the Americans fishing themselves. Great Britain had simply admitted an American right and had made no stipulations as to how the inhabitants of the United States should profit from this right; and, in conclusion, it was contended that the term "inhabitants of the United States" was used only for the purpose of eliminating other foreign nationals.

The decision of The Hague was ingenious. The right of the United States to hire fishermen of other nationalities was admitted, but foreigners "employed as members of the fishing crews of American vessels" were to "derive no benefit or immunity from the Treaty." In other words, Americans were given the privilege of hiring whom they liked, but Great Britain was assured at the same time of a perfect right to refuse access to her waters to any foreigners or British citizens serving on American vessels. These rights were, of course, inherent in each nation as a sovereign state, and the Hague decision did no more than reiterate a platitude of international law.

The third question was defined thus:

> "Can the exercise by the inhabitants of the United States of the liberties referred to in the said article be subjected without the consent of the United States to the requirements of entry or report at customs-houses, or the payment of light, or harbor, or other dues, or to any other similar requirement, or condition or exaction?"

As interpreted by the British case, the question was whether or not "American fishing vessels were entitled to frequent the British coasts, bays, creeks, and even harbors, to land upon British territory, and to exercise all the privileges accorded to trading vessels, and yet to be exempt from the supervision which all nations exercise over all vessels (not only foreign, but their own) coming into their harbors and discharging upon their territory: and exempt also from contribution to the upkeep of lights necessary to the navigating of the waters."

The United States here admitted that it had not contended that the Convention of 1818 had given American fishing vessels the right to carry on commercial or trading activities in British ports. But after Great Britain had thrown open her colonial trade to the nations of the world, it then rested with the United States government whether or not American fishing vessels were to be allowed also to trade. The United States admitted, however, that when engaged in commercial ventures, her ships should pay harbor and light dues. When the vessels were engaged solely in fishing, no such obligation existed. British fishing vessels were not compelled to pay these taxes, and Americans were supposed to enjoy equal rights and immunities. Finally, both Lord Elgin and Sir Edward Grey had admitted that any such discrimination was unjust.

The British reply to these arguments was based on practical and geographical conditions. In a country such as Newfoundland it was quite impossible to prevent illicit trade by vessels that claimed to be engaged only in fishing. In view of this fact, the Newfoundland government announced that American vessels must report at customhouses that their character might be determined. It was also held to be logical that ships that were assisted by lights and flag signals should contribute to the maintenance of these necessities.

Taking cognizance of the fact that the necessity of reporting at customhouses might frequently cause unnecessary hardship and delay, the Hague Tribunal decided that American fishing vessels should report "if proper conveniences for doing so were provided." The obligation, moreover, was simply to report, and did not necessitate the obtaining of formal clearance papers. In regard to light and harbor taxes, "American vessels were not to be subject to dues not imposed upon Newfoundland fishermen."

The fourth question presented to the tribunal was somewhat different in character. Questions One, Two, and Three had dealt with American rights on the treaty coast: Question Four was concerned with certain special privileges extended to American vessels in other British waters. It was proposed as follows:

"Under the provision of the said Article, that the American fishermen shall be admitted to enter certain bays, or harbors, for shelter, repairs, wood, or water, and for no other purpose whatever, but that they shall be under such restrictions as may be necessary to prevent their taking, drying, or curing fish therein, or in any other manner whatever abusing the privileges thereby extended to them, is it permissible to impose restrictions making the exercise of such privileges conditional upon the payment of light, or harbor, or other dues, or entering or reporting at customs-houses or any similar conditions?"

The British case here reiterated the arguments used in Question Three, and pointed out that every vessel entering a harbor, whether under legal right or merely by privilege, was obliged, unless especially exempted, to pay all customary dues and to observe the regular formalities suitable to that act. The convention gave no special exemption to American craft, but on the contrary exposed them "to such restrictions as may be necessary to prevent . . . their abusing the privileges . . . extended to them." And, in fact, it was not until 1905 that any objection had been raised to the imposition of such restrictions.

The American reply was practical and conclusive. Due to the extended coastline of Newfoundland, and the few customhouses in operation, the necessity of reporting every time that an American vessel was driven in for shelter would cause a great deal of inconvenience—frequently necessitating a detour of fifty or one hundred miles to reach the nearest customhouse. Moreover, such a regulation would not "be necessary" to prevent "the taking, drying or curing of fish" within the prohibited area.

Here it appears that the right of the British authorities to issue regulations was undeniable, but these regulations should not be of such a character as to destroy the value of the privilege given to American ships. The local authorities were undoubtedly entitled to the knowledge of the presence of foreign vessels in their territorial waters, but care should be taken not to impose such rules as would unnecessarily hinder American fishermen engaged in the honest pursuit of their calling. On these grounds of common sense and humanity the tribunal decided that the imposition of restrictions making compulsory a report at a customhouse was not permissible. Nor was the levying of light and harbor dues. On the other hand, if an American vessel remained in British waters for forty-eight hours, the captain must report in person or by telegraph to a customs official "if reasonably convenient opportunity therefore is provided."

Question Five ranks with Question One as one of the two most important problems before the tribunal.

"From where must be measured 'the three marine miles off any of the coasts, bays, creeks, or harbors' referred to in the said article?"

The primary importance of the division involved resulted in a great expenditure of time, argument, and oratory. Fortunately, the matter lends itself to concise analysis.

The question was one of definition. The United States claimed that the expanse of territorial water was to be measured at three marine miles from a line that followed the sinuosities of the coast, with the exception of those bays and harbors which were less than six miles wide at the mouth (thus being entirely territorial). Great Britain argued for a literal interpretation of the convention. To the British lawyers a bay was a bay regardless of size or particular configuration. According to this definition, the line separating territorial waters from the open sea should be drawn parallel to another line joining the headlands of the coast. This same problem had arisen in connection with the argument over the Alaskan boundary. An exact interpretation of the wording of the convention undoubtedly upheld the British case, and so the tribunal awarded. "In the case of bays the three miles are to be measured from a straight line drawn across the body of water, at the place where it ceases to have the characteristics and configuration of a bay. At all other places the three marine miles are to be measured following the sinuosities of the coast." Realizing, however, the impracticability of this decision, the tribunal, through a doubtful interpretation of Article IV of the Root-Bryce agreement, advised the adoption of the rule heretofore used—particularly in the case of Conception Bay. This plan was that all partially enclosed bodies of water measuring ten miles or less from headland to headland should be considered to be territorial waters, or, for the purpose of this decision, bays. Certain other bays which were even larger were also recognized (apparently on historical grounds) as territorial waters.

This decision was not assented to by Judge Drago, who contributed a lengthy dissenting opinion.

Question Six was submitted as follows:

"Have the inhabitants of the United States the liberty under the said Article or otherwise to take fish in the bays, harbors and creeks of that part of the southern coast of Newfoundland which extends from Cape Ray to the Ramean Islands, or on the western and northern coasts of Newfoundland from Cape Ray to the Guispon Islands, or on the Magdalen Islands?"

This problem arose from a discovery of Sir Robert Bond in 1905, which had apparently never been considered before that time, and was from the British standpoint the weakest of the cases prepared. By a careful analysis of the wording of the convention, Sir Robert Bond had found that whereas American fishermen were given the liberty to fish "on the coast, bays, harbors and creeks from Mount Joly on the southern coast of Labrador . . ." they were given similar privileges only on the "coast" of Newfoundland and on the "shores" of the Magdalen

Islands. Here, argued the British case, was a clear distinction, and under the liberty to fish on the "coast" and "shores," American fishermen could not enter the bays, harbors, and creeks behind. In other words, they must confine themselves to the British territorial water outside the shore line, which, by the decision in Question Five, was to be drawn from headland to headland. A weak attempt was made to prove that this distinction had been undisturbed by negotiators in 1818.

Inasmuch as the American fishermen depended on these bays for bait fish, the decision was distinctly important, and the argument of the United States was sufficiently clear to convince the tribunal of its justice. Root and his assistants proved conclusively that no such distinction had been thought of in 1818, and that no just basis could be found for the British claim. As one eminent American scholar has written, "the question was political rather than legal, and seems to rest on no substantial basis of law or fact."

The tribunal ruled, very briefly, thus: "American inhabitants are entitled to fish in the bays, creeks and harbors of the Treaty coasts of Newfoundland, and the Magdalen Islands."

Another section of Question Six follows:

"Are the inhabitants of the United States whose vessels went to the Treaty coast for the purpose of exercising the liberties referred to in Article I of the Treaty of 1818 entitled to have for those vessels when duly authorized by the United States in that behalf, the commercial privileges of the Treaty coast accorded by agreement or otherwise to United States trading vessels generally?"

Stated in other terms, do American fishing vessels command the privileges generally accorded commercial craft? Can a single ship be at once a fishing vessel and a trader? Had Great Britain the right to close her ports to fishing schooners which sought to engage in commercial enterprises?

Great Britain contended that American fishermen could claim

no liberties in British waters except those conferred by the Convention of 1818; that no commercial privileges were then granted; and that the treaty did not give rights to vessels as vessels.

The United States replied that the treaty did not deny commercial privileges—that it did not concern itself with commerce at all. By other and later decrees Americans were given the right to carry on trade with the British colonies, and the United States, being a sovereign power, had the right to permit any of its subjects to act in a commercial capacity, even though that person were at the same time a fisherman. No stipulation in the treaty forbade inhabitants of the United States to act as traders and fishermen at one and the same time. American fishing vessels had American registry and were therefore entitled to trade under the American flag, and this was not forbidden by any existing agreement. All this, of course, entirely overlooked the right of Great Britain, also a sovereign nation, to close her ports to any vessels except fishing craft as agreed to in the Convention of 1818.

The British case was chiefly concerned with the practical problem involved. If an American vessel were allowed to trade and fish at the same time, all of the safeguards insisted upon in the Treaty of 1818 would be useless. The Americans would be able to establish their headquarters on British soil and fish or trade as occasion suited. Endless confusion would ensue. A fishing vessel was a fishing vessel, and apart from the liberties granted in 1818 it had no rights in British waters. Moreover, by international law, Great Britain (or any other state) could close its ports to foreign ships or any particular class of foreign ships, and consequently the imperial government (or the government of Newfoundland) could forbid all American trading vessels that also engaged in fishing to enter her harbors. American fishing vessels could use them only in accordance with the Treaty of 1818.

The decision of The Hague recognized the right of American vessels to fish, or to trade, but stated that these rights could not be used concurrently. This decision was, beyond all doubt, legally sound, and practically sensible. Any other award would have resulted in constant discord and endless confusion.

This ended the duty of the Hague Tribunal. As can be seen, the decisions handed down were, in almost every case, based upon a compromise, which found some justification in each case. The chief end in view was to settle the problems in a practical and workable manner, in order to obviate further collisions. Although this award was, on the whole, satisfactory to both parties, it was decided, as had been provided for in Article X of the Root-Bryce agreement, to revise the Hague decisions. For this purpose a joint commission met at Washington, and on 20 July 1912 announced a final and definite settlement. The modifications agreed upon by this commission were not of vital import, but were designed to eliminate all possible charges of injustice, and to provide machinery to deal with any further trouble that might arise in the future.

The final agreement may be summarized as follows:

Article 1. All future laws for the regulation of fisheries passed by Canada, Great Britain, or Newfoundland shall be promulgated and come into operation within the first 15 days of November each year, unless intended to apply to the conduct of fishing between the period from November to February, when it shall be promulgated at least six months before the first of February. These laws shall be published in the London *Gazette*, the Canada *Gazette*, and the Newfoundland *Gazette*. The dates fixed here, for promulgation, may be altered after ten years, on the agreement of the Permanent Mixed Fishery Commission. If the government of the United States should object to any such laws, as inconsistent with the Treaty of 1818, it may notify the government of Great Britain within forty-five days and may request that the said law be submitted to the Permanent Mixed Fishery Commission for decision. If the law is not contested, or if it is contested, but declared to be reasonable, it shall come into force: if declared unreasonable it shall not be applicable to the inhabitants of the United States. A Permanent Mixed Fishery Commission shall be established for Canada and another for Newfoundland. The United States shall appoint one member to each, and all shall be appointed for five years. The third member in each case shall be agreed upon by the two national members, or failing such agreement, shall be appointed by the Queen of Holland. The two national members must be summoned by Great Britain within thirty days from the date of the protest by the United States. If they are unable to agree, a third member shall be added, and a majority decision shall be final and binding.

Article 2. In the matter of bays it is agreed that "the limits of exclusion shall be drawn three miles seaward from a straight line across the bay in the part nearest the entrance at the first point where the width does not exceed ten miles." Here follows a definite settlement in regard to certain well-known bays, specifically excluding from this agreement any connection with Hudson Bay.

Article 3. It was agreed that the declaration of any or all the bays on the coast of Newfoundland, does not require consideration at present.

Article 4. This agreement to be ratified by the President and Senate of the United States and by His Britannic Majesty.

This final settlement was received with approbation in the four countries involved, and the whole course of the arbitration formed a most pleasing example of the possibilities of international adjudication when each side is willing to make concessions and to agree upon a just decision. The fisheries question had been a cancerous growth in the international relations of the English-speaking peoples, and at times had threatened to become malignant; yet by a few months of earnest and peaceful endeavor the danger was eliminated. To Lord Bryce, Elihu Root, and Sir

Edward Grey belong primarily the credit of this splendid achievement—assuredly a proof of the pragmatic value of interesting men of character in the conduct of international affairs.

The legal aspects of the fisheries problem were settled by the adjudication of the Hague Tribunal. The practical regulations to govern the conduct of the industry, however, were still somewhat uncertain. For the time being, Canada was content to allow the *modus vivendi* that had been effective since 1888 (see p. 225) to remain in effect. This was satisfactory also to the United States, and when the Underwood Tariff Bill of 1913 was enacted, it appeared as though a real era of good feeling were about to be inaugurated.

For some years after 1912 the problem of the northeastern fisheries remained quiescent, and the representatives of the two countries were able to devote some much-needed attention to such other problems as the protection of sockeye salmon on the Fraser River, the threatened extermination of the halibut off the coast of Alaska and northern British Columbia, the fisheries of Lake Champlain, the protection of the sturgeon fisheries in the Great Lakes, rules for the lobster industry of Nova Scotia, and the international protection of whales.

Under the pressure of war conditions, an agreement was reached early in 1918 by which the fishing vessels of each country were to be accorded in the ports of the other all the privileges enjoyed by domestic vessels.

On 2 September 1919 a treaty was signed at Washington providing for the protection of the sockeye salmon of the Fraser River. This industry had been steadily losing ground for many years, very largely as a result of the methods employed by American fishermen in taking the salmon before they entered the river. The treaty was received with great pleasure in British Columbia, though it was soon proved to be inadequate for its announced purpose.

During the Washington Conference of 1921, Sir Robert Borden, the leader of the Canadian representatives, took up with the American officials the question of a new treaty to regulate the international fisheries. A conference was arranged to consider the situation. On 15 July the United States canceled its war legislation, which had allowed Canadian vessels free access to American ports. This proved to be a signal for the renewal of some of the old difficulties. Within a week nine American vessels were seized by Canadian patrol boats for poaching in forbidden waters. The situation was further complicated by the enactment of the Fordney Tariff Bill, which raised an almost prohibitive wall against the importation of Canadian fish.

On 26 July the conference arranged by Sir Robert Borden reported, and although its recommendations were not adopted, they are worthy of serious consideration, as they undoubtedly point the way to the only really satisfactory solution of this most involved problem. The recommendations may be summarized as follows:

1. The markets of both countries should be made available to the fishermen of both, on equal terms.
2. The Treaty of 1818 should be so amended as to allow the fishing vessels of either country to enter and clear from the ports of either country.
3. The fishing vessels of either country should be allowed to dispose of their catches, and purchase bait, ice, coal, nets, lines, oil, provisions, and all other supplies in the ports of either country.
4. A treaty for the more adequate protection of the Fraser River sockeyes should be enacted.
5. A closed season for Pacific halibut should be enforced, between 16 November and 15 February, each year for at least ten years.

Canada would, of course, gain more from such an agreement than would the United States, but in the long run it would prove beneficial to the fishing industries of each country. The embattled cannery industries of Washington and New England, however, were unwilling to endorse such proposals, and in this attitude they were supported by the ultra-protectionist administration of President Harding.

Although irritated by the American cancellation of the war-time privileges, and the enactment of the Fordney tariff, the Canadian government continued to apply the rules of the *modus vivendi* in the hope that the American policy might soon be modified. During 1922 and 1923, however, opposition to this one-sided condition developed in Canada. During the session of the House of Commons in the latter year, vigorous expression was given to the Canadian feelings on this matter. Mr. Duff (Nova Scotia), speaking on this subject, declared:

"The Fordney Bill, as I have said, was very injurious to the people of Nova Scotia. For instance, the business in which I am most interested, fish, is hard hit, a duty of $1.60 per hundred pounds having been imposed on salt, dry fish . . . and on fresh fish, herring, mackerel, and so on a prohibitive duty of two cents a pound. . . . It is no wonder that all over Nova Scotia and the other two Maritime Provinces the fishermen are leaving for the United States, because they find that under the Fordney Tariff they cannot make a living."

Mr. Martell voiced the common sentiment when he pointed to the following solution:

"We have a weapon, I believe, in our hands. . . . [American vessels] are enabled by means of this licensing system to come into Canadian ports and use our ports to transship their catch, take bait, buy their nets, twine and all their other supplies and outfit and ship their goods through to the United States in bond . . . whereas when our own fishermen come in from the banks, if they wish to sell to the United States, which in days gone by took 40% of their catch, they are obliged to pay two cents a pound duty on fresh fish, which is practically a prohibitive rate. The United States vessels, I believe, would not be able to successfully

245

prosecute the catching of fresh fish if they were not allowed the use of our Canadian ports. . . . If they were denied that privilege I really believe that it would be conducive to the United States authorities negotiating with the Dominion government for reciprocity, at least on fish."

As a result of continued protests, the Canadian government finally notified the United States that after 31 December 1923 the privileges heretofore extended to the United States fishing vessels in Canadian ports would be discontinued. At the same time Ottawa issued a statement explaining that for upwards of thirty years Canada had granted these privileges to the United States, but that except for a brief period (1918–21) during which American war legislation had made the privileges reciprocal, the United States had done nothing to assist the Canadian fishermen. Canada had waited for over two years after the repeal of the American war legislation in the hope that the United States might again enact the rules of that time. "In this hope Canada has been disappointed. The government of the United States has not only not made provision for the restoration of the arrangements of 1918, but has by tariff provisions imposed additional duties upon Canadian fish. . . . From the action of the United States authorities the obvious conclusion was reached that little or no value was attached by the people of the United States to the privileges that Canada had been voluntarily extending for so long a period." These privileges in consequence were now to be withdrawn. It was ten years before they were restored, and the restoration was then only partial, extending the right of purchase of bait, ice, seines, and other supplies. These privileges have been renewed annually by Order in Council since 1933.

The fact is that the acute stage in the fisheries dispute between Canada and the United States gradually disappeared as the methods employed in the sea fisheries changed. In particular, the situation was affected by the introduction of Diesel-powered trawlers, which can sail great distances from home ports without the necessity of shipping crews and of obtaining bait and other supplies from ports in the vicinity of the fishing-grounds. Thus, the value of port privileges for the United States vessels on the Atlantic coast greatly diminished. Where port privileges were still of value, as in the halibut fishery on the Pacific, the need was reciprocal, and common privileges were granted by both sides. For a considerable period this was effected by legislation passed annually in each country and made applicable on a reciprocal basis. In 1950, by treaty, the privileges thus granted were put on a continuing basis subject to termination on twelve months' notice.

With the entry of Newfoundland into the Canadian federation, it was necessary to extend fishery privileges on the Atlantic banks to other foreign fishing vessels, particularly those of Portugal, in line with the pre-confederation practice in Newfoundland.

As a result of the commercial agreements of 1935 and 1938, there has also been some relaxation in the United States tariff policy on Canadian fishery products, which has been of the greatest importance to the Canadian fishing industry.

The outstanding fisheries problems between Canada and the United States during this period—and this is likely to be even more true in the future—have been in the field of conservation of the fisheries resources, and here the interests of the two countries are for the most part mutual.

On the Pacific coast the effect of the fur-seal agreement between Canada, the United States, Japan, and Russia has been preserved by a separate provisional agreement between Canada and the United States following the abrogation of the 1911 agreement by Japan in 1941.

The halibut convention that was originally signed in 1923 has been revised twice, once in 1930 and again in 1937. The result has been to give the International Fisheries Commission additional powers required for the preservation of this fishery. Discussions are now under way between the two governments with a view to still further revision.

A new and more effective convention for the protection, preservation, and extension of the sockeye salmon fisheries in the

Fraser River system was signed in 1930 and has already made a great contribution toward the protection and development of this industry.

In connection with the fisheries of the northeast Pacific, particularly the sockeye salmon and halibut fisheries, developed and maintained by the joint efforts of Canada and the United States, the two countries have during the past few years been closely allied in seeking an acceptable method of co-operation with other countries of the Pacific to ensure that the sacrifices involved in developing these fisheries to their highest sustained level of productivity will not be in vain. It is a very difficult problem, as these are for the most part high-seas fisheries and thus under international law open to the fishermen of all nations. Yet it is abundantly clear that both fisheries would long since have been utterly destroyed had it not been for the self-denying practices enforced on their own people by the governments of the United States and Canada. It would be manifestly unfair to allow foreign fishermen, who have made no contribution to the protection and development of the resource, to profit from and eventually destroy the results of the self-denial of the countries most directly concerned. Various proposals for a solution of this impasse have been suggested, but the problem is still far from solved.

On the Great Lakes, after many years of futile efforts to bring about a satisfactory agreement on conservation measures, a treaty between the two countries similar to the halibut treaty on the Pacific coast was signed in 1946. Although this treaty has not to date been ratified because of the opposition of certain local fishing interests in one of the states bordering on the Great Lakes, there are hopes that this opposition will subside and that the treaty will be brought into effect.

In the northwest Atlantic where, besides Canada and the United States, a number of European nations have exploited the fisheries of the international banks, Canada and the United States have co-operated in bringing about a multilateral convention between nine countries, providing for the constitution of an international commission for the scientific investigation of those stocks of fish that support the international fisheries of the area. Although this commission has not the regulatory powers of the two commissions on the Pacific coast, nevertheless it may recommend to the participating governments regulatory measures which they can adopt. The convention has been ratified by the required number of nations and is now in force.

Although the fisheries controversies of the past between Canada the United States have been moderated as a result of easier access to the available resources and the expansion of markets, this does not mean that problems do not exist. Any threatened denial of present markets would in all probability resuscitate some of the old and engender new controversies. Such a development might also lead to the partial or even complete nullification of the valuable co-operative efforts of the two countries toward the fullest utilization of their common fishery resources.

In the long range, it is as true today as it was three decades ago that final settlement of the fisheries problems between Canada and the United States will be achieved only when equal access to the resources is accompanied by like access to the markets of both countries. But in these days of floating canneries and long-distance mother ships, the new problem of the just allocation of rights in the fisheries on the high seas will present difficulties even more trying than those which troubled so long the relations between the United States and Canada. In facing these new problems, however, the peoples of these two North American countries will have common interests at stake and can be expected to substitute co-operation for the friction that has marked their past activities in this domain.

8

One Hundred Years
of Commercial Intercourse

---

1. Reciprocity and Tariffs, 1854-1911

It is now a platitude that economic interests constitute the most important factor in the business of international relations. There was a time when ambassadors, ministers, and other diplomatic representatives devoted themselves primarily to what was described as "high politics" and to the social, representational, and prestige functions appropriate to their status. Today, however, the successful diplomat, whatever his other qualifications, must be a competent man of business.

In the history of the relations of Canada and the United States the significance of the economic factors has been particularly clear and has been generally recognized. The American Revolution, the War of 1812, the various boundary disputes, the swinging tides of immigration and emigration, as well as the persistent debate over tariff and exchange problems, have all been the direct result of, or integral elements in, the economic development of North America. Today Canada and the United States have a larger trade than any other two countries in the world. Over seven billion dollars has been invested in Canada by American citizens, and Canadians own over one billion dollars' worth of American securities. Each country is the other's best customer, and each has a tremendous stake in the commercial welfare of its neighbor.

For the larger part of the history of the last hundred and fifty years the economic factors in the relations of the two countries may be summarized in the following generalizations: (1) the desire of the industrial and manufacturing interests of the United States to gain control of the vast storehouse of Canadian raw materials; (2) the attempts of these same interests to break down the Canadian tariff against manufactured articles, to the end that American goods might capture the Canadian market; (3) the bitter opposition, especially in the Western and Southern states, to any lowering of the American duties on raw materials—a step that would bring Canadian grain, minerals, dairy products, and fish into serious competition with the commodities of the American farmer, miner, and fisherman; (4) the desire of the Canadian farmer to gain freer access to the American market, and to purchase his supplies at the lowest figure regardless of the place of manufacture; (5) the fear of the Canadian industrial interests that any lowering of the national tariff on manufactured products would result in their extermination by their more powerful, highly developed, and favorably situated competitors in the United States. In both countries, but particularly in the United States, the high-tariff interests have generally maintained control. The American customs wall has been the admiration of protectionists throughout the world. But one result of this policy has been that Canadian goods, whether manufactured or in the raw, throughout the larger part of this period have faced great difficulties in obtaining effective access to the American consumer, with resulting economic distress to those Canadian producers who, like the fishermen of the Maritime Provinces, look to the United States as their logical market.

Within recent years, however, and especially since the beginning of the Second World War, the significance of the tariff as an element in Canadian-American relations has greatly diminished. The growth of cartelization through the establishment of branch factories in Canada or through equally effective contacts and agreements between United States and Canadian firms has resulted in a decline in the competitive element in both industrial and commercial circles. The effect of the Ottawa agreements of 1932, of the reciprocal trade agreements of 1935 and 1938, and, more important still, of the Hyde Park and similar arrangements developed during and after the war, has been to ensure a more rational division of markets (though this has not always been of benefit to the consumer). The tremendous expansion of Canadian industry has made it evident that, given anything like an equal market demand, Canadians can hold their own with even the most efficient of American corporations.

The history of independent commercial intercourse between Canada and the United States goes back only to the middle of the nineteenth century. It was between the years 1840 and 1849 that Canada first took over the active control of her own economic life. During this decade the last remnants of the Navigation Laws were abolished, and Great Britain, whose adoption of the policy of free trade seriously injured Canadian commerce, was henceforth treated in the matter of tariffs as a foreign state. Having lost its tariff preference in the British markets, Canadian trade came almost to a standstill, and the United Provinces were forced to turn to the United States for aid. The desire for reciprocity became more and more insistent and vigorous and during the great depression of 1849 a strong movement in favor of annexation developed in Montreal. But Canadians preferred reciprocity to annexation, and they even went so far as unilaterally to lower the Canadian tariff on American goods in the hope that the United States would follow suit. This example of homeopathic magic, however, was not effective. During this period of financial stringency, Lord Elgin reported that

"If things remain on their present footing . . . there is nothing before us but violent agitation ending in convulsion or annexation. No measure but the establishment of reciprocal trade between Canada and the United States, or the imposition of a duty on the produce of the States when imported into England, will remove it."

England, however, would not modify the application of her new economic philosophy even for the benefit of her premier colony, and all Canadian efforts were soon directed toward the achievement of a reciprocal agreement with the United States. Congress was not enthusiastic. American attitudes and reasoning were mixed and contradictory; Southern delegates felt that such an agreement would lead to the annexation of Canada—the admission of many "free" states. The Representatives and Senators from the North, on the other hand, believed that the commercial pressure resulting from the refusal of the United States to grant reciprocity would lead most surely to the political union the North desired. For six years negotiations were continued without success, until in 1854, as a result of the realistic and highly efficient diplomatic methods of the Governor-General of British North America, the Elgin-Marcy Treaty was drawn up and ratified. It is generally believed that the avenues of approach that finally led to this goal were social rather than economic or political. The treaty was described by a contemporary observer as having been "floated through on a sea of champagne." In so far as this is true, it might almost be described as an example of the end justifying the means, for both countries profited greatly from the treaty.

It must now be noted, however, that the United States government, having decided to support the reciprocity agreement, did some "floating" on its own account. A special agent was sent into those parts of the Maritime Provinces and Newfoundland which were opposed to, or lukewarm concerning, reciprocity. He subsidized newspapers and individuals with funds supplied by Washington and did a great deal to produce the favorable attitude with which the various provinces greeted the treaty. This episode is so little known that it is worth particular attention.

The Elgin-Marcy Treaty was made acceptable to the United States by the inclusion of certain stipulations giving to American fishermen full privileges in the Atlantic coast fisheries. Lord Elgin, moreover, adopted the Northern argument and succeeded in convincing the Southern Congressmen that failure to enact such an agreement would result in the annexation of Canada. The natural inclination toward freer trade inherent in the agricultural South was gratified. The products of forest, farm, and mine were placed on the free list by both countries; American vessels were allowed to use the St. Lawrence River, and Canadians were given similar privileges in Lake Michigan. The treaty was designed to run for ten years, and subsequently was to be subject to abrogation by either party on one year's notice.

The result of this treaty was an immense stimulus to trade in both Canada and the United States. The economic life of the two countries became more closely integrated. Commodities were imported by the United States from Canada at one point in the long boundary line, and goods of the same type were exported to Canada at another point. Canadian fish, lumber, and farm products found a ready market in the large cities of the Northern and Eastern states; American manufacturers had access to greatly expanded sources of raw materials, and the cost of living was perceptibly lowered in both countries. In 1854 the total value of Canadian–United States trade was $3,480,000; in 1856, the first complete year after the signing of the treaty, this total was raised to $57,000,000. Throughout the period the treaty was in force the United States exported $363,000,000 worth of goods to Canada, and the British provinces exported $268,000,000 worth to the United States.

The treaty was not, of course, the only factor in the rapid increase in trade that took place between the two countries. In both, but especially in the United States, the process of industrialization was undergoing a rapid acceleration. The demands of the Civil War, moreover, accelerated the industrialization of the United States in the same way that the requirements of the two World Wars speeded that same process in Canada two or three generations later. This was accompanied by the tremendous development in the field of transportation, both domestic and external, that was the result of the more effective utilization of steam and coal. The United States was now going through its second, and much more important, revolution. From an agrarian republic it was becoming an industrial empire. Moreover, population was growing with unprecedented rapidity, not only in North America but in Great Britain and the more industrialized areas of the continent of Europe. All these changes stimulated trade generally and had a direct bearing on the growth of commercial intercourse among all Western countries, including Canada and the United States. Without the Elgin-Marcy Treaty, however, there would have been no such expansion in North American trade as did in fact take place.

As the result of notice given a year earlier, the reciprocity treaty was terminated by the United States on 17 March 1866.

It cannot be doubted that the primary factor in bringing to an end this mutually advantageous agreement was the hostility aroused in the United States by the attitude (real or imagined) of Canada during the American Civil War. The tone of many Canadian papers, the Confederate raids from Canadian soil, the absence from Congress of the members from the agricultural and low-tariff states of the South, and a sudden raising of the Canadian tariff on certain manufactured articles, all tended to estrange American friendship and to make the people of the United States anxious to terminate the existing commercial arrangements that so greatly benefited Canada—even though they had been highly profitable to the United States as well. As Charles Francis Adams declared, the abrogation of this treaty was "the result rather of a strong political feeling than of any commercial consideration." [1] The argument most frequently used by opponents of the treaty in the United States was that Canada had violated the spirit of

---

[1] Dr. O. D. Skelton summarized the reasons for the American action as follows: "In 1864 the cumulative effect of anger at British and Canadian sympathy with the South; rising protectionist sentiment, pressure of internal taxation, aggrieved sectional interests, and the absence from Congress of the low-tariff southerners led the United States to give notice of the abrogation of the Treaty of 1854." *General Economic History, 1867–1912*, p. 127.

the agreement by raising her duties on certain manufactured articles, thereby damaging American trade. What had really happened was that Canadian manufacturers had been slowly expanding, and, fearful of extermination unless protected against their larger American rivals, they had demanded and in 1858 and 1859 some of them received tariff assistance. This action had so frequently occurred in the United States that American politicians should have recognized it in another country. Indeed, during this same war period the American tariff rates had also undergone a process of elevation, and the newly organized Republican Party made an exaggerated form of tariff protection one of the major elements in the platform upon which it sought to obtain and retain political power.

The Canadian action was certainly a violation of the spirit of the treaty, though it was legally defensible. Two other motives were to be found for the American action: the first was retaliation for Canada's action in making American vessels pay tolls on the Canadian canals; and the second was the frequently expressed desire to force Canada, by depriving her of all trading privileges, to agree to annexation. The American House of Representatives protested in 1867 against the formation of the Dominion of Canada, which occurred in that year. Their contention was that this organization of a new state was a violation of the Monroe Doctrine. They saw in this northern Union a barrier to their hopes of annexation.

Canada was still anxious to continue the agreement, and in spite of domestic criticism of this "truckling" to an unfriendly neighbor, the Confederate Council on Commercial Treaties, composed of representatives of all the British colonies in North America, sent a commission to Washington early in 1866 in an effort to save the treaty. This delegation received a distinctly hostile reception, and, their mission failing, the treaty expired on 17 March.

The termination of the reciprocity treaty dealt a heavy blow to American-Canadian trade, which fell from $60,000,000 in 1865 to $50,200,000 in 1867 and $48,900,000 in 1868; and this in spite of the tremendous expansion of industry, commerce, and population then going on throughout the continent. The insistent and increasing demands of westward expansion shortly led to an improvement in conditions in the United States, but in Canada the comparable movement came much later and the effects of the American tariff policy were seriously felt.

For some time after the termination of the reciprocity treaty Canadian tariffs were allowed to remain at the old level. Canadians, according to George Brown, "assumed that there were matters existing in 1865–1866 to trouble the spirit of American statesmen for the moment, and they waited patiently for the sober second thought which was sure ere long to put all things right." The great majority of Americans expected, also, that the high rates imposed during the war would be lowered on its conclusion. In the end, however, the vested interests that had been built up during the war years proved to be too strong, and session after session of Congress passed without any serious attempt to lower the tariff walls.

Meanwhile personal and diplomatic negotiations were continued. In 1869 Sir John Rose, Minister of Finance in the Macdonald Cabinet, who played a very prominent part in developing all the commercial and economic policies of this period, proposed at Washington a treaty which would have practically unified the economic life of the two nations, and which embodied discrimination against Great Britain itself. This proposal was almost immediately denounced in the Canadian House. Hope was aroused when it was announced in Canada that Premier Macdonald was to be one of the five British commissioners charged with the negotiation of the Treaty of Washington in 1871. Despite his most earnest endeavors, however, this treaty included no provision for reciprocal trading relations. The British delegates wanted a treaty at any cost and were little anxious to assist the Canadian Premier in bartering fishery rights for trading privileges. In the agreement the fishery question was treated by itself; Canadian claims for indemnity for the Fenian raids were disregarded; and reciprocity was not mentioned. Indeed, Senator Sumner, having drawn up a bill for $2,500,000,000 against Great Britain (on account of the *Alabama* and other British activities that, he claimed, had prolonged the war), proposed to buy Canada with a part of this sum. His offer was not accepted. The treaty was received with protests by Canada, to be accepted finally as a sacrifice borne by the Dominion for the benefit of the Empire.

In 1874 the Liberal administration of Alexander Mackenzie made a most notable attempt to secure the enactment of a mutually beneficial trade agreement. At the instigation of the Canadian government, Sir Edward Thornton, British Minister at Washington, and George Brown were empowered to enter into negotiations with the Americans with a view to stimulating trade with Canada. The resulting agreement (largely the product of Brown's peculiar ability) was received with considerable favor even in the protectionist press of the United States. The Brown-Fish Agreement, as it was known, dealt with the problem of the fisheries and raw materials as they had been dealt with in the Treaty of 1854; the canals and rivers were thrown open as arranged in the Treaty of Washington, and Canada agreed to enlarge her waterways further; the coasting trade of the Great Lakes was to be free to ships of either nation; and finally, a considerable list of manufactured articles was made exempt from tariff dues. The treaty was to run for twenty-one years, and subsequently subject to three years' notice of abrogation. But advantageous as this agreement would undoubtedly have proved to both participants, and in spite of an unusually favorable reception in the American press, the United States Senate, controlled by industrial and commercial interests that felt the concessions made by Canada were not sufficient, at first postponed a decision and finally refused to accept the proposal.

Throughout this period, and until the Taft-Fielding agreement was enacted in 1911, the activating force urging closer commercial relations came from Canada, although the Canadian pressure for a reciprocity agreement declined in fervor with the growth of prosperity during the last few years of the nineteenth century and the early years of the twentieth. To Washington, the Dominion was of small importance—a colony that would one day break with England and inevitably become a part of the all-powerful United States. Why, then, should American legislators take the trouble of ameliorating Canadian conditions while that country retained its colonial status? Let Canada progress as best she could, that she might enter the Union the more readily when the ordained time arrived. When Canada was ready to enter a complete *Zollverein*, Congress would be ready to receive her; but the bargaining for and limited profits of restricted reciprocity were not worth the trouble. For Canada, on the other hand, access to the American market was of real importance. Comparatively isolated from the other large consuming areas of the world, and unassisted by any preferential treatment in Great Britain, the economic life of the country was dependent to a dangerous degree upon American demands for Canadian raw materials.

Faced with repeated rebuffs in their efforts to obtain free access to the American market, Canadians were, however, forced into efforts to find other solutions for their commercial difficulties. In the years of depression following 1873, they began to experiment with the expedient of a high protective tariff.

In the words of the Rowell-Sirois Report, looking back at this period from the vantage point of posterity, "falling hopes and falling prices" brought about the raising of tariffs. "The time has come," said the Canadian Minister of Finance, "when we are to decide whether we will simply be hewers of wood and drawers of water. . . . The time has certainly arrived when we must consider whether we will allow matters to remain as they are, with the result of being an unimportant and uninteresting portion of Her Majesty's Dominions, or will rise to the position which I believe Providence has destined us to occupy."

The "National Policy" of Sir John A. Macdonald was promulgated in 1879, and although he made an offer of reciprocity, the underlying principle of his new policy was a determination to "go it alone." If the United States was not willing to agree to "reciprocity of trade," it must encounter a "reciprocity of tariffs." From this time on, the urgency of the Canadian desire for lower tariff barriers along the United States border began slowly to decline, and although it never disappeared and in fact always retained a prominent position among the objectives of Canadian policy, it did not occupy the predominant place in Canadian minds that it had held earlier.

In 1883 the United States gave the required two years' notice of termination of the fisheries agreement negotiated by A. T. Galt in 1874, and consequently in 1885 this century-old problem again became a matter of dispute. The resulting dissatisfaction made some form of agreement necessary, and Canada once more suggested reciprocity, pointing to the satisfactory conditions in the fishing industry during the period of reciprocity from 1854 to 1866. In President Cleveland's second term the willingness of the Democratic Party to adopt a more liberal trading policy, particularly in relation with Canada, became more clearly emphasized. A reciprocity agreement was actually prepared, but the President was unable either to persuade or to coerce the Senate into giving its consent, and this attempt to better conditions failed as had its predecessors. The protectionists were still firmly entrenched in the Capitol at Washington. Even the power of the White House could not dislodge them.

As the depression of 1873–8 had led Canada to demand tariff protection as a sovereign remedy, so the stringency of 1884–9 induced the demand for commercial union with the United States. This term meant exactly what it denoted: the complete union of Canada and the United States in all matters pertaining to commerce and to trade. Identical tariffs were to be imposed on all foreign goods, while free trade was to exist between the two countries. Customs and excise duties were to be pooled and distributed on the basis of population. The leaders in this movement were Erastus Wiman, a Canadian, resident in the United States, and S. J. Ritchie, an American capitalist with large interests in Canada. Starting in 1887, the campaign for commercial union shortly brought to its standard such papers as the Montreal *Witness* and the Toronto *Globe*, and though its advocates were disheartened by the triumph of high protection when the Republicans returned to power in the American elections of 1888, in the modified form of "unrestricted reciprocity" it became the platform upon which the Liberals fought the election of 1891. The Conservative leaders, though at first tending to favor the proposed union, gradually turned against it as disloyal to the imperial ties, and on the eve of election they announced that plans were under way for a settlement of all outstanding grievances between the United States and Canada, including the re-enactment, with necessary modifications, of the reciprocity agreement of 1854. The disclosure that several leading proponents of commercial union were also favorable to annexation practically nullified the chances of a Liberal victory, and a Conservative majority was again returned.

The years 1892 to 1895 were characterized in both the United States and Canada by an acute increase in the financial depression that was endemic during the period from 1873 to 1896 in both Canada and the United States. During this time conditions were, of course, very much worse in Canada than in the more self-sufficient Republic. It was indeed the darkest era of Canadian history and was marked by a loss of population to the United States that constituted an almost unbearable drain on the resources as well as on the morale of the people of the Dominion. The National Policy, the construction of the transcontinental railway, the determined development and maintenance of a language of imperial patriotism as exemplified in Macdonald's "A British subject I was born, a British subject I will die," were but parts of the courageous resistance that Canadians were putting up against the magnetism of American economic and political institutions. In the end the defenses held, though Canadian nationalism was inevitably substituted for imperialism; but there were many dark moments along the way. In 1891 and 1892 conditions were so bad that renewed efforts to obtain a reciprocity agreement were undertaken in spite of the hostile atmosphere that was known to exist in Washington. A delegation was sent to the United States capital in 1891, but Secretary Blaine refused even to receive it. In the following year another commission was sent, but as the American Secretary of State insisted upon the assimilation of the Canadian to the American tariff, and discrimination against Great Britain, the discussions were unproductive.

It should be noted that during this period between 1866 and 1897 the political power of the manufacturing interests of Canada as contrasted with that of the agricultural community was steadily increasing. The Conservative Party, which preeminently represented the industrial interests in Parliament, was frequently and flatly accused by the Liberals of making only halfhearted attempts to gain reciprocity with the United States. Indeed, the Conservative leaders were finally forced to admit that they were prepared to grant free entry only to *raw products*. This, of course, was of little value to the United States, which desired a market for its *manufactured* goods.

In 1897 President McKinley, taking cognizance of the many matters disturbing the harmony of the two nations, proposed the appointment of a joint high commission to discuss and settle the Alaskan boundary, the question of Bering Sea, the fisheries problems, and reciprocity. This commission first met in August 1898, and its discussions continued until February 1899, when, unable to agree on the Alaskan problem, it disbanded with but little accomplished on any of the issues that had been raised.

Dr. Skelton has well characterized the difficulties of this period:

"The conditions were not favorable for a broad and statesmanlike settlement of the outstanding issues, consistent with the economic advantage and political independence of both countries. The United States, throughout this period, was still dogmatically protectionist, still prosperous, still provincial, still prodigal of resources; the 'muck-raker' and foreign complications and wealthy malefactors had not yet disturbed her complacency. The organized anarchy of the check and balance system, carried to its illogical extreme in a Constitution which kept executive, Senate and Representatives normally at loggerheads, still made negotiation difficult and ratification a gamble."

With the opening of the twentieth century, American-Canadian relations underwent a sudden and dramatic metamorphosis. The disappearance of the American frontier, the opening of the Canadian West, the rapid depletion of certain American resources as the result of the activities of wasteful and unscrupulous exploiters, the growing American demand for markets and for raw materials, the adoption by the Canadian government of modern advertising methods in its campaign for immigrants—these and other factors tended to increase the importance of Canada in the eyes of American manufacturers, farmers, and financiers. Within the Dominion itself a new spirit began to be manifested. The increased domestic demand for Canadian goods, the growth of local industry, a realization of the immense potential wealth of the western provinces, combined to develop among Canadians a new buoyancy and optimism, a determination to justify the oft-repeated words of Sir Wilfrid Laurier: "The nineteenth century belonged to the United States, the twentieth century belongs to Canada." [2]

In spite of, or perhaps in some measure because of, the trials and hardships of the last half century, Canada had grown from a weak and puny infant to a strong and lusty youth. Feeling more confidence in its own ability and more assurance of its future success, the Dominion ceased its practice of organizing political pilgrimages to Washington. The vast emigration of young Canadians to the United States was gradually ceasing, and, in contrast, Canada was beginning to provide homes for the more adventurous of American farmers and to give employment and residence to American engineers and promoters. More rapid and convenient methods of transportation were opening ever wider markets to the Canadian producer, and the importance of the United States in this respect was correspondingly lessened.

[2] First used in a speech delivered in Massey Hall, Toronto, on 20 May 1902.

A feeling of confidence began to pervade the whole country; every branch of national life was expanding; Canadians were beginning to thrill with pride in their new-found strength. They became less sensitive to the slights of the United States, and somewhat less interested in the actions of their mighty neighbor. At the same time, however, trade with the United States was rapidly increasing. (See chart, p. 278.)

The great accumulation of capital resulting from the extraordinary industrial development of the nineteenth century made it inevitable that American financiers should look beyond the boundaries of the United States for opportunities for profitable investment. Canada, possessing almost untouched resources, inhabited by an industrious and competent population, but seriously handicapped for lack of capital, was the logical field of exploitation.

As Canadian self-confidence increased, so American interest in Canada developed; pilgrimages to Ottawa succeeded the pilgrimages to Washington. Nor were reasons for this change difficult to find. The tremendous immigration into the United States since the Civil War had resulted in the rapid occupation of the West; the best farm lands were taken; many of the forests and mines had come into the power of unscrupulous corporations and were being rapidly depleted. So great had been the industrial development that new and increasing supplies of raw materials were becoming ever more necessary; and foreign markets must be developed for the finished product, or American industry would be seriously affected. Both as a depository of raw materials and as a growing market for manufactured articles, Canada was taking a more prominent place. American industrialists suddenly realized that no nation in the world was better supplied than Canada with the resources of nature, while only Germany and Great Britain now exceeded Canada in the amount of imports from the United States. As a corollary to the increased industrial preoccupation of the Republic, the manufacturing interests had established a firmer control over the legislative and executive

264

departments of the American government. It was, then, only logical to expect, when the industrial leaders of the country should demand the negotiation of a reciprocity agreement with Canada (on the basis of American manufactures for Canadian raw materials), that Congress should accede to the request. For once the consumers' interests ran parallel to those of the capitalistic promoter, for real reciprocity with Canada would mean cheaper food for the American public.

Thus, as the United States began to look more favorably toward prospects of closer trade relations with the Dominion, Canada was undergoing a development that increased the national self-confidence and tended to remove some of the urgency from Canadian interest in American policy. The whole issue was crystallized by the Payne-Aldrich Tariff of 1909 and brought to a definite issue in the Canadian elections of 1911.

2. *Reciprocity in 1911*

In the Payne-Aldrich Tariff the United States for the first time embodied the principle of maximum and minimum rates. The minimum rates were to be the general and permanent duties, while an addition of twenty-five per cent of the value of the commodity was added to form the maximum rate—a club with which to force concessions. The higher duties were to be enforced at the discretion of the President against all nations discriminating against American goods. In Canada this threat was considered grossly unfair. Although the United States admitted that the British preference did not constitute discrimination, the American negotiators demanded that Canada accord to the United States terms as favorable as those given France in an agreement made in 1910. But as the American tariff was already very much higher than that of Canada, the Canadian government looked upon the American threat as quite unjustifiable.[3] American commissioners who came to Ottawa in March 1910 were told that the Canadian government would not make the concessions demanded, and a tariff war seemed inevitable. Fortunately the people of neither country were in a mood for such an insane procedure, and when Democratic candidates favoring reciprocity with Canada showed unexpected strength in American elections, the Republican administration changed its course and after a discussion with W. S. Fielding, Canadian Minister of Finance, President Taft declared Canada to be eligible for the minimum rates. Fielding promised certain minor reductions and agreed to enter negotiations for a general discussion of reciprocity.

In March 1910 President Taft sent Charles M. Pepper, John G. Foster, and Henry C. Emery to Ottawa to discuss tariff problems with Fielding. In November of the same year Foster and Emery were replaced by Henry M. Hoyt. The American representatives were "authorized to take such steps for formulating a reciprocal arrangement as might be necessary and to receive and consider any proposition which the Canadian government might care to submit." These discussions were adjourned to Washington in January 1911, and on the 26th of that month agreement was reached. Products of the farm, dairy, sawmill, and mine were in most cases placed on the free list, as also were fish and their by-products. Substantial reductions were to be made in the tariffs on meat, flour, coal, agricultural implements, and many manufactured articles. The agreement was to be made effective by concurrent legislation, not by treaty.

These proposals met with strong opposition from many members of the Republican Party in Congress. They could not easily forget the protectionist doctrine they had so steadily upheld. The Western farmers and lumbermen objected to the admission of Canadian cereals and forest products. The fishing interests of the United States feared Canadian competition in the markets

---

[3] As remarked by Skelton, this is "A sound criticism . . . but not to the point in the discussion of modern protectionist warfare, where ethics and etiquette have never been conspicuous."

of Boston, Seattle, and San Francisco. On the other hand, the "regular" Republicans voted with the administration as they had been trained, and the Democrats, delighted at the division in their opponents' ranks, and naturally tending toward freer trade, supported the proposals of the President. The powerful financial interests of the East, feeling that reciprocity would facilitate their endeavors to obtain control of the Canadian market, liberally assisted in the campaign; indeed, their campaign had started long before. The border states sent delegations to Secretary Knox protesting vigorously against a tariff war with Canada, and favoring reciprocity. An attempt was made in some quarters to convince the American public that reciprocity would ultimately lead to the annexation of Canada. This idea was particularly stressed by the Hearst publications, and unfortunately the statements of many responsible Americans, who should have been better acquainted with the situation, followed the same line. President Taft himself made an incredible blunder while in the process of outlining one of the strongest arguments, from the American point of view, for reciprocity. "The amount of Canadian products that we would take," he declared, *"would make Canada only an adjunct of the United States.* It would transfer all their important business to Chicago and New York, with their bank credits and everything else; and it would increase greatly the demand of Canada for our manufactures." Partially true, but surely an impolitic statement to make in regard to American relations with a proud and sensitive neighbor.

The Reciprocity Bill was passed by the House of Representatives, but the Senate failed to act before adjournment on 4 March. President Taft immediately called a special session and, assisted by the Democrats and the weather, the bill was passed on 22 July.

Almost half a century had passed since the abrogation of the first reciprocity treaty between the United States and Canada. During that time the renewal of the agreement of 1854–66 had been a cardinal principle of Canadian policy. Time after time Canadian proposals of reciprocity had been refused by the United

States, but now, at long last, the objective of Canadian diplomacy seemed about to be achieved. The United States had expressed its readiness to engage in a mutual reduction of tariffs; all that remained was for Canada to implement the agreement she had tried so long and so vainly to achieve.

At first glance the result of the Canadian general election of 1911 seems to be an inexplicable phenomenon. Why should a country turn so suddenly and so completely against a policy that had been advocated by both its political parties and by practically every class of its citizens for over fifty years? It is true that for a decade or more Canada had been less dependent than formerly upon American trade for her prosperity; and it is also true that certain Conservative leaders who were in close touch with the manufacturing interests of Montreal and Toronto had been somewhat lukewarm in their advocacy of reciprocity; but the great majority of the Canadian people, regardless of party or class, had been educated to the belief that reciprocity with the United States would mean prosperity in Canada. Yet in the election of 21 September 1911 the Conservative Party, whose whole campaign was based on opposition to reciprocity, won 133 seats to 88 for the Liberals.

The real explanation of this apparently sudden alteration in Canadian policy is to be found in two facts: the hostility of the manufacturing and financial interests of Ontario and Quebec, and the latent hostility of Canadians to the United States. Opposition to the agreement was organized, advertised, and subsidized by the great railroad, manufacturing, and banking interests of eastern Canada. All their propaganda would have been useless, however, had it not been for the anti-American sentiment that characterized the Canadian people in much the same way that during the nineteenth century hostility toward Great Britain had been a national characteristic of the people of the United States. However regrettable the revival of anti-American feeling may have been and however unjustified by contemporary conditions, it is beyond dispute that this prejudice was the vital factor in the defeat of the Taft-Fielding agreement of 1911.

Because of its importance as marking the end of an era in Canadian-American relations, and because of the insight that it gives into the present Canadian attitude toward the United States, a somewhat extended consideration of this election is clearly demanded.

The attitude of the United States can be stated very briefly. American opinion was obviously divided, but the subject was not then an issue of paramount and extreme importance. Canada, after all, was a comparatively small neighbor, and in letting down the bars to the north the manufacturers, or even the primary producers of the United States, were not running a very serious risk. The former at least would gain much more than they would lose. But in either event it was not a problem of life and death.

Nevertheless, President Taft was faced by the prospect of a rupture within the ranks of his own party, and it had taken all of his forensic ability and all the influence of his office to force the bill through the Senate. In his determination to crown a mediocre administration with at least one real achievement, he toured many sections of the country, pointing out "the peculiar relations existing between Canada and the United States" which "justify a different policy as to imports and exports from that which obtains in regard to European and Oriental countries." He further declared that "if, by reciprocal arrangements we can make the commercial bond closer, it will be for the benefit of both nations." Eugene R. Foss, seeking Congressional honors in Massachusetts, stated the attitude of American advocates of reciprocity thus succinctly: "We need Canada more than she needs us. In a few years we shall have to beg for favors that now she might willingly grant."

The political argument based on loyalty to the Empire largely overshadowed the economic aspects of the reciprocity question in Canada. Nevertheless, the latter aspects were not completely slighted. As might be expected, Canadian farmers and producers of raw materials generally favored the bill, for it promised them a wider market and higher prices. This applied to the mine-owners in the British Columbia coal region, although the Nova Scotia miners did not profit because of the close relation between the railroads and coal-producers of the Eastern United States. Canadian millers, packers, brewers, and canners were opposed to the agreement because they would have to raise their payments for raw materials to the level of the American industries of the same class. Canadian manufacturing interests greatly feared, and with justice, the competition of American firms, and the banks of Canada were too closely involved in Canadian industrial life to oppose the manufacturers. The railroads of the Dominion, particularly the all-powerful Canadian Pacific, feared the substitution of north-and-south for the existing east-and-west lines of shipment and joined in the opposition. Sir William Van Horne, one of the builders of the Canadian Pacific Railway and himself an ex-American, expressed the view of his colleagues when he said: "I am going out to bust this thing."

Proponents of the agreement argued logically that reciprocity would allow greater specialization in each country; that the complementary seasons would result in a greater variety of cheap fruits and vegetables; that transportation charges would be lighter because of the possibility of utilizing the nearest source of supply regardless of its geographic situation in relation to the boundary; and, finally, that the agreement would result simply in an enormous expansion of the home market.

Conservation became a magic word in Conservative circles during the campaign. Reciprocity, declared the followers of R. L. Borden, would result in denuding Canada of its natural resources to feed the hungry maw of American industry. The United States had wasted and destroyed her own timber; had taken only the best from her own mines; and had exterminated the fish that once had thronged her waters. Now she was preparing the way to exploit the resources of Canada. Under reciprocity Canada would become "a mere feeder to the Hill system—the back yard and lumber camp of New England."

Important as were the arguments to be made against reciprocity on the basis of commercial inexpediency, the Conservative Party early chose a different method of attack. Spending little time on a discussion of the economic factors involved, it declared in unequivocal terms that reciprocity was but the first step to annexation; that a vote for Laurier was a vote against the King; and that a ballot cast for the Conservative Party was a ballot cast against union with the United States. This issue became the center of the campaign, and in spite of the repeated denials of any such tendency by all Liberal leaders, tens of thousands of Canadian voters went to the polls on 21 September firmly convinced that the fate of the Empire rested upon their ballots.

Too much stress can hardly be laid on the assistance given the anti-reciprocity forces of Canada by the more vocal expansionists of the United States. Conservative editors searched the pages of the *Congressional Record* and delved in the files of the more bombastic section of the American press, and their gleanings made excellent irritants to disturb the minds of an already excited public. "Canadian annexation," said Senator McCumber, "is the logical conclusion of reciprocity with Canada." "We are preparing to annex Canada," declared the Speaker of the House of Representatives. The New York *American* represented the attitude typical of all Hearst publications: "Eventually, of course, Canada will come in," said the editor. "That will be when we want her." To this assertion a Canadian editor made the obvious reply that Canada was "united in a bond that extends from England around the world and back again to England . . . the answer from the Canadian people is that Canada is, and intends to remain, British." Congressman Samuel McCall, of Massachusetts, declared himself of the opinion that under reciprocity "the inevitable day will be more quickly reached when the two countries will be politically one." Congressman Prince, of Illinois, was unusually frank: "Be not deceived," he advised his northern neighbors. "When we go into a country and get control of it, we take it." Senator Cummins, of Iowa, was even more brief, stating: "I am for the annexation of Canada." The hope of Representative Madden, of Illinois, was that Canada "may become part of us, as it should be," while the famous railroad magnate James J. Hill rejoiced that "reciprocity will stop the union of the British Empire." Champ Clark's expressed desire to see the Stars and Stripes float over the whole continent, and the famous "adjunct" speech of President Taft, made splendid fuel for the fires of hostility blazing in Canada.

When American political leaders began to understand the damage these declarations were doing the cause of reciprocity, an attempt was made to minimize the issue. Secretary Knox stated: "The United States recognize that the Dominion of Canada is a permanent North American political unit and that her autonomy is secure. . . . There is not the slightest probability that their racial and moral union will involve any political change, or annexation, or absorption." President Taft in his message urging ratification took pains to make clear that the agreement "in its intent and terms was purely economical." The Liberal Party of Canada, and all who favored closer economic relations between the two countries, joined in the same chorus. They declared it an insult to Canadians to argue that a mere commercial agreement would make them false to their imperial obligations and their fealty to the Crown. They "scouted all ideas of political or commercial annexation by the United States and protested their entire and whole-hearted loyalty to the empire."

These assurances from the United States and from Canadian Liberals did not, however, satisfy the voting public. The Conservative Party, well supplied with campaign funds by the financial interests, was able to carry on a propaganda that thoroughly convinced a majority of Canadians that the election offered only a choice between "the Union Jack or Old Glory." Sir James Whitney, Premier of Ontario, expressed the current Canadian opinion of the American designs when he said: "There is not an American who does not hope away down in his heart that Canada will some day be a part of the United States and feel that reciprocity is the first step in this direction. It is the means by which annexation will be reached most quickly." Commenting on this statement, a Western paper expressed another conviction commonly held by the Canadian people: namely, that reciprocity was a method employed by the United States to secure "control of Canada's vast natural resources, and of dominating the Dominion at first commercially, and then, afterwards, politically." George E. Foster saw in reciprocity "a menace to national solidarity," and the Conservative Party declared its platform to be "the historic policy of high protection," and "loyalty toward England." "Commercial Union is another name for commercial control," wrote a Conservative pamphleteer. "Commercial control means the reduction of Canadian ports to mere subsidiaries of Boston and New York. Permit that and Canadian nationality is hopelessly emasculated; and the partnership in the empire becomes a subsidiary affair also. When that point is reached there is no need to talk of annexation. It will take care of itself." "The adoption of the Reciprocity pact," wrote a western Canadian editor, "means the disruption of the Empire."

Although a large majority of the leading statesmen of Great Britain favored any movement toward freer trade on the part of the Dominion,[4] there were prominent Englishmen whose fears were identical with those of the Canadian Conservatives. Preeminent among the latter was that ardent imperialist Rudyard Kipling, and his widely circulated appeals had no little effect on Canadian opinion.[5] The final appeal of R. L. Borden, leader of the Conservative Party, to the Canadian electors struck again the note of national and imperial patriotism: "I beg Canadians to

[4] Asquith, Lloyd George, Haldane, Chamberlain, Balfour, and Bryce all declared their sympathy with the movement for reciprocity.

[5] Kipling wrote: "I do not understand how nine million people can enter into such arrangements with ninety million strangers . . . and at the same time preserve their national integrity. It is her own soul that Canada risks today. Once that soul is pawned for any consideration, Canada must inevitably conform to the commercial, legal, financial, social, and ethical standards which will be imposed upon her by the sheer admitted weight of the United States. Whatever the United States may gain, and I assume that the United States proposals are not wholly altruistic, I see nothing for Canada in Reciprocity except a little ready money that she does not need, and a very long repentance." Victoria *Colonist*, 20 September 1911.

cast a soberly considered and serious vote for the preservation of our heritage, for the maintenance of our commercial and political freedom, for the permanence of Canada as an autonomous nation of the British Empire."

It would be erroneous to suggest that reciprocity was the only issue in the election of 1911. No government can stay in power for fifteen years, as that of Sir Wilfrid Laurier had done, without making enemies and without stains on its record. The Laurier administration had not escaped, and during the campaign Liberal failures and mistakes were not overlooked. The plan of organizing a Canadian navy was also attacked: by the Conservatives who wished to make a direct contribution to the British Admiralty, and by the Nationalists in Quebec who wanted no naval expenditure of any sort. For the first time Sir Wilfrid Laurier was faced by real opposition in his own province, and the activities of Henri Bourassa and his Nationalist followers contributed in no small measure to the defeat of the government. But, making every allowance for these issues, the vital question in the minds of the majority of the Canadian people was that of reciprocity.

The election was held on 21 September, and resulted in an overwhelming victory for the Conservative Party. A Liberal majority of 44 in a House of 221 members was converted into a Conservative majority of 45. Eight Cabinet ministers were defeated. "The Ghosts of the United Empire Loyalists stalked triumphant through the corridors of Ottawa." [6] For the next twenty years reciprocity was no longer an issue.

In commenting on the election Canadian journals, while admitting the strength of the anti-administration sentiment, which had been accumulating for fifteen years, and while laying full stress on the French-Canadian opposition to the Laurier navy policy, yet were practically unanimous in declaring that fear of American encroachment had been the determining factor in the Liberal defeat. The election was "Canada's decided Declaration of Independence." One of the most influential and, at that time,

---

[6] F. H. Soward, quoted in Keenleyside: "American Economic Penetration of Canada," *Canadian Historical Review*, March 1927, p. 36.

comparatively independent papers in Canada declared that the choice was between "Imperialism and ultimate Continentalism, and the realization of this had an immense influence on the result. Unmistakably the country had decided against Continentalism in trade or politics." The economic value of reciprocity was invariably questioned by Conservative journals, but "even these practical considerations counted for less in the contest than the determination of the people to permit nothing to be done which would weaken the bonds of Empire." The Toronto *Globe,* for nearly a century the leading organ of Liberalism in Canada, stated: "The people of Ontario do not like their neighbors to the south. That is emphatically the lesson of yesterday's election. Liberals in tens of thousands . . . joined the Conservatives . . . to show their objection to having any 'truck or trade with the Yankees.' The campaign orators of the Conservative Party builded better than they knew when . . . they appealed to the people of this province to save Canada from the Americans."

In the United States, naturally, much less interest was taken in the defeat of reciprocity. After all, Canada, while important to American trade, was only one country, and the failure of the reciprocal agreement was not by any means a fatal or even a very serious blow. Sorrow and some perplexity were expressed over the reasons that led Canada to take such action, but in general the issue was minimized, and the result explained by local political conditions in the Dominion.

As subsequent discussions and actions in Parliament showed, the election of 1911 did not permanently settle the question of reciprocity between Canada and the United States. It was inevitable that it should arise again, and when it did so in the form of the trade agreements of 1935, it received almost equally approving support from Conservative, Liberal, Progressive, and Labor members of the Canadian Parliament. Canadians, having asserted their independence in 1911, were more than willing to obtain the benefits of freer trade when at last the opportunity was again presented.

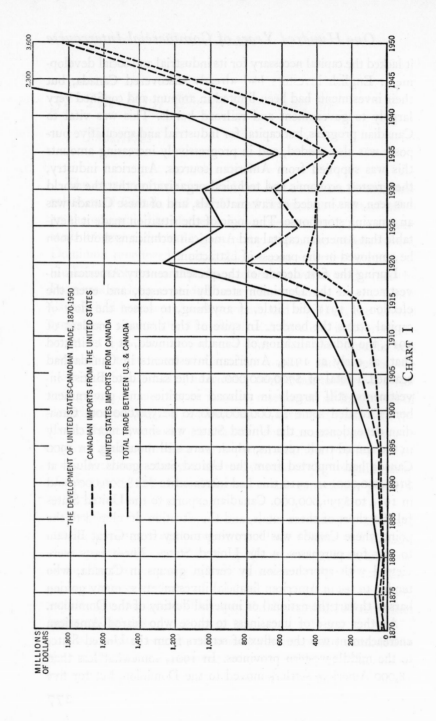

MILLIONS OF DOLLARS

THE DEVELOPMENT OF UNITED STATES-CANADIAN TRADE, 1870-1950

- - - CANADIAN IMPORTS FROM THE UNITED STATES

- - - UNITED STATES IMPORTS FROM CANADA

——— TOTAL TRADE BETWEEN U.S. & CANADA

CHART I

Canada and the United States

Summary of the Trade of Canada with the United States, 1868–1950

Fiscal Years	Merchandise Imports	Merchandise Exports
1868	$ 22,660,132	$ 25,349,568
1869	21,497,380	26,717,656
1870	21,697,237	30,361,328
1871	27,185,586	29,164,358
1872	33,741,995	32,871,496
1873	45,189,110	36,714,144
1874	51,706,906	33,195,805
1875	48,930,358	27,902,748
1876	44,099,880	30,080,738
1877	49,376,008	24,326,332
1878	48,002,875	24,381,009
1879	42,170,306	25,491,356
1880	28,193,783	29,566,211
1881	36,338,701	34,038,431
1882	47,052,935	45,782,584
1883	55,147,243	39,513,225
1884	49,785,888	34,332,641
1885	45,576,510	35,566,810
1886	42,818,651	34,284,490
1887	44,795,908	35,269,922
1888	46,440,296	40,407,483
1889	50,029,419	39,519,940
1890	51,365,661	36,213,279
1891	52,033,477	37,743,430
1892	51,742,132	34,666,070
1893	52,339,796	37,296,110
1894	50,746,091	32,562,509
1895	50,179,004	35,603,863
1896	53,529,390	37,789,481
1897	57,023,342	43,664,187
1898	74,824,923	38,989,525
1899	88,506,881	39,326,485
1900	102,224,917	57,996,488
1901	107,377,906	67,983,673
1902	115,001,533	66,567,784
1903	129,071,197	67,766,367
1904	143,329,697	66,856,885
1905	152,778,576	70,426,765
1906	169,256,452	83,546,306
1907 *	149,085,577	62,180,439
1908	205,309,803	90,814,871
1909	170,432,360	85,334,806
1910	218,004,556	104,199,675
1911	275,824,265	104,115,823
1912	331,384,657	102,041,222
1913	436,887,315	139,725,953
1914	396,302,138	163,372,825

279

Summary of the Trade of Canada with the United States, 1868–1950 (Continued)

Fiscal Years	Merchandise Imports	Merchandise Exports
1915	$ 297,142,059	$ 173,320,216
1916	370,880,549	201,106,488
1917	665,312,759	280,616,330
1918	792,894,957	417,233,287
1919	750,203,024	454,873,170
1920	801,097,318	464,028,183
1921	856,176,820	542,322,967
1922	515,958,196	292,588,643
1923	540,989,738	369,080,218
1924	601,256,447	430,707,544
1925	509,780,009	417,417,144
1926	738,568,000	475,881,000
1927	836,532,000	475,028,000
1928	914,713,000	489,303,000
1929	948,446,000	503,496,000
1930	659,094,000	402,350,000
1931	396,355,000	266,268,000
1932	241,351,000	174,101,000
1933	210,651,000	185,409,000
1934	302,433,000	231,696,000
1935	323,194,000	286,444,000
1936	384,151,000	375,832,000
1937	509,316,000	398,309,000
1938	467,767,000	260,172,000
1939	489,103,000	339,956,000
1940	713,248,000	423,541,000
1941	993,519,000	553,526,000
1942	1,333,541,000	716,731,000
1943	1,443,952,000	1,024,307,000
1944	1,440,749,000	1,259,898,000
1945	1,177,559,000	1,124,932,000
1946	1,441,614,000	883,388,000
1947	2,073,747,000	1,095,102,000
1948	1,912,174,000	1,553,561,000
1949	1,940,395,000	1,512,128,000
1950 †	1,829,737,000	1,770,308,000

* Nine months ended March 31.
† Jan.–Nov. Includes Newfoundland and Labrador beginning Jan. 1950. Data 1926–50 prepared in the U. S. Department of Commerce, by International Economic Analysis Division, Office of International Trade, from basic data of the Bureau of the Census, Feb. 1951. "Exports" include re-exports.

years before the outbreak of the First World War over 100,000 annually crossed the border. The result gave a distinctly republican tinge to many of the settlements on the Canadian prairie. Between the years 1901 and 1911 (the census in Canada is taken in the years ending in 1) the American-born population of Canada increased by almost exactly 175,000. Of this increase more than 106,000 was provided by the returns from the three Prairie Provinces. In the latter year the American-born formed 3½ per cent of the population of Manitoba, over 14 per cent of the population of Saskatchewan, and almost 22 per cent of the population of Alberta. This trend grew much more pronounced between the census year 1911 and the outbreak of the World War in 1914. It was not surprising, therefore, to find ex-Americans playing an important part in all the activities of life in the Canadian middle west.

The First World War did more than any other single factor to hasten the "Americanization" of Canadian industry. A vast increase in the demand for Canadian goods, both raw and manufactured, was united with the interruption of the flow of British exports of both capital and commodities to the Dominion. During these years the total value of Canadian exports increased as follows:

1912	$ 314,000,000
1913	377,000,000
1914	455,000,000
1915	461,000,000
1916	779,000,000
1917	1,179,000,000
1918	1,579,000,000

As increased prices were partially responsible for this increase, it will perhaps be more accurate to show the rise in actual volume of Canadian exports. Taking 1912 as the base, the index figures of exports by volume rose as follows:

1912	100
1913	127
1914	119
1915	186
1916	242
1917	220
1918	174

Canada was forced to look to the United States for much of the capital that made possible this increase in productivity, though domestic war loans and taxes brought Canadian revenues to a figure that would have been inconceivable a few years earlier. As a result of borrowings in New York, it is estimated that by 1920 the total of American investments in Canada was in excess of $1,300,000,000. During the same period the Canadian holdings of Great Britain remained constant or began to decline. And this was not the end. The fact that the pound sterling was at a discount during the postwar years, while the American dollar was selling at a 7 to 15 per cent premium, gave a further advantage to American investors in Canada—an advantage of which they made wide use. For a time at the end of the war the reconstruction of Europe brought demands for both consumption and capital goods that kept the Canadian economy going—though many of these exports were financed by Canadian loans. But it was not long before the postwar depression, which had only been delayed, again forced Canada to look abroad for aid. As early as 1918 it was estimated that American investors owned approximately thirty per cent of all Canadian industry. After 1918 the movement of American capital across the border continued unabated. By the end of 1924, American investments, according to the United States Department of Commerce, totaled $2,538,-000,000, or over $300,000,000 more than the total of all other foreign holdings. By 1 January 1928, the total American investment was slightly over $3,000,000,000 and it was increasing at the approximate rate of $250,000,000 a year. During the great depression the investment of new funds declined to a much lower figure, but by the beginning of the Second World War United States investments in Canada totaled approximately $4,-000,000,000. Early in 1952 they were estimated at over $7,000,-000,000.

An important aspect of the American financial investments in Canada after the First World War was the establishment of branch factories by American enterprises. Such a factory enjoyed certain very definite advantages: it had free access to the Canadian market, it profited by the British preference, and it benefited from special trade agreements such as that between Canada and France. The automobile and similar industries found a further incentive in the fact that the Canadian tariff rate on parts was less than that on complete machines, with the result that assembling plants were economically profitable.

Estimates as to the number of such factories varied greatly. As early as 1925 it is probable that there were 700 branch factories fully owned by parent companies in the United States, and at least 900 other establishments were partially or completely controlled by American capital. One estimate placed the total at 1400.

Apart from its general high percentage of control, American capital during the postwar years played a particularly significant role in certain selected branches of Canadian industry. The following table throws an interesting light on the situation as it existed in 1920:

Industry	Percentage of capital held in		
	Canada	Great Britain	United States
Electrical apparatus	36.	12.	49.
Meat packing	57.	0.2	41.4
Rubber	40.	2.	50.
Patent medicines	12.	1.8	86.
Paint and varnish	44.	1.5	47.
Motorcars	39.	—	61.
Motorcar accessories	6.5	—	93.5
Brass & copper castings	55.	—	44.9
Condensed milk	48.5	0.5	40.
Refined petroleum	46.7	0.2	53.1
Sugar	67.2	8.4	17.2
Pulp and paper	68.	4.	24.

In addition, American investors held some 41 per cent of the capital invested in Canadian steel furnaces and rolling mills, and approximately 52 per cent of that in copper smelting.

Although American investments in Canada were most extensive in the field of industry, the Canadian bond market also began to attract American capital in considerable quantities. By 1928 the total national wealth of Canada was estimated at some $25,600,000,000, of which United States investors were estimated to hold some $3,000,000,000, or about 8.5 per cent.

Canada and the United States

It should not be overlooked, however, that at the same time Canadian investors were increasing their own foreign holdings at a rather remarkable rate. Not only were Canadian banks and insurance companies investing heavily in foreign securities, but private individuals were showing an ever-widening interest in the offerings of foreign bonds and stocks. It is natural that a considerable percentage of the surplus Canadian funds should go into American industrial enterprises or governmental bonds. The following table, prepared by Professor Kenneth W. Taylor, gives the approximate figures for 1928, on the eve of the great depression:

Canadian Investments Abroad, 1 January 1928

	Total	In U. K.	In U. S.	In O. C.
Govt. loans and balances	$ 43,000,000	....	$ 7,000,000	$ 36,000,000
Balances of chartered banks	270,400,000	....	162,200,000	54,200,000
Foreign securities held by chartered banks	89,000,000	37,000,000	22,000,000	30,000,000
Insurance and trust companies	267,000,000	15,000,000	165,000,000	87,000,000
Direct R. R. and indust. invest.	268,000,000	2,000,000	151,000,000	115,000,000
Miscellaneous investments	425,000,000	10,000,000	215,000,000	200,000,000
Total	$1,362,400,000	$118,000,000	$722,200,000	$522,200,000

During the 1930's Canada was a net exporter of capital, partly through direct investment in foreign securities and in part through the repurchase of Canadian securities held in foreign hands. This movement was made possible and accelerated by the fact that Canada was now reaching the stage of maturity that made possible not only the export of accumulated capital, but the export also of managerial ability, which in turn provided favorable opportunities for the Canadian investor.

This movement was, of course, continued through the Second World War although its form changed. In these later years Canadian exports of capital were largely in the form of loans and "mutual aid" or outright gifts. But of this more will be said later.

The Underwood Tariff of 1913 had marked the first definitely downward movement in American customs dues since the Civil War. It was received with great rejoicing in Canada, especially the reductions on livestock, meats, diary products, wheat, potatoes, and pulp and paper. There was an immediate increase in sales to the United States, and Canadian development was measurably affected by this enactment. Unfortunately the First World War brought other factors into the commercial arena.

During the First World War trade conditions in North America as elsewhere were quite abnormal and a study of the figures contains little that is of permanent significance. The situation may be summarized by stating that European demand was, in most lines, vastly increased, while goods that had heretofore been supplied by European states were now produced in Canada or the United States, and imported by one from the other.

After the war European conditions gradually returned toward normal, and Canadian-American trade began a process of deflation. From 1920 to 1923 this deflation, as far as Canada was concerned, was in part the result of patriotic prejudice. During and immediately after the war the United States became increasingly unpopular in Canada, while there was a great stimulus given to British imperialism. This feeling was increased by American legislative enactments, such as the Jones Shipping Act, which tended to hinder international commerce; the Panama Tolls Bill; the Fordney Emergency Tariff; and, finally, the Fordney-McCumber Tariff of 1922. During these years the United States was adopting the policy of isolation in commercial almost as thoroughly as in political affairs. The reaction against the Wilsonian concept of American leadership in a co-operative effort to establish and maintain a just peace was paralleled by the narrow and indefensible action of the industrially and economically most powerful country in the world in raising tariff rates under the depressing trio, Harding, Coolidge, and Hoover, that set new altitude records in the history of tariff barriers. An incidental result, of course, was the inability of Britain and other debtor countries to pay the interest and principle on their indebtedness to the United States, because they were so firmly barred from selling in the American market. Fordney, Mc-Cumber, and their colleagues thus not only did their best to stop any real development of multilateral world trade, but at the same time gravely exacerbated the political tensions that had arisen between the friends as well as the enemies of the World War days. This combination of circumstances and events assisted the efforts that were being made for various reasons to persuade Canadians to buy within the Empire. The percentage of Canadian imports received from the United States compared with the percentage received from Great Britain during the immediate postwar years was as follows:

	From United States	From Great Britain
1918	82.3	8.4
1919	81.6	8.0
1920	75.3	11.9
1921	69.0	17.3
1922	69.0	15.7
1923	67.4	17.6
1924	67.3	17.2
1925	64.0	19.0
1926	65.8	17.7

Although Canadian-American trade declined from a war-time and immediate postwar high of some $1,200 million in 1918, 1919, and 1920 and $1,300 million in 1921 to approximately $800 million in 1922 and $900 million in 1923, the great progress of the North American economy was reflected in the succeeding years. The record of 1921 was equaled in 1927, was exceeded in 1928, and rose to $1,450 million in 1929.

During these years the exchange of goods between Canada and the United States normally left the former with a deficit on the visible exchange averaging some $260 million, and the "unfavorable" balance was increasing toward the end of the period. The tripartite arrangement by which Canada sold to Britain and bought from the United States was firmly established as the pattern of north Atlantic trading.

4. *Depression and Reciprocal Trade Agreements*

In 1929 a wholly new factor altered the climate in which Canadian-American commercial relations were being conducted. The appearance of European recovery after the First World War had been accepted as fact, but no hard core of reality underlay the appearance. The fever of speculation that began to rise in the United States in 1925 broke in October 1929 with a crash that continued to resound for the better part of the next decade, not only in the United States itself but throughout the whole commercial world. Whatever merits President Herbert Hoover's recovery measures may have possessed—and the Reconstruction Finance Corporation, designed particularly to aid small business, is the only important survivor—they were powerless to halt the downward spiraling of New York Stock Exchange prices, which, with doubtful logic, were believed to reflect the state of national economic health. Not even the election of Franklin D. Roosevelt to the Presidency in 1932, and the return of courage inspired by his inaugural pronouncement: "The only thing we have to fear is fear itself," had any immediate effect in restoring equilibrium to the market.

The panic created throughout the United States had a somewhat delayed reaction in Canada, where overexpansion had been serious but less pronounced. The internal position of the economy remained strong enough to permit the completion of a number of Provincial developments begun during the boom. The downswing in the American business cycle was too prolonged, however, for any market as responsive as Canada's to withstand. The loss of billions of dollars of investment eventually forced Canadians into the vortex with their neighbors.

287

The shock of the great depression aggravated, and was in turn aggravated by, the "agricultural protectionism" resorted to by a Republican Congress in the Hawley-Smoot Tariff Act of 1930. This legislation was deeply resented in Canada, where people felt that it was like hitting a friend when he was down. Retaliation was swiftly forthcoming in the tariff proposals presented in the Dunning budget which was accepted by the Canadian Parliament in May 1930. The new restrictions were frankly advocated as a stiff reply to the "ungenerous" policy of the United States. Pointedly directing its strictures against American tariff increases on meat, poultry, and other agricultural or processed products, the Liberal government adopted what was called the "countervailing principle." This meant that the Canadian tariff was raised in certain specified instances to match the burden imposed on Canadian exports. The Minister of Finance also proposed that the British margins of preference be widened. When enacted, Schedule A of the 1930 tariff bill allowed 589 out of 1,188 items to enter free under British preference. The budget debates were uncompromising in their references to giving the United States "a friendly jolt," and to the duty of the government, "in the interest of furthering our industrial establishment," so to manage Canadian fiscal policy that workers were not left in idleness and forced "to emigrate in order to earn a living."

The desire to expand this policy of retaliation against the United States and at the same time to defend with tariff bars the suffering industries of Canada were major factors in bringing the Conservatives to power in the Canadian elections of 1930. Like his right-wing counterparts in the United States, Prime Minister R. B. Bennett advocated the closing of all possible doors and insisted that as far as possible imports be limited to goods that Canada could not produce. The tariff was to be used as a weapon: he promised to "blast" his way into foreign markets. In some cases even British preferential rates were increased. The Bennett tariff policies were, of course, assailed by the Labor, Progressive, and Liberal opposition, who accused the government of "asking

288

the manufacturers to press their own tariff needs at as high a level as they desired."

Given the conditions existing in the United States at that time, it is unlikely that any action, or lack of action, on the part of Canada would have had any significant effect on American policy. The fact was, however, that both the American and the Canadian tariff changes in 1930 not only failed to contribute to the restoration of the world's shattered equilibrium, but probably extended and prolonged the effects of the depression. The trade figures for the period 1928–33 (see table, p. 280), influenced by the depression and aggravated by the erection of American-Canadian tariff walls, are eloquent of the plummeting progression of the neighboring economies.

The new tariff barriers were not, of course, the only or even the most significant factors in the reduced volume of trade that marked the early years of the new decade. The general slowing down of economic activity in both the United States and Canada meant inevitably a reduction in the rate of exchange of commodities between the two countries. But the tariff bickering was psychologically important and received a great deal of editorial and forensic attention.

The sudden change in Canada's economic life caused by the depression was the more unfortunate in the light of developments that had given great promise in the years before 1929. The vastly cheaper means of transportation via the Panama Canal had lowered the cost of shipping British Columbia's lumber to Eastern ports from $27.30 per thousand feet in 1920 to $10.11 in 1929, with a consequent doubling of output. Similarly, the reduction in water freight rates on grain shipments through the Canal had extended the marketing range of wheat from Alberta and Saskatchewan. Of tremendous potential importance was the rise in the provision of hydroelectric power in Ontario and Quebec from 2,000,000 to 4,800,000 horsepower between 1920 and 1930, and the application of these new facilities to the extraction of ores and the processing of wood in the pre-Cambrian area of the two major provinces. Capital investments in roads and highways had resulted in a tourist trade which in 1929 was estimated at $300,000,000, or more than the value of any single commercial commodity.

The fact that, without any actual alteration in the productive capacity of either country, the crisis of 1929 should have dangerously affected the economic structure of both the United States and Canada was evidence that the root of the crisis lay neither in one nor in the other of the two countries. It was, rather, to be found in Europe, where the destruction caused by the First World War combined with the financial and economic decisions taken by the victors at its close had so undermined the stability of the European economy that any hope of effective and early recovery was soon abandoned.

Britain, with the pound overvalued and her trade gravely impaired, was most adversely affected by heavy withdrawals of foreign capital. Had she been able to liquidate holdings in central Europe, recovery might have been possible, but liquidation was no longer feasible. Credits were frozen, loans in default, and a moratorium had eventually to be declared on German reparations. London abandoned the gold standard in September 1931 and some seventeen countries closely linked to Britain followed this example within the year.

The effect of the international crisis was particularly severe on countries which, like Canada, were dependent on raw-materials exports, and resulted in stringent unilateral action designed for national protection. But new and unprecedented controls were introduced by almost every country. Some of these took the form of drastic quota restrictions, others of licensing systems or similar regulatory measures. Britain, for example, in November 1931, put into effect an Abnormal Importations Act to run for a period of six months. This measure gave authority for Orders in Council imposing duties not to exceed 100 per cent ad valorem on foreign manufactured goods, and duties of 50 per cent ad valorem on some fifty designated articles. The Import Duties Act of 1 March 1932 fixed a duty of 10 per cent ad valorem on goods not otherwise subject to duty, but it exempted a number of products of value to Canada, notably wheat, cotton, cattle, wool, certain ores and minerals, and all shipbuilding materials.

These and similar import restrictions elsewhere produced a striking phenomenon, for although world production of food-stuffs was higher in 1933 than it had been in 1929, world trade in agricultural commodities had fallen by almost 20 per cent.

In the United States, farmers by the thousands lost title to their lands and homes in foreclosure proceedings, and the federal government instituted desperate measures to stabilize farm hold-ings and prices. The Canadian farmers, particularly the wheat-growers, were similarly hit. The bumper crop of 1928 had brought Canadian producers $612,000,000, but for each of the years 1931–3 their income fell to about $170,000,000. In De-cember 1932, according to Professor Vernon C. Fowke, "No. 1 Northern wheat, the best grown in Canada if not in the world, sold at Fort William for less than 40 cents a bushel, which, after deducting transportation and handling charges, represented a price to the farmer of 25 cents or less." Canadian suppliers of newsprint, unorganized and less powerful than their buyers in the United States (who normally constituted 85 per cent of their market), saw demand fall by 30 per cent as capacity increased by one fifth. Bankruptcy in the industry was widespread.

Perhaps the worst effect of the great depression was the stimu-lus it gave to those autarchical tendencies which are latent in every country and which almost inevitably come into play to the general detriment of the international trading community when-ever unexpected and severe pressures are exerted on the national economies.

The Canadian government, faced with mounting unemploy-ment, turned to the largest remaining comparatively free-trade area for its market and convened an Empire Economic Confer-ence at Ottawa in the summer of 1932. As a result of this confer-ence Canada entered into bilateral trade agreements with the United Kingdom, New Zealand, Australia, Southern Rhodesia, the Union of South Africa, and the Irish Free State. With Australia, for example, Canada worked out a pattern of Empire preference that involved levying a 25 per cent duty on non-Australian rice until such time as Australia should be able to supply Canadian requirements; a similar arrangement was evolved for Australian peanuts. With the Union of South Africa Canada formalized commercial relations for the first time on a treaty basis.

The United Kingdom, while continuing preferences and exemptions already in force, provided for additional benefits to Canada by imposing new and increased duties on competing foreign imports. These were chiefly in the field of agricultural and dairy products, but the list included copper. In return, Canada agreed to widen the margin of preference on British imports. Tariff changes were made on 225 items, on 223 of which the British margin of preference was increased. The number of articles placed on the free list was extended by more than fifty. In general, manufactured goods of a class or kind not produced in Canada were made free. The British, however, "reserved the right to remove duties on foreign wheat, copper, lead and zinc at any time Empire producers were unwilling or unable to provide United Kingdom requirements at world prices."

With the non-self-governing colonies and protectorates Canada agreed that tariff schedules should be based on the principle that protective duties be made amenable to adjustment as ability to produce and relative costs of domestic production underwent changes. The Canadian Tariff Board was instituted at this time, to exercise supervision of such details in future, and "to give sympathetic consideration" to the eventual abolition of exchange dumping duties.

As was to be expected under the circumstances, Canadian increases in the margin of United Kingdom preference "were most substantial in lines where the position of the United States had been most dominant." In the classes of goods covered by the Ottawa agreements Canada's trade with the United States had amounted to far more than that with the United Kingdom: approximately $36,000,000 as against $14,000,000.

The negotiations in Ottawa were watched with a rather jaundiced eye by the officials in Washington to whom the Empire preferences had always been a source of annoyance and concern. Yet as an effort to switch Canadian trade from the United States to the United Kingdom and other Empire and Commonwealth areas, the Ottawa agreements cannot be said to have been a great success. They did undoubtedly affect the course of trade in a minor degree for a few years, but whether this compensated for the animosity they aroused in the United States—particularly with reference to the application of the most-favored-nation clause—is an imponderable that can never be determined with assurance. Certainly the Ottawa agreements did not achieve all that their authors had hoped and promised.

The year 1934 appears in retrospect to have been a turning-point toward revival. Not only did it mark the start of the American Reciprocal Trade Agreements Program, with which the name of Secretary of State Cordell Hull became synonymous, but in that year also the United States and Canada recognized and admitted the necessity of bettering and cementing their commercial relations. Actually, no other choice was possible, for, as W. A. Mackintosh pointed out in 1939, isolation could not exert a strong appeal in Canada for very long. As he said, "The position of Canada affords no basis for debate. Economically Canada has been reared in a world economy. She exists in a world economy or she does not exist. Her exports and her tourist trade contribute directly anywhere from 25 to 38 percent of her national income. . . . The deep and abiding interest of North America must be in a program of world co-operation and world order." By the middle of the decade the need for readjustment in Canadian-American tariffs was widely recognized.

The efforts to expand the principle of autarchy in the economic affairs of the two countries were obviously and increasingly proving to be a detriment to both. As early as the spring of 1933, the bellicose Prime Minister Bennett had sought to pave the way to reopen negotiations with Washington. At that time he had found that a condition of further negotiations would have to be an adjustment in the rate base used by Canada in estimating ad valorem duties. This he was as yet unwilling to consider. Although Bennett had once said that "rates made in the United States" could never be made the basis for Canadian tariffs, he would not accept the fact that rates made in Canada on the basis of purely arbitrary juggling of invoices before the application of ad valorem duties were equally unacceptable to American exporters.

Discussions were not wholly abandoned, but it was not until after the victory of Mackenzie King and the Liberal Party in the Canadian elections of 1935 that a really determined effort was made to reach a solution with the United States. On 15 November 1935 an agreement was signed in Washington that in effect re-established reciprocity between Canada and the United States. Under the terms of this agreement the United States granted concessions on some ninety-nine products in exchange for similarly "substantial" concessions by Canada. The year 1911 was at last forgotten.

Some idea of the trend of Canadian trade in the years prior to the agreement can be gained from percentages furnished by the United States Tariff Commission in its Introduction to the text of the 1935 Trade Agreements Act. In 1928, the United States supplied 67.6 per cent of goods imported into Canada, the United Kingdom supplied 13.9 per cent, and other countries 18.5 per cent. In 1934, Canadian imports from the United States stood at 56.8 per cent of the total; those from the United Kingdom constituted 22 per cent, and those from other countries 21.2 per cent.

Concessions made by the United States under the 1935 agreements included a reduction of duties on fifty-nine items, the reductions ranging from 20 to 50 per cent of former rates. Farm products headed the list of important items affected, and among these were not only cattle, dairy products, and poultry, but cheese, maple sugar, apples, grass and clover seed, certain vegetables, and hay. Quota limitations were placed on certified seed

294

potatoes, and duty reductions on four of the principal dairy products were limited to specific quotas. Fish and forest products, minerals, manufactured and miscellaneous products completed the list of concession items, but continued free entry into the United States was bound on a great many others. Among these were such important items as fresh and frozen herrings and lobsters; pulpwood, wood pulp, standard newsprint paper, shingles (under quota limitations), and other nonprocessed wood; crude gypsum, asbestos and artificial abrasives, nickel ore, matte, certain chemicals, and undressed furs.

Concessions made to Canada under the agreement were for the most part only on commodities of which Canada was the principal supplier to the United States. Concessions made by Canada fell into two classes: reductions of from 10 to 100 per cent of former duties, with some relatively unimportant articles transferred to free entry; and reductions in Canadian rates under the most-favored-nation provision, of from 10 to 25 per cent, with some of greater magnitude.

Of items granted reductions, farm products included fresh and canned fruits and vegetables of practically every kind, timothy seed, and corn not for distillation. Corn for certain manufacturing purposes was already free and was so bound under the agreement. Of fish products, the most important item was oysters. Miscellaneous manufactures included wood and paper products; miscellaneous iron and steel manufactures, a very large item; agricultural machinery, electrical apparatus, building stones, dolls and toys. Rate reductions under the most-favored-nation clause included a wide variety of items, from pork products, furniture, engines, aircraft, automobiles and parts, to dry medical and pharmaceutical preparations, boots, shoes, jewelry, phonographs and records. Free entry into Canada was bound on a large number of items, including certain newspapers and magazines, lower-priced farm tractors, typesetting and typecasting machines, and other less ponderable products.

A note from the Canadian Legation to the United States government provided relief in the matter of arbitrary valuation for the assessment of ad valorem duties. The most-favored-nation treatment accorded any non-British country was also granted the United States, and with it went removal of the 10 per cent discriminatory tariff on transit of imports from non-British countries through United States ports.

The signing of the 1935 Trade Agreements Act represented, in Canada, a victory for the Liberal government, which was returned to power in that year. Ironically, despite the Conservative feeler put out to the Americans earlier, the major opposition party now criticized the new agreements, claiming that Canada had not sufficiently pressed its advantages in the negotiations. But the Liberal majority in Parliament, aided by popular support, left no doubt of the passage of the act, and Mackenzie King's government met the Conservative charges with the reminder that the increase in Canadian purchasing power would more than justify the concessions.

The government claim was indeed borne out, as trade figures for the first year of the act's operation showed. Compared with their total in 1935, the United States products on which Canadian tariffs were reduced increased by 24 per cent; those unaffected by the agreement showed an increase of only 8 per cent. On the export side, Canadian products not included in the concessions rose 24 per cent in volume, as against a rise of 65 per cent in duty-reduction imports to the United States. The American concessions on farm products from Canada effectively undid the wrongs Canadians had so long associated with the Hawley-Smoot Tariff Act of 1930, and these concessions were to prove extremely valuable in the following year, when the American farm states suffered a severe drought.

The 1935 agreement was subject to termination by unilateral action, and any "severe exchange depreciation" by either signatory would be considered prejudicial to the agreement's continuing in force. Most novel of all the aspects of the agreement was the introduction of quotas into North American trade operations. When any product so limited passed the quota designated, the higher rate of duty previously existing went automatically into force.

The psychological significance of the trade agreements of 1935 transcended their value commercially, great though that was. With minor exceptions and as contrasted with the previous conditions, conciliation may be said to have marked the atmosphere ever since in the commercial relations between the two countries. In the changed economic climate of the later thirties, the position of Canada in the "North Atlantic Triangle," as the distinguished historian John Bartlett Brebner has described it, was undergoing a change. The geometric figure, from being isosceles, was shifting to a right-angled triangle at whose far point lay England and at whose base angles stood the North Americans.

The United States, under President Roosevelt's astute direction, was engaged in a kind of political logistics, and as the trend from anarchy to autarchy grew unmistakable in central Europe, the administration in Washington began concentrated moves in the direction of hemispheric solidarity. Within this framework the Trade Agreements Act with Canada became a keystone in the Good Neighbor edifice that Secretary Hull was busily erecting in North and South America.

A supplementary Trade Agreement between Canada and the United States was signed at Washington on 17 November 1938, and became provisionally effective in both countries on 1 January 1939, to continue in force for three years.

In 1937 the dutiable imports to the United States from Canada were $155,233,000 and the duty-free imports, $238,009,000, a total some $20,000,000 above that of the year before. Under the second Trade Agreement rates of duty lower than those in effect in 1935, before the first Agreement, were fixed on imported commodities valued in 1937 at $120,500,000 and constituting 77 per cent of all dutiable imports. In addition, the 1935 rates were bound against increase on commodities valued at $3,300,000, or about 2 per cent of the dutiable total. Quota limits were placed on the operation of rate reductions in the case of

297

seven dutiable commodities (cream, milk, seed potatoes, table potatoes, calves, cattle, and fillets of cod), of which imports into the United States were valued at $14,200,000.

The United States Tariff Commission, in its summary of the effects of the agreements, noted that "Excluding whisky, the imports from Canada of commodities on which duties were reduced by the agreement (as compared with 1935 rates) were valued at $99.2 millions, and the imports from all countries at $121 millions, the imports from Canada representing 82 per cent of the total."

The years from 1935 to 1948 have been called "the King era" in Canada, and their coincidence with so much of the "Roosevelt era" in the United States can scarcely be overlooked. But in view of the deteriorating world situation, it is doubtful that anything short of the close Canadian-American co-operation achieved during this period was possible. As the shaky system of collective security broke down in Asia and in Europe, the ties linking the democratic English-speaking peoples were strengthened until by 1939 an Anglo-American trade treaty had crowned a succession of reciprocal agreements.

The United States, under the farsighted leadership of President Roosevelt, was during this period engaged in a determined effort to build an area of mutual prosperity based on expanded trade among all the American and western European countries. To this program the negotiation of the broadly inclusive trade agreement with the United Kingdom was an essential climax.

By the success of these negotiations the ties linking the democratic English-speaking peoples had been so strengthened that it was possible for J. B. Brebner to write: "The greatest triangular exchange of commodities in the world had thus been 'frozen' in the patterns of reciprocal advantage by three carefully drawn treaties."

The commercial position of Canada at the outbreak of war in Europe in 1939 was well summarized in Book I of the *Report* (1940) of the Royal Commission on Dominion Provincial Relations, appointed by Order in Council in 1937. Pointing to Can-

ada's "particularly important place in the world economy," the
Report continued,

> "Although containing less than one per cent of the
> world's population, Canada ranks sixth among the leading
> world traders, first among debtors, fifth among creditors,
> third or fourth among security dealers, and first in tourist
> trade—in fact, she ranks high in all the major activities
> which make up the balance of payments. On a per capita
> basis the Canadian figures in all these transactions sub-
> stantially exceed those of the leading world economic pow-
> ers—United States, United Kingdom, Russia, Germany,
> France, Japan. . . . Industrially Canada is ranked eighth
> in the world (although only thirtieth in population); Ca-
> nadian railways are the fourth largest in the world; and the
> volume of shipping from Canadian ports is about the fourth
> largest. . . .
>
> "To summarize, Canada's position in both her trade and
> other financial relations with the outside world is largely
> that of her position in relation to the United States and the
> United Kingdom. This position is similar to that of a small
> man sitting in a big poker game. He must play for the full
> stakes, but with only a fraction of the capital resources of his
> two substantial opponents. . . . It is scarcely necessary to
> add that if the international trading system in which the Ca-
> nadian economy was designed and built as an integral part
> should be further restricted, a new appraisal (which would
> be distressing) must be made of Canadian resources and the
> Canadian position."

This was the position of Canada before the Second World
War. Changes since 1939 have greatly increased the importance
of the Canadian place in the world economy. During the last
fifteen years Canada has expanded its industrial output, proportionately, as much as the United States did in the hundred years
from 1839 to 1939. During the same fifteen years, and more
particularly since 1947, Canada has vastly increased its known

resources of mineral and other natural wealth. Discoveries of enormous deposits of high-grade iron ore in Quebec and Labrador, the world's largest deposit of titanium in Quebec, a doubling of what were already the greatest known reserves of asbestos, and a constantly and rapidly expanding utilization of the Canadian hydroelectric potential of over 50,000,000 horsepower [7] have all contributed to the conviction that Canada's era of progress has just commenced.

Commercial relations during the Second World War are dealt with elsewhere. After its successful conclusion, Canada participated in the formulation of the charter of the International Trade Organization, and was one of the Big Three in deliberations leading to the General Agreement on Tariffs and Trade signed in Geneva in 1947. Concessions made by Canada under this agreement were of very considerable value to the United States, none more so than "one long requested by industry": removal of the fifty-cent per ton duty on anthracite coal, which had been in force since 1932.

The Report of the United States Tariff Commission on *Operations of the Trade Agreements Program*, dated 1950, noted that while the 1939 trade agreements with Canada were still in effect, "Canada imposed severe quantitative restrictions on imports." Although established during and immediately after the war with the primary purpose of enabling the Canadian government to increase its reserves of United States dollars, the controls were expected also to restore Canada's trade with the United Kingdom and western European countries to somewhere near its prewar level. They attained, however, only the objective of protecting Canadian holdings of United States dollars. Throughout 1948 and 1949 the United Kingdom and western Europe continued to supply far less than what had been their normal proportion of Canadian imports; the share supplied by the United States, on

---

[7] Just over 13,000,000 horsepower are now in use and expansion is taking place at the rate of almost 1,000,000 per year.

the other hand, continued to exceed that of the immediate prewar years (in 1949 it was 70.7 per cent).

Canadian government holdings of United States dollars and gold reserves had reached nearly a billion dollars by the end of 1948, mounted to 1.1 billions in 1949, and were approaching 2.3 billions in June 1950, when the outbreak of hostilities in Korea carried Canadian-American relations around another sharp turn, to be integrated on new and somewhat more difficult terms.

The lessons to be drawn from this review of Canadian-American economic and commercial relations are clear and important. The two countries constitute the greatest international trading community in the world. Although Canada has a population of only 14,000,000 people, it buys each year more American goods than any other three countries in the world—more than most of Latin America combined. In addition, Canada supplies the United States with commodities—nickel, pulp, paper, uranium, to mention only a few—that the great Republic needs and cannot obtain in suitable quantities elsewhere. Canada is moreover the locus of a very large part of American foreign investment—over $7 billion dollars out of a world total of about $20 billion. In return, Canadians hold some $1.1 billion worth of American securities. All these figures are steadily and rapidly rising.

This tying together of the two economies continues at an accelerating tempo. In the year 1950, American companies invested some $167 million in Canadian subsidiary companies and $363 million in Canadian enterprises, a total of $530 million for the single year. It is estimated that United States investors control approximately twenty-five per cent of Canadian industry as well as owning considerable equities in enterprises still under Canadian control. United States investors drew $325 million in interest and dividends from Canada in the year 1948.

On the other hand, Canadian investment in United States securities is much greater per capita than that of Americans in Canada.

301

It is also of interest to note that in the very important field of railway transportation Canadian companies operate and control over 8,000 miles of line in the United States, whereas American railroads have corresponding rights on only 1,550 miles in Canada.

Under these circumstances, it is essential on both sides that the commercial and financial relationships of the two countries be carried on with meticulous care, understanding, and fundamental friendship. The values at stake are now too great to excuse carelessness or the indulgence of irritation. Properly managed in an atmosphere of conciliation and with the application of intelligence, this economic relationship, which already exceeds in dimensions that between any other states in history, can also set an example of profitable and enlightened self-interest.

9

Immigration and Emigration

I. Introduction

The constant and two-way movement of immigrants across the international boundary has been a characteristic phenomenon of the history of the United States and Canada. For almost two centuries the people of the two countries have crossed and re-crossed the international boundary in response to the beckoning finger of opportunity. Today approximately nine out of every one hundred living persons born in Canada are resident in the United States, while more than 300,000 persons of United States birth have made their homes north of the border.

In 1950, the Report of the Commissioner of the United States Immigration and Naturalization Service indicated that over the 131 years from 1820 to 1950, immigrant Canadians admitted to the United States numbered 3,177,446, a total greater than that of immigrants from England. The movement has been an uneven one, and the totals for different periods have shown a wide variation. According to United States figures, the influx (including Newfoundlanders) for the last three decades, for example, has varied as follows:

1921–30	924,515
1931–40	108,527
1941–50	171,718

Canadian emigration to the United States began very early in the history of that country, and the movement of Americans to Canada was in progress even before the Revolutionary War. Although American immigration to Canada was important during the years following the Revolution, when the richly productive lands of Upper Canada enticed many settlers across the border, this movement died down soon after the War of 1812, because of the hostility aroused in the United States by that struggle, the opening of the regions west of the Alleghenies, and the rapidly improving means of communication and transport to the Western plains. After the American Civil War the emigration of youthful Canadians to the rapidly expanding Union was the skeleton in the closet of Canada's national pride. Attracted by the high wages paid in the industrial centers of New England, by the greater opportunities for commercial or professional success, or by the accessibility of the excellent farm lands of the American Middle West,[1] the enterprising and ambitious youth of Canadian birth was easily tempted to cross the border and seek fortune and fame in the great Republic.

It was not until the opening of the twentieth century that American immigration to Canada again reached notable proportions. Between 1896 and 1914 many farmers from the central regions of the United States, influenced by the immigration policy of the Canadian government and attracted by the extraordinary qualities of the wheat belt of Manitoba, Saskatchewan, and Alberta, moved to the north of the 49th parallel and took up homesteads in the Prairie Provinces.

But the outbreak of war in 1914 brought to an end the first era of great expansion in the Canadian west. Immigration from Europe ceased abruptly, and the number of immigrants from the United States was drastically reduced. During succeeding years the stream across the international boundary diminished at times

---

[1] At this time western Canada was almost unexplored and had little or no connection with the original centers of Canadian population. The first through railway was opened only in the eighties; the farm land, now so extraordinarily productive, was almost inaccessible. The free land of the United States was, on the other hand, very easily reached and was in direct communication with the Eastern markets.

to little more than a trickle, though it has never stopped entirely. It has always been and is still true that whenever the promise of economic opportunity glows more brightly on one side of the boundary than on the other the movement expands in rapid response and citizens of one country move to the other with almost the same easy disregard of political boundaries that characterized their fathers before them.

What effect this mutual exchange of citizens has had, or what effect it may have in the future, is a matter for individual interpretation; but there can be little doubt that the influence of the migrants has already played a significant part in drawing the peoples of the two countries together. There are comparatively few Canadians today who have no relatives in the United States, and American citizens are brought into frequent contact with ex-Canadians or persons of Canadian descent in their academic, religious, professional, labor, athletic, and business organizations.

Throughout the nineteenth century neither the American nor the Canadian government was sufficiently interested in the problems of immigration to gather the accurate and detailed records that would make the movement really intelligible to the modern investigator. Even in recent years the relatively complete records of border crossings give no accurate indication of what proportion of the movement in either direction can be attributed to persons intending to take up *permanent* residence across the line. Often the putative immigrant cannot himself define his ultimate intention. Owing to differing standards and classifications, statistics for the two countries are not always comparable. Enough information is available, however, to give some idea of the numbers and categories of those composing the tide of international migration on this continent, and to allow of reasonably defensible generalizations concerning it.

2. *Canadian Immigration into the United States*

Canadian immigration into the United States has been largely concentrated on New England, New York, and the north-central states of the American Union. Within recent years there

TABLE I

Immigration to the United States from Canada, 1871–1950

Year	Number	Year	Number	Year	Number
1871	47,082	1905	2,168	1928	73,154
1872	40,176	1906	5,063	1929	64,440
1873	37,871	1907	19,918	1930	63,502
1874	32,960	1908	38,510	1931	21,687
1875	24,051	1909	51,941	1932	7,929
1876	22,471	1910	56,555	1933	6,135
1877	22,116	1911	56,830	1934	7,873
1878	25,568	1912	55,990	1935	7,695
1879	31,268	1913	73,802	1936	8,018
1880	99,706	1914	86,139	1937	11,799
1881	125,391	1915	82,215	1938	14,070
1882	98,295	1916	101,551	1939	10,501
1883	70,241	1917	105,399	1940	10,806
1884	60,584	1918	32,452	1941	11,280
1885	38,291	1919	57,782	1942	10,450
1886–98		1920	90,025	1943	9,571
	No record	1921	72,317	1944	9,821
1899	1,322	1922	46,810	1945	11,079
1900	396	1923	39,295	1946	20,434
1901	540	1924	70,064	1947	23,467
1902	636	1925	100,895	1948	24,788
1903	1,058	1926	91,019	1949	24,516
1904	2,837	1927	81,506	1950	21,885

has also been a considerable movement of Canadians to California and Washington. Detroit, New York, Boston, and Los Angeles have larger populations of persons of Canadian birth than have most of the cities of Canada. Historically Nova Scotia and New Brunswick were forced by geographic conditions to use

306

Boston as their principal depot of supplies, and it was quite natural that ambitious sons of maritime families, dissatisfied with the limited opportunities of their native provinces, should have looked to Boston or New York rather than distant Toronto or Montreal as the scene of their life activities. To the French-speaking Canadian, also, the attractions of New England have been irresistible. The early introduction of the factory system, and the comparatively high wages paid in textile centers such as Lowell, Woonsocket, and Pawtucket, were most inviting to the young man accustomed to the meager salary of an agricultural laborer in Quebec. A few years of toil in the textile mills for Pierre, and of domestic service in a New England family for Marie, and enough money would be saved to return in state to Canada, or to found a family in Massachusetts or Vermont. This movement began early in the nineteenth century; and by 1850 there were 147,711 persons living in the United States who claimed Canada as their place of birth.

Although the migration of Canadians across the border slackened during the period of the Civil War, the immense industrial and commercial expansion which followed that conflict resulted in a strong stimulus to the movement.

But the industrial and commercial interests of the United States were not alone in receiving a new impetus from the necessities of the Civil War period: agriculture also was benefited by the increased demands for food and raw materials. Thus, when Canadian immigration began again at the close of the war, one current of the stream was directed toward the farm lands of the north-central states. By 1870 the Canadian-born population of the United States had increased to 493,464. Then for thirty years the movement of Canadians into the States reached new high levels, and the fact that many of these emigrants were the more able and ambitious members of their respective Canadian communities, while advantageous to the United States, was a subject of bitter complaint in Canada. A feeling of hopelessness born of the long period of depression seemed to pervade the Provinces, and it was not until the opening of the twentieth century that confidence in their national destiny began to be restored to the people of Canada. Table II gives the measure of this nineteenth-century emigration.

TABLE II

Number of Canadian-born in the United States

1870	493,464
1880	717,157
1890	980,938
1900	1,179,922
Increase, 1870–1900	686,458

Thus, in a period of thirty years, the number of Canadian-born residents of the United States increased by an average of approximately 23,000 annually. When it is realized that during this same period the native-born population of Canada itself increased only from 2,892,763 in 1870 to 4,761,815 in 1900; and that in the latter year the number of Canadian-born persons residing in the United States was almost one fourth the number of the same birth in Canada itself, the serious effects this migration entailed for the people of the Provinces become readily apparent.

After 1900 the movement of the Canadian population tended inward, toward its own "last, best West." This was due to the impact of certain fairly obvious changes in the national economy, among them the great railway expansion to and in the west, an increased appreciation of the potentialities of the Canadian wheat belt, and the propagandist activities of the Canadian government, which both attracted immigrants from all parts of the world and instilled in Canadians themselves a new enthusiasm for their northern homeland. The election of Wilfrid Laurier and the Canadian Liberal Party in 1896 struck a note of confidence and self-reliance that soon resounded throughout the Provinces. The opening of the west as well as the industrial awakening of the east offered more worthy opportunities to youthful energies and ambitions. No longer were Canadians forced by lack of opportunity to emigrate to the United States in order to find scope for their business or professional abilities.

With most of the farm lands of the United States already occupied (the "frontier" is generally said to have disappeared in 1890), Canadian and soon American farmers began to turn with increasing interest to the vast regions west of Lake Superior and north of the international boundary. Industrial and commercial expansion opened new fields for the young engineer, tradesman, and lawyer, while the growing population made increasing demands for the doctor, the clergyman, and the professor. Between 1900 and 1910 the number of Canadian-born persons in the United States increased by only 24,715 to a total of 1,204,637, while by 1920 the total had actually decreased to 1,124,925. Table III, moreover, demonstrates clearly that this diminution occurred principally in the agricultural communities. The really significant figures, those for the north-central states, show a decrease of almost 100,000 in the number of Canadian-born between 1900 and 1920.

TABLE III

Canadian-born in the United States by Geographical Divisions,
1900–10

Geographical Division	1900	1910	1920
United States, total	1,179,922	1,204,637	1,124,925
North Atlantic States	650,617	674,608	614,556
South Atlantic States	6,920	8,681	13,041
North Central States	422,323	375,989	334,597
South Central States	10,262	12,179	11,969
Western States	89,800	133,180	150,762

The outbreak of the First World War marked the beginning of the end of the practically unrestricted movement of immigrants across the border between Canada and the United States. It is true that the exchange of population went on during the war years, but it was on a greatly reduced scale, and largely in answer to the special demands of conditions created by the war. The Allied nations were insatiable in their need for food, munitions, and supplies, and the economies of the United States and Canada expanded to meet that need. Competition for labor was keen and continent-wide, and the net results seem to have been that during the war years American farmers moved into the Canadian

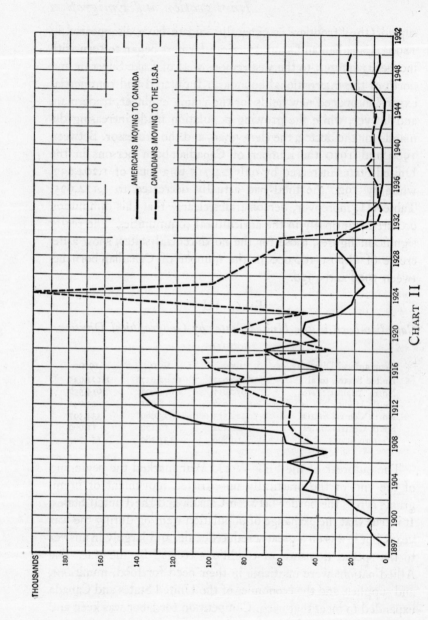

THOUSANDS

180

160

140

120

100

80

60

40

20

0

1897 1900 1904 1908 1912 1916 1920 1924 1928 1932 1936 1940 1944 1948 1952

AMERICANS MOVING TO CANADA

CANADIANS MOVING TO THE U.S.A.

CHART II

west, while Canadians in greater numbers moved to the industrial areas of the northeastern and central states. But it was the early movement into the Canadian west that set the keynote for the decade and resulted in the decrease of Canadian-born in the United States revealed by the census of 1920.

As an aftermath of the war, and of the difficult period of postwar readjustment, however, both countries embarked for the first time on rather complicated programs of immigration control.

The United States after 1893 had begun the registration of aliens arriving at Canadian seaports en route to the United States, but arrivals over land borders did not begin to be reported until 1904, no official record was kept until 1907, and it was only in 1924 that real barriers were raised against the admission of immigrants from Canada.

The postwar decade was marked by an economic boom that ended with the financial crash of October 1929 and the subsequent acute depression. The boom started first in the United States, pulling thousands of Canadians to the great American cities and industrial areas. As conditions improved in Canada, however, this southward movement gradually diminished until 1924. In that year, immigrant quotas, applied for the first time to immigrants entering the United States across the Canadian border, had the immediate effect of encouraging the one phase of the movement which remained unrestricted: namely, the emigration from Canada of the Canadian-born. But that movement, too, was diminishing in volume when the crash of 1929 brought immigration virtually to a standstill, and many expatriate Canadians returned to their original homes. As a result, the Canadian-born population of the United States rose only from 1,124,925 to 1,286,389 between 1920 and 1930.

Throughout the first part of the next decade, Canada and the United States alike suffered the ravages of the great depression, and these were accentuated in both countries by persistent drought in the prairie grainlands. Unemployment of unprecedented proportions became a nightmare to both peoples and governments. The situation was reflected dramatically in the ensuing exchanges of population. Alien public charges were repatriated, and European immigrants whose entry was found to have been irregular were deported to their homelands. The movement of expatriate Canadians to their homes in Canada continued, while almost as many Americans returned to the United States. The census of 1940 revealed that Canadian-born in the United States had decreased in the ten-year period by 242,270.

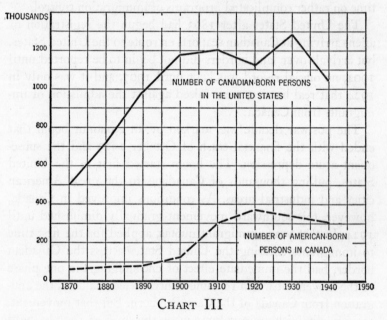

CHART III

Before the close of the decade the grim days of the thirties had culminated in the outbreak of the Second World War. The high degree of co-operation and integration that was subsequently developed in matters of military and economic defense between the United States and Canada as the two countries recognized the extent of their shared strategic interests resulted in an increasing tendency to look upon the whole continent north of the Rio Grande as one economic unit. That situation has changed little throughout the troubled postwar years.

Within the framework of such an intimate association it would be reasonable to expect a relatively free interchange of peoples. Millions of Canadians and Americans yearly cross the common border as tourists or visitors. But while the events of the last two decades have caused population shifts in other countries on a scale never before experienced, and while European immigration to both the United States and Canada has been increasing since the war, North American migration has shown a relative stability that is almost unique. In the United States and in Canada industrial expansion and enormously increasing productivity have created virtually full employment, keeping to a minimum the number of those who cross the border in the hope of finding greener pastures in more distant fields. The constant and two-way movement goes on, but the swinging tide has lost much of its impetus. The numerical balance now, as so often before, is in favor of the United States; but Canada today is in a period of high and increasing activity, developing with tremendous rapidity an industrial machine that has no counterpart in any comparable country. It is not inconceivable that the balance of migration may, in the future, shift again in favor of the northern nation.

The preceding pages have dealt with the history and the physical measurement of immigration into the United States from Canada. More important, perhaps, to the welfare of the recipient state is the quality of the immigrants and the extent of their social and political adjustment in the country of their adoption. An examination of the movement from this standpoint discloses many interesting facts. It reveals, for example, additional reasons for Canada's discontent in reference to the vast emigration of the period from 1870 to 1900. Apart from the French-Canadian laborers and the fishermen and mechanics from the Maritime Provinces, Canada lost during those decades many of those who, by their exceptional qualifications for business or professional life, would have done much to speed the development of their native country. The second great exodus, in the years following the end of the First World War, had many similar characteristics. Large numbers of highly trained professionals, products of

Canada's excellent educational institutions, sought employment south of the border, where greater economic activity offered more in the way of financial reward. In the academic world the situation has been most extraordinary. The faculties of the better American universities are honeycombed with Canadian scholars, and many ex-Canadians reached the top of the academic pyramid. The number of university presidents and deans of Canadian origin would constitute an imposing record.

More recent immigration from Canada appears to be following somewhat the same pattern. Among 18,043 immigrants of Canadian birth entering the United States during the fiscal year ended 30 June 1950, the largest single group, numbering 2,612, was made up of "professional and semi-professional workers," followed by "clerical, sales and kindred workers" numbering 2,457. This is, of course, not taking into account a group of 9,455 listed as having "no occupation" and consisting largely of wives and children. Of actual workers, the professional classes made up 30 per cent.[2] These figures, which are typical of recent years, while representing a drain on the talent and character of the Canadian population, do not in any real measure justify the complaints still so commonly heard in Canada that the United States is draining off the best Canadian youth. There was certainly some basis for such complaints in the period from 1870 to 1895, and again in the 1920's, but the old refrain lacks most of its pertinence in the circumstances of 1951. The fact is that a country of over 14,000,000, with the standards of education now existing in Canada, can well afford the loss of trained men and women in these relatively insignificant numbers, particularly when it is recognized that a considerable proportion of these "immigrants" will, in fact, return sooner or later to the land of their birth. In the meantime they are good representatives of Canada in the United States, most of them are adding to their knowledge and resources, and they are contributing to the common cause of North American development. An annual "loss" of this magnitude should not necessarily be a cause for regret; and certainly

[2] Report of the U. S. Immigration and Naturalization Service, 1950.

it provides little justification for the continued complaints of Canadian critics. French Canadian-born immigrants are not today so readily distinguishable as they once were. In so far as they can be identified, they are usually to be found in the categories of skilled workers and foremen, semiskilled workers, and laborers other than farm workers.

The Canadian-born immigrants have shown a high degree of assimilability in employment, and can today be found in practically all occupational groups. Geographically, too, they are widely scattered, being identified in every state of the Union. But the great majority of them are still concentrated in relatively small areas. Table IV shows their distribution by states in each of the census years from 1890 to 1940, and makes it clear that in the latter year nearly half the Canadian-born population could be found in three states: Massachusetts, with 223,873; Michigan, with 158,416; and New York, with 123,737. Twelve states had less than 1,000 Canadian-born, and sixteen more states had less than 5,000.

The 1950 census of the United States showed a population shift of some magnitude from the Central and Eastern to Western states, and although classification of this most recent census by country of birth or origin is not yet available, there is reason to believe that the Canadian-born have participated to some considerable extent in this internal migration. Nevertheless, the statistical record will no doubt show that nearly eighty per cent of all Canadian-born in the United States continue to live in the states bordering on Canada, plus Massachusetts, Connecticut, and Rhode Island in the East, and California and Oregon on the Pacific coast.

This tendency to "bloc" or concentrate in certain areas is a characteristic of the Canadian immigrant to the United States that is not equally shared by the Americans in Canada, who are distributed more evenly over a wider area. The centers of Canadian settlement in the United States have been determined largely by the types of early migrations, and the concentration has been brought about by later immigrants who settled where

TABLE IV

Canadian-born in the United States by States, 1890–1940

(Compiled from Reports of the United States Census. Figures for years prior to 1910 include persons born in Newfoundland.)

Division and State	1940	1930	1920	1910	1900	1890
United States	*1,044,119*	*1,286,389*	*1,124,925*	*1,204,637*	*1,179,922*	*980,938*
New England:						
Maine............	60,990	73,995	74,420	76,223	67,077	52,076
New Hampshire...	42,272	50,992	52,312	57,878	58,967	46,321
Vermont.........	19,735	27,194	24,885	26,058	25,655	25,004
Massachusetts....	223,873	289,496	263,478	297,369	293,169	207,601
Rhode Island.....	30,747	39,325	36,482	41,954	39,277	27,934
Connecticut.......	31,025	37,863	24,679	26,757	27,045	21,231
Middle Atlantic:						
New York........	123,737	149,148	112,804	123,551	117,535	93,193
New Jersey.......	14,526	16,665	10,396	9,135	7,132	4,698
Pennsylvania......	13,412	16,617	15,100	15,683	14,760	12,171
E. North Central:						
Ohio.............	21,071	27,345	24,670	23,692	22,767	16,515
Indiana..........	5,588	6,267	5,147	5,838	5,934	4,954
Illinois...........	33,256	43,988	38,773	45,751	50,595	39,525
Michigan.........	158,416	203,783	165,902	172,863	184,398	181,416
Wisconsin........	11,622	15,613	19,400	24,996	33,951	33,163
W. North Central:						
Minnesota........	22,060	27,216	33,862	41,121	47,578	43,580
Iowa.............	4,962	6,353	8,944	11,619	15,687	17,465
Missouri..........	4,096	5,460	6,562	8,069	8,616	8,525
North Dakota.....	8,721	12,509	15,743	21,507	28,166	23,045
South Dakota.....	2,176	3,414	4,462	6,010	7,044	9,493
Nebraska.........	3,024	4,410	5,780	7,335	9,049	12,105
Kansas..........	2,764	4,068	5,352	7,188	8,538	11,874
South Atlantic:						
Delaware.........	512	479	453	504	298	309
Maryland........	2,642	2,307	1,894	1,430	1,230	1,020
Dist. of Columbia..	2,924	1,729	1,726	1,161	906	655
Virginia..........	1,929	1,647	1,947	1,360	1,130	780
West Virginia.....	848	980	981	872	711	374
North Carolina....	1,005	948	663	543	480	355
South Carolina....	331	280	271	282	204	159
Georgia..........	1,023	1,104	965	801	759	609
Florida...........	9,368	8,189	4,141	1,728	1,202	1,151

TABLE IV. *Canadian-born in the United States by States,*
1890–1904 (Continued)

Division and State	1940	1930	1920	1910	1900	1890
E. South Central:						
Kentucky........	853	934	903	1,070	1,208	1,173
Tennessee........	848	949	988	1,156	1,045	1,020
Alabama.........	722	919	904	833	706	620
Mississippi........	303	365	406	450	420	345
W. South Central:						
Arkansas.........	560	715	893	1,074	1,093	947
Louisiana........	899	1,009	1,186	1,191	1,034	762
Oklahoma........	1,654	2,146	2,489	2,871	1,807	420
Texas...........	4,100	4,563	4,200	3,534	2,949	2,866
Mountain:						
Montana.........	8,569	11,193	14,700	13,842	13,826	9,040
Idaho...........	4,098	4,529	4,961	5,371	2,923	1,791
Wyoming.........	974	1,144	1,440	1,431	1,248	1,314
Colorado.........	4,165	5,845	7,642	9,581	9,797	9,142
New Mexico......	515	618	738	1,023	764	681
Arizona.........	1,590	2,037	1,964	1,827	1,269	732
Utah............	1,434	1,192	1,471	1,690	1,331	1,222
Nevada.........	841	955	1,181	1,847	1,032	1,662
Pacific:						
Washington.......	42,306	48,269	43,179	39,482	20,284	17,412
Oregon..........	16,492	17,946	13,800	12,409	7,508	6,460
California........	95,741	101,677	59,686	44,677	29,818	26,028

others of their kind had gone before them. Thus there is a heavy concentration of French-speaking Canadians in New England, which has been the destination of emigrants from Quebec since the early migrants first found employment in the textile mills and the homes of that region. Table V gives the number of French Canadian-born in the whole of the United States in each of the census years from 1890 to 1940, and shows the high percentage of those who, over the years, have made their homes in the New England states. Table VI reveals how thinly they were scattered through the other states of the Union in 1940.

As between rural and urban areas, Canadians again are less evenly distributed than the United States population as a whole, tending more strongly to be urban dwellers, being similar in this

TABLE V

Concentration of French Canadian-born in the New England States

Census Year	United States	French Canadian-born in New England States	Percentage
1890	302,496	205,761	68.0
1900	394,461	275,377	69.8
1910	385,083	278,156	72.2
1920	307,786	240,385	78.1
1930	370,852	264,261	71.2
1940	273,366	195,000	71.3

TABLE VI

Canadian-born in the United States, French and other, by Divisions, 1940

Division	Canada-French	Canada-other
United States, total	273,366	770,753
New England	195,000	213,342
Middle Atlantic	23,890	127,785
East North Central	29,950	200,003
West North Central	7,281	40,522
South Atlantic	2,013	17,669
East South Central	233	2,493
West South Central	715	6,498
Mountain	2,589	19,597
Pacific	11,695	142,844

TABLE VII

Urban and Rural Distribution for total population, all foreign-born, and Canadian-born: 1940

Class	United States Number	Percentage	All foreign-born Number	Percentage	Canadian-born Number	Percentage
Total	131,669,275	100.0	11,419,138	100.0	1,044,119	100.0
Urban	74,423,702	56.5	9,134,318	79.9	796,066	76.2
Rural-						
nonfarm	27,029,385	20.5	1,371,206	12.0	167,465	16.0
farm	30,216,188	22.9	913,614	8.1	80,588	7.8

respect to the foreign-born of other countries living in the United States. This is made clear in Table VII. French Canadian-born show an even stronger tendency to live in cities, 214,962, or 78.6 per cent, of a total of 273,366 in 1940 being classified as "urban," and only 6.4 per cent in the "rural farm" category. Among United States cities in 1940, Detroit, New York, Boston, Los Angeles and Chicago, in that order, had the greatest Canadian-born population. (See Table VIII.)

Generally speaking, the tendency to "bloc" is not a desirable characteristic in the immigrant population. With English-speak-

TABLE VIII

Cities of the United States having more than
5,000 Canadian-born: 1940

Name	Number
Detroit, Mich.	74,137
New York, N. Y.	35,500
Boston, Mass.	33,143
Los Angeles, Calif.	27,755
Chicago, Ill.	21,578
Buffalo, N. Y.	13,735
Seattle, Wash.	12,545
San Francisco, Calif.	8,615
Somerville, Mass.	7,808
Rochester, N. Y.	7,760
Lowell, Mass.	7,471
Portland, Oregon	7,029
Worcester, Mass.	7,020
Fall River, Mass.	6,782
Cambridge, Mass.	6,662
Providence, R. I.	5,668
Springfield, Mass.	5,604
Minneapolis, Minn.	5,450

ing Canadians, however, there is no problem of integration. Their cultural, political, and religious background is similar to that of the majority of their American neighbors, and they soon make themselves at home, mingling freely with the people of the communities into which they have moved. Intermarriage is frequent, speeding the process of complete assimilation. Naturalization is less frequent with them than with the immigrant population from Britain, Germany, Scandinavia, and the Low Countries, but this is very likely due less to a reluctance to accept a new citizenship than to the proximity of their former homes and the ever present possibility of some day going back.

The French-speaking Canadian immigrant, though he is now

more likely than before to speak English, brings with him a different cultural background. His life centers largely in his home and his church, and religious and family ties are very strong. Efforts are made to preserve his traditional language and his cultural inheritance generally by the establishment of parochial schools and colleges, by French-Canadian books and newspapers, by societies and organizations, and by all the other influences that strengthen his association with other French-speaking Canadians both in the United States and in the Canadian province that he very often continues to call "home." It is not surprising, therefore, to learn that the French-speaking Canadian immigrant buys a home less frequently than his English-speaking compatriot, and shows less tendency to acquire citizenship in his adopted country, although, on the average, he has resided there over a longer period. A recent sampling of the population showed that only 56.1 per cent of the French-Canadian stock were naturalized, while 60.8 per cent of other Canadian residents had become United States citizens. As has previously been indicated, both are below the general average for immigrants in the United States.

Two other aspects of social relations are important in any study of immigrant population: literacy and criminality. For the first, no statistical record is available since the 1930 census, when it appeared that 3.3 per cent of the Canadian-born in the United States were illiterate. This was about the same as for the population of the United States as a whole. Taken separately, however, English-speaking Canadians had a much lower illiteracy rate, 0.6 per cent, being second only to the Scots in this respect. When it is noted that the illiterates in 1930 were largely among the older population groups, it is reasonable to assume an even higher degree of literacy among those of Canadian origin in the United States today.

The inadequacy of the available figures on the immigrant and his participation in crime was recognized by the Senate Committee on the Judiciary in its Report on the Immigration and Naturalization Systems of the United States, 1950. Nevertheless, the available figures used by the Bureau of the Census reveal that in the institutional census years of 1910, 1923, and 1933 the Canadian-born were well down in the list of foreign-born white prisoners, on the basis of commitments to penal institutions. In the years 1940, 1945, and 1946, however, when only the statistics on commitments for felonies were used, the Canadian-born ranked second in 1940 and third in 1945 and 1946. It is noted, however, that foreign-born whites, including Canadians, do not exceed their proportion of the total population in general commitments for crime.

In connection with Canadian-American migrations, mention must always be made of the "Canadian channel" through which for many years a stream of European immigration flowed into the United States. Even today, with immigrant quotas being carefully observed, many who are not Canadian-born are included in the Canadian movement. In the fiscal year that ended 30 June 1950, among 21,885 immigrants who entered the United States from Canada, 3,842 were other than Canadian-born. Many of these had spent considerable time in Canada, and had no doubt been sufficiently influenced by their Canadian associations to be all but indistinguishable from their fellow Canadian immigrants.

Canadian immigration has been a significant factor in the growth of the American population. There are today more than 3,000,000 persons of Canadian derivation in the United States. Within the present pattern of North American development, however, it is reasonable to suppose that any future movements from Canada will, in comparison with the size of the general population, be relatively insignificant. The quality of their contribution to the cultural and economic progress of their adopted country may be expected to continue to be of greater significance than their numbers.

321

3. American Immigration into Canada

The first important influx of Americans into what is now Canada occurred in the decade before the American Revolution. Long before this the expansive New England frontier was thrusting toward the northeast. New Englanders had focused their attention on the French settlements in Acadia—present-day Nova Scotia and New Brunswick—and at the beginning of the eighteenth century they had been instrumental in bringing about the conquest of the area. In 1713 the war was ended by the Treaty of Utrecht, and by its terms the whole region, with the exception of what is now called Cape Breton Island, was joined to the First British Empire.

Because of the grant to the Scotsman Sir William Alexander in the time of James I, this area, which the French called Acadia, was known in the British world as Nova Scotia. For forty-odd years after 1713 Nova Scotia was neglected by the British, and the French Acadians continued to till their fertile lands around the Minas Basin. They hoped to be allowed to remain the Neutral Acadians of Nova Scotia. In time of war, however, this French group constituted in the eyes of the British an unreliable and proportionately large part of the population. To offset this alien element, Halifax was founded in 1749.

In the early 1750's, war with France, the final great duel for North America, seemed inevitable. Governor Lawrence of Nova Scotia did not feel that he could accept the responsibility of allowing the French Acadians to continue in the province and determined upon their expulsion and dispersal. Longfellow in pathetic verse, but with perhaps something less than historical objectivity, has described the results.

The land left vacant by the forceful and tragic expatriation of the Acadians became the next object of Governor Lawrence's policy. The New England frontier seemed to provide the answer. In proclamations spread throughout New England, he offered this land on generous terms to the North American pioneer. At first these offers met with little response. After 1759, however, a variety of circumstances combined to make the offer more attractive. There was land hunger on the New England frontier, and a depression had followed the cessation of hostilities in North America. Politically, Nova Scotia had not been attractive to New Englanders, as it lacked a representative assembly. In 1758 an assembly was granted. The early 1760's saw a considerable influx of New Englanders into Nova Scotia, and the movement continued. On the eve of the American Revolution, New Englanders made up between two thirds and three fourths of the population of Nova Scotia.

These people in Nova Scotia, as in the Middle West of the United States, left the indelible imprint of their institutions, their attitudes, and their way of life. As Thomas Chandler Haliburton, creator of the character Sam Slick, and a man sensitive to the essential Nova Scotian temperament, remarked a half century later: "The old stock comes from New England and the breed is tolerably pure yet, near about one half applesarce and tother half molasses." The long struggle of the War of Independence put a peculiar and painful strain on these people. It is an irony of history that these New Englanders, who had replaced a people whose aspiration it had been to maintain neutrality in the face of the Franco-British struggles, now found themselves, as the Revolutionary struggle deepened and became ever more bitter, aspiring toward their own kind of neutrality. Neutral Yankees of Nova Scotia had replaced neutral Acadians of an earlier day. The good citizens of Yarmouth, Nova Scotia, put the case plaintively in 1775:

"We do all of us profess to be true friends and loyal subjects to George our King. We were almost all of us born in New England, we have fathers, brothers and sisters in that country divided betwixt natural affection to our nearest relations and good faith and friendship to our King and Country, we want to know if we may be permitted at this time to live in a peaceable state, as we look on that to be the only situation in which we with our wives and children can be in any tolerable degree safe."

Yet neutrality did not satisfy all these people. There was a good deal of sympathy for the revolutionary cause, and had not geography and British sea power imposed their mandate, it is not impossible that Nova Scotia would have become a fourteenth colony in revolt and a fourteenth state in the federal Republic.

The second great influx of Americans into Canada came as a result of the American Revolution. There were a variety of reasons for Loyalist migrations, and among the powerful motives operating were those common to the North American pioneer.

The Loyalists took two main routes in their removal from their old homes: one route by sea to the province of Nova Scotia (divided in 1784 to form the provinces of Nova Scotia, New Brunswick, and Cape Breton), and the other route by land into the province of Quebec. The first migration was by far the larger. New York had become a Loyalist center during the years of the Revolution, and when peace came in 1783 it was necessary to make some provision for these people who had by force or through conviction suffered so much for their British allegiance.

The British post at New York, unlike other such posts in the Northwest, was evacuated promptly at the peace. There was much vacant land in the border province of Nova Scotia, which had for so long looked toward both New England and New France. It was a land with a long history of disputed boundaries and divided loyalties—a land of bitter conflict. It had known neutral Acadians, neutral Yankees; and was now to accept a large admixture of people who had been unwilling or unable to remain neutral in the last great struggle for North America. As in the past it had been an outpost between British North America and New France, so now, following the great schism of the eighteenth century, it was to be an outpost between the United States of America and a new British North America. A maritime region of great beauty and diversity, it drew its inspiration and quickness from the sea, and today its population, varied and talented, illustrates in a marked degree the strain and stress of North American politics and geography.

In 1783 there was a "spring fleet" and a "fall fleet" from New York to take the Loyalists to their new homes. One observer declared: "Nova Scotia is the rage. Everybody, all the world, moves on to Nova Scotia." It was confidently predicted that Nova Scotia would be made the envy of all American states. Indeed, there was much to give substance to this belief. The Loyalists who went to Nova Scotia were, on the whole, drawn from the group on the Atlantic seaboard characterized by property, education, and superior social standing. They belonged to an old and settled society and became pioneers most unwillingly. They achieved the measure of success they did in pioneering only after tragic suffering. One of these Loyalists, whose grandson became the Finance Minister in the later Dominion of Canada, told one of her descendants: "I climbed to the top of Chipman's hill and watched the sails disappearing in the distance, and such a feeling of loneliness came over me that, although I had not shed a tear through the war, I sat down on the damp moss with my baby in my lap and cried."

As a result of these mass population movements, some 20,000 Loyalists went to Nova Scotia, some 14,000 to New Brunswick, 600 to what is now the province of Prince Edward Island, and 400 to Cape Breton. The total was around 35,000.

By eighteenth-century standards this was mass migration. Shelburne, Nova Scotia, today a sleepy provincial town, was, in the autumn of 1784, next to Philadelphia, Boston, and New York, the largest city on the continent north of Mexico. The Loyalists dispersed themselves, however. There was a good deal of moving around within the new British North American Maritime Provinces, and some moving back to the United States. But the end result was a very large addition of population, and, significantly, that population was American. It has left its imprint down to the present day.

This population movement completed a process. It was the last eastward thrust of population along the Atlantic seaboard. During the next generation the population filled in the valleys opening out to the sea. The excitement, the color, the drama of the American Revolution have obscured the general character of this movement. It is a mistake to think that the Revolutionary struggle accounts for the peopling of this northeastern section of Canada. The preliminaries of the Revolution and the course it ran in fact interrupted a great North American pioneer movement for almost a generation. What the Revolution did was to impose upon a general pattern a selective process, political in nature. The northeastern region of Canada would have been peopled by Americans in any case. The course of history determined that rather than being settled by willing Americans, it was settled by unwilling ones.

The second route that the Loyalists took was the natural way into the old province of Quebec. The British authorities were adamant against allowing the Loyalists to settle in the region north of Lake Champlain in the area of the Eastern Townships and the old seigniories. There were two main reasons for this: to settle Loyalists in this region would have complicated relations with the French, and, in addition, the border character of the region made its future most uncertain. Consequently, Governor Haldimand insisted upon a removal of the Loyalists to a more remote and inaccessible frontier. In the main the Loyalists settled along the north shore of Lake Ontario, east of St. Francis, and, coming across from Detroit, in the present districts of Amherstburg and the Thames River.

There were far fewer Loyalists who came overland into what is now the province of Ontario than there were Loyalists who had gone to the Maritime Provinces. Of real Loyalists there cannot have been more than seven thousand. There were "Early" and "Late" Loyalists. The motives of the Late Loyalists were more closely related to pioneer activities and had little if any political significance. They illustrate a pioneer movement and not a political exile. The term "Late Loyalist" came to have a most derogatory connotation. The Loyalists who came northward across the border were quite different in background from those who went to Nova Scotia. They were mostly pioneer farmers. Governor Hope said in 1786 that few Loyalists in Canada were persons of great property or consequence, and another observer declared that they were "mostly farmers from the back parts of New York province." They were part of the North American frontier, and where they led, other pioneers followed.

For three decades after 1783 there was a flow of American settlers into British North America. By all odds the most important movement in these years was overland into the old province of Quebec, which was divided in 1791 into Upper Canada, present-day Ontario, and Lower Canada, present-day Quebec. In the early years after 1783 it was difficult to discriminate between Loyalists and pioneer farmers. But later the migration had a clearly defined character; it had become part of the westward movement of the North American frontier.

The westward migration, which explains so much in the distribution of North American population, has too often in the past been conceived in terms of two westward movements—an American movement and a Canadian one. This is not a true historical concept. There have not been parallel American and Canadian westward movements; there has been a single North American westward movement. An understanding of this fundamental fact in the dynamics of population movements is necessary before any real understanding of the intermingling of the Canadian and American people is possible. Canadians from the beginning united with Americans in their assault on the continent. To the North American frontiersman, good land meant much and political sovereignty little.

From the early 1790's onward, the movement of Americans into Upper and Lower Canada was part of the North American westward movement. The expansive frontiers of New England and New York found their outlet more naturally in the Canadas than in their own Northwest. The Constitutional Act of 1791 gave the framework of government and the guarantee of representative institutions. Montreal provided a market for potash, that essential product of the agricultural frontier. Both Upper and Lower Canada actively sought settlers in the United States. Land was cheaper in Canada, and the Indian troubles that beset the Old Northwest in these years were largely absent in Canada. Indeed, the pioneer route to the Old Northwest was more difficult and dangerous than that to the Canadas. The economic stagnation following Jefferson's embargo in 1807 added to the impetus northward and westward into British North America. Looking backward in 1816, the editor of the Montreal *Gazette* wrote: "If the two last Presidents are entitled to the honour of monuments anywhere upon the globe, it surely is at Montreal."

The result was that Americans in large numbers came into the Eastern Townships and advanced westward along the north shore of Lake Ontario. These were pioneer communities, and these Americans understood pioneer techniques. Nationality was no bar to entry or to the taking up of lands. The British authorities valued the skills, the tenacity, the industry these people brought. These factors bulked large and political sentiments played a minor part. Bishop Stewart declared that the Americans made the best settlers in a new country. Revolutionary soldiers returned once a year to the United States to collect their pensions. A common way of life developed.

There are no official records through which we can learn with exactness the size and scope of this movement. The writer of an authorized gazetteer, however, in 1812 reckoned that eight out of every ten persons in Upper Canada were Americans or of American descent. One quarter of this number were Loyalists or the children of Loyalists. But these people were settled for the most part on the north shore of Lake Ontario or in the Niagara peninsula. The people on the north shore of Lake Erie and in the upper Thames Valley were almost without exception from Pennsylvania, New Jersey, or New York. Since originally the Loyalists did not amount in numbers to more than seven thousand and since in 1812 the population of Upper Canada was about one hundred thousand, this province, which had been opened to accommodate Loyalists, appeared on the eve of the War of 1812 to be more American than British. On both sides of the international line it seemed that the inevitable result of war would be to join Canada to the federal Republic.

By 1812 the eastern half of the shores of Lake Erie were filled in by settlement on both the Canadian and the American sides. The war between Canada and the United States, which began in June of that year, had two fundamental effects upon the frontier: it diverted settlement and the westward movement south of the Lakes, and it promoted an anti-American spirit in Canada, particularly among the Loyalist population and the British official element. This was most apparent in Upper Canada, where danger from a possibly disloyal element seemed greatest.

After the war the easygoing official attitude toward the entry and the taking up of land by Americans in Upper Canada was replaced by more rigorous regulations and an effort to attract settlers from the British Isles. It was hoped to make the province more essentially British. In 1815 the Colonial Office directed that no further lands be granted to persons of American nationality, and an effort was made to prevent such people from coming in, in so far as this was possible. In 1817 the administration of the nationality laws was tightened. This had the effect of lowering the price of land in Upper Canada and was highly unpopular in the province. The policy was characterized as "the deadliest thrust ever made by folly at the prosperity and welfare of Upper Canada." The Assembly of the province was only prevented from passing a vote of censure through prorogation. In spite of this discouragement, however, settlers from the United States still continued to enter and establish their homes in Upper Canada.

The panic of 1819 interrupted the westward movement in both Canada and the United States. By the time the movement again became vigorous, about 1825–6, the Erie Canal had been completed, making available an all-American water route to the interior. From the 1830's on toward the end of the century, the goal of westward-moving pioneers became not Canada but the

Western states of the United States. A variety of factors produced this result: the existence of the Erie Canal; the political troubles of the 1830's in the Canadas; the depression of 1837, combined with the fear of further insurrections following the rebellions of that year. But most important of all, Canada had no middle west; it had instead a Pre-Cambrian shield.

The shield was a lopsided triangle. Its northern points were Labrador and the Arctic east of the great Mackenzie River. It came down close to the St. Lawrence as that river emptied into the Atlantic, and toward the west the good lands failed some hundred miles north of Lake Ontario. It followed the north shores of Lakes Huron and Superior and then struck northwestward to the mouth of the Mackenzie River. It completely severed the St. Lawrence lowlands from the western plains, and it was generally unsuited to agriculture. During the glacial period it had been swept clear of its topsoil. Professor D. G. Creighton has written: "It was a solemn country, with that ungainly splendour evoked by great, crude, sweeping lines and immense and clumsy masses. The marks of age and terrific experience lay heavy upon it. It was an elemental portion of the earth, harshly shaped by the brutal catastrophes of geological history." It has been said that the greatest gift Canada ever made to the United States was the gift of its good topsoil from this whole gigantic region.

Consequently, the North American westward movement was deflected across Michigan and south of the Great Lakes. By 1852 the railways had reached Chicago, and by 1854 the section of the New York Central between Buffalo and Detroit had been completed. This railway followed the old track of the pioneer, but it came after the great movement into Canada had spent itself, and instead of bringing Americans into Canada, it took Canadians into the United States, following the North American frontier. The West for Canadians and for Americans was the West of the United States.

Broadly speaking, it may be said that between 1783 and 1850 southern Ontario had many Americans, that between 1840 and

ments to other parts of Canada. Economic expansion in British Columbia attracted both labor and capital from the United States. Ontario, too, experienced an influx of American immigrants during that period. Some of these had responded to the lure of the fabulous wealth they hoped to find in the mining regions north of Lake Superior; others thought they saw opportunities in the newly opened region of the Rainy River; and still others followed American capital into Canada as more and more branch plants were established across the border by American manufacturers.

While the First World War put an abrupt end to immigration from Europe and slowed down considerably the movement from the United States, nevertheless American farmers continued to move into the Canadian west, and the development of the prairie farmlands went on apace. By the end of the war Canada was the world's greatest exporter of wheat.

But now the agrarian pioneer stage of Canada's development was drawing to a close, and a basic change in the Canadian economy was taking place. Industry had gained in importance during the war, and it continued to expand during the decade of the twenties, concurrently with the increasing exploitation of Canada's natural resources—minerals, forests, and water power. A distinct movement from rural to urban areas became evident. When immigration from Europe began again, it was restricted to those who would buy land or accept farm or domestic employment; but at the 1931 census it was revealed that 60% of the new arrivals had found their way to the cities.

But great as was the economic activity in Canada, that of the United States far surpassed it, and many of the recent arrivals from the United States responded to the lure of the great cities across the border. Although immigration from the United States continued in diminishing volume throughout the decade, Canada's American-born population decreased by nearly 30,000.

The high point in postwar immigration to Canada was reached in 1929, when some 165,000 immigrants were admitted, of whom 30,000 were from the United States. But once again a major world catastrophe—this time the financial crash of 1929—stemmed the immigrant tide, and it had just begun to rise again when the Second World War broke upon a still-troubled world. The 1941 census disclosed another decrease of more than 30,000 in the American-born population of Canada, although the British and European-born elements showed an even greater decrease. The extent of the outward movement during the years of depression was all too clear.

Immigration from Europe was, of course, at a standstill during the first half of the forties; and when it began again after the close of hostilities, the first groups admitted were the wives and dependents of Canadian service personnel, close relatives of persons living in Canada, and displaced persons or refugees, who came in groups destined to employment as farmers, miners, woods workers, and domestics. A plan to encourage the immigration of Netherlands farm families—bona fide farm settlers—was a move designed to replenish the Canadian farm population, depleted by an expanding industrialization. As growing economic activity increased Canada's absorptive capacity, classes of admissible immigrants were widened; and the decade ended with European immigration again being actively encouraged, though on a carefully selective basis.

Through all this activity, immigration from the United States remained at a uniformly low level. Even the oil "boom" in Alberta, which brought large quantities of American capital into Canada, failed to attract more than a handful of Americans classified as immigrants. The smaller "independent" oil companies are now almost completely staffed in all branches by Canadians, and the largest western operator reports only 17 United States citizens out of a total employee roll of 1,230. The ratio of American personnel engaged in the Alberta oil industry today is estimated at about ten per cent.

During the calendar years 1946–50, immigrants admitted to Canada numbered 430,389, of whom only 43,833 were from the United States. During the same period some 30,000 citizens returned to the United States. Official estimates of the Dominion

Bureau of Statistics placed the population of Canada in December 1950 at approximately 14,000,000, an increase of some 2,500,000 over 1941. These estimates give no indication of the composition of the population by country of birth or origin, and the picture will be fully revealed only by the results of the 1951 census. Nevertheless it seems fairly obvious that, in spite of the general population increase, the number of American-born in Canada will be found to have changed little since the opening of the decade, when it stood at 312,473.

TABLE XIII

*American-born in Canada, by Provinces, 1871–1941 **

Year	Canada	Prince Edward Island	Nova Scotia	New Brunswick	Quebec	Ontario
1871	64,613	350	2,239	4,088	14,714	43,406
1881	77,753	609	3,004	5,108	19,415	45,454
1891	80,915	582	3,238	4,278	18,524	42,702
1901	127,899	764	4,394	5,477	28,405	44,175
1911	303,680	829	4,802	5,766	29,843	55,676
1921	374,022	1,215	7,016	8,268	42,122	70,729
1931	344,574	1,380	7,222	8,794	49,406	72,525
1941	312,473	1,335	8,633	7,952	50,229	71,847

Year	Manitoba	Saskatchewan	Alberta	British Columbia	Yukon	Northwest Territories
1871	166					
1881	1,752			2,295		116
1891	3,063			6,567		1,961
1901	6,922	2,705	11,172	17,164	6,707	14
1911	16,328	69,628	81,357	37,548	1,891	12
1921	21,644	87,617	99,879	34,926	557	46
1931	17,903	73,008	78,959	34,706	526	145
1941	15,740	54,617	65,682	35,903	367	168

* *Eighth Census*, Vol. I, Table 21.

But 312,473 American-born comprised 2.7 per cent of the population of Canada in 1941, while the 1,044,119 Canadian-born in the United States in 1940 formed only 0.78 per cent of the American population. Presumably, then, the influence upon the Canadian people of the American immigrant population has been relatively greater than that in the United States of a much

TABLE XIV

*Gainfully Occupied American-born in Canada, by
Occupations, 1941* *

Occupation	Males	Females	Total
All (not including Active Service)	119,626	21,030	140,656
Agriculture	51,896	1,234	53,130
Fishing, hunting, trapping	764		764
Logging	1,832	1	1,833
Mining and quarrying	2,079		2,079
Manufacturing	17,359	2,256	19,615
Construction	5,677	6	5,683
Transportation and communication	8,111	369	8,480
Trade	10,441	1,869	12,310
Finance	1,277	49	1,326
Service	10,847	11,633	22,480
Professional	5,014	4,029	9,043
Public	1,236	104	1,240
Recreational	471	46	517
Personal	4,126	7,454	11,580
Clerical	4,087	3,396	7,483
Laborers (not previously included)	5,046	182	5,228

* *Eighth Census*, Vol. VII, Table 12.

larger group of immigrants born in Canada. Moreover, the American-born in Canada are very evenly spread, not only through all the provinces, but through counties and municipalities as well. Table XIII makes clear the comparative evenness of the distribution by provinces.

This wide geographic distribution, in itself, allows the greatest possible opportunity for the mingling of the immigrant and the native populations, and no doubt hastens the Canadianization of the newcomer, whose influence must, at the same time, be felt among those with whom he is associating. Here, no doubt, is one of the factors that have contributed to the comparatively wide knowledge of the United States that one finds generally among the Canadian people.

In employment, too, the American-born are evenly distributed, being found in every occupational group in percentages that are very close to those for the Canadian-born. As might be expected, the largest number are in agriculture, followed by professional and other services, manufacturing, and trade. Table XIV gives the measure of this distribution as reported in the 1941 census. Table XV, however, compiled from Canadian immigration records, reveals a decided shift away from agriculture in recent years, with relatively fewer immigrants in the farming classes, and more whose occupations are shown as "skilled," "unskilled and semiskilled," and "trading."

Canada has benefited much from the influx of scientific, technical, and other trained personnel from the United States, along with the import of American capital and the establishment of "branch plants," all of which have contributed enormously to the rapidity and the diversity of Canadian industrialization.

TABLE XV

*Immigration to Canada from the United States by Occupations, 1946–50 ***

Occupation	1946	1947	1948	1949	1950	Totals
Farming	662	511	404	281	267	2,125
Unskilled and semi-skilled	546	557	500	595	526	2,724
Skilled	758	864	729	758	708	3,817
Clerical	401	422	346	343	498	2,010
Professional	500	537	383	477	467	2,364
Trading	777	788	524	623	620	3,332
Female domestics	57	65	29	21	37	209
Other	1,271	1,053	876	861	823	4,884
Total workers	4,972	4,797	3,791	3,959	3,946	21,465
Dependent wives	2,936	2,471	2,010	2,057	2,009	11,483
Dependent children	3,561	2,172	1,580	1,728	1,844	10,885
Total dependents	6,497	4,643	3,590	3,785	3,853	22,368
Grand totals	11,469	9,440	7,381	7,744	7,799	43,833

* Official Canadian immigration records.

It has been suggested that the even distribution of the American-born in Canada has had some influence on their rate of naturalization. Certainly that rate is high—74.2 per cent of the American-born population being naturalized Canadians in 1941, as compared with 71.5 per cent of the total foreign-born, although some of the individual foreign-born groups show a considerably higher rate. It will be recalled that only 58.4 per cent of the Canadian-born (French and other) in the United States had taken the citizenship of their adopted country. The explanation is probably to be found in the original *intention* of the immigrant. The average American who moves to Canada does so with the intention of remaining there permanently; the Canadian tends to go to the United States to obtain temporary employment. Approximately 10,865 American-born have become naturalized Canadian citizens in the period since the 1941 census.

The tendency of an immigrant population to identify itself easily with a new community might naturally be presumed to result in a considerable degree of intermarriage within that community. This has been so with the American-born in Canada. Data available on marriages in Canada show the nativity or birthplace of the marriage partner to be a matter of almost complete indifference to the American-born bride or groom. It is interesting to note, too, that the proportion of the American-born who are married comes very close to that of native Canadians.

On the basis of literacy, the American immigrant has proved a very desirable addition to the Canadian population, only 1.31 per cent of the American-born being illiterate as compared with 2.99 per cent of the native Canadian population.[3] The American-born immigrant, in fact, has a lower rate of illiteracy than any other foreign-born element of the population except the British. His relations with the law, as well, testify to his desirability as a citizen. In 1941, there were 371 convictions for indictable offenses for each 100,000 of the population in general, but only 291 for the American-born. In 1949, when for the first time figures were available on the basis of birthplace of the number of persons convicted, rather than total number of convictions, the ratio between the general rate and the rate for the American-born appears to be about the same, though an exact rate is impossible to calculate at any point in the intercensal period.

The American-born, then, on almost every basis of comparison, are shown to be a valuable asset in the Canadian population. And what of the future? Canada is in a period of high activity.

[3] 1931 census. No later figures are available, although age and other factors involved make it reasonable to suppose the rate would now be even lower.

Her industrial production and employment are at record levels. Her mineral and forest resources and her vast potential of hydro-electric power are being extensively developed. Recent and substantial discoveries in oil and natural gas, high-grade iron ore, and deposits of titanium and uranium give promise of an unprecedented expansion in many new fields of Canadian industry. New capital is finding its way to Canada, and nonresident investment has reached new heights.

But Canada needs manpower as well as money if the promise of the future is to be fulfilled. Her capacity to absorb new people is great. It is a situation likely to attract the adventurous and enterprising American, who is always to be found where new frontiers offer rewarding opportunities. At the same time, the more agreeable climate in certain parts of the United States and the magnetic attraction of its great metropolitan areas will almost certainly continue to exact their annual tribute from among the people of Canada. This constant exchange will undoubtedly continue to increase mutual knowledge and understanding among the Canadian and American people, promoting that spirit of goodwill and co-operation which has, to so great an extent, characterized the recent relations between these two countries of the North American partnership.

10

The Effects of the First World War

1. Canada and American Neutrality, 1914-17

Although the ultimate results of Canadian-American collaboration in the First World War were probably beneficial, the immediate effect on the attitude of Canadians toward the United States was almost wholly bad.

It is arguable that as there were no permanent ill effects, and as Canadian governmental policy was never seriously affected by the popular hostility toward the United States, the whole matter might now well be forgotten. But the fact is that for some years the effects of the war and postwar attitudes and activities of the United States exerted an important influence on Canadian-American relations. This fact, moreover, is significant in its illustration of the tense sensitivity of the Canadian people to events in the United States. It was not until the impact of the great depression made itself felt in both countries that the strong though superficial hostility created in Canada by the events of the war was submerged in the mutual suffering of the early thirties.

Canada's part in the First World War had stimulated the

slowly growing sense of national consciousness among the Canadian people, and it hastened the recognition of their country as an independent state, both at home and abroad. The rather spectacular contribution of Canadian naval, military, and, above all, air personnel, created a new interest in and respect for Canada in the United States. This somewhat superficial, though very real interest was solidified in business and governmental circles by the substantial economic contribution made by Canada to what was ultimately recognized as the common cause.

But the immediate effect on Canadian opinion of certain wartime and postwar events in the United States was deplorable and evoked a measure of Canadian hostility that was reminiscent of the bitterness of earlier periods in Canadian-American relations. Even ten years later neither time nor a clearer perspective had entirely healed the wounds. The fact that Canadians were always sensitive to American actions, that the national inferiority complex from which they suffered during their colonial days made them ever ready to find, emphasize and dilate upon what they considered flaws in the American way of life offers only a partial explanation of the violence of the anti-American sentiment that developed in Canada during and after the First World War.

The American people did not realize the deleterious effect that the war strain produced on the Canadian attitude toward the United States. This was not at all surprising. After the war Americans believed, when they thought of it at all, that Canada was and should be grateful for the assistance of the United States—assistance that made inevitable the defeat of Germany and her allies. Throughout the war, American newspapers had abounded with flattering references to Canadian valor; after the United States entered the struggle the two countries co-operated at home as on the battlefield, and American soldiers gave their lives in the common cause. There was, moreover, much positive evidence of Canadian good will. Northern newspapers greeted American entry into the war with enthusiastic acclaim; distinguished Canadian visitors to the United States stressed the "cousinly" relationship, and pointed with ever more dramatic (and ever more boring) enthusiasm to three thousand miles of undefended border. American officials visiting in Canada were received with normal courtesies and cordiality.

To the American whose knowledge of international relations was confined to the reports of the daily and weekly press, the truth about the Canadian attitude was hard to believe. Dislike of the United States seemed illogical and absurd. And yet the American who visited Canada and kept in touch with Canadian opinion between 1915 and 1930 could be under no illusions. To him the attitude of the majority of Canadians was provoking, painful, and quite unfair, but he did know the truth. The fact was that most Americans knew very little about Canadian affairs and were not particularly interested in them. In consequence, the prairie fire of Canadian hostility passed unnoticed among the American people as a whole.

In Canada, however, the situation was very different. In 1920 it was much more true than it is even today that Canadians could not escape the shadow of the United States. American influence could be discerned in almost every aspect of Canadian life. Canadians could not, if they would, ignore their great neighbor. The result was a comparative unanimity of opinion among Canadians regarding the United States and its activities. This situation made it quite possible for the American people seriously to offend Canadian opinion without ever being aware of the fact. This explains the situation developed by the war. Of all the countries in the world, Canada watched most closely and felt most keenly the actions and attitudes of the United States. When these actions or attitudes seemed to be critical of or hostile to the Allies or their cause, Canadians reacted more quickly and more strongly than any other people.

Before 1914 the world had been repeatedly assured, and many Canadians were inclined to believe, that the United States—whatever its other faults—was somewhat more idealistic, more peace-loving, more considerate in its relations with small and oppressed states, than were the majority of strong and vigorous nations. The policies espoused by John Hay, the arbitration

344

treaties negotiated by William Jennings Bryan, the friendly urbanity of President Taft, the splendidly idealistic phrases of Woodrow Wilson, and the persistently high moral tone that marked the utterances of official America had been leading Canadians to the belief that the United States was, in very truth, a vital force for good in international affairs. It is true that many citizens of the Dominion did not love the United States—the fate of reciprocity had proved that—but a steadily increasing number of them were offering their respect. Having worked off a certain amount of ill will by their votes in 1911, it is probable that Canadians as a whole were, in 1914, more friendly to the United States than they had been at any previous period. Then came the World War, and in the tense atmosphere of that struggle the new friendship was sorely tested.

In order to understand the war-fostered growth of Canadian antipathy toward the United States, it is necessary to recapture something of the atmosphere of those lurid years from 1914 to 1918. Canada entered the European conflict on 4 August 1914;[1] on that day Sir Robert Borden, the Canadian Prime Minister, cabled to London an offer of every assistance that his country could supply.

The violation of Belgian neutrality was, for the majority of Canadians, the real justification for their participation in the war; and the failure of the United States to protest against that breach of international law marked the first change in the Canadian attitude toward the Republic. Canadians did not expect the United States to enter the war, but they did expect a protest from the government that had so often and so emphatically proclaimed its allegiance to the principles of international law. Accustomed to the tone of high morality and idealism that had characterized American public oratory, the people of Canada looked to Washington for an unequivocal denunciation of the German action. Feeling so intensely the righteousness of their cause, raised to

---

[1] Canada was legally in the war, as a part of the British Empire, without any action on her part, but, if it had desired, Ottawa might have declared its independence and neutrality and Britain would have been powerless, and probably unwilling, to resort to coercion.

the heights of moral integrity by a consciousness of the sacrifice soon to be demanded of them, Canadians were amazed by the inexplicable silence of the United States; they felt that in its great test the idealism of the Republic had faltered. Of the divided opinion in the United States, of the conflicting official reports as to the actual facts of the invasion of Belgium, of the later disclosures of French and Russian participation in the responsibility for the advent of war, of the powerful influences in the United States that demanded strict impartiality on the part of the President, of the social and political consequences that might have followed a protest to Germany—of all these things Canadians knew and cared little; to them the issue was clearly marked, and the United States had failed the peace-loving nations.[2]

Upon the outbreak of the war the American people naturally congratulated themselves on being well out of it. Looking on the conflict as a purely European affair, engendered by the "European system," the citizens of the United States, being normal human beings, were gratified at their isolation. But expression of this attitude—not always in a humble tone—gave rise to the second great cause of Canadian bitterness. The declaration of Newton D. Baker, Secretary of War, that the United States was "now in the dominant moral position in the world" was greeted with sarcasm north of the international boundary, for among Canadians it was felt that they, rather than the Americans, had recognized and accepted the task of fighting to maintain the moral standards of civilization. Martin Glynn, temporary chairman of the National Democratic Convention, declared on 14 June 1916: "Wealth has come to us, power has come to us, but better than wealth or power we have maintained for ourselves and for our children a nation dedicated to the ideals of peace, rather than to the gospel of selfishness and slaughter." Nor was Glynn the only American who prided himself "on some moral

[2] It must be understood that these statements refer to the great majority—but not all—of the Canadian people. Many of the leading newspapermen and political leaders recognized the real difficulties that faced the United States—the indifferent masses in the Middle West, the vast alien population, the historic policy of nonintervention in Europe.

quality that . . . was inherent in the attitude of neutrality."
Canadians resented being told that their sons were dying to uphold the "gospel of selfishness and slaughter," and refused to
think of themselves as occupying a moral plane lower than that
of Democratic machine politicians.

The propaganda carried on by the Irish and German elements in the American population, while directed against England, found its most sensitive audience in Canada, and Canadians, judging the nation by the individual, tended to accept these
attacks as typical of the American attitude.

As the war progressed, a new condition developed. The
United States, hitherto a borrowing country, was steadily taking
rank as a powerful creditor nation. Loans to the belligerents—
although at first opposed by President Wilson as unneutral—
were made in immense figures. War orders from the Allies were
creating a condition of unprecedented prosperity; high wages
and enormous dividends were the commonplaces of the day;
extravagance and reckless expenditure marked American society.[3]
In Canada, on the other hand, although profiteers were reported
—and later proved—to be making fortunes from paper shoes,
shoddy uniforms, and decayed bacon, the people as a whole were
forced to endure a period of rigid economy. Comparison of the
prevailing conditions in the two countries was everywhere obvious and insistent. Every month added to American wealth, to
American expressions of satisfaction at being free; while every
month Canada faced her growing debt, her casualty lists, her
dead.

Another factor influencing American-Canadian relations may
at first glance seem somewhat absurd, but it was, nevertheless, of
real importance. The topical news films shown in Canadian
theaters were of American origin and of interest chiefly to
American citizens. Thus when Canadian audiences gathered for

[3] "The demand for luxuries was equalled only by the craze for entertainment—
futile brains were busied with the innovation of new dancing steps rather than the
issues of the European War. Cabarets were crowded—and the general atmosphere of
the country was heavy with amusement and money-making." Seymour: *Woodrow Wilson and the War* (New Haven: Yale University Press; 1921), pp. 67-8.

347

a few hours in an attempt to forget the constant strain under which they lived, they were frequently greeted with pictures of American "preparedness" parades, of the American expedition into Mexico, of the National Guard on summer maneuvers. The irony of such pictures to those whose sons and brothers were dying by the hundred in the real war produced its inevitable and evil result. Canadian newspapers, also, were forced to rely very largely on American press associations for their news. It was the dissatisfaction which this condition aroused that later resulted in the establishment of the Canadian Press.

These facts did not become widely known in the United States, and Americans, in consequence, failed to understand Canadian opinion, because Canadian newspapers, political leaders, and industrial spokesmen insisted on ignoring or belittling the existence of anti-American sentiment. Early in the war Canadian newspapers were requested to tread gently when dealing with the United States, and this suggestion was very generally observed. Public officials, regardless of their personal inclinations, were bound by their duty to the nation—and the nation's welfare demanded apparent friendship with the United States.

The people of Canada knew little of the class and national cleavages of the United States. Throughout the war, in spite of the neutrality proclamation, American opinion was overwhelmingly on the side of the Allies. Millions of Americans joined with Canada in the belief that the Allied forces were contending for the more righteous cause—that German victory would result in the triumph of the military ideal. As a result of this conviction, American periodicals and political leaders, in the vast majority of cases, favored the Allied cause.

But the speeches of Woodrow Wilson and William Jennings Bryan and the notes of the President to the warring powers increased the Canadian hostility. Canadians felt that the Great War was a strife of moral as well as of physical powers; yet President Wilson declared that "With its causes and objects we are not concerned." In the election of 1916, Canadians were almost unanimous in their desire to see Charles E. Hughes vic-

torious, and they were greatly disappointed when the final returns showed a reversal of the earlier reports. As most Canadians viewed it, the United States in 1916 re-elected a President who had sacrificed the national honor in order to keep his country "out of war"; a man who represented the popular attitude in being unable to distinguish between the objectives of the two belligerents. The demand made by President Wilson that Americans should be neutral in thought as well as in deed was not the least of Canadian grievances.

Walter Hines Page, United States Ambassador to London and a vigorous Anglophile, wrote on this subject: "The President suppressed free thought and free speech when he insisted on personal neutrality. To the minds of official Washington, Germans and English are alike foreign nations who are now foolishly engaged in war." Vice President Marshall inanely boasted that he had read no Orange Paper, Blue Paper, White Paper, or other partisan document, for fear that he would become unneutral. "The mass of American people," declared Page, "find themselves forbidden to think or talk and this has a sufficient effect to make them take refuge in indifference." Secretary Franklin K. Lane stated that the President told the Cabinet that he wished to see neither side win, "for both had been equally indifferent to the rights of neutrals."

The *Lusitania* notes of President Wilson, and the repetitive correspondence resulting from other submarine activities, because of their length and ineffective character, gradually became subjects of sarcastic comment among Canadians. Even the newspapers went so far as to question the wisdom of the President's course. One editor declared: "We fear that the United States is not cutting a very dignified figure before the eyes of a condemning world these days." The Victoria *Times* in outlining the history of American protests over the *Lusitania* affair said: "The honor of the United States would have stood higher if, from the very commencement of the war, it had constituted itself the guardian of international law, instead of waiting until its own interests were affected." The United States, of course, was convinced that it had been the one nation in the world that *had* upheld the dictates of international law, but Canadians could not forget the violation of Belgium and America's failure to protest. "During the course of the war," wrote the editor of the Vancouver *Sun*, "the United States government has received so many rebuffs that one finds it hard to know just what the words of national honor have come to mean."

The Canadian people naturally took the side of the British government in the prolonged and bitter arguments concerning the legality of the Allied blockade, and the British definition of contraband. The United States was criticized for the severity of the notes written to Great Britain, notes that were couched in terms almost as vigorous as those used in the official protests to Germany for far more serious violations of international law— more serious because German activities endangered and destroyed American lives, whereas the British interference with American trade entailed only financial losses. There can be no doubt that Britain did extend its interpretation of the maritime rights of belligerents far beyond any previous practice, but after the United States entered the war, the Allied policy became still more inclusive and severe.

One episode at this time was perhaps more important than any other in arousing popular feeling in Canada—the action of American destroyers in standing by or, at the request of the German submarine *U-53*, changing their position, while the undersea craft sank a number of British and other vessels just off the eastern coast of the United States. It would, obviously, have been an unneutral action for the American war vessels to have intervened, but public opinion takes little notice of the technical demands of law in such a case. Blood, it seemed, no longer was thicker than water.

These were the outstanding causes that aroused and sustained Canadian animosity toward the United States between August 1914 and April 1917. That this attitude was based largely on misunderstanding and on a very inadequate appreciation of the real conditions in the United States did not lessen its potency.

It was unfair, unbalanced, and unjust; it took no heed of American difficulties, was critical only of failures; it did not recognize the signs of friendship, was conscious only of opposition. Yet it was completely understandable; it was, indeed, inevitable; for as America waxed richer and stronger, Canada suffered, fought, and sacrificed her prosperity and her sons. America counted her profits while Canada buried her dead.

It was, of course, eventually recognized even in Canada that between 1914 and 1917 American opinion, in spite of the President's demand that the people of the Republic should be neutral in thought as well as in action, was preponderantly and strongly pro-Ally.

2. The War Partnership and Its Aftermath

The United States entered the war in April 1917 and received a tremendous welcome from the hard-pressed Allied powers. Not only did the latter recognize the influence that would be exerted by America's financial, military, and naval co-operation, but they also rejoiced in the effect that America's decision would produce on neutral opinion and on the verdict of history. A Canadian editor well expressed the feeling of all the Allied powers when he wrote: "Canada has been waiting and watching, hoping and praying, that you would not be too proud to fight for the rights of humanity; and that you would recognize the essential difference between the German cause and ours. All Canada, all the British Empire, and all the Allies feel as if a tremendous victory had been won."

The Dominion government formally welcomed the United States as a comrade-in-arms on 19 April when in the House of Commons Sir George Foster and Sir Wilfrid Laurier joined in hailing the era of good feeling which the American declaration of war presaged.

It would not be true to suggest, however, that the American declaration of war at once removed the critical irritation that had embittered Canadian feeling. Privately, if not in public, the view was often expressed that the United States had waited and profited during the heat of the struggle and was now about to claim the victory as well. As time went on, however, and as American soldiers, too, began to give their lives in the common cause, this bitterness was slowly purged away. Official co-operation between Canada and the United States—the pooling of grain, fuel, power, and transportation resources, the underwriting of a Canadian loan by bankers of New York—produced a good effect on the public mind. Canadian recruiting detachments were welcomed in the United States, while a reciprocal agreement was ratified to facilitate the return of draft-evaders. A Canadian War Mission was established at Washington, and in many other ways the activities of the two countries were co-ordinated for efficiency. Immigration regulations were relaxed and thousands of American farmhands crossed the border to assist in harvesting the Canadian crops. Officially and publicly, at least, the two nations were on better terms than ever before in their history, and on the American side this attitude extended through almost all classes of society—in so far as they ever thought of Canada. The statement of ex-President Roosevelt, on 15 August 1917 that "We have no right to consider ourselves as standing level with Canada in this fight for democracy until we have placed 5,000,000 men in the field" did much to mollify Canadian sentiment. The nobly expressed idealism of President Wilson and his plans for co-operation with the war-shattered states of Europe aroused a popular response among the people of Canada.

Barely had this happy result been attained, however, when all the old prejudices were revived by the end of the war and the disillusionment of the postwar years.

Few periods in the history of mankind have been so prolific in the generation of international strife as the months that followed the Armistice of 1918. Scarcely had the war ended and the external pressure been removed, when centrifugal forces began to sever the bonds welded by the conflict. The scores of new problems aroused by the intrigues and mistakes of the conference at Versailles were accentuated by American repudiation of one of the few hopeful results of the four years of devastation and suffering and by the accentuated nationalism that was the form taken by the American reaction against the sacrifices and co-operation of the war period. But there was another and a more immediate cause for the revival of Canadian ill feeling.

It is probable and natural that most of the Allied nations emerged from the war convinced that victory was primarily due to their own efforts. This conviction was expounded at various places and times by military and naval leaders of the different powers. Unfortunately, in the United States a certain section of the public undertook to proclaim the prominent part played by the American forces in a manner that was particularly provocative, and Canadians, being the nearest neighbors, felt the full effect. It cannot be too strongly insisted upon that nowhere, not even in Canada itself, was the display of the "We Won the War" and "The Yanks Did It" posters more roundly condemned than among the better elements in the United States. But Canada, whose half-million soldiers (according to the official Canadian figures) [4] had suffered more casualties than the whole

[4] General Clark in the Canadian House of Commons gave the following figures for the last hundred days of the war. Quoted from *Hansard*, by the New York *World*, 21 May 1922:

	Canada	United States
Troops engaged	105,000	650,000
Days of operations	100	47
Casualties	45,830	100,000
Prisoners taken	31,537	16,000
Guns captured	623	468
Machine guns taken	2,842	2,864
Trench mortars taken	336	177
Territory freed (sq. miles)	610	336
Villages freed	228	150
German divisions defeated	47	46
Maximum advance (miles)	86	34

of the American army; who had taken more guns, more ground, more prisoners, and had fought for two years longer; was bitterly critical of the juvenile boasts of these enthusiastic American patriots. Yet this was not, after all, a particularly heinous offense. The American people had not suffered enough to be chastened, and a certain exuberance was to be expected and might well have been excused. Unfortunately, it happened to be cities like Seattle, Los Angeles, and Detroit—cities that were particularly well known to Canadians—in which the most unrestrained celebrations were staged.

Thus in a few short weeks was undone much of the good that had been accomplished by the months of co-operation and mutual sacrifice during the war. And the revival of Canadian ill will in an intensified form was largely due to nothing more serious than the exuberance and lack of taste of a small part of the American people.[5] On such a precarious foundation does international friendship rest—when nations speak the same language and live so close together.

There were a number of other causes that contributed to the maintenance of Canadian irritation during the postwar years. Important among these were the unfavorable rate of exchange, the American tariff policy, the revival of Anglo-Irish strife and the role played therein by the Irish-Americans and their sympathizers, the problem of the Allied debts, and the attitude of the United States toward the League of Nations.

The rate of exchange was an obviously absurd basis for the maintenance of international ill feeling, but unfortunately the majority of the Canadian people were not economists. Moreover, it was unpleasant, even if profitable, to hear American tourists paying their bills in Canadian shops with what some of them proudly referred to as "real" money. Even a Canadian who was not an economist could catch that inference.

The Underwood Tariff of 1913 had given Canada a great

---

[5] It should also be noted, however, that President Wilson was the outstanding opponent of separate representation for Canada at the Peace Conference and in the League of Nations, and that this attitude was hotly resented in Canada.

many valuable concessions by opening the American market to a large number of Canadian commodities. These favors were almost all rescinded by the Fordney Emergency Tariff of 1921 and the McCumber Tariff of 1922. To Canadians this seemed like a rather gratuitous injury. The United States, as a result of the war, had become the wealthiest nation in the world, the rate of exchange was vastly in her favor, her sales in Canada far exceeded her purchases there, and yet she was not satisfied. The Canadian press united in denouncing the riot of protectionism represented by these two bills, while Premier Taschereau of Quebec threatened to retaliate by a prohibition of pulpwood exports—an action that would stifle many American mills and newspapers.

The ubiquitous Irish question had played its part in Canadian-American relations ever since the middle of the nineteenth century. The renewed discussion of this problem after the First World War, and its effect on the American attitude toward Great Britain, were of some political and international importance. These were the days of the Irish War Loans in the United States, of the Black and Tans, and of Irish Republican Army atrocities in the unhappy island. Canadians generally had little sympathy for Irish republican ideals, but they did believe that Ireland should be given the *de facto* independence of "Dominion status." Almost without exception Canadians looked upon any interference from the United States as unwarranted and impertinent. Canadians have never recognized the peculiar interest America has taken—and naturally taken—in this problem, due not only to the presence of over five million persons of Irish descent in the United States, but also to the essential justice of the Irish cause.[6]

The difficulties raised by the inter-Allied debts were among the most prominent causes of international discord in the postwar years. As a debtor nation Canada was prepared to pay the sums for which she was legally responsible, but the prospect was not

[6] The American census of 1920 showed 1,037,233 Irish-born residents of the United States.

a pleasant one. In a long and carefully prepared article for the New York *Times,* one of Canada's leading financiers well summarized Canadian sentiment in this matter in the summer of 1922. The statement, in part, read as follows:

"(1) That the debt is legally owing is certain.

"(2) The claim that the debts are not morally due is based on one contention only—that unless these debts be cancelled the United States will not have borne her equal share of the burdens of the war—Americans will naturally resent even the suggestion that their country may not have paid her way, but this question must be quietly discussed if we are to understand the position taken by the rest of the world.

"(3) The United States had a vital stake in the war from its very beginning, though it took some time for her people to realize it. . . . But it is not suggested that the American government contribute anything towards expenditures made prior to the time it officially entered the struggle.

"(4) Had the United States intervened at the time of the *Lusitania* incident the war would have been shortened by two years, millions of lives and tens of billions of dollars would have been saved, the condition of Europe would not be what it is, and the problem of these debts would not have arisen.

"(5) These considerations, however, have a sentimental value only. The case against the validity of these debts merely claims that when the United States declared war she took her place by the side of the Allies and became responsible for her reasonable share from that time on.

"(6) The United States was unprepared and had to raise, train, equip, and transport her armies. She could, for long, render little aid except financial. The Allies had to hold the enemy back with but little assistance from her in man power. The Allies could supply the men but had already bled their people white financially. The United States could not supply men but had a plethora of wealth, much of it obtained by supplying materials to the Allies.

"(7) The services of the men placed by the Allies in the fighting during those twelve months were given to the common cause. The hundreds of thousands of lives were given, for alas, they cannot be restored. Must the contribution of the United States be on a different basis and be considered a loan to be repaid? Are dollars more valuable than lives?

"(8) The financial assistance of the United States was of inestimable value, but if the money be repaid with interest, as demanded, do the Americans consider that the effective contribution of their country was in proportion to her population or wealth, or in harmony with her dignity? Are they content to owe their safety and victory to the sacrifices of others without bearing their fair share?"

It is difficult in these days when national and international debts are computed in figures of astronomical proportions to recall the bitterness with which the war-debt problems were debated in the 1920's.

Among Americans there were at least three typical attitudes toward this problem of the inter-Allied debts. One was represented by the query that was generally attributed to President Coolidge: "They hired the money, didn't they?" From this point of view the whole problem reduced itself to the simple terms of a legal and financial transaction, and failure to carry it out would weaken the whole basis upon which the economic fabric of modern society was founded. Another group favored partial or total cancellation as an aid to economic sanitation, or as a further contribution of America to the cause for which the Allies fought. A third group, revolted by the spectacle of postwar Europe, desired to use the debts as a means of keeping certain European nations in such a condition of impecuniosity that they would be unable again to resort to war.[7] The problem was

[7] The terms finally proposed to France and Italy resulted in considerable scaling down of the amount to be repaid. Shortly after the treaty with Italy was signed, the dictator of that state proposed an Italian air force that would "obscure the sun," and an army of five million men.

357

a good deal more involved from an American than it was from a Canadian point of view. With the best will in the world, an intelligent American would find his powers taxed to discover the just and humane course to follow.

Last, and perhaps most important of all in its effect on postwar Canadian opinion of the United States, was the attitude of America toward the League of Nations and the international questions involved therein. The Covenant of the League of Nations was prepared at Paris largely through the efforts of President Wilson and his American colleagues. This document was intended to embody the highest aspirations of a war-sick world. It was ratified by all the signatory powers except the United States, where a combined drive by certain progressives and the forces favoring nationalistic isolation succeeded in defeating the efforts of President Wilson and the Democratic Party. Of course, there were many other issues involved in the election of 1920, but revival of the traditional American policy of isolation was an inevitable psychological reaction from an unsatisfactory adventure into a European struggle. Many Americans felt that they had been cheated in the result of the war; that they had been inveigled into it by Allied (particularly British) propaganda, and that they had been used to "pull the chestnuts out of the fire" for the rapacious imperialists of Europe. The vast majority of the American people went into the war in the firm belief that they were crusading, fighting in one last war that would end all wars. Yet scarcely had the war ended when the Allies fell to quarreling over the spoils; they maintained armies on a scale far exceeding prewar standards, and carried on sporadic military operations in Russia, Asia Minor, Ireland, and the Far East. The disillusionment produced by these conditions was already well started in 1920, and in their disgust Americans returned again to their policy of isolation.

To many Canadians, however, the defeat of the pro-League party in that year appeared to be due purely to selfishness—the determination of America to follow her own course, regardless of the needs, hopes, or pacific aspirations of the remainder of the world. Color was given to this interpretation by the actions of the new Harding administration. A separate treaty was negotiated with Germany which retained for the United States all the benefits conferred by the Treaty of Versailles, and denied all the obligations undertaken by signatories of the general treaty. The tripartite agreement by which Great Britain and America were to guarantee aid to France in case of an unprovoked attack was also denounced by the United States Senate. After the elevation of Senator Harding to the Presidency, the typical expression of the isolationist journals was the cryptic phrase: "The League is dead." Forthwith the State Department not only refused to aid the League in its many humanitarian projects, but actually failed to acknowledge receipt of letters and dispatches from the Secretariat. Later Secretary of State Charles E. Hughes did reply— but forwarded his communications through the diplomatic agents of other countries rather than recognize the existence of the League Secretariat.

From a Canadian viewpoint this attitude of the United States was consistent with her attitude on the debt question: America wanted all the benefits of the war with none of the obligations. The League—the one great attempt to end war—was prevented from reaching its full strength by the refusal of the United States to do her part. Whether or not this criticism was justified is quite beside the point. The important fact is simply that this was the Canadian opinion, and that it explained in some measure the skepticism with which for many years Canadians viewed American professions of a unique or exceptional interest in the maintenance of international law and the willingness to sacrifice for the principles of justice among the nations. Only the practice of Lend-Lease, the generous postwar assistance in the development of the resources of western Europe, and the Point 4 Technical Assistance program of the United States have done much to restore the old belief in a philanthropic and idealistic America.

With the passage of the years this Canadian hostility toward the United States slowly disappeared. Above all, the effects of the great depression contributed largely to this end. The bursting of the American bubble in 1929 had a chastening effect on the United States and aroused a mutual sympathy between that country and its neighbor and companion in misfortune. An even more important factor in the growth of better feeling in Canada was the development of national self-consciousness and the ending of the old colonial sense of inferiority that had for so long plagued and debilitated the Canadian spirit. The establishment of independence in every realm of official and cultural activity was the outstanding event of the postwar years in Canada. The old inferiority complex gradually disappeared, the idea of annexation became a dead issue. Canadian diplomatic representation in Washington and elsewhere reflected the true birth of the nation, and characteristic developments in art, education, and even in business were signs of a new national life. Canada could never hope to equal the United States in size or power; but Canada in these years did come of age. The new self-confidence was reflected in a willingness to relinquish the old concentration on criticism of the United States. Before the outbreak of the Second World War, Canadians had almost completely recovered in their relations with their neighbor from the wounds created by the first world conflict. It was only in an occasional intellectual or colonial backwater that the old hostility could still be discovered.

II

The Second World War and After

I. Introduction

In contrast with the immediate effects of the war of 1914–18, the results of the Second World War on the relations between Canada and the United States were almost wholly beneficial. This was due to a number of causes.

In the first place, the United States played a much larger role in the years between 1941 and 1945 than in the First World War. The enthusiasm and the excitement of American participation in the conflict against the forces of the Kaiser were not tempered except in individual cases by any very serious suffering or loss. But in the years between Pearl Harbor and the final surrender of Germany and Japan, the United States went through a period of tragic and bitter suffering. At the same time the American people began to realize something of the extent and gravity of the responsibilities being forced upon them by the position of the United States as the strongest power in the modern world. These tempering factors, combined with the close and prolonged co-operation between the United States and the other democratic powers, brought to the American people an appreciation of the virtues of their comrades-in-arms and of the interdependence of the nations comprising the free world. As a result, at the end of the war there was little evidence of the flamboyant and boastful spirit that characterized some elements of American society in 1918 and the succeeding years.

This change in atmosphere in the United States was reflected in the attitude of the Canadian people toward their southern neighbors. Canada's entrance into the war had been marked by a sense of bitter resignation and harsh resolve. In September 1939 there was none of the holiday spirit of August 1914. Canadians realized that there was a stern and distasteful task to be performed. They also realized that the mismanagement and appeasement of the years preceding the outbreak of war placed some of the responsibility for that conflict on the democratic governments including their own. They did not expect the United States to enter the war at once and they were, in fact, agreeably surprised by the clear position in support of the democratic cause which was adopted by President Roosevelt and by the American administration.

But more important than all these things in its influence on the Canadian attitude was the fact that between 1918 and 1939 Canada and Canadians had come of age. The old inferiority complex had almost entirely disappeared. The events of the early thirties had shown that even the United States was not invulnerable to the influence of the business cycle and the peoples of the two countries had been drawn together by the common suffering of the great depression. The fact that in spite of its limited population Canada was one of the half-dozen great trading countries of the world and that internal conditions had so progressed that Canada stood high in the roster of nations in all the indices of economic and social development gave to the Canadian people a maturity of outlook that wiped out most of their old sensitivity toward external criticism or disregard.

2. *The Collapse of Collective Security*

No other international conflict was ever more fully advertised in advance or more clearly foreshadowed by preceding events than the Second World War.

The seizure of the government in Italy by Mussolini and his Black Shirts in the early twenties was a plain invitation to the totalitarian forces in every land to prepare for the usurpation of power at home and the practice of a policy of bellicosity and aggrandizement abroad. In 1931, with the world struggling against the effects of universal economic distress, the Japanese abandoned their efforts to establish a democratic and peaceful state and began again on their program of imperialistic expansion in Asia. When the League of Nations and the United States greeted the rape of Manchuria with only mild expressions of disapproval, the pattern of appeasement and the route to war were more clearly defined. When the Japanese delegates stalked arrogantly out of the League, Hitler, on the verge of power in Germany, was an interested and careful observer. His own rule was soon established on the apparently successful pattern of police terror at home and threats of war abroad. In 1935 Mussolini commenced his attack on hapless Ethiopia and roared his defiance at the timorous and divided governments of the other powers. Throughout 1936, 1937, and 1938 Hitler continued his outrages in Europe with an increasing confidence and a growing appetite for power that was fed rather than satiated by the bloody sacrifice of Spain and the cynical betrayal of Czechoslovakia. And all the time Japan continued on its program of developing a "Sphere of Co-Prosperity" in Asia.

For much of the fourth decade of the century most of the democratic powers, gripped by internal depression, were ruled by governments that suffered from a sense of frustration and a

363

vitiated morale that was not offset by any firm moral commitments, intellectual genius, or concentration of will.

No man was more clearly conscious of these developments and conditions in the realm of national and international affairs than the remarkably intelligent and politically acute President of the greatest of the great powers. Franklin D. Roosevelt not only foresaw the looming catastrophe but did everything that was possible within the wide range of his exceptional capacity to prepare his own people for the major part that they would inevitably have to play in meeting the attack of despotism and aggression. At the same time he sought to strengthen the American position abroad by drawing closer the bonds of friendship with all democratic peoples. Above all, he directed his efforts toward the development of a firm system of hemispheric and continental defense.

Although the immediate danger in the years before the war was concentrated in Europe and to a lesser extent in the Far East, the more thoughtful people of the Western Hemisphere viewed with increasing apprehension the unfolding of a procession of events that carried obvious implications for their own future. This fact facilitated the development of a closer integration of the policies of the United States and the Latin-American republics. It was also responsible for the gradual drawing together in what was at first an implicit and later became an explicit alliance between the United States and Canada. Winston Churchill's famous statement in 1940 that those "two great organizations of the English-speaking democracies, the British Empire and the United States, will have to be somewhat mixed up together in some of their affairs for mutual and general advantage" was true, above all, of Canada and the United States.

In spite of the intimate and friendly relationship between the American and Canadian peoples, the arrangement of an alliance between Washington and Ottawa presented a difficult problem. In its relations with the Latin-American countries the United States was dealing with governments that had no firm constitutional or political ties with foreign states. In the case of Canada,

however, the American government had to recognize the significance of the bonds that still united Ottawa to London, Canberra,
New Delhi, Wellington, and Pretoria. It is true that by 1939 the
principle of the divisibility of the Crown had been confirmed in
practice and was in some measure recognized by foreign states.
But although the legal ties uniting the British nations were thus
dissolving, the emotional and sentimental bonds remained intact. This meant that although the United States could enter
what was in fact a defensive alliance with the Latin-American
republics without the intrusion of any complicating factors, a
similar arrangement with Canada did imply a definite if remote
danger of involvement in foreign complications. An irresponsible
government in Canada, relying on the protective power of an
understanding with the United States, could have embarked
upon or encouraged the United Kingdom to embark upon military adventures that might conceivably have involved serious
implications for the United States. Fortunately, no such irre-
sponsibility was ever manifest in Ottawa.

As the black shadow of Hitler gradually spread across
Europe, closer and more frequent contacts were established and
maintained between the responsible leaders of the United States
and Canada. When Mackenzie King was re-elected and again
became head of the government in the autumn of 1935, the
formal contacts between the two capitals were supplemented by
the intimate friendship of the Prime Minister of Canada and the
President of the United States. This friendship played a role in
subsequent events which will be fully recognized only when the
personal as well as the state papers of Roosevelt and King are
made available to historians. Enough is already known, however,
to justify the statement that the friendship between these two
men exerted an influence that affected not only the relations of
Canada and the United States but the whole course of world history during one of its most fateful decades.

Speaking at Queen's University on the 18th of August 1938,
President Roosevelt made the first formal commitment of the
United States to aid in the defense of Canada when he said: "I

365

give to you assurance that the people of the United States will not stand idly by if domination of Canadian soil is threatened by any other Empire."

Two days later Prime Minister King announced the complementary Canadian obligation when in a speech at Woodbridge he said: "We, too, have our obligations as a good friendly neighbour, and one of them is to see that, at our instance, our country is made as immune from attack or possible invasion as we can reasonably be expected to make it, and that, should the occasion ever arise, enemy forces should not be able to pursue their way, either by land, sea, or air to the United States, across Canadian territory."

Although not embodied in formal or official undertakings and though either or both might be subsequently denied by legislative decision, these two statements made explicit the defensive union of the two great American powers. Each assertion gained its strength from the fact that it did represent the state of opinion in the country on behalf of which it was made. How important this was to be and how extensive the steps taken to implement these promises, the events of the next few years were clearly to disclose.

3. *Permanent Joint Board on Defense*

The United Kingdom declared war on Germany on 3 September 1939. The Canadian declaration came exactly one week later. The changed position of Canada in the world and the recognition of that change by the government of the United States were both illustrated by the attitudes and actions of Washington during the intervening week.

Under the Neutrality Act of 1935, Americans were prohibited from exporting arms, munitions, or implements of war to any country recognized by presidential proclamation as being in a state of war. On 5 September 1939 the President issued a proclamation extending the provisions of the Neutrality Act to the belligerent nations, including the United Kingdom, Australia, India and New Zealand. It was not until 10 September, however, that, following the separate Canadian declaration of war, a similar proclamation was issued adding Canada to the roster of belligerents. So greatly had the situation changed since President Wilson had argued against the recognition of Canada as a signatory of the covenant of the League of Nations.[1]

There were no significant developments in the relations of Canada and the United States during the months of the "phony war." A critical re-examination of the position of the two countries, however, followed immediately upon the lightning conquest of Holland and Belgium and the collapse of France. In the dark days of June 1940 there were close and intimate contacts between Roosevelt and King. During this time the President repeated his earlier assurances that the United States would defend Canada against any external attack. In the meantime he did what he could within the limitations of the neutrality legislation to assist Canadians to prepare their own defenses.

By midsummer of 1940 the fascist tide had engulfed most of western Europe, and the triumphant Nazis, firmly established on the French coast, were preparing for the invasion and subjugation of Britain.

Across the Channel the people of the United Kingdom, though determined to resist to the end, found themselves guarded only by a small army, which since Dunkirk was almost devoid of supplies,[2] a powerful navy, and an efficient but meager air force. It was recognized that if the Germans could land in

---

[1] There is an as yet unconfirmed story that President Roosevelt telephoned to Prime Minister King to ask whether Canada should or should not be included in the original list of combatants. He is said to have added that if he had to choose between offending Canada and the British Foreign Office he would choose the latter every time. There is nothing inherently improbable or out of character in this story, but it has not been confirmed or denied by any official source.

[2] The two Canadian divisions then in England were the only units that could be described as well equipped, and even their equipment was far from complete.

force on the English coast, no defense, no matter how heroic, could stand against them. When on 8 August the German air attack began and waves of German bombers sought to drive the Royal Air Force from the skies and to destroy the aerodromes and land defenses of Britain, there were few informed observers who believed that the British Isles could long be held. Among those who feared, and in fact expected, the worst, was the President of the United States. Accepting the exaggerated estimates of Colonel Lindbergh and others, he was convinced that even if the Luftwaffe lost five aircraft for every British fighter shot down, the Germans would in the end be left with thousands of planes when the Royal Air Force was completely destroyed. No one knew better than Roosevelt the danger that would then threaten an almost defenseless North America. The future of the whole of the still free world was plainly in jeopardy.

During the early days of the crisis Mackenzie King had refrained, on political grounds, from a personal visit to Washington, and he and the President had relied on letter or telephone conversations and on the exchange of messages by personal emissary. As the situation abroad grew more and more desperate, however, arrangements were made, on the suggestion of King, for a meeting with the President at Ogdensburg, New York, on 17 August. There, in the private railway car of the President, the two statesmen, who had already committed themselves to the principle of joint defense, met to consider the implementation of their public statements. Of the necessity of co-operation no one could be in doubt. To Canadians it was obvious that their meager resources of population and military equipment were incapable of protecting the vast riches of their national domain. To informed Americans it was equally clear that the United States in its condition of unpreparedness could not easily protect itself against a serious attack based on or directed through Canada. Co-operation was as inevitable as it was imperative.

Following a prolonged discussion, Roosevelt and King on 18 August issued the following statement:

368

"The Prime Minister and the President have discussed the mutual problems of defence in relation to Canada and the United States.

"It has been agreed that a Permanent Joint Board on Defense shall be set up at once by the two countries.

"This Permanent Joint Board on Defense shall commence immediate studies relating to sea, land, and air problems including personnel and material.

"It will consider in the broad sense the defense of the north half of the Western Hemisphere.

"The Permanent Joint Board on Defense will consist of four or five members from each country, most of them from the services. It will meet shortly."

Thus was established a body unique in the history of international relations. Canada and the United States had long practiced, had indeed originated, the technique exemplified in the Permanent Joint Board on Defense through the establishment and successful operation of the International Joint Commission, which was set up in 1909. But the new Defense Board was unique because it brought together in the common interest and in common planning a belligerent and a neutral power. The difficulties inherent in such a situation are obvious and had constantly to be kept in mind. In spite of these difficulties, however, the Board functioned effectively as an advisory body and the results of its work soon began to be evident through the progress made in the integration of the defenses of the North American continent. Among the more dramatic of the activities undertaken as a result of Defense Board initiative was the construction of the Alaska Highway. The building of this road from railhead at Dawson Creek in northeastern British Columbia to Fairbanks, Alaska, was an epic example of applied energy and skill. Another program of a similar character was the construction of the Northwest Staging Route—a line of airfields built by Canada and expanded with American help from Edmonton to

369

Nome. Along this route thousands of aircraft were rushed to the assistance of Russia in the critical years of the conflict. At the end of the war Canada repaid the United States for American expenditures on these airfields. Similarly, on the eastern edge of the continent, American and Canadian co-operation located sites, established airfields, and opened new channels for the movement of men and planes across the Atlantic.

Throughout the whole period of the war, the Defense Board continued to operate as the chief instrument for the direct co-ordination of the defensive military policies of the two countries. It was not designed to act as an operating agency, nor was it in a position to participate directly in the discussions on over-all problems of world strategy and offensive action that developed after the entrance of the United States into the war. Canada participated in the discussions of such matters in two ways. The Prime Minister and the Minister of National Defense took part from time to time in discussions of problems of fundamental strategy with the political leaders of the United Kingdom and the United States. In addition, senior Canadian military, naval, and air officers were established in Washington where they were in constant contact with the British and American members of the Combined Chiefs of Staff, a body organized to advise the Allied governments on matters of military policy and to ensure the effective execution of agreed plans. As a result of the organization and effective functioning of the Combined Chiefs of Staff and of adequate arrangements for Canadian access to that body, the significance of the role of the Permanent Joint Board on Defense gradually declined, following the entrance of the United States into the war and, in particular, as the democratic powers passed from defensive to offensive action. With the conclusion of the conflict the Board, as was foreshadowed in the use of the word "permanent" in its title, continued in existence, and it is now the chief channel of contact on service matters between the two countries. The threat of a new war coming from a new source has given to its work a renewed significance that is again of the greatest importance.

4. *Economic Co-operation*

The Second World War marked the definite emergence of Canada as a major industrial power. The transition from an agricultural to a primarily industrial community had started in World War I and had continued slowly in the intervening years. But the demands of World War II accelerated the change in an almost unbelievable manner. By 1943 agriculture, in spite of a 60 per cent increase in output, accounted for only 20 per cent of the net value of Canadian production. Before the war, Canada had very little in the way of an industrial machine that could be described as a war potential. The aircraft industry was producing only small planes, and these at a rate of less than one a week. No ocean-going vessel had been built for twenty years. But by the end of 1943, Canadian industry was producing 80 fighting aircraft and 6 seagoing ships each week, as well as "10,-000 tons of chemicals and explosives, 4000 military vehicles, 450 armoured cars and tanks and large quantities of other war material. Canada had become the fourth industrial country among the United Nations, with the two largest blast furnaces in the British Empire, a rate of industrial production double the pre-war rate, a steel production double that of pre-war, an aluminium production six times pre-war." [3] Canada was also producing gun barrels, optical glass, and a whole series of articles that had never before been thought of as within the range of Canadian interest or capacity.

The practice of consultation and co-operation worked out in the Defense Board technique was not confined to the military, naval, and air aspects of the war. Of equal, if not greater, importance was the financial and economic collaboration that sought to

[3] Higgins and Lerner: "Trends and Structure," in G. W. Brown, editor: *Canada* (United Nations Series; Toronto, 1950), p. 259.

unify the production and supply activities of the two countries for the more efficient prosecution of the conflict. It became evident almost as soon as the war had started that the ordinary diplomatic and other channels of contact between the two countries were not designed for nor competent adequately to handle the peculiar and complex circumstances of two continent-spanning nations at war. Special machinery—boards, agencies, committees —was created to meet specific needs.

Canadian trade has traditionally been marked by an excess of exports to the United Kingdom and an excess of imports from the United States. This deficit in United States trade was relatively unimportant as long as it was balanced by convertible surpluses in sterling and other currencies. With the outbreak of war, however, this traditional arrangement was immediately upset when Britain took drastic steps to protect its foreign exchange by suspending the convertibility of the pound.

The Canadian government, in turn, endeavored to defend its position by reducing the funds available for nonessential purchases in the United States. In June 1940 an exchange tax of ten per cent was imposed on all imports from non-British countries. A new graduated excise tax was applied in such a way as to reduce the imports of American automobiles or automobile parts. Until the collapse of western Europe, British imports from Canada had shown only a limited expansion, but after May and June of 1940 the appalling danger with which they were faced convinced the British government and industrialists alike that their previous opposition to the development of Canadian war plants must be abandoned. In its effort to meet the ensuing demands, Canadian industry had to rely in part upon United States materials and supplies. It was estimated that about thirty per cent of the content of the rapidly expanded Canadian output of munitions was imported from the United States. As Britain was soon unable to pay for Canadian goods, in either gold or American dollars, the position of Canada vis-à-vis the United States became more and more critical. As the need for United States funds increased, the supply radically declined.

372

To meet this situation the Canadian government could dispose of American securities held by Canadians, or Canada might have accepted lend-lease aid. The first procedure would have provided only a temporary solution; the latter would have complicated Canadian relations with the United States for many years to come and it was, in any event, a solution that did not appeal to the sensibilities of the Canadian people. The Minister of Finance expressed the Canadian view when looking back three years later he said: "We never wished to ask the U. S. for lend lease assistance—we always felt that, as a nation in a favoured position, free from the ravages of war, we were in duty bound to stand on our own feet and indeed to share with the U. S. in assisting other less fortunate of our allies in carrying on the war against the common enemy." It is worth while emphasizing that almost alone among the Allied powers Canada did not at any time during the war accept lend-lease assistances from the United States. On the contrary, under a different title, mutual aid, Canada supplemented the United States lend-lease program by extending similar help to Britain and other Allied nations. Before the end of the war Canada had given to Great Britain and other allied nations over four billion dollars' worth of Canadian goods and services.

The difficulties of the Canadian exchange situation were fully recognized in the United States as well as in Canada, and frequent discussions between the financial authorities and the political leaders of the two countries were devoted to an examination of various proposals for a solution of the problem. The solution was found and was announced on 20 April 1941, in what has become generally known as the Hyde Park Declaration. Speaking from President Roosevelt's home in New York State, the President and Prime Minister King announced on that date the conclusion of an agreement on financial and economic matters that related not only to long-term policies but to certain immediate steps that were to be taken to overcome the Canadian exchange difficulties. The importance of this agreement is so great that its full text is worth review. The official announcement said:

"Among other important matters, the President and the Prime Minister discussed measures by which the most prompt and effective utilization might be made of the productive facilities of North America for the purposes both of local and hemisphere defence and of the assistance which in addition to their own programs both Canada and the United States are rendering to Great Britain and the other democracies.

"It was agreed as a general principle that in mobilizing the resources of this continent each country should provide the other with the defence articles which it is best able to produce, and, above all, produce quickly, and that production programs should be co-ordinated to this end.

"While Canada has expanded its productive capacity manifold since the beginning of the war, there are still numerous defence articles which it must obtain in the United States, and purchases of this character by Canada will be even greater in the coming year than in the past. On the other hand, there is existing and potential capacity in Canada for the speedy production of certain kinds of munitions, strategic materials, aluminum, and ships, which are urgently required by the United States for its own purposes.

"While exact estimates cannot yet be made, it is hoped that during the next twelve months Canada can supply the United States with between $200,000,000 and $300,000,000 worth of such defence articles. This sum is a small fraction of the total defence program of the United States, but many of the articles to be provided are of vital importance. In addition, it is of great importance to the economic and financial relations between the two countries that payment by the United States for these supplies will materially assist Canada in meeting part of the cost of Canadian defence purchases in the United States.

"In so far as Canada's defence purchases in the United States consist of component parts to be used in equipment

374

and munitions which Canada is producing for Great Britain, it was also agreed that Great Britain will obtain these parts under the Lease-Lend Act and forward them to Canada for inclusion in the finished articles.

"The technical and financial details will be worked out as soon as possible in accordance with the general principles which have been agreed upon between the President and the Prime Minister."

The most significant aspect of the Hyde Park Declaration was the provision for the allocation between the two countries, on a co-operative basis, of the responsibility of making specific contributions to each other's efforts in the common cause. This agreement of co-operation in the economic realm was a natural corollary to the establishment of the Permanent Joint Board on Defense in the field of military action.

In order to carry out the principles enunciated in the Hyde Park Declaration, steps were taken to establish co-operative working arrangements, and here again the Joint Board principle was employed. The first of the new boards became known as the Materials Coordinating Committee and consisted of officials appointed by the Office of Production Management in the United States and of the Wartime Industries Control Board in Canada.[4] The duty of the Materials Coordinating Committee was to exchange information on the available supplies of raw materials in the two countries, to provide for the utilization of these supplies for the maximum benefit of both, to co-ordinate civilian restrictions and controls on the use of scarce materials in the two countries, and, in general, to ensure the most effective use of the available supplies for the mutual benefit and the maximum prosecution of the war effort.

Almost at the same time that the Materials Coordinating Committee was set up, negotiations initiated by Canada, through the Department of External Affairs, culminated in the estab-

---

[4] Steps looking toward the development of such a practical contact in the munitions field had been suggested by the Permanent Joint Board on Defense in the middle of February 1941. It had also been under discussion through diplomatic channels.

lishment of the Joint Economic Committees of Canada and the United States. In this instance the arrangement varied from the Joint Board procedure; there were now two committees, one Canadian and one American, each with a separate life and on occasion meeting as an individual unit. Nevertheless, the significant part of the terms of reference of the committees related to their joint activities and was expressed as follows:

"The Government of Canada and the Government of the United States of America . . . announced that they have established joint committees of inquiry to explore the possibility of a greater degree of economic co-operation between Canada and the United States. They will be known as the Joint Economic Committees.

"The Committees have been instructed to study and to report to their respective governments on the possibilities of (1) effecting a more economic, more efficient, and more co-ordinated utilization of the combined resources of the two countries in the production of defence requirements (to the extent that this is not now being done) and (2) reducing the probable post-war economic dislocation consequent upon the changes which the economy in each country is presently undergoing.

"It is the common belief of the two governments that such studies and reports should assist the governments and peoples of each country in formulating policies and actions for the better utilization of their productive capacities for the mutually greater welfare of each, both in the present emergency period and after the emergency has passed.

"This joint inquiry marks one further step in the implementation of the declaration made by Prime Minister Mackenzie King and by President Roosevelt at Hyde Park on April 20, 1941."

The work of the Joint Economic Committees never fully justified the expectations that might reasonably have been based

on their announced terms of reference. Some useful discussion
of problems of co-ordination in such fields as agriculture, labor
exchange, prices, shipping, foreign exchange, tariffs, and war production did take place, but action in these fields was generally
the result of the assignment of the problem concerned to some
other agency. In fact, the Joint Economic Committees themselves recommended the establishment of what was known as
the Joint War Production Committee, which was created in
October 1941, and which, in fact, took over most of the immediate wartime responsibilities that had originally been considered
to be within the area of responsibility of the Joint Committees
themselves. Nor did the Committees make any really significant contribution to the discussion of "the probable post-war economic dislocation consequent upon the changes which the economy in each country is presently undergoing." What meager
thinking was ever undertaken in this field was directed through
other channels.

The responsibilities of the Joint Economic Committees were,
of course, only advisory and they had no administrative or executive authority. They confined themselves to rather general considerations and failed to play the role that more imaginative
and determined direction might have developed. They did some
useful work but failed to take advantage of many of the opportunities to which they might have devoted their attention. When
they gradually disintegrated and were finally disbanded in 1944,
they had long ceased to play any really significant role in Canadian-American relations. They were the one exception to the
roster of dramatically successful agencies that were created to
ensure the maximum co-ordination of the wartime economies of
the two great nations.

On the other hand, the Joint War Production Committee,
"operating through a series of sub-committees consisting of
senior production officials concerned with specific problems," performed a very significant function in ensuring the integration
and in stimulating the effective exploitation of the productive
resources of the two countries. A further strengthening of the

bonds uniting the two economies followed the establishment, two years later, of a Joint Agricultural Committee, which maintained a continuous review of the production and distribution of food and other agricultural products.

Before the end of 1941 the basis had thus been laid for a measure of economic and military co-operation between Canada and the United States that has no counterpart in the history of voluntary action between two independent and democratic countries. The joint-board principle, which is historically a North American contribution to the history of international relations, was being utilized to a degree that could almost be described as excessive. There were, of course, many difficulties to be overcome in the co-ordination of the war efforts of the two countries, and many conflicts of interest and disputes at the operational level were recorded during the course of the conflict. Through the joint boards and committees, however, a machinery had been established for the solution of almost any problem that might arise.

Operationally the economies of the two countries were bound even more closely together by the exchange of personnel in industrial and scientific establishments and by the close contacts maintained at the departmental level by the appointment of Canadian financial and other specialists as attachés in Washington and a similar assignment of American officials to the United States Embassy in Ottawa.

The Hyde Park agreement worked so effectively that, though it cannot be said that it solved all the financial problems that existed or developed between Canada and the United States during the war, it did ensure that no such problems would seriously or permanently hamper the wartime operations of the Canadian economy. While primarily designed to benefit Canada, it was, within its compass, equally beneficial to the United States.

One of the difficulties that had to be overcome in order to facilitate the maximum utilization of the joint resources of the two countries was that presented by the tariff impediments to the exchange of essential materials. This was a matter to which the

Joint War Production Committee had devoted attention in its first meeting when it declared that

> "Legislative and administrative barriers including tariffs, import duties, customs, and other regulations or restrictions of any character which would prohibit, prevent, delay or otherwise impede the free flow of necessary munitions and war supplies between the two countries should be suspended or otherwise eliminated for the duration of the war."

This declaration was approved by the Canadian government and by President Roosevelt, and it was, in fact, generally implemented throughout the war by tariff adjustments in Canada and by administrative expedients in the United States.

An obstacle more important than a tariff barrier to transborder trade was the adoption of export control by both belligerents. That such controls were essential to the effective prosecution of the war and, in particular, to ensure the denial of useful commodities to enemy countries was, of course, apparent early in the conflict. The situation was complicated, however, by the fact that it was not always possible to convince manufacturers or even government officials that Canadian or American needs, as the case might be, were more important than the requirements of their own country. Moreover, the fact that prices started higher and increased faster in the United States than in Canada presented a great temptation to Canadian exporters whose commodities were required at home but who could find greater profits by sales abroad.

The solution of the problems created by these circumstances was not always easily attained, but the generally friendly and co-operative attitude that characterized the relationship of the officers in charge of the controls and procurement services in the two countries did ensure that the difficulties would be kept within manageable proportions. The significance of this personal and friendly contact was well described by S. D. Pierce, a Canadian official who was particularly concerned with economic relations between the two countries during the war, in the following terms:

"The official pronouncements, the committees, and the practical achievements do not adequately represent the degree of co-operation achieved. The intangibles have been equally important but more difficult to set out. There has been the open exchange of confidences between the Americans and the Canadians, the warm welcome, the freedom from formality, the plain speaking, and the all-pervading friendship. Neither is it easy to enumerate the conditions which made the high degree of co-operation possible. Co-operation was, of course, a sensible course to follow. It stood on its own merits. However, common sense is not always able to prevail over sovereignty, and self-interest, and special national interests. That the course was followed, or at least adopted so readily and successfully, is due in part to the friendly disposition that existed, attributable no doubt to our common background of language and culture and to the close trade and industrial relationship; in part it is due to the fact that our approach to problems is similar. We both attach much importance to facts and figures, the Americans perhaps more than we. They are fond of brass tacks, of talking turkey, and of claiming they are from Missouri. We do not take it amiss when the United States asks us to present facts and figures in support of a requirement, we do not feel that our prestige is lowered, or that it is beneath our dignity to corroborate our request."

The importance of this friendly relationship was never better exemplified than in the working out of the problems of price control and rationing. The fact is, of course, that neither Canadians nor Americans suffered any appreciable hardship from food or indeed other rationing during the war. On the whole North Americans ate more food during the war than before it started and general consumer purchases rose appreciably with the impact of war wages and full employment on the national economies.

Generally speaking, the Canadian authorities, who were, of course, faced with very much the easier task, managed the problem of price controls and rationing more effectively than was the case in the United States. Nevertheless, there were occasions on which Americans accused the Canadians of failing to adopt the same measure of austerity as was being practiced in the United States. In other instances Canadians visiting in the United States were astonished at the availability of goods that had largely disappeared from Canadian shops. The explosive quality of disputes on such matters as these, between nations that were supposedly united in their acceptance of the hardships imposed by the war, was fully recognized in both countries, and rigorous efforts were made to ensure that parallel policies were pursued. This effort was continued into the period of readjustment after the war when rationing and control were gradually removed in both countries. These steps were not always taken precisely together in spite of the announced and very real efforts that were made to keep the programs synchronized as far as the particular circumstances would permit. On the whole, however, the procedures were so handled that little excuse was given to the people of either country to complain about the policies of the other.

5. Scientific Co-operation

Another area in which a considerable measure of productive co-operation was developed between Canada and the United States during the war was found in the exchange of scientific knowledge and personnel. Here the Canadian contribution went far beyond the share that might, proportionally, have been expected. In the period of crisis the generally high standard of Canadian education, reflected in the quality and number of the research personnel and facilities, brought results of inestimable value to the national war effort and to the Allied cause. In the secret war on the scientific front Canada played a notable part.

Canadian scientific and technical contributions to the war effort were in the beginning hampered and in the end strengthened by the fact that Canada was not a major power [5] and that the Canadian units were not separately supplied and equipped. In the words of Dr. C. J. Mackenzie, president of the National Research Council, "it was early aparent that if we did develop a new arm, a new device, a new plane it would never be used unless adopted by the United Kingdom forces; and we took a firm stand then that if we were to work officially we must start on every problem with the full knowledge available to our Allies; and, further, that we must work cooperatively on common problems."

This policy was accepted by Great Britain and the United States, with results that went far beyond the most optimistic expectations of either the Canadians or their collaborators. The name of Canada, to quote Dr. Mackenzie again, became known scientifically in the Second World War as it had become known for military prowess in the First World War.

It would be out of place to try to cover the whole field of the Canadian scientific contribution to the winning of the War, but a few outstanding examples will indicate the value of the work done by the northern ally.[6] Canadians made a number of critically valuable contributions to the development of radar; their work on the proximity fuse was described by the official war science historian of the United States as one of the "three or four most extraordinary scientific achievements of the war." Almost equally important contributions were made to the development of RDX, in the field of chemical warfare, in aviation medicine, in food maintenance, and finally in the broad field of atomic

---

[5] Although the Canadian contribution far exceeded that of any country except the United States, the United Kingdom, and the U. S. S. R.

[6] The material summarized here is treated at much greater length in the admirable volume *Scientists at War,* by Wilfred Eggleston, a distinguished figure in Canadian journalism and academic life.

energy. Canada is still one of the three great partners—with the United States and the United Kingdom—that are engaged in keeping the Western World ahead of any possible competitors in the realm of nuclear fission. Not only does Canada stand second in the world in its known resources of uranium; its research and manufacturing facilities in the field of atomic energy are exceeded in importance only by those of the United States, Great Britain, and, presumably, Russia.

The purpose of including these facts here is simply to illustrate the importance of the application of co-operation in this as in other fields. Without such combined efforts as were developed by Canada and the United States during the war, not only would Canada have lost opportunities for effective utilization of the discoveries of others, but the United States and the other Allies would have failed to profit by what proved to be the very great potential that Canada had to offer in this aspect of the common effort.

6. Political Relations

Political relations between Canada and the United States during the war were dominated by the fact that, with few exceptions, the people of the two countries entertained similar views in regard to the necessity of removing the totalitarian threat with which the free world was confronted. It is true that prior to the war small groups of semi-fascist character had developed in both countries. It is also true that in Canada there was still some measure of hostility toward participation in a "British" war on the part of some elements in the province of Quebec. This opposition, however, was infinitesimal in comparison with the difficulties that had been created by the introduction of conscription during the First World War, and there were few of the political leaders among the French-speaking Canadians who did not real-

ize and accept the necessity of destroying the Nazi-Fascist re-
gimes. Similarly in the United States there was a nucleus of
bitter isolationists who were prepared, for example, to argue that
President Roosevelt had invited, if he had not actually caused,
the Japanese attack on Pearl Harbor. But in both countries the
overwhelming weight of public opinion was firmly united behind
the principles for which the United Nations were fighting. There
was almost equal agreement on the broad lines of policy to be
followed.

Given this fundamental identity of purpose, supplemented by
a steadily growing recognition of their common interest, the
foundation was laid for a constantly increasing North American
unity in thought and action. This unity was further strengthened
by a sense of dangers shared and of common suffering and loss.
There was never a time in which the two peoples were more
closely united in firm and broad bonds of friendship.

It was fortunate also that in both countries there were men
in positions of authority, starting with the President and the
Prime Minister, who found it easy to collaborate on a basis of
personal friendship as well as of national policy. Mackenzie
King's prolonged contacts with Americans and residence in the
United States were matched by President Roosevelt's wide
knowledge of Canadian affairs and his summers at Campo Bello
Island in New Brunswick. Both men, moreover, were among
the most articulate political leaders of their generation and they
found it easy to express in appropriate and moving terms the
national friendship of which their personal relationship was an
effective symbol.

But of infinitely greater importance than these immediate
circumstances is the fact that the American and Canadian peoples
had over the years come to an intimate knowledge and mutual
respect. Faced with somewhat similar problems, arising from
their geographical and historical environments, they have responded in similar though not identical ways to the problems
they have shared. As nations they have far more in common than
they have points of difference. In many respects there are greater

differences within each country than there are between them. The traditional New Englander is much more like the typical Canadian than he is like the average citizen of Arkansas or Georgia. The basic unity of outlook and interest in the two nations made it inevitable that, faced with a critical threat to their common inheritance, they should find themselves united on every vital issue; that the war should bring them more closely than ever before to a course of mutual action based on mutual ideals and resulting in an enhanced mutual esteem.

7. *Relations after the Second World War*

Since the end of the war the United States and Canada have entered a new era in their relationships. The wartime co-operation in military and economic affairs has been largely maintained. Today, according to Brooke Claxton, Canadian Minister of National Defense, "the general staffs of Canada and the United States have complete agreement on doctrine, plans and preparations for the joint defense of North America." The Permanent Joint Board on Defense continues to function. There is a sustained interchange of military personnel for training and experience. Canada has standardized the equipment of her forces on American rather than British models.

In economic matters a postwar continuation of the Hyde Park thesis still underlies the production and exchange activities of the two economies and there is constant, close, and sympathetic consideration of the problems with which they are individually or jointly confronted. In 1949, when the threat of war again became a matter of direct and close concern to all free peoples, a joint Canadian and United States Industrial Mobilization Planning Committee was established to provide for the exchange of information if joint action should again become essential. The one great failure in the field of economic co-operation has resulted from the repeated refusal of the United States Congress to agree to participate in the development of the power and navigation potentials of the St. Lawrence waterway. It is now likely that Canada will proceed with this project as a national undertaking—a step that its importance will amply justify.

The social contacts and personal intercourse between the two people have never been so intimate and constant. Over forty million people now cross the international boundary every year, and the number is steadily growing. The movement of magazines, books, radio programs continues unabated—most of it in the northerly direction. The friendship between the peoples has never been so deep or firmly grounded.

But politically the situation has changed and the importance of the change is of historic significance.

When Canada and the United States first announced their union in defense in 1938, the League of Nations was dying, the United States was still predominantly isolationist in philosophy, the free world was divided, weak, and fearful.

Today the United Nations is in being, the United States is in full and active membership, and the democratic powers, though faced with a new menace in the East, are united and resolved. As the action taken in Korea has proved, they are determined now as they were never determined before to defend, if necessary by arms, the principles to which they have subscribed.

Supplementing the new world-wide organization and designed to compensate for the weaknesses inevitable in its efforts to function under present circumstances, there have been established regional associations that are of the greatest importance in the present context of international affairs. The United States and the republics of Latin America have drawn closer together in arrangements for mutual defense. Of even greater importance is the establishment of the North Atlantic Alliance.

Speaking of the way in which the use of the veto was hamstringing the work of the Security Council, the Prime Minister of Canada, Louis S. St. Laurent, said in 1947 that the nations of the free world "in their search for peace and cooperation will not and cannot accept indefinitely and unaltered a Council which was set up to assure their security, and which . . . has become frozen in futility and divided by dissension. If forced they may seek greater safety in an association of democratic and peace loving states willing to accept more specific international obligations in return for a greater measure of national security." The alliance now embodied in the North Atlantic Treaty Organization was the result of this conception, and the Canadian Prime Minister was one of the chief architects of the new defensive agreements. The decision of the United States to join in the North Atlantic Treaty Organization ensured the power and the continuance of the new design, and the appointment of General Eisenhower as Supreme Commander of the Allied forces gave emphatic proof of the determination of the partners in the Organization to make a reality of their undertaking.

In all the international postwar arrangements the United States, of necessity, has taken and must for long retain the leadership of the free nations. There is no possible substitute. If the United States were to withdraw into a recast shell of isolation, the free world would disappear—and so, within a reasonable time, would the United States itself.

As a result of these facts, it is inevitable that all the democratic peoples should watch with the closest attention every act and every policy that originates in Washington. But no other country is so deeply concerned as Canada, no other is in so good a position to keep informed on every change that takes place in the United States. Canada has always been affected by United States action or policy; today Canadian existence depends on that policy and action. As a result, every important development in the political or economic life of the United States is immediately noted and assessed in Canada; its significance becomes at once a subject of Canadian debate. Eventually this will lead to increased understanding, but its immediate effect may be to arouse critical comment in Canada, which at times may provoke occasional resentment in the United States. Americans not understanding the cause and extent of Canadian interest in their affairs will tend to overlook Canadian approval, but may object to Canadian criticism.

The people of the United States are not adjusting themselves easily to their new responsibilities as citizens of the strongest power in the world. The diversity of their views on international affairs is exceeded only by the vigor with which they are expressed. Neither the United States itself nor the other democratic powers can long afford a continuance of this disunity which may destroy them all.

Thus, at the very time when Canadian-American relations have reached the highest level of understanding and cordiality in their history, a real complication has been introduced into those relations as the result of the new threat to the peace of the world, and of the divided American reaction to that threat. Instead of being able to relax in the sunshine of friendship and relative prosperity Canadians have been forced to quicken their anxious interest in every change in American opinion or policy. In such an atmosphere it is inevitable that occasional frictions will develop.

Douglas Abbott, Canadian Minister of Finance, clearly expressed the concern of his countrymen, and at the same time their fundamental trust in the quality of the government and people of the United States in an address dealing primarily with the economic relations of the two countries in 1948. In concluding a speech in St. Louis he said:

"Canadians are realists. We recognize and are proud of the growing importance of our country in international affairs. But that pride does not blind us to the simple truth that your country occupies a central place in the world today. You emerged from World War II as a giant among nations. In your hands rests the power and the means for world leadership—and with that power rests responsibility. The destitute and the oppressed of the world look to you for leadership and support. No other country can begin to do what you can do. Great Britain and Canada can help—

but they cannot lead. Only the United States can lead the world out of the sorry conditions which now prevail. Only the United States can provide the leadership and the help that can make the world the sort of place that your people and our people want to live in. Much depends on your internal strength, economic stability and moral stamina. We who know you well know that you are not unmindful of your responsibilities. We know, with confidence, that you will accept the challenge with determination and vigour. On your response depends the welfare and freedom of mankind."

More recently in an address in Toronto on 10 April 1951, L. B. Pearson, Secretary of State for External Affairs, commented on current problems, and in particular Canada's relations with the United States, in the following terms:

"The present situation of war without warfare may continue for years. . . . We must be sure, so far as we can ever be sure, that the United Nations remains the instrument of the collective policy of all its members for the preservation of peace and the prevention or defeat of aggression and does not become too much the instrument of any one country. I am not suggesting that this has happened or is going to happen, but it is something that we should guard against. . . .

"I do not think that we should be asked, in the United Nations or elsewhere, to support automatically policies which are proposed by others if we have serious doubts about their wisdom. We must reserve the right, for instance, to criticize even the policy of our great friend, the United States, if we feel it necessary to do so. There are, however, two reservations to this. First, we must recognize and pay tribute to the leadership being given and the efforts being made by the United States . . . and realize that if this leadership were not given we would have little chance of success in the common struggle. Secondly, we must never forget that our enemy gleefully welcomes every division in the free democratic ranks and that, therefore, there will be times when we should abandon our position if it is more important to maintain unity in the face of the common foe. This reconciliation of our right to differ and the necessity for unity, is going to be a tough problem for anyone charged with responsibility for foreign policy decisions in this, or indeed in any free country.

"This brings us squarely up against . . . the question of Canadian-American relations in this two-power world of conflict. It is, I think, one of the most difficult and delicate problems of foreign policy that has yet faced the Canadian people, their Parliament and their Government.

"With the United States our relations grow steadily closer as we recognize that our destinies, economic and political, are inseparable in the Western hemisphere, and that Canada's hope for peace depends largely on the acceptance by the United States of responsibility for world leadership and on how that responsibility is discharged. With this closeness of contact and with, I hope, our growing maturity goes a mutual understanding and a fundamental friendliness. This makes it possible for us to talk with a frankness and confidence to the United States, which is not misunderstood there except possibly by a minority who think that we shouldn't talk at all, or who complain that if we do, our accents are too English! But we need not try to deceive ourselves that because our close relations with our great neighbour are so close, they will always be smooth and easy. There will be difficulties and frictions. These, however, will be easier to settle if the United States realizes that while we are most anxious to work with her and support her in the leadership she is giving to the free world, we are not willing to be merely an echo of somebody else's voice. . . . In our turn, we should be careful not to transfer the suspicions and touchiness and hesitations of yesteryear from London to Washington. Nor should we get unduly hot and bothered over all the pronouncements of journalists or generals or politicians which we do not like, though there may be, indeed *are* some on which we have a right to express our views especially when those pronouncements have a direct effect on action and policy which we have undertaken together. More important, we must convince the United States by action rather than merely by word that we are, in fact, pulling our weight in this international team. But this does not mean that we should be told that until we do one-twelfth or one-sixteenth, or some other fraction as much as they are doing in any particular enterprise, we are defaulting. . . . I can explain what I mean by an illustration. The United States would certainly have resented it, and rightly so, if we in Canada had called her a reluctant contributor to reconstruction in 1946 because her loan to the United Kingdom was only three times as large as ours, while her national income was seventeen or eighteen times as large. In our turn, most of us resent being called, by certain people in the United States, a reluctant friend because Canada, a smaller power with special problems of her own, ten years at war out of the last thirty, on the threshold of a great and essential pioneer development, and with half a continent to administer, was not able to match, even proportionately, the steps taken by the United States last June and subsequently, which were required by United Nations decisions about Korea; decisions which, I admit, caught us by surprise.

"The leadership then given by the United States rightly won our admiration, and the steps that she has taken to implement them since, deserve our deep gratitude. . . .

"There may be other ripples on the surface of our friendship in the days ahead, but we should do everything we can in Canada, and this applies especially to the Government . . . to prevent these ripples becoming angry waves which may weaken the foundation of our friendship. I do not think that this will happen. It will certainly be less likely to happen, however, if we face the problems frankly and

391

openly of our mutual relationship. That relationship, as I see it, means marching with the United States in the pursuit of the objectives which we share. It does *not* mean being pulled along, or loitering behind.

"Nevertheless, the days of relatively easy and automatic political relations with our neighbour are, I think, over. They are over because, on our side, we are more important in the continental and international scheme of things, and we loom more largely now as an important element in United States and in free world plans for defence and development. They are over also because the United States is now the dominating world power on the side of freedom. Our preoccupation is no longer whether the United States will discharge her international responsibilities, but how she will do it and how the rest of us will be involved." [7]

These quotations are taken from the first public address directly devoted to the subject of Canadian-American relations that has been delivered by a Canadian foreign minister in many years. The fact of the speech as well as its content is symptomatic of the greatly increased interest that Canadians are taking in this subject.

The common attitude of Americans toward Canada is almost invariably friendly, and the assumption that Canadians are essentially the same as citizens of the United States is so firmly ingrained among Americans that there is in the Republic a tendency to believe that Canada will naturally take the same attitude as the United States not only on all basic problems in foreign affairs but on all details as well. In general this assumption is justified, but because it is not and never will be wholly true, it should not be adopted as a working hypothesis nor be allowed to establish a frame of mind, particularly by those charged with governmental, journalistic, or other serious responsibilities in the United States. Americans should remember the strength

---

[7] This address was delivered just before the dismissal of General MacArthur and it reflected the Canadian fear that the American general would, by his continued disobedience, involve the Western World in an all-out war with Russia.

—indeed, on occasion the violence—of their own domestic arguments on foreign affairs during the last generation and should not be surprised that Canadians may also have vigorous views of their own. On the average, Canadians are very much more interested in and, because of their historical connections abroad and the necessities of their present circumstances, are generally better informed about foreign affairs than Americans are. Fortunately, the study of this subject is increasing very rapidly in the United States.

This having been said, it should be added that though the United States may, on occasion, have been guilty of assuming automatic support from Ottawa, there has, at least since the election of President Roosevelt in 1932, been very little in the way of an attempt to force or demand Canadian co-operation. The days when an American President tried to keep Canada out of individual membership in the League of Nations or a Secretary of State successfully blocked efforts to invite Canada to participate in the Pan American Union are past. Presidents Roosevelt and Truman, the State Department, senior officials of other branches of the United States government, and even the military leaders of the United States have in general been very much aware of Canadian sensitivity and have been careful in their observance of all appropriate proprieties in their contacts with Canada. Pessimistic Canadians sometimes worry over the possibility of their country becoming a *de facto* colony of Washington, now that it has become *de jure* independent of London. There has been little if anything in the recent conduct of American officials to justify this fear.

The fact is that Canada is now too important to the United States, and too strong in her own right, to make a domineering attitude on the part of the United States either wise or practicable. Apart from a few of the more bellicose and irresponsible elements in the American press, these facts are generally understood in the United States.

Canada and the United States are engaged in a partnership made inevitable by history, geography, and modern communications. It is a partnership of two countries and two peoples who are equal in rights, equal in quality, but unequal in size and power. The United States is and will probably always remain the senior partner and as such will carry the greater responsibility. In the dangerous and difficult world of the 1950's this is a burden profound in all its implications. But Canada as the junior partner has a proportionate, perhaps even more than a proportionate, responsibility to bear. The successful conduct of the affairs of the two nations will not be an easy or an automatic task. But in facing it both countries will have the proud record of their past to sustain them.

Canadians and Americans have met many problems and have achieved an extraordinary record of success in their solution. Between them these two governments and peoples have

—taken a continental wilderness and made it the most productive area on earth;

—quarreled over boundaries, fishing rights, tariffs, but for almost a century and a half avoided war;

—established between them a volume of trade that far exceeds that of any other two nations in the world;

—created a material standard of life that has no counterpart in either ancient or modern times;

—joined in the two most appalling wars in history and fought successfully in defense of the dignity and rights of free men and nations;

—invented and used between them a wholly new type of machinery for the maintenance of peace and the just settlement of disputes;

—convinced most of the world that neither separately nor together do they endanger the independence of any nation or the rights of other men;

—contributed on a scale beyond all precedent to the alleviation of human suffering in other lands and to the development of peoples and regions that need external aid.

To say that this is a record of which the American and Canadian people can be proud is to understate the facts. But it is not a record that is closed or ended. The future lies ahead; in that future the two peoples in their own relations and in their contacts with the remainder of the world can be expected to continue the course they have so well begun.

8. Retrospect

The first edition of this book concluded with a series of notes, under the general heading "Recent Developments," that included comments on annexation, the then newly established Canadian Legation in Washington, the territoriality of the waters of Hudson Bay, the International Joint Commission, and Canada's relationship to the Monroe Doctrine and the Pan American Union. Most of these matters are now subjects of historical rather than current interest.

Annexation of Canada by the United States is no longer a subject of informed discussion. It is sometimes mentioned as a desirable possibility by the more ignorant practitioners of American journalism or is revived with malicious intent by such aberrant agencies as the Hearst or McCormick press. In Canada the issue is dead, killed by the growth of Canadian nationalism and the continued influence of French Canada.

The establishment of a Canadian Legation in Washington and of an American Legation in Ottawa marked the first tentative steps in the organization of a Canadian foreign service that has now spread embassies, legations, and consular offices in all parts of the world where Canadian interests require attention. Both Canada and the United States have been well served over more than twenty years by a series of competent and in some cases distinguished ministers or ambassadors in each other's capitals.

The territoriality of the waters of Hudson Bay has continued to be asserted by Canada and has not been challenged by any other power. It can now be accepted as established.

The proposal that Canada should join the Pan American Union, or what is now known as the Organization of American States, has lost most of the urgency that once attended its discussion. Canada, the United States, and the republics of Latin America are now united in a wider association, and little purpose would be served, though certainly no harm would be done, by Canadian participation in the regional association. Similarly, the position of Canada as a beneficiary of the Monroe Doctrine has lost most of its significance through the more concrete alliance that has been established with the United States and through the general protection that is afforded by membership in the United Nations.

9. *International Joint Commission*

The International Joint Commission is still a successful operating agency, effective in action and unique in constitution. Its significance was strongly underlined by the enlarged application of the principle on which it was based by the creation during the war of a whole series of agencies in its image. It is still one of the most important, most satisfactory, and most thoroughly unique developments in the history of international relations.

It is unfortunate that the existence and labors of this Commission are not better known. It is quite probable that the vast majority of the people of Canada and of the United States have never heard it mentioned, and yet it is one of the most interesting developments in the international relations of the twentieth century. It is an entirely unique organization, and one that deserves far more recognition than it has ever received.

The International Joint Commission originated in an effort to develop a satisfactory method of dealing with the innumerable problems that were constantly arising as a result of the geographic and political relationships of the two countries. It was particularly designed "to prevent disputes regarding the use of boundary waters," but the terms of its creation also included the statement that it was intended "to settle all questions that are now [1909] pending between the United States and the Dominion of Canada involving the rights, obligations, or interests of either in relation to the other or the inhabitants of the other; along their common frontier, *and to make provision for the adjustment and settlement of all such questions as may hereafter arise*." The tenth article of the treaty provides specifically that "The Senate of the United States and His Majesty's Government with the consent of the Governor-General-in-Council may by joint consent refer to the Commission any question or matter of difference that may arise between them or the inhabitants of the two countries." Thus the Commission is, in actual fact, a permanent tribunal for the settlement of whatever problems may arise between Canada and the United States. The only limit to its power is to be found in the possible unwillingness of the Senate or the Canadian Cabinet to submit to it problems of vital importance.

The most important factor in the original creation of the Commission was the necessity of having some joint authority to settle problems that were annoyingly frequent along the international boundary. At a number of points along the frontier, rivers cross from one country to the other; elsewhere rivers and lakes form the boundary, and islands were subjects of dispute; along the St. Lawrence, difficulties were very frequent; problems of water power and water supply were constantly arising.

The genesis of the Commission may be found in the International Waterways Commission established in 1902. The duties of this body were very limited, being restricted to the investigation of the lake and river waters along the border. They were expected to report on lake levels, condition of the water, the reasons for and effect of diversions, and similar subjects. This

Commission did excellent work, but its powers were too limited and by the Treaty of 1909 it was agreed to create the present International Joint Commission. This treaty, in addition to the organization of the Commission, provided for free navigation of all boundary waters, including Lake Michigan and all canals uniting boundary waters, provided for the protection of those who were injured by diversion of these waters, and gave the Commission serious responsibilities in relation to levels, obstructions, diversions, or pollution.

During the forty-two years of its existence the Commission has disposed of a large number of problems, any one of which under the old system of diplomatic intercourse, might have dragged along indefinitely, and would certainly have been attended with possibilities of serious friction. Among the more important problems undertaken have been the Sault Ste. Marie water-power cases, which involved the levels of Lake Superior and consequently the interests of the cities on its shores; the Lake of the Woods investigation; the Trail Smelter arbitration; the St. Lawrence River navigation and power investigations; and the diversion of the waters of the St. Mary and Milk rivers for purposes of irrigation in Montana and Alberta.

The Commission as now organized consists of six members, three appointed by the President, three by the King. They meet as a single body, with an American chairman presiding when the meeting is in the United States; a Canadian in the chair when the session is in Canada. There are two fixed meetings annually: in Washington in April, in Ottawa in October; but other meetings are held at frequent intervals.

Up to the present there have been no cases submitted to the Commission which involve its general powers. It is to be hoped that a precedent of this sort will be established in the near future. But whether employed or not, the power is there, and it is quite conceivable that it may yet prove of real importance in the history of American-Canadian relations. This will be the more likely if an intelligent and informed public opinion can be developed in the two countries to understand, to strengthen, and to support the work of this unique organization in the realm of international affairs.

10. Conclusion

Canada and the United States have lived as neighbors for over one hundred years without resort to war. During that time problems have arisen that were not easy to remove, and yet the good sense of the two peoples has triumphed and the fragile bonds of peace have not been broken. The difficulties have not all been ended, but there is today less reason than ever before to contemplate the possibility of serious strife between the Republic and its northern neighbor.

The future relations of Canada and the United States should be characterized by a growing intimacy and understanding, an increased co-operation, and a mutual respect. A still greater development of trade and an increased ease and frequency of personal intercourse are inevitable in view of the growth of population and the rapid improvement in means of transportation. It is not unreasonable to believe that these changes will make for an ever more soundly based friendship. Unless some totally unforeseen catastrophe intervenes, the peaceful record of the past hundred and fifty years should be maintained on an even higher plane during the century to come. In a war-racked world Canada and the United States must continue to prove that peace is not an impossible ideal, that states can best maintain their national honor not by resorting to the law of the jungle, but by reasoned and constructive friendship, conditioned by understanding, governed by justice, and founded on peace.

Selected Bibliography

The most exhaustive bibliography of Canadian-American relations is contained in the twenty-five volumes of the Carnegie Series on "The Relations of Canada and the United States." The final volume of this series, J. B. Brebner's *North Atlantic Triangle* (New Haven and Toronto, 1945), pp. 329-341, has an excellent critical bibliography. E. W. McInnis in *The Unguarded Frontier* (New York, 1942), has a worthwhile "Note on Bibliography," pp. 371–377, which has the special merit of containing references to the periodical literature. *The Canadian Historical Review* publishes in each issue a list of "Recent Publications Relating to Canada" which is very useful, listing, often with a brief description, recent studies and monographs on Canadian-American Relations.

The following bibliography is a selective one and confines itself to significant works published largely since 1940.

BREBNER, J. B., *North Atlantic Triangle* (New Haven and Toronto, 1945).

This volume was the last of the Carnegie Series to be published. It is, however, in no sense a summary of the Series, though as Professor Brebner says ". . . its main outlines have been used as a partial framework or blue print for that Series." It is a work with a character and high merit of its own, which make its publication a memorable event in the relations of Canada and the United States.

Canada and the United States

BRODIE, B. "Strategic Implications of the North Atlantic Pact," *Yale Review*, XXXIX, 193–308 (1949).

BROWN, G. W. (ed.), *Canada*, United Nations Series (Toronto, 1950).

A collaborative work by a group of Canadian scholars on various aspects of Canadian life, historical, economic and constitutional. American parallels are often brought in and form an interesting feature of the work.

BURT, A. L., *The United States, Great Britain and British North America from the Revolution to the Establishment of Peace after the War of 1812* (New Haven and Toronto, 1940).

In some ways a continuation of the author's earlier work *The Old Province of Quebec* (Minneapolis, 1933), this work is by all odds the most detailed and best account we have of the period covered. The work is based on wide ranging research and contains many original and provocative "revisions."

COATS, R. H., and MACLEAN, M. D., *The American Born in Canada: A Statistical Interpretation* (Toronto and New Haven, 1943).

This work should be related to the works by Hansen and Truesdale (see below) for a true understanding of the movement of population across the Canadian-American border.

Conference on Canadian-American Affairs: *Proceedings*. Under the joint auspices of the Carnegie Endowment for International Peace, the St. Lawrence University and Queens University, 1935, 1937, 1939, 1941. The *Proceedings* were published by Ginn and Company.

The holding of these biennial conferences, as Professor Brebner has remarked, ". . . has meant that in both countries statesmen and men of affairs, as well as publicists and scholars, have entered the present world conflict with a living sense of an interplay which was far too little known a decade ago."

COREY, A. B., *The Crisis of 1830–1842 in Canadian-American Relations* (Toronto and New Haven, 1941).

An excellent study of the background of the Webster-Ashburton Treaty, being particularly strong on extradition and the strategic aspects of the boundary problem.

CRAIG, G. M., "The American Impact on the Upper Canadian Reform Movement before 1837," *Canadian Historical Review*, XXIX, 333–352.

Based upon research for a doctoral dissertation, this article is an important contribution to our understanding of the background of the Rebellions of 1837 in terms of the American influence.

DAWSON, R. M., *Canada in World Affairs: Two Years of War 1939–1941* (New York, 1943).

A good study of Canadian relations with the United States and Great Britain during the early years of World War II. This work should be read in conjunction with Soward's work. (See below).

ELLIS, E. L., *Reciprocity 1911: A Study in Canadian-American Relations* (New Haven and Toronto, 1939).

This is our best study of a most important theme in Canadian-American relations. The work develops with clear logic and force.

GLAZEBROOK, G. P. DE T., *A History of Canadian External Relations* (London, New York, Toronto, 1950).

This work together with the author's *Canadian External Relations: to 1914* (Toronto, 1942), and *Canada at the Paris Peace Conference* (Toronto, 1942), forms an important contribution to our knowledge of Canadian foreign policy.

GRAHAM, G. S., *Sea Power and British North America 1783–1820* (Cambridge, Massachusetts, 1941).

A study of the continuation of mercantilist policies after 1783. A field poorly covered otherwise, except for H. T. Manning, *The British Colonial Government after the American Revolution 1782–1800* (New Haven, 1933).

HANSEN, M. L., completed and prepared for publication by J. B. Brebner, *The Mingling of the Canadian and American Peoples* (New Haven and Toronto, 1940).

This is an original work of high merit and rare charm, based upon enormous research, but with a wide popular appeal. It is one of the best studies in the whole Carnegie Series.

HARRISON, W. E. C., "Canadian-American Defence," *International Journal*, V, 189–200 (1950).

HOWARD, G. B., "United States Defence Procurement in Canada," *International Journal*, V, 315–324 (1950).

HUGHES, E. C., *French Canada in Transition* (Chicago and Toronto, 1943).

This is a study of urbanization in Quebec and its human, economic and social problems.

INNIS, H. A., *The Cod Fisheries: The History of an International Economy* (New Haven and Toronto, 1940).

A full-scale study of an international industry, carried through on a chronological plan. This is a basic study and unique in its field. The period covered is 1497–1938.

JAMES, R. W., *Wartime Economic Co-operation: A Study of Relations between Canada and the United States* (Toronto, 1949).

This work is the best and most elaborate account of the complex boards and agencies which handled the integration of Canadian and American economic relations during World War II. It is very strong on the institutional side and individuals do not emerge.

KERR, W. B., *The Maritime Provinces of British North America and the American Revolution* (Sackville, New Brunswick, 1941).

This covers much of the same ground as J. B. Brebner in his *Neutral Yankees of Nova Scotia* (New York, 1937), but the author sets himself the task of tracing "the conditions and events which led the provinces to stay within the empire."

LANCTOT, G. (ed.), *Les Canadiens français et leurs voisins du sud* (Toronto and New Haven, 1941).

This is a collaborative work covering the whole period. It is uneven in merit, being perhaps best in its treatment of 1867–1937 and in its treatment of the Americanization theme.

LANDON, F., *Western Ontario and the American Frontier* (Toronto and New Haven, 1941).

A study of American influence in this area and a great achievement in the writing of intellectual and social history in Canada. Canadian-American relations would be greatly elucidated if we had more of this kind of writing.

MANNING, W. R. (ed.), *Diplomatic Correspondence of the United States: Canadian Relations, 1784–1869* (Washington, 1940–1943).

The most complete printed collection of documents available for the earlier period. This work may well be bracketed with *Treaties and Agreements Affecting Canada in Force between His Majesty and the United States of America, with Subsidiary Documents 1814–1925* (Ottawa, 1927).

MARTIN, C., *History of Prairie Settlement and "Dominion Lands" Policy* in *"Canadian Frontiers of Settlement"* (Toronto, 1938).

A thorough study, developing many interesting parallels between Canadian and American policies toward the public lands.

McINNIS, E. W., *The Unguarded Frontier: A History of American-Canadian Relations* (New York, 1942).

This is an excellent integrated study of Canadian-American relations down to the involvement of the United States in the Second World War.

McINNIS, E. W., and REID, J. H. S., *The English Speaking Peoples* (Toronto and Vancouver, 1948).

The chapters on Britain and the Empire are by Reid and those on Canada and the United States are by McInnis. This work is an interesting effort to weave together the diverse tendencies of a complex theme.

MERK, F., *Albert Gallatin and the Oregon Problem: A Study in Anglo-American Diplomacy* (Cambridge, 1950).

The best account we have of this important aspect of Canadian-American relations.

404

MORTON, W. L., *The Progressive Party in Canada* (Toronto, 1950).

A valuable contribution to the study of political parties in Canada. The main emphasis is upon the development of progressivism in Western Canada.

PRITCHETT, J. P., *The Red River Valley 1811–1849: A Regional Study* (New Haven and Toronto, 1942).

This study deals with one of the many regions of special interaction along the boundary of the United States and Canada.

Royal Commission: *Report on Dominion Provincial Relations* (Ottawa, 1939).

Book I: A detailed survey of Canadian development from 1867 to 1939 with attention to the political, constitutional and economic aspects. This volume is most thought-provoking, and is an example of the kind of work much needed in Canadian historiography.

Book II: Contains the recommendations of the Royal Commission.

Book III: This is largely devoted to the statistics of public finance. There are, more or less forming an integral part of the *Report*, twenty other studies by experts for which the Commission does not take responsibility.

Royal Commission: *Report on National Development in the Arts, Letters, and Sciences* (Ottawa, 1951).

This eagerly awaited work has caused and will continue to cause a great deal of discussion in Canada. It deals in a full and free way with the many cultural contacts Canada has with the United States, and raises the problem, as C. Hartley Grattan has phrased it, of Canada's "Cultural Sovereignty."

Royal Commission: *Studies: A Selection of Essays Prepared for the Royal Commission on National Development in the Arts, Letters and Sciences* (Ottawa, 1951).

SHARP, P. F., *The Agrarian Revolt in Western Canada: A Survey Showing American Parallels* (Minneapolis, 1948).

This work with the same author's "When Our West Moved North," *American Historical Review*, LV, 286–300, brings out clearly the agrarian discontent of the frontier which spilled over into Canada in the late 1890's and early 1900's. These works may well be compared with John Hicks' *The Populist Revolt* (Minneapolis, 1931), for further parallels.

SHOTWELL, J. T., "A Personal Note on the Theme of Canadian-American Relations," *Canadian Historical Review*, XXVIII, 31–43.

An after-dinner address of charming anecdote and reminiscence by one who has made a tremendous contribution to a proper understanding of Canadian-American relations.

SOWARD, F. H., *Canada in World Affairs: The Pre-War Years* (New York, 1940).

――――― *Canada in World Affairs: From Normandy to Paris 1944–1946* (Toronto, 1950).

Canada and the United States

These two volumes together with the work of Dawson, op. cit., cover the recent international relations of Canada in an admirable manner.

STACEY, C. P., "The Myth of the Unguarded Frontier, 1815–1871," *American Historical Review*, LVI, 1–18 (1950).

This article, a part of a larger uncompleted study, puts the Rush-Bagot Treaty in a new light, and studies subsequent developments in border defense.

STEVENSON, J. A., "Canada, Free and Dependent," *Foreign Affairs*, XXIX, 456–467 (1951).

TANSILL, C. C., *Canadian-American Relations 1875–1911* (New Haven and Toronto, 1943).

The most detailed study of Canadian-American diplomatic relations available for the period covered. This work is based on enormous research and, though perhaps not wholly without bias, is indispensable.

TRUESDELL, L. E., *The Canadian Born in the United States: An Analysis of the Statistics of the Canadian Element in the Population of the United States, 1850–1930* (Toronto and New Haven, 1943).

A pioneer study and the companion work to that of Coats and MacLean, op. cit.

WEBB, W. P., "Ended: 400 Years of Boom," *Harper's*, CIII, 25–33 (October 1951).

An interesting and provocative article which relates the destiny of Canada and the United States to the Great Frontier and its disappearance. A second article will follow.

Index

i

Index

ii

Index

Index

Index

Index

Index

A NOTE
ON THE TYPE USED

The text of this book has been set in a modern adaptation of a type designed by William Caslon, the first (1692–1766), greatest of English letter founders. The Caslon face, an artistic, easily read type, has had two centuries of ever increasing popularity in our own country—it is of interest to note that the first copies of the Declaration of Independence and the first paper currency distributed to the citizens of the new born nation were printed in this type face.

The book was composed, printed and bound by Kingsport Press, Inc., Kingsport, Tennessee.

A NOTE
ON THE TYPE USED

The text of this book has been set in a modern adaptation of a type designed by William Caslon, the first (1692–1766), greatest of English letter founders. The Caslon face, an artistic, easily read type, has had two centuries of ever increasing popularity in our own country—it is of interest to note that the first copies of the Declaration of Independence and the first paper currency distributed to the citizens of the new-born nation were printed in this type face.

The book was composed, printed and bound by Kingsport Press, Inc., Kingsport, Tennessee.